Praise for *Starring Tom Cruise*

"The contributors analyze Cruise's appearance, his affect, the surrounding discourses, and films' presentation of the actor in ways that illuminate the various aspects of his stardom and the society and industry that have made him a star for forty years."
—Cynthia Baron, author of *Denzel Washington*

"Love him or loathe him, there is no denying that Tom Cruise has been one of the world's biggest movie stars for a long time. As such, he deserves serious scholarly attention, and this book provides it with fifteen smart essays that adroitly address just about every imaginable facet of the star's cultural, sexual, and symbolic resonance."
—Gaylyn Studlar, author of *This Mad Masquerade: Stardom and Masculinity in the Jazz Age*

"Sean Redmond's first-rate edited collection offers detailed consideration of the most important roles in Cruise's successful decades-long career. This wide-ranging volume also covers essential new ground for the analysis of contemporary Hollywood stardom. Its insightful cross-disciplinary examination of the star's perpetual border crossing makes this book an unmissable read. Stars like Tom Cruise never seem to lose their shine. This book enables us to understand why."
—Virginia Luzón-Aguado, *Harrison Ford: Masculinity and Stardom in Hollywood*

"This is a book that star studies has wanted, even if we didn't know it—a wide-ranging set of reflections on the desirability, authenticity, and dogged agelessness of contemporary Hollywood's ubiquitous genre king. As equally attuned to the white, masculine normativity of Tom Cruise as to his performative excess, sexual indeterminacy, and spiritual eccentricity, this book advances star studies by elucidating a changing Hollywood landscape through the cultural continuity of its most tenacious star."
—Misha Kavka, professor of cross-media culture, University of Amsterdam

Starring Tom Cruise

Contemporary Approaches to Film and Media Series

A complete listing of the books in this series can be found online at wsupress.wayne.edu.

GENERAL EDITOR

Barry Keith Grant
Brock University

Starring Tom Cruise

Edited by Sean Redmond

WAYNE STATE UNIVERSITY PRESS
DETROIT

Copyright © 2021 by Wayne State University Press, Detroit, Michigan, 48201. All rights reserved. No part of this book may be reproduced without formal permission.

ISBN (paperback): 978-0-8143-4718-8
ISBN (hardcover): 978-0-8143-4717-1
ISBN (ebook): 978-0-8143-4719-5

Library of Congress Control Number: 2020948830

Cover design by Katrina Noble

Wayne State University Press
Leonard N. Simons Building
4809 Woodward Avenue
Detroit, Michigan 48201-1309

Visit us online at wsupress.wayne.edu

CONTENTS

Acknowledgments   ix

Introduction   1
Sean Redmond

I. Desiring Tom Cruise

1. Adolescence and Its Psychological Phases in Tom Cruise's 1980s Teen Films   19
   Patrick O'Neill

2. Gazing at Tom Cruise   36
   Sean Redmond

3. Losing Cruise Control: Disenchantment of Tom Cruise's Star Image in *Eyes Wide Shut*   53
   Defne Tüzün

4. "Nothing Is 'Impossible' if You're Tom Cruise": Scientology, Spiritual Neoliberalism, and the Tom Cruise Closet   71
   Brenda R. Weber and Sasha T. Goldberg

5. Searching for the "Desert of the Real" in the Films of Tom Cruise   94
   Loraine Haywood

II. Genre Cruise

6. The American Everyman Goes Irish: Gender, Genre, and Ethnicity in *Far and Away* — 115
   Carlos Menéndez-Otero

7. Cruising the Vampire: Hollywood Gothic, Star Branding, and *Interview with the Vampire* — 133
   Sorcha Ní Fhlainn

8. Cruising into the Future: The Redemption of "Authentic" Masculinity in the Science Fiction Films of Tom Cruise — 152
   Linda Wight

9. Cruising the Closed World: The Cold War and the Cyborg in *Top Gun*, *Mission: Impossible*, and *Minority Report* — 169
   Alex Wade

10. Cruising Stardom in Hollywood Franchising: Tom Cruise as Franchise Star in the *Mission: Impossible* and *Dark Universe* Storyworlds — 187
    Tara Lomax

III. Aging Cruise

11. Tom Cruise as Father and Son — 211
    Adam Daniel

12. "How am I supposed to do this?": The Impossibility of Tom Cruise's Masculine Performance in the Face of His Aging Star Body — 226
    Ruth O'Donnell

13. Starring Tom Cruise as (Desperately Defying) Aging Action Star — 243
    Glen Donnar

14. The Authentically Bruised Cruise: Tom Cruise,
    Mission: Impossible, and Extreme
    Performative Labor 262
    Justin Owen Rawlins

15. Aging for Life: Tom Cruise in the Era of
    Functional Fitness 279
    Michael DeAngelis

    Filmography 297
    Contributors 299
    Index 303

ACKNOWLEDGMENTS

With sincere thanks to Barry Keith Grant for commissioning this collection and Marie Sweetman for her support and guidance during its development.

To my students, colleagues, friends, and family who have had listen to me opine about the pleasures and perversion of a film starring Tom Cruise: this book is for you.

>ALGREN: I have questions.

>KATSUMOTO: Questions come later.

INTRODUCTION

Sean Redmond

La Petite Mort

In the penultimate "final ride" scene to *The Last Samurai* (Edward Zwick, 2003), Tom Cruise (Nathan Algren) and Ken Watanabe (Lord Katsumoto Moritsugu) face the mechanization of the modern Japanese army while on horseback and with only swords to fight with. The scene, beautifully filmed through a mixture of elegiac slow motion, landscape long shot, and facial close-up, captures the free-flowing movement of the samurai and their horses, in tune and consort with the natural environment. This naturalized and romanticized movement is contrasted against the clinical lines and rapid fire of the near stationary army, led by a general who eschews the noble tradition that Algren and Katsumoto are meant to represent. After the samurai warriors have been mowed down by machine-gun fire, the scene ends with Katsumoto, already wounded, committing seppuku with Algren's help. As he does so, the soldiers kneel in respect.

This suicide scene is played out with remarkable sexual layering: lying next to each other, almost in a loving embrace, Algren agrees to Katsumoto's request for a noble death. As they rise from the ground, Algren gently pushes or caresses the sword into Katsumoto's stomach. This action brings the two star actors together in a coupling embrace, where they stare intently, at first, into each other's eyes. Katsumoto then rests his head on Algren's shoulder to witness the cherry blossoms falling from the trees behind him. He whispers, "Perfect." In many respects the scene is awash with homoerotic, male-bonding aesthetics and carries forward the screen action codes of male, masculine friendship, and heroic sacrifice. However, Cruise's polysemic star image—his always in-between gender and liminal sexuality—casts this engagement as romantic and sexual. Katsumoto's death here is a type of *petite mort*. The surplus value of Cruise's star image, one that endlessly border crosses, set within this coupling terrain, renders this embrace and the insertion of the sword, a queer one. It is Cruise here who is being identified as "perfect," if only because he collapses and reconfigures gender and sexual binaries and fulfills the latent desires of the film.

There are, of course, other Cruise star indicators that signify in *The Last Samurai*. There is the presence of the white savior myth that finds Cruise at the "head" of the samurai warriors, involved in a civilizing process. At the same time, the mixing of racial and ethnic backgrounds is meant to fetishize the East and spice up and ennoble Cruise's white idealized star image. The film draws on Cruise's physicality and skilled athleticism in action and fight scenes, and it inserts him into a heterosexual romantic narrative with Taka (Koyuki Kato), the wife of a samurai slain by him, if only to lessen and to make safe the queer heartbeat of the film. Finally, *The Last Samurai* draws on both the hegemony of the Hollywood male star and the transitional appeal of Cruise: the film was a bigger success in Asia, and Japan in particular, making $120 million in Japan alone (Box Office Mojo 2020).

What *The Last Samurai* offers us is the representational and discursive scaffolding to begin to understand the way the Cruise star image centrally functions. It shows us that a film starring Tom Cruise will have certain narrative coordinates and ideological traces, star signs, and performative echoes that the chapters in this book work to explore and unearth. *The Last Samurai* demonstrates the complex appeal of Cruise's *petite mort* star image.

Why *Starring Tom Cruise*?

The Cruise star image seems to be always on the point of expiration. He is one of the most successful Hollywood film stars of the last thirty-five years, with a cumulative worldwide box office of nearly $8 billion (The Numbers 2020), and yet his appeal has also waxed and waned, particularly in North America, while in Asia he continues to remain incredibly popular. These geographical shifts and differences in popularity tell us about the way American star icons travel, carrying the American dream to "foreign" markets, in new and highly energized global arenas. *The Last Samurai*, as noted above, tapped into and opened up these transnational cultural spaces for Cruise and was deliberately engineered to appeal to the Japanese market. In a very real sense, then, Cruise begins to allow us to see how star texts work within these new forms of global cultural productions.

With regard to North America, there is a rise and fall trajectory to his star image. Cruise was the leading film star of the 1980s and early 1990s in terms of not only box office appeal but also media coverage, endorsements, and promotions. Further, he became the ideological center for the representation of white, idealized masculinity. Finally, Cruise took on a number of "serious" film roles, connecting him to dramatic cinema through his work with auteurs such as Paul Thomas Anderson (*Magnolia*, 1999) and Stanley Kubrick (*Eyes Wide Shut*, 1999). This performative regeneration of the Cruise star image began with *Rain Man* (Barry Levinson, 1988) where he appears opposite renowned method actor Dustin Hoffman, who plays the part of Raymond, an autistic savant. Cruise, in the role of fast-dealing salesman Charlie, draws on aspects of his masculine star self but also enables, as P. David Marshall argues (1997, 112), for his star text to now become "a moniker that has a certain guarantee of quality, a brand-name status that not only includes his promise of alluring filmic masculinity, but is also symbolic of serious and quality films."

Cruise's appeal lessened in North America, and Europe to a degree, for a number of reasons. First, new generations of cinemagoers found new, generally younger stars to identify with. As Cruise aged, his fans aged with him and they are not consistent cinemagoers. Second, Cruise starred in a number of bland star vehicles that repeated without invention his role type from earlier films, such as the poorly received and underperforming *Days of Thunder* (Tony Scott, 1990) and *Far and Away* (Ron Howard, 1992). Third, Cruise's private life began to warrant, or at least attract, a great deal of attention, whether it be through his connection to Scientology, his numerous failed marriages, or the "queer space" he was positioned within through fan work and gossipmongering. This set of counterdiscourses ran in opposition to his star image, or, more complexly, they "revealed" what was already there.

Cruise's star text is in part based on authenticity. The affective registers we see onscreen supposedly carry this realness forward. This is matched by action performance codes, where Cruise literally puts his body on the line, undertaking his own stunts. Audiences know this, of course, because the marketing and promotion texts that circulate around Cruise foregrounds this/his muscly and heroic authenticity. For example, his broken ankle that happened as he jumped a building on the set of *Mission: Impossible—Fallout* (Christopher McQuarrie, 2018) became the narrative image of the film, authenticating Cruise's masculinity. Cruise is nearly always at the point of expiration as he jumps from helicopters, climbs up skyscrapers, and drives a car or motorbike at breakneck speeds. As Erin Meyers (2009, 905) writes, authenticity "gives the illusion of knowing the 'truth' about what a star is 'really like.' More important, once the celebrity is positioned as 'authentic,' the values and ideologies she symbolizes also become 'real' and culturally resonant." However, when such authenticity is openly called into question and circulates freely in discourse, then the coherency or consistency of the star text begins to crumble.

For Cruise, this began to ostensibly be the case since his star text was increasingly felt to embody an *inauthentic* authenticity: one that was performatively clinical and cold and that was attempting to mask or conceal something much more fluid that lay beneath his performativity. Barry King (2008), for example, reads Cruise's emotional and confessional 2005 appearance on *The Oprah Winfrey Show*—where he revealed his impassioned love for actress Katie Holmes—in the light of the adverse response to his membership of the Church of Scientology. The appearance on the show becomes, then, an attempt to reposition Cruise as authentically heterosexual and essentially, warmly romantic. What this "para-confession" does is to function as a "commercially efficacious self-disclosure" (130). The love confession also reveals, through its spectacle and emotional excessiveness, the liminality that sits at the corporeal center of Cruise's star image.

One can read Cruise's performance on *The Oprah Winfrey Show* as a "closet" moment (Sedgwick 1990): an attempt to shore up his heterosexuality at a time when it was being questioned and lampooned outside of official discourses. However, Cruise's performance here, as with many of his film roles, does not register as heterosexually authentic or "real" but instead as stage managed and phony. The performance's excessiveness draws attention to his plasticity and theatricality and opens up the ability to view him queerly, whereby there is an "open mesh of possibilities, gaps, overlaps, dissonances and resonances, lapses and excesses of meaning when the constituent elements of anyone's gender, of anyone's sexuality aren't made (or can't be made) to signify monolithically" (Sedgwick 1993, 8). Cruise is very often an invincible action hero and/or dreamy romantic lead in his films and yet finds himself in homoerotic and homosocial relationships that unsettle and undermine these heterosexual scripts. When he kisses his female leads, for example, there is a sterility to the act, as in *Eyes Wide Shut*; or it is a violent act, as in *Vanilla Sky* (Cameron Crowe, 2001); or the person being kissed registers as "male," as Charlie (Kelly McGillis) does in *Top Gun* (Tony Scott, 1986). As the exemplary male Hollywood star of the last forty years, such a fracturing of the heterosexual self undermines binaries, revealing them to be merely performative. The Cruise star text cracks open the egg of patriarchal culture, showing us the messier but inviting yolk of gender and sexual identity. This very act of unmaking binaries returns us to the *petite mort* conception that starts this introduction since there is the death of the binary in these reconfigurations, even as the life of "new" sexual formations emerge in and through Cruise's star image.

Star studies has itself suffered a partial death or, as Martin Shingler and Lindsay Steenberg (2019, 445) put it, has gone through a "mid-life crisis." This is in part to do with the rise of celebrity studies and of fame culture and the argument that stars could now be understood only within these metaframes. There was also a critical take on the single "star" case study and of textual analysis used to mine that star, with the argument being made that it did not pay enough attention to cultures of production and the political economy (Turner 2004). This is not the view of this author, who feels in part responsible for this "death" since he started, with Su Holmes, the journal *Celebrity Studies*, whose very title seems to make stardom invisible.

Stars still operate as powerful producers of meaning, desire, and attraction. They are found in site-specific arenas, and their mythologized "aura" is circulated and experienced in different ways to those who operate outside the cinema agora. That is not to say, however, that celebrity has not got something important to say about stardom. Clearly, they entangle and connect, particularly in the spaces of the social media. Further, textual analysis was never a method that simply stayed *inside* the text; it always systematically reached out connecting with production and consumption matters. The methods of close textual analysis are also incredibly robust and deeply intimate, revealing and exposing the ideological tissue that sits beneath its skin. Its forensic lens is always extractable: good close textual analysis does not simply reveal something about the "text" in question but the culture that produced it.

So, it is hoped, intended, that this collection shows how important star studies is not just for understanding the ideological, commercial, and cultural significance of one star—Tom Cruise—but also for elucidating the way masculinity, ethnicity, sexuality, and commodity relations function in contemporary society. It also intends to advance star studies through the cross-disciplinary way that Cruise's star image is unmasked in its pages. Scholars writing for this collection approach the Cruise star image through various vectors and frames: and they are revelatory in nature. As such, they not only demonstrate the very best traditions of close "star" textual analysis but also move the approach to the star forward. This is *why Tom Cruise*.

Structure

The collection is divided into three parts, each one focusing on a specific textual and contextual aspect of Cruise as a star, performer, and embodied actor. The sections, nonetheless, speak to one another, and chapters within them are in conversation with one another, so that readings build and at times contest. The breadth of Cruise's acting career is under the lens here, from his early teen romances in the 1980s to the blockbuster aesthetic he embodies in the *Mission: Impossible* franchise series. The collection, however, does not attempt to cover every film, of which there are forty-nine, including those currently in production. Rather, it examines the key film texts that reveal and conceal his ideological and performative traces. However, it should be noted that there is a deliberate *concentration* of chapters that deal with his contemporary action roles, particularly through the *Mission: Impossible* franchise series, which has seen his star text on the "rise" again. This concentration enables the volume to undertake a 360-degree "deep focus" lens to these action roles, enabling the textual analysis undertaken to spend detailed time with the aspect that they each focus on.

The three sections of the volume take us through the core aspects of Cruise's star image. In part 1, we explore the ways that he is connected to affective and psychological registers, to the intoxicating perfumes of attraction and desire, and the complex and contradictory ways he embodies masculinity and heterosexuality. In part 2, we place Cruise within the codes and conventions of genre filmmaking and the way they intersect with the star vehicle. Cruise becomes monomythical, heroic, authentic, romantic; at the same time, he struggles to hold these platforms and ideologies together. In part 3, we look at the way that Cruise is both an ageless totemic figure and an aging star, his body centrally the conduit for eternally youthful masculinity and a signifier of that which must ultimately fail. We connect these strands to wider discursive texts, recognizing that film roles are not the only site for understanding the star image of Tom Cruise.

Part 1: "Desiring Cruise"

In the first section, the authors focus on the way Cruise's star image and his film and media performances are built on a desiring gaze, on forms of sexualized and romanticized identifications. The desiring of Cruise is, however, nearly always complicated by perverse narrative arcs and liminal character relationships and by the extra-diegetic material that fans, viewers, and critics read back into the film text in question. Desiring Cruise is a problematic and at times perverse activity. Further, desiring Cruise is problematized by the "lack" that sits at the center of his fantasy star image and because of the simulations upon simulations that define him and for which he stands—the plasticity of the star image. The chapters take Cruise through the central arc of his career and draw on different theoretical and illustrative material to do so.

In "Adolescence and Its Psychological Phases in Tom Cruise's 1980s Teen Films," Patrick O'Neill investigates the embedded and translated psychologism of Tom Cruise's teenage screen persona. Analyzing three 1980s teen films—*Losin' It* (Curtis Hanson, 1983), *Risky Business* (Paul Brickman, 1983), and *All the Right Moves* (Michael Chapman, 1983)—O'Neill argues that Cruise's screen persona can be examined by linking his characters' behavior and textual relationships to issues concerning the lived experience of adolescence, including one's sexuality, virginity loss, and acts or notions of youth rebellion. O'Neill's chapter is concerned with analyzing the internal, psychological forces that motivate and shape Cruise's characters and the stories they are connected to, but the reading is also usefully set against the changing sociopolitical landscape of the Reagan era.

This periodization is also taken up in "Gazing at Tom Cruise," in which Sean Redmond explores the looking regimes that Cruise is often put under in three films from the 1980s, *Top Gun*, *Jerry Maguire* (Cameron Crowe, 1996), and *Born on the Fourth of July* (Oliver Stone, 1989). Redmond suggests that when viewers are asked to gaze at Tom Cruise, a high degree of gender and sexual ambivalence crystalizes, which undermines the masculine and heterosexual codes that are seeking to define him. *Top Gun* offers up hyperbolic images of a hypermasculine and heterosexual Cruise, coupled with highly charged homosocial and homoerotic male relationships. Redmond argues that "these excessively coded images ultimately undermine the heterosexual script the film tries to run with." *Jerry Maguire* attempts to "fix" Cruise's desirability and heterosexual orientation within the conventions of the romantic comedy, but through excessive, racially coded visual gesturing, the film ultimately reconfigures the desire that is on offer. Redmond suggests that in *Jerry Maguire* the "real love story, the real regime of gazing it unleashes, is between two men of different races." *Born on the Fourth of July* offers the viewer a "broken" image of Cruise, whose role as a disabled Vietnam vet is meant to be anything but desirable. However, narratively and contextually speaking, the films draws on the honed and youthful star image of Cruise to haunt the disability representation that follows. What *Born on the Fourth of July* offers the viewer, Redmond suggests, "is a perverted form of desiring or gazing at Tom Cruise." These are perversions, in fact, that sit at the queer heart of his star image.

This idea of perversion is further taken up in Defne Tüzün's chapter, "Losing Cruise Control: Disenchantment of Tom Cruise's Star Image in *Eyes Wide Shut*." Tüzün suggests that *Eyes Wide Shut* purposely uses Cruise's star image to sabotage the film's eroticism, since his ability to find pleasure or express desire is constantly undercut and frustrated. Through the course of the film, the sexual frustrations and the symbolic failures that Cruise's character experiences as an overconfident doctor come to mirror or entangle with his star image: they are a perfect fit since, as Tüzün argues, Cruise is a liminal figure who often registers in symbolic terms as impotent. *Eyes Wide Shut* "reinforces" the "ambiguity" of Cruise's star image, "at first highlighting [its] extraordinariness . . . but later undermining it by revealing its artificiality and constructedness."

In "'Nothing Is "Impossible" if You're Tom Cruise': Scientology, Spiritual Neoliberalism, and the Tom Cruise Closet," Brenda R. Weber and Sasha T. Goldberg explore the idea of the closet through Cruise's relationship to and involvement with Scientology. Weber and Goldberg argue that the commingled branding between Cruise and Scientology fuses through "a strict and uncompromising adherence to self-improvement . . . which promises superhuman results." Cruise becomes superhuman—a desired alpha male—through his involvement with Scientology, while Scientology finds a superhuman in Tom Cruise. This enables Scientology to present itself as a technological church that enhances human capability to godlike levels. Nonetheless, Weber and Goldberg suggest that the oxymoronic mediated reputation of Scientology—positioned as it is in both ridiculousness and eccentricity—also creates a representation of the closet that is defined by the spectacular and the circumspect. In this chapter, they bring Cruise out of the closet.

In "Searching for the 'Desert of the Real' in the Films of Tom Cruise," Loraine Haywood takes a broadly Lacanian approach to the way that the idealized Tom Cruise symbolically functions. For Haywood, the Cruise film text enters the breakdown in the symbolic order and restores its inherent inconsistency through heroic sacrifice. His films stage the breaking down of the American dream and its ideas of utopia, but these are then restored at the film's conclusion through his symbolic agency. Haywood suggests that Cruise performs as "the double of himself, but he also doubles as the empire—America" and "its dream of a 'Savior' and the fulfillment of the prophetic utopian vision that is the continuation of its founding narrative." The importance of Tom Cruise in this imaginary cinematic history of America is a "translation of his body as a text, a map, and a story that keeps the illusion of wholeness in America's vision of empire."

Part 2: "Genre Cruise"

In this section of the collection, the authors place Cruise within the structures of film genre, articulating his star image in terms of the codes and conventions of the films he appears in. The authors bind this articulation to questions of gender and sexuality, national and ethnic identity, star branding, and ideological and cultural context. The genres under analysis are the western and migrant melodrama picture, the Gothic film, science fiction, and the Cold War thriller.

In "The American Everyman Goes Irish: Gender, Genre, and Ethnicity in *Far and Away*," Carlos Menéndez-Otero explores the Cruise star persona through the notion of problematic fit. *Far and Away* draws on the codes and conventions of the western genre, on classically romanticized notions of the Irish, and on the heroic action and romanticism of the Cruise star image to create a high-concept film that is intended to appeal to audiences globally and to the Irish diaspora particularly. However, Menéndez-Otero argues that while the film aligns certain Cruise qualities with the textual operations of the film, including desiring physicality, there is ultimately tension between the type of idealized white masculinity that he embodies and the class signifiers of Irish ethnicity. Further, in its attempt to ethnicize him, *Far and Away* seeks "to conceal the violent history of the West and deny the existence of white privilege in America," all the while opening up the space to see Cruise as the very embodiment of such privilege.

Sorcha Ní Fhlainn also explores the problem of inserting the Cruise star image into a subversive film that is adapted from an incredibly successful novel, and one with a large fan base. In "Cruising the Vampire: Hollywood Gothic, Star Branding, and *Interview with the Vampire*," Ní Fhlainn compares the queer aesthetics and relationships of the Gothic film with the two central thrusts of Cruise's film performativity: as an idealized, heterosexual star and one whose masculinity and heterosexuality opens itself up to queer sentiments. The chapter contextualizes the controversy that followed Cruise's casting in the film, suggesting it may have been a purposeful "attempt to straighten the narrative and/or dampen the queer-edginess so established in Anne Rice's *Vampire Chronicles*." Ní Fhlainn argues that "Cruise's turn as Lestat still commands fascination as a timely constellation between his star image, the queering power of Rice's source material, and Hollywood's reinvigoration of adapting Gothic literature for the screen."

In "Cruising into the Future: The Redemption of 'Authentic' Masculinity in the Science Fiction Films of Tom Cruise," Linda Wight takes a cluster of Cruise-led, early twentieth-century science fiction films to argue that they "chart the movement of the male protagonists from crisis to redemption." Exploring five films—*Vanilla Sky*, *Minority Report* (Steven Spielberg, 2002), *War of the Worlds* (Steven Spielberg, 2005), *Oblivion* (Joseph Kosinski, 2013), and *Edge of Tomorrow* (Doug Liman, 2014)—Wight argues that the Cruise star vehicle has long articulated both concerns about masculinity in crisis and an admired masculine ideal. The Cruise science fiction picture uses the masculine ambiguity of his star image to first represent everyman, unable to act or not fully skilled to do so, and to then find his masculine superideal in heroic acts and actions. Cruise embodies an "authentic" heroic masculinity, even in an uncertain and threatening future. His masculinity stands for the security of today and for tomorrow.

Alex Wade explores Cruise's masculinity through the lens of futuristic, fusion technology while suggesting that his star power originated in the folding times and spaces of the Cold War. In "Cruising the Closed World: The Cold War and the Cyborg in *Top Gun*, *Mission: Impossible*, and *Minority Report*," Wade suggests that Cold War technologies, real and imagined, are drawn into the Cruise picture both to offer technological visual excess—the triumph of spectacle—and to show and evidence their assimilation into everyday life. Using Paul N. Edwards's 1996 *The Closed World: Computers and the Politics of Discourse in Cold War America* as its departure point, the chapter explores how technologies in the films *Top Gun*, *Mission: Impossible*, and *Minority Report* embed, embody, and ultimately become part of "Cruise's on-screen characters, generating a type of ageless cyborg-human." For cyborg Cruise, Wade suggests, "age is just a number, merely information, his star power the closed world transfer between the screen, the talk-show couch, and commerical—if not critical—adulation."

Cruise, of course, exists in a range of overlapping franchise and transmedia contexts. His star image moves in and between generic forms and media platforms, something that Tara Lomax explores in her chapter, "Cruising Stardom in Hollywood Franchising: Tom Cruise as Franchise Star in the *Mission: Impossible* and *Dark Universe* Storyworlds." Lomax examines how as a franchise star, "Cruise articulates a complex interplay of stardom, legal-industrial proprietary, and storyworld development." While his role in the *Mission: Impossible* franchise works successfully as a star-vehicle that markets Cruise's star brand as a heroic action hero, his starring role and influence in *The Mummy* (Alex Kurtzman, 2017) arguably stifled and detracted from the narrative and generic coherency of the monster picture and potential longevity of the *Dark Universe* franchise since Cruise became the narrative image of the film. Focusing on the dynamic between stardom and franchise storyworld development, Lomax argues that there are creative and industrial shifts in how the interplay of stardom, intellectual property (IP), and narrative is negotiated in "contemporary Hollywood."

Part 3: "Aging Cruise"

In the final section, the authors look at the (lack of) aging in the Cruise star vehicle, each taking a different approach to the question of his authenticity, embodiment and movement, and to familial/patriarchal roles he takes on. The chapters focus on the contemporary action films but weave an analysis that allows us to see how Cruise's star image and publicity machine work in and across his career, forming around the vectors of masculinity, sexual vulnerability, and the uneven actions of heroism. Cruise does not seem to age, and yet his star image is inherently connected to roles and performances that draw attention to his agelessness or to the way, almost paradoxically, he embodies characters that are defined by their age. Cruise star images embody a linear temporality and yet also resist the aging process. He is beyond age and yet the very marker of aging.

In "Tom Cruise as Father and Son," Adam Daniel examines fatherhood and sonhood both through the roles that Cruise has played and his own complicated familial relationships as both a son and a father. The chapter centrally explores Cruise's representation of fatherhood in three films, *War of the Worlds*, *Minority Report*, and *Eyes Wide Shut*, contextually linking this reading to Cruise's own fatherhood of three children. Daniel suggests that "by examining the choice of roles he has undertaken, his oeuvre can arguably be read as both a reflection of his personal reckoning with his complicated familial dynamics and as a cultivated staging of performative sonhood and fatherhood." Cruise's filmography may be understood as one that explores "his troubled relationship with his father and his complex and, in some respects, difficult relationships with his children."

This vexed question of Cruise's aging/ageless masculinity is something that Ruth O'Donnell also directly explores, drawing a set of conclusions slightly different from Daniel's with regard to Cruise's ability to be a believable patriarchal father figure. In "'How am I supposed to do this?' The Impossibility of Tom Cruise's Masculine Performance in the Face of His Aging Star Body," O'Donnell explores the incredulity and suspicion that greets the physicality of Cruise, suggesting that age anxiety "stems less from his aging per se than from the growing disconnect between his chronological age and his star persona, which is predicated on notions of boyishness and his positioning as a figural son (symbolized at the familial or social level)." If the Cruise star image suffers from Peter Pan syndrome, then his aging body can only draw attention to this phallic and symbolic lack: "While he may grow older, he will never ascend to the role of patriarch."

In "Starring Tom Cruise as (Desperately Defying) Aging Action Star," Glen Donnar draws on on-set news, gossip and publicity, and promotional materials from a number of recent films, including the three *Mission: Impossible* films—*Ghost Protocol* (Brad Bird, 2011), *Rogue Nation* (Christopher McQuarrie, 2015), and *Fallout*—and *The Mummy*, to interrogate enduring narratives about Cruise's aging body as it manifests within a very particular "spectacular" stardom. Tom Cruise's most recent films prominently feature him performing ever-more outlandish stunts and ever-greater physical exertions: an embodied signifier of his undiminished authenticity and supposed youthfulness. However, Donnar argues that what is also revealed in the wider marketing and promotional material is how his body increasingly fails, gets injured. In so doing, "both Cruise's renowned stunt work and the on-set injuries he has laudably overcome now evidence anxieties about undeniable aging rather than its undaunted defiance."

Justin Rawlins also explores the increasingly vital function of Tom Cruise's performative stunt labor to his overall star image in his chapter, "The Authentically Bruised Cruise: Tom Cruise, *Mission: Impossible*, and Extreme Performative Labor." Using reception studies to survey the paratexts—the studio promotion of *Mission: Impossible* films and Cruise as well as the critical reactions to both—Rawlins argues "that these discourses and representations orbiting *Mission: Impossible* and Cruise collectively constitute an interpretive framework for understanding performance outside of the films themselves." Rawlins contends that "the persistent emphasis on Cruise as a stunt-centric actor and producer . . . is especially integral to publicity materials for more recent *Mission: Impossible* installments and entwined with the series' durability and profitability." Referencing his disastrous string of media appearances in 2005 as a touchstone for the fissures that emerged in his public image and which undermined Cruise's authenticity and threatened his professional viability, Rawlins further suggests "that these paratexts surrounding both star and franchise have been essential in establishing his performances as stunt centric and thus have become at least as important a venue as the films themselves in repairing his compromised star image."

Michael DeAngelis takes us beyond the Cruise film text to look at the phenomenon of "functional fitness." In "Aging for Life: Tom Cruise in the Era of Functional Fitness," DeAngelis examines what is commonly known as Tom Cruise's age-defying tactics by demonstrating their consonance with the philosophy and practices of the popular workout phenomenon known as functional fitness. "Here, Cruise's authenticity can be recuperated through the cultural context of a contemporary predisposition to framing body transformation and preservation in terms of contemporary public health discourse, thereby largely evading the 'self-serving' narcissism often associated with the process of bulking up." His commitment to physical self-improvement authenticates his star image since it aligns with popular health discourses and foregrounds "authentic self-determination."

PostScript: ". . . but not today"

In the trailer for *Top Gun: Maverick* (Joseph Kosinski, 2020), we find Cruise as Maverick some thirty-four years on from his having become a flight instructor at the elite Naval Fighter Weapons School at Naval Air Station Miramar. It is clear he has remained a maverick, having never been promoted beyond captain, albeit with a heroic "checklist" of awards and citations, read out by the sneering two-star rear admiral (Ed Harris), who is Maverick's superior. The trailer visually and narratively alludes to the first film through its high-sheen military aesthetic, combat scenes, and character iconography—Cruise is seen putting on a bomber leather jacket and aviator sunglasses and driving off on his motorcycle under a warm orange sun. The central montage of the trailer extends this allusion as we witness honed male bodies playing beach volleyball and a squad of pilots breaking into song in the local bar—all lifted from the first film. The trailer is full of nostalgia, a nostalgia that feeds off and reseeds the Cruise star image: it utilizes his authenticity—it is Cruise flying the military jet in the trailer—and places him within a narrative that explicitly temporalizes him. The generation who watched the first film at the time of its release have aged with him, and yet maverick has remained the same—a rebel outlier within a military machine, unable to fully mature.

At the end of the trailer the unnamed rear admiral says to Maverick, "The end is inevitable, Maverick, your kind is headed for extinction." Maverick responds, "Maybe so, sir, but not today." One can read these lines of dialogues in multiple ways: it suggests the imminent death of the Hollywood movie star, of the Cruise star image, and the/his resistance to giving in to the change it demands. Cruise is refusing to age, to be moved from his position as high-concept movie star.

The dialogue, of course, also touches on the bureaucratization of action and the need to rein in mavericks who threaten the system. In a very direct way, the dialogue replays that from *Dirty Harry* (Don Siegal, 1971), in which cop Harry Callahan (Clint Eastwood) refuses to play by the book, then seen as a critique of an American political system that had gone soft on crime. *Top Gun: Maverick* has been produced during the age of Trump, a maverick president, and the militainment aspect of the film resonates with his warmongering and desire for military parades and to make "America's military the best in the world" ("President Donald J. Trump" 2017). Maverick embodies the new Trumpian age of war spectacle and fuck-you diplomacy.

Nonetheless, there is another way to read these lines of dialogue. Maverick is a queer character, his identity connected to deeply homosocial and homoerotic relationships that ultimately overloaded the original film so that desire centrally circulates in and between the male characters. The "your kind" quotation outs Maverick and the Cruise star image as always predicated on queer intersections. That he will not die today, not give into hate speech, is a resistance to heteronormativity. And that is potentially "perfect."

Works Cited

Box Office Mojo. n.d. "The Last Samurai." IMDbPro. Accessed May 15, 2019. www.boxofficemojo.com/release/rl3593176833/weekend/.

King, Barry. 2008. "Stardom, Celebrity, and the Para-confession." *Social Semiotics* 18 (2):115–32.

Marshall, P. David. 1997. *Celebrity and Power: Fame in Contemporary Culture*. Minneapolis: University of Minnesota Press.

Meyers, Erin. 2009. "'Can You Handle My Truth?': Authenticity and the Celebrity Star Image." *Journal of Popular Culture* 42 (5): 890–907.

"President Donald J. Trump Will Make the American Military Great Again." National Security & Defense Fact Sheet, December 12, 2017. www.whitehouse.gov/briefings-statements/president-donald-j-trump-will-make-american-military-great/.

Sedgwick, Eve Kosofsky. 1990. *Epistemology of the Closet*. Berkeley: University of California Press, 1990.

———. 1993. "Queer and Now." In *Tendencies*, 1–22. Series Q. Durham, NC: Duke University Press.

Shingler, Martin, and Lindsay Steenberg. 2019. "Star Studies in Mid-life Crisis." *Celebrity Studies* 10, no. 4 (October): 445–52.

The Numbers. n.d. "Tom Cruise." Nash Information Services. Accessed May 15, 2019. www.the-numbers.com/person/540401-Tom-Cruise#tab=summary.

Turner, Graeme. 2004. *Understanding Celebrity*. Thousand Oaks, CA: Sage.

I
Desiring Tom Cruise

1
ADOLESCENCE AND ITS PSYCHOLOGICAL PHASES IN TOM CRUISE'S 1980S TEEN FILMS

Patrick O'Neill

Tom Cruise's movie apprenticeship began in the 1980s teen genre in films that are the focus of attention here: *Losin' It* (Curtis Hanson), *Risky Business* (Paul Brickman), and *All the Right Moves* (Michael Chapman), all produced in 1983. Despite the formulaic nature of these films and comedic tone of *Losin' It* and *Risky Business*, a close analysis using an adolescent psychological approach produces an alternative insight into the teenage Cruise screen persona, most notably in relation to issues of sexuality, loss of virginity, risk-taking, peer pressure, and rebellion. One model that resonates is research carried out by G. Stanley Hall in 1904, who was one of the first scholars to critically examine youth psychology. He outlined the "storm and stress"[1] phases of adolescence; Jeffrey Arnett (1999, 317–22) updates this notion, which characterizes behavior displayed by young people: "conflict with parents" (and adults), "mood disruptions," and "risk-taking"—all behaviors that the Cruise character demonstrates in these films.

The methodologies used relating to adolescence and its psychology as applied to the films in this chapter need some explanation. It would be a bold

---

1 "Storm and stress" is the English translation of the German phrase *Sturm und Drang*, whose origins lie in German literary history of the eighteenth century. It refers to individual extremes of emotion in the face of perceived rationalist thought.

claim, without justification, to suggest that the films could critically engage with disciplines outside of the arts, which often rely on scientific, empirical, and statistical data in the literature. The aim is to bypass these data and view the findings in broader and more holistic terms and then to modify and apply them to a fictional character and narrative. It is also important to examine how this interpretation of the Cruise persona compares with other debates in the wider scholarly literature and how it differs. This is developed throughout the analysis, so a brief insight here is useful. Existing work on Cruise focuses on issues such as psychoanalysis and the sociopolitical landscape of the 1980s (O'Donnell 2012); gender, the body, and the gaze (Rall 1993); masculinity in binary terms (Peberdy 2010); masculinity, performance, and stardom (Studlar 2001); masculinity and queerness and how this is conveyed through mise-en-scène (Bruzzi 2013); and the comedic and ironic tone of *Risky Business* set against the capitalist Reagan era (Bernstein and Pratt 1985). Therefore, this investigation, while still acknowledging the textual issues these writers discuss, is more concerned with debates originating from scientific and empirical sources on adolescence, which do not refer to cinema in their scholarly literature. The goal is to produce an interdisciplinary work that offers an innovative contribution to the analysis of films and their characters. Moreover, this approach allows educators and students alike the opportunity to use these teen films and the Cruise persona as a vehicle to research and study adolescent psychology from a new, media-related perspective.

Youth in Society and Film Genre

Before the analysis, a brief insight into the sociopolitical landscape of the 1980s and issues relating to film genre is helpful. While *Losin' It* is set in 1965,[2] *Risky Business* and *All the Right Moves* take place in the 1980s, which,

---

2   Although *Losin' It* is set a different period (1960s) and the issues pertaining specifically to the Reagan era are not relevant, the Cruise character's behavior and motivations still draw comparison in relation to other 1980s teen films and their adolescent issues. Furthermore, the intertitle in the film's opening credits, albeit an anachronism that riffs on *Star Wars* made just a few years earlier—"A Long Time Ago in a High School Not So Far Away"—places the film within the 1980s teen genre.

under Ronald Reagan's presidency (1981–89), was marked by a neoliberal free-market economy, deregulation, privatization, and tax cuts for the middle and upper classes. Dubbed "Reaganomics," this promoted social mobility, individualism, the accumulation of wealth, materialism, and conspicuous consumption. The expression "Greed is good"[3] became synonymous with this decade as a more aggressive form of capitalism meant that white-collar professionals prospered under this economic ideology. But the manufacturing and heavy industry sector suffered because of these policies, and blue-collar communities experienced recession and unemployment, creating a growing rich–poor divide in the United States in the 1980s. The Cruise character in *Risky Business* is the son of affluent parents who are success stories in the Reagan era. In *All the Right Moves*, he is the son of a steelworker who faces unemployment in a town that becomes marginalized during this period.

The films were part of the 1980s teen genre, which reached its peak during this epoch and has been referred to by Jonathan Bernstein (1997) as "the golden age" of teen cinema. During the 1970s, several commercially successful youth-oriented films such as *American Graffiti* (George Lucas, 1973), *Grease* (Randal Kleiser, 1978), and *Animal House* (John Landis, 1978) alerted the Hollywood studios to the growing popularity of the genre. By 1979, about 80 percent of ticket sales were bought by teenagers and those in their twenties (Maltby 2003, 74). Young people had more disposable income than ever before and wanted to watch films that reflected their own experiences. *All the Right Moves* was a serious drama that focused on romance, whereas *Losin' It* and *Risky Business* were part of the teen subgenre—the teen sex comedy—which was characterized by vulgar sexualized humor, including penis jokes, nude bodies, and characters indulging in promiscuous and casual sex, often attempting to lose their virginity. *Porky's* (Bob Clark, 1981) and *Fast Times at Ridgemont High* (Amy Heckerling, 1982) were the two biggest box office hits of this subgenre. Others included *Little Darlings* (Ron Maxwell, 1980), *The Last American Virgin* (Boaz Davidson, 1982), and *Getting It On* (William Olsen, 1983). Timothy Shary (2002, 229) points out these provocative titles "were indicative of the increasingly direct sexual marketing of youth films." Lesley Speed (2010, 821) refers to them as "vulgar

---

3 "Greed is good" is spoken by Michael Douglas's character, Gordon Gekko, the ruthless stockbroker in Oliver Stone's *Wall Street* (1987).

teen comedies [that contain] acts of hedonism at parties, excessive drinking, having sex . . . [and] ridiculing authority figures." The often-graphic content of these films was made possible because of a more liberal approach to film censorship, introduced in 1968. The new film ratings board, the Motion Picture Association of America, replaced the conservative Hays code, which set strict moral guidelines in terms of film content. Explicit sexual and violent scenes and use of profanity were now permitted in feature films. Shary (2005, 35) explains that these changes in relation to teen films "meant more movies dealing with sex, drugs, violence and the honest expression of disdain for adults." These changes in film content ran parallel to changes in Western society. The so-called sexual revolution of the 1960s promoted liberal attitudes toward sex, challenging more conservative values. The drug-fueled, hippie counterculture redefined youth; feminist and gay liberation groups began to emerge, and youth were becoming politicized, protesting against the Vietnam War and supporting civil rights movements. Reflected in the films investigated in this chapter are Thomas Hines's (1999, 27) observations about the evolving nature of the teens and sexuality from the 1960s onward: "Young people increasingly socialized in groups, and they saw sex not so much as a prelude to marriage but as a form of personal exploration and intimate communication. . . . Virginity was no longer prized."

Losin' It

A boyish-looking Tom Cruise was in his early twenties playing a high school teenager when he starred in *Losin' It*. His character, Woody, is one of three middle-class teens from Los Angeles who travel over the border to Tijuana in Mexico to party and lose their virginity. On the surface, the film is a rather unsophisticated and crude tale about hormonally charged teenagers being unruly in another country. But the boys' episodes of sexual initiation can be viewed more critically in terms of the adolescent experience in relation to risk-taking behavior, represented through a cinematic lens. Jeffrey Arnett (1999, 319) writes that "adolescents have higher rates of reckless, norm-breaking, and anti-social behavior than either children or adults . . . [and] are more likely to cause disruptions of the social order and to engage in behavior that carries the potential for harm to themselves and/or the people around them." This gives an early insight into the Cruise persona in terms of risk-taking, something that is a feature of many of his characters in future films. Woody and his friends take to the bars and haunts of Tijuana seeking casual sex, which leads to them incurring the wrath of the Mexican locals. His two friends, Dave (Jackie Earle Haley) and Spider (John Stockwell), depict a more aggressive style of macho behavior: the obnoxious and narcissistic Dave is introduced in the opening scene posing in his bedroom, seminaked and flexing his muscles in front of the mirror; Spider is hotheaded and is involved in a couple of violent incidents. Bernstein (1997, 8) describes the males in the aforementioned *Porky's* as "a group of young male studs . . . blustering but inexperienced and foul mouthed—in feverish pursuit of sex," a description that equally applies to Dave and Spider. This resonates with the concept of masculinity offered by Stella Bruzzi (2013, 115), who writes about Cruise's *Top Gun* (Tony Scott, 1986) "as a performance, a show put on for an imaginary crowd."

But analyzing Woody in terms of his status within the high school stereotype system reveals another side to the Cruise persona, and unlike in many of his later screen roles, it is not one that is based on an exaggerated form of physicality and masculinity. Murray Milner Jr. (2014) writes about the different cliques and groups in the American high school, and Woody could fall into a couple of the categories: although he is part of a group that displays more of a toxic form of maleness ("jocks" [40], who are usually white, heterosexual, narcissistic, and highly noticeable alpha males), Woody could also be described as a "pretend hoodlum" (42) who might look like his jock friends but who is in fact "reasonably well behaved" (43). He is revealed as more nuanced, sensitive, and less macho, foreshadowing his persona in *All the Right Moves*. In his opening bedroom scene, unlike Dave, the clean-cut Woody looks in the mirror, carefully combs his hair, stands up straight, and avoids any macho posturing.

Developing these two opposing attitudes through an adolescent psychological lens can bring the subject of young males' experience of sexual initiation into a sharper, more analytical focus. Examining the Cruise persona in binary terms echoes Donna Peberdy (2010, 231), who, writing about his character in *Magnolia* (Paul Thomas Anderson, 1999), outlines his screen persona in the context of masculinity being a performance shaped by binary forces that "are bipolar, simultaneously exhibiting hard and soft modes" . . . between . . . "Wild Man to Wimp." This structuralist notion is applied here to examine the Cruise persona, but where it differs is that this research inscribes a psychological dimension supported by adolescent real-life experiences, whereas Peberdy relies primarily on spectacle and the physical body within a cinematic landscape. Consequently, a closer investigation reveals something that departs from the orthodox representation of the Cruise persona. While being depicted as "soft" in terms of masculinity and sexuality, Cruise's character development can be located within Laura Carpenter's (2002) empirical research on adolescence. She writes about first-time adolescent sexual experiences and loss of virginity in oppositional terms in the context of it being a "gift" or "stigma" (345), reflecting the concerns and attitudes of teens when confronted with the "do I, don't I?" dilemma. The notion of sex as stigma can be associated with Dave and Spider (and those in *Porky's*) whose predatory sexual conduct is evident in the film: they are adolescents who "express disdain for virginity, engage in sexual activity primarily out of curiosity and desire for physical pleasure" (346). J. Bernard (1981) reinforces this attitude, stating that "young men attach more importance to individuality and had a more impersonal attitude towards sex" (cited in De Gaston, Weed, and Jensen 1996). Treating sex as a "gift" is generally associated with female characters in the 1980s teen comedies; these young women are more interested in relationships, romance, and, at times, preserving their virginity. Although they are exceptions in the genre, some males, like Cruise's Woody, are also seen, initially, treating sex in this way. Woody has the opportunity to lose his virginity with a Mexican prostitute in *Losin' It* but decides against it because he experiences a sense of fear that could be described in more of a psychological context as "heterosexual social anxiety . . . defined as anxiety arising from real, anticipated, or imagined interactions with others of the opposite sex" (Leary and Dobbins 1983, 139). Woody does go on to lose his virginity to an older woman, Kathy (Shelley Long), and the Cruise sexual persona continues to be framed by the "gift" approach to sex, as their encounter is depicted as intimate (although, nevertheless, it turns out to be no more than a casual fling and they go their separate ways). In contrast, Ruth O'Donnell's (2012) portrayal of this scene places it within an Oedipal and psychoanalytical framework, citing Melanie Klein's work on the archaic mother figure and relationship to the male child. The "gift" attitude to sex derives less from theoretical and abstract concepts, reflecting instead empirical research carried out based on real-life sexual experiences of adolescents.

Cruise's Woody removes himself from any dangerous situation involving adolescent risk-taking (which is not the case with his character in *Risky*

Business). Despite Dave's and Spider's machismo in their attempts to have sex, they fail to do so. Dave tries to seduce one of the local girls by spiking her drink with a Spanish fly (an aphrodisiac) and is punished for this by the girl's brother. Spider ends up in jail after becoming involved in a barroom brawl. Adolescent risk-taking here produces a crisis in masculinity: treating sex as a "stigma" results in the failure of the male sexual quest, and characters suffer negative consequences in their pursuit of sex. Conversely, Cruise's sensitive character treats sex as a "gift" and depicts a nonthreatening "soft" form of masculinity, a characteristic he demonstrates in later films, like *All the Right Moves*, *Rain Man* (Barry Levinson, 1988), and *Magnolia*. (The Cruise characters in *Rain Man* and *Magnolia* start off as cynical and macho but by the final act are more sensitive and empathetic.)

Risky Business

Cruise's first leading role was in *Risky Business*, which established his star persona. It was a box office hit and the tenth-highest-grossing American film in 1983 (Box Office Mojo n.d.). He plays the ironically named Joel Goodson, the only child of wealthy parents, living in a mansion in the suburbs of Chicago. Like in *Losin' It*, adolescent sexuality is initially viewed through the Cruise character in terms of him being a shy, virginal teenager. Under pressure from his friends to lose his virginity, he contacts a prostitute, Lana (Rebecca De Mornay), and experiences his sexual awakening. It is more stylistically inventive than *Losin' It* and not as hackneyed in its depiction of teenage adolescence, with the Cruise character being more acutely observed and nuanced.

His persona is immediately evident in the opening scene of *Risky Business*, which features a stylized aesthetic containing a dream sequence, a kind of narrative flashback. His face is shot in extreme close-up as he stares into the camera, addressing the viewer—a visage not to too dissimilar from the fresh-faced look in *Losin' It*. But he displays more of an attitude here: wearing sunglasses and cigarette hanging from his mouth, there is an immediate sense of youthful rebelliousness. O'Donnell (2012) considers this scene in terms of its extratextual qualities—branding and consumption—and discusses the Ray-Ban sunglasses that Cruise wears in relation to the male narcissism that emerged in the image-obsessed 1980s advertising landscape. She points out that sales of this brand soared after Cruise donned them in

Risky Business, helping promote his star status beyond the cinematic text (50–51). But the scene and his persona can be viewed in more behavioral terms relating to adolescent sexuality. Cruise's voiceover describes an erotic recurring dream where he enters his neighbor's house, approaches a naked girl who is in the shower, and then finds himself in a school classroom, where he is late for an exam. This again induces the adolescent fear of sex (and education), and the "heterosexual-social anxiety" referred to above reflects the view that sexuality "poses fundamental challenges for young people" (Crockett, Raffelli, and Moilanen 2001, 371) in terms of coping with feelings of desire, hormonal changes, and the different attitudes of those around them. Furthermore, the dream sequence can be interpreted as a visual representation of "non-coital sexual behavior," defined as an "erotic fantasy" that is "the most common sexual behavior in adolescence" (372). So while Cruise's star persona is being created by the sexualized images seen both on the screen and in a broader cultural context,[4] a psychological intervention contributes to a more internal understanding of the motivations and impulses of his character and identity.

In the next scene, Joel is with his friends. They mock him for being a virgin, which highlights a key feature of adolescent life: peer pressure. As Bradford B. Brown, Donna Rae Clasen, and Sue Ann Eicher (1986, 521) point out, "Conformity to peers is often considered one of the hallmarks of adolescent behavior [and] the adolescent's need for affiliation with a group of peers is manifested by group norms, and . . . the group itself is strengthened when members exert conformity pressures on each other." Pressure for Joel to conform is what creates the initial tension in the narrative; the development of his sexual persona depends on him losing his virginity not just to satisfy his carnal urges but also to reinforce the teen group identity. Teenage peer pressure is more common in issues relating to sexuality than to any other aspect of young peoples' lives (Brooks-Gunn and Furstenberg 1989). Joel is pressured by one of his friends to make the most of his parents going away for the weekend.

Just before Joel's parents leave, his father, the patriarchal figure of authority in his life, lays down the law with strict instructions on what Joel is not to do while they are away (particularly not play the stereo too loudly).

---

4 Cruise was named "the Sexiest Man Alive" in the celebrity magazine, *People*, in June 1990.

"My house, my rules," he tells his son—a handy trigger for Joel's youthful rebellion and transgressive behavior. Matthew Bernstein and David Pratt (1985) write about the film's comedic and ironic implications, pointing to its setting in the capitalist Reagan era of the 1980s and the privileges this entails for rich kids like Joel. Elizabeth G. Traube (1992, 78) describes the persona of Cruise and others (e.g., Matthew Broderick in *Ferris Bueller's Day Off*; John Hughes, 1986) in the 1980s teen genre in romantic terms, as a "roguish heroes: boys who prefers play to work, who succeed through tricks or daring . . . and, routinely subvert established conventions and repressive authority"—traits that are evident in the films released soon after *Risky Business* that came to galvanize his screen presence, such as *Top Gun*, *The Color of Money* (Martin Scorsese, 1986), and *Days of Thunder* (Tony Scott, 1990). Where Traube and others eschew any psychological motivation behind the construction of his persona, the study of adolescence and its phases adds to the existing debates by offering a broader insight into the screen identity of Cruise. Joel's nature resonates with J. A. Hadfield's (1962, 183) "storm and stress" paradigm as it relates to rebellion: "Adolescents have the reputation of being rebellious and disobedient. . . . They are setting out to form their own views and gain their own independence. They are no longer willing to submit without question to the authority even of their parents." Echoing this, M. R. Gray and L. Steinberg (1999, 239–40) refer to this form of rebellion as a process of "individuation" whereby a "young person develops a clearer sense of himself and herself as psychologically separate from their parents."

So Joel begins his transformation from a shy, vulnerable virgin to a more sexually active adolescent. Left alone in the house, he dances with exaggerated confidence in the huge front room, establishing his sexual presence (though at this stage it is more of a performative example of masculine bravado) and inviting the viewer's gaze into this corporeal act. He is half-dressed, in oxford shirt, socks, and underpants, and he dances and pantomimes to Bob Seger's "Old Time Rock & Roll." With music on full blast (disobeying his father's orders), his act of teenage rebellion becomes a physical spectacle. Veronika Rall (1993, 95–96), drawing on the writings of Laura Mulvey and studies relating to psychoanalysis and the gaze, comments on sexual close-ups of his body that convey an image of male exhibitionism and narcissism, replete with homoerotic leanings, "which [invite] the female as well as the male gaze." The scene is an early example that helped establish the Cruise persona. This sexual transformation can be viewed more clinically in adolescence as the "initiation phase" (Van Noorden and Bukowski, 2011, 600), which is characterized by the adolescent's sexual identity evolving and expanding.

The fantasy tone of the film and the fear-of-sex theme continue in a scene in which Joel dreams that while he is making love to the "babysitter," the house is suddenly surrounded by armed police who order him to come out. Neon-red flashing lights saturate the screen, suggesting something transgressive and deviant is taking place. His parents are also there, pleading with him to obey the police. This scene invokes the fear that adolescents experience about sex; in this case, being caught "in the act" by adult and parental authority figures induces an acute sense of embarrassment. The scene is highly stylized and treated comically, belying what it could reveal regarding the difficulties young people have to face when shaping a sexual identity. Adolescent sexuality, Ian McMahan (2009, 412) notes, "is generally treated as a source of problems, rather than as an integral part of human development."

When Joel first meets Lana, the sex is not portrayed as awkward or embarrassing, as it was with Woody's failed attempt with the Mexican prostitute in *Losin' It*. Instead, the dream-like tone reinforces the teenage fantasy. Bernstein and Pratt (1985, 36) refer to the symbolic and dramatic nature of Joel and Lana's encounter in visual terms: Joel's home is the "house-prison" in which he is held captive by his father's strict directives, and when Lana enters the house, "the living room doors swing open onto the patio with a burst of wind." Aesthetically, there is a soft-porn feel to the scene as Cruise's sexual presence is intensified.

These encounters and incidents establish the blueprint for the Cruise persona in terms of masculinity, body image, and sexual presence, both in and out of the cinema. When referencing the dancing/front room scene, O'Donnell (2012, 103) notes: "It is a teenage display of egocentrism and self-pleasure, one that laid the groundwork for the persona of the young Cruise and shot him to fame." But internal adolescent forces that remain hidden from a textual analysis continue to contribute to the psychology behind his persona. The fears that Joel experiences—losing his virginity, peer pressure, and the presence of adult and parental figures intruding on his sexual fantasies—are typical of the teenage anxieties, or "knots" (Friedenberg 1963, 3), that occur in the relatively short, emotionally fraught, and often sexually chaotic coming-of-age process that marks the transition from youth to adulthood.

Joel's adolescent risk-taking sees him damaging his father's Porsche, which he was forbidden to use. His questionable judgment also brings him into conflict with Lana's pimp, Guido (Joe Pantoliano), who demands money for her services. Lana convinces Joel to go into business together in order to pay for the car's repairs and pay off Guido, so they turn his parents' house into a brothel for one night. Joel invites his equally rich and hormonally charged friends, and Lana provides the women—the night is a financial success. Our "roguish hero" (Traube, 1992, 78) becomes, in the words of Gaylyn Studlar (2001, 176), a "hustler . . . narcissistic . . . overconfident," one who showcases "a stubborn disobedience to patriarchal values." Bernstein and Pratt (1985), observing Joel and Lana's success as mini-capitalists (albeit unlawful ones), link sex and entrepreneurship to the "greed is good" Reagan era.

At the same time, Joel's sexual persona evolves: once mocked for being a virgin, he now becomes a kind of pimp and a hero to his friends. In a sense, Cruise's Joel can be viewed as an early comic incarnation of the sex guru he plays in *Magnolia*, Frank T. Mackey. The comically played-out brothel scene portrays sex as a "stigma," as many of Joel's friends lose their virginity without any emotional involvement—and also without any of the consequences that Spider and Dave suffered in *Losin' It*. The film never judges Joel or his transgressive behavior, which is played for laughs—after all, his daring and rebellious nature are key factors in constructing Cruise's screen presence. But if we bracket the comedic elements of this scene, we cannot help but view it framed by the knowledge that adolescent sexual activity has the potential to incur negative consequences, STDs and unwanted pregnancies just two among them. In the real world, McMahan (2009, 421) reminds us, "a great many adolescents are misinformed or uninformed about sex, its possible risks, and ways they can reduce or avoid those risks." But in the fantasy world of Hollywood teen cinema, sex has no unhappy consequences. Unlike the experience of his friends, Joel's sexual relationship with Lana embodies the "gift" of emotional attachment (though the relationship does not last), but even more, because "teens often do not differentiate between sex and love, . . . sex may be used as means to attain status and acceptance" (Miller and Benson 1999, 111). That Joel's hero status remains unchallenged by his friends is one of the key factors of his appeal to his fans and the wider media. It is this "status and acceptance" from his peer group that is instrumental in creating the nascent Cruise sexual persona.

All the Right Moves

In *All the Right Moves*, Cruise is cast against type and plays the lead role in a teen film that departs from the comedy and sexual permissiveness of *Losin' It* and *Risky Business*. This serious sports-related drama centers on a working-class town (a pointed contrast to the affluent suburb where Joel lives in *Risky Business*) whose main employer, the steel mill, is under threat of closure and struggling to survive in Reagan's America. Cruise plays Stefen Djordjevic, who lives with his older brother and widowed father, both of whom work at the mill. He is a high school football player hoping for a scholarship to study engineering at college. There's little gross-out humor and there are few scenes of teens prowling for casual sex; instead, Cruise's persona demonstrates a more sensitive and romantic side through his "gift" relationship with a steady girlfriend, Lisa (Lea Thompson). Although Steff can be seen as a jock, it is not in the stereotypical *Porky's* way: he is a conflicted, vulnerable, and troubled teen, representing the "mood disruptions" phase of adolescent "storm and stress" (Arnett 1999, 320–21). He is also thoughtful and compassionate. This is a different screen persona for Cruise, one that does not rely on comedic hijinks, an extroverted personality, sex appeal, and body image but rather on more temperate and introspective features. Traube (1992, 75) describes his performance in *All the Right Moves* as "decent, honest, and industrious." However, audiences did not warm to this "serious" Cruise persona, and the film was a box office flop.

Another aspect of adolescence seen in Steff in relation to the "storm and stress" model is played out through the conflict between him and his football coach (Craig T. Nelson). Their frequent clashes escalate to the point where the coach blocks Steff's chance to graduate. Initially, Steff ignores his father's advice on how to handle these conflicts, but by the end of the film, he, unlike Joel in *Risky Business*, eventually submits to adult authority. Adolescent rebellion threatens but is never fully released. Instead, a more conservative ending plays out in which a blue-collar teen comes to understand that hard work and conformity to adult values are what it takes to succeed. McMahan (2009) documents risk factors that can negatively affect levels of achievement and progression of teens from less well-off backgrounds, including "growing up in a single parent household . . . [and] family economic stresses, such as having a parent laid off or unemployed" (301), and Cruise's Steff serves as a case in point. One mitigating factor, McMahan notes, is "consistent parental discipline" (301), and this is reflected in the positive influence of Steff's father, who helps curb his rebellious spirit (unlike the father in *Risky Business*, who after laying down the law to his son is largely absent).

Performative masculinity is not a key feature of *All the Right Moves*, but there are instances of drinking, partying, and male bonding on the football field; the male body is not generally sexualized and put on display like in *Risky Business*. In the film's opening sequence, a semi-naked Steff wakes up in his bedroom. His muscled torso is prominent as he begins working out. O'Donnell (2012, 51) refers to this image as another example of "exhibitionist masculinity," but examining the scene through a different lens, one that takes into consideration the impact of sports on adolescent development, allows for a different perspective. Here, Steff's identity is not defined by losing his virginity and gaining hero status among his friends but by self-discipline and focusing on his studies in order to achieve his goal of getting into college on a football scholarship. Cruise's Steff is a representation of someone for whom sports is a "significant factor in the development of . . . identity, self-esteem, and competence" (Danish, Taylor, and Fazio 2001, 97)—characteristics aligned with success and the American dream in the 1980s.

Steff's relationship with his girlfriend, Lisa, reveals the more romantic side of adolescent relationships and a more sensitive side to the Cruise identity—witnessed briefly in *Losin' It*—but here his character is less naïve, vulnerable, and more mature. Their union is portrayed as stable and committed, and there is no dream-like, fantasy imagery that frames their interactions, like in *Risky Business*. They discuss the significance of trust, responsibility, love, and their future together. Their adolescent romantic development, which characterizes their relationship and the Cruise persona here, moves from the "affection phase," in which "adolescents seek new relational depths and substance from their romantic relationships" to the "bonding phase," in which "issues related to commitment" are key emotional features (Van Noorden and Bukowski 2011, 601). If we view the Joel who dances to Bob Seger in *Risky Business* as being in the "initiation phase" of adolescence, where the focus is on "self-exploration" (600), the bonding phase of Steff in *All the Right Moves* represents an evolution of the Cruise sexual/romantic persona. This also supports textual analysis of his changing persona: his narcissism and reliance on fantasy imagery, on full display in *Risky Business*, give way to a more restrained, focused, and mature depiction in *All the Right Moves*.

When Steff and Lisa are heavily petting in his car, he is ready to lose his virginity, but she is not, in what is a tender moment between the couple. Steff is empathetic and displays none of the aggressive attitudes displayed by many of the teenage characters in typical teen sex comedies. When they do have sex, there is but a brief shot of their nude bodies before the camera cuts away to another scene. Here, the Cruise sexual persona offers a portrayal more conservative and less explicit than the one on display in the highly stylized, dream-like aesthetic of *Risky Business*. Sex and romance between teenagers in *All the Right Moves* are ultimately depicted as a positive, healthy experience, in contrast to some of negative descriptions in the adolescent literature. The scenes reflect a thoughtful maturity, along the lines of what Julia A. Graber, Pia R. Britto, and Jeanne Brooks-Gunn (1999, 376) report in their findings of young people's attitudes about sex and relationships: "Many adolescents are entering into sexual relationships and are faced with the task of regulating this behavior and identifying its meaning in the context of the relationship."

The portrayal of masculinity and adolescence in *All the Right Moves* through the Cruise character leans toward old fashioned and traditional; it is far removed from the narcissism of *Risky Business*'s Joel and his rich, privileged friends, who are not held accountable for their rebellious antics because their parents are ineffective and mostly absent. The working-class Steff is portrayed as industrious, hardworking, and optimistic—qualities that were endorsed in the Reagan era in order to succeed. His lack of autonomy within the adult world contrasts sharply with Joel's unfettered freedom and omnipotence—traits that were rewarded in box office returns.

Conclusion

Applying an adolescent psychological rather than a strictly textual approach to three early Cruise films shows a thread of different adolescent phases that links one film to the next. Whether his characters are grappling with risk-taking behavior, peer pressure, or the loss of virginity in a comedic or dramatic genre, together they form a cohesive basis for the construction of Cruise's screen persona.

Risky Business established Cruise's star persona, and *All the Right Moves* demonstrated he could act in more dramatic pictures (although the latter was not as commercially successful). Nevertheless, these performances—others include *Born on the Fourth of July* (Oliver Stone, 1999), the aforementioned *Magnolia*, and Stanley Kubrick's *Eyes Wide Shut* (1999)—proved that he did not always have to rely on the familiar characteristics of his star persona to achieve recognition. Future research focusing on his later roles could benefit if viewed in light of adult psychological phases, which continue to shape and contribute to the Cruise screen persona.

Works Cited

Arnett, Jeffrey Jenson. 1999. "Adolescent Storm and Stress, Reconsidered." *American Psychologist* 54 (5): 317–26.

Bernstein, Jonathan. 1997. *Pretty in Pink: The Golden Age of Teenage Movies*. New York: St. Martin's Press.

Bernstein, Matthew, and David Pratt. 1985. "Comic Ambivalence in 'Risky Business.'" *Film Criticism* 9, no. 3 (Spring): 33–43.

Box Office Mojo. n.d. "Yearly Box Office, 1983 Domestic Grosses." Accessed April 1, 2019. www.boxofficemojo.com/yearly/chart/?view2=releasedate&view=opening&yr=1983&p=.htm.

Brooks-Gunn, Jeanne, and Frank F. Furstenberg. 1989. "Adolescent Sexual Behavior." *American Psychologist* 44 (2): 249–57.

Brown, Bradford, B., Donna Rae Clasen, and Sue Ann Eicher. 1986. "Perceptions of Peer Pressure, Peer Conformity Dispositions, and Self-Reported Behavior among Adolescents." *Developmental Psychology* 22 (4): 521–30.

Bruzzi, Stella. 2013. *Men's Cinema: Masculinity and Mise en Scène in Hollywood*. Edinburgh: Edinburgh University Press.

Carpenter, Laura. 2002. "Gender and the Meaning and Experience of Virginity Loss in the Contemporary United States." *Gender and Sexuality* 16 (3): 345–65.

Crockett, Lisa J., Marcela Raffelli, and Kristen L. Moilanen. 2001. "Adolescent Sexuality: Behaviour and Meaning." In *Blackwell Handbook of Adolescence*, edited by Gerald R. Adams and Michael D. Berzonsky, 371–92. Oxford: Blackwell.

Danish, Steven J., Tanya E. Taylor, and Robert J. Fazio. 2001. "Enhancing Adolescent Development through Sports and Leisure." In *Blackwell Handbook of Adolescence*, edited by Gerald R. Adams and Michael D. Berzonsky, 92–108. Oxford: Blackwell.

De Gaston, Jacqueline F., Stan Weed, and Larry Jensen. 1996. "Understanding Gender Differences in Adolescent Sexuality." *Adolescence* 31 (121).

Friedenberg, Edgar Z. 1963. *Coming of Age in America: Growth and Acquiescence*. New York: Vintage.

Graber, Julia A., Pia R. Britto, and Jeanne Brooks-Gunn. 1999. "What's Love Got to Do with It? Adolescents' and Young Adults' Beliefs about Sexual and Romantic Relationships." In *The Development of Romantic Relationships in Adolescence*, edited by Wyndol Furman, B. Bradford Brown, and Candice Feiring, 364–95. Cambridge: Cambridge University Press, 1999.

Gray, M. R., and L. Steinberg. 1999. "Romance and the Parent–Child Relationship." In *The Development of Romantic Relationships in Adolescence*, edited by Wyndol Furman, B. Bradford Brown, and Candice Feiring, 235–65. Cambridge: Cambridge University Press.

Hadfield, J. A. 1962. *Childhood and Adolescence*. Harmondsworth, UK: Penguin.

Hall, Stanley G. 1904. *Adolescence: Its Psychology and its Relations to Physiology, Anthropology, Sociology, Sex, Crime, Religion, and Education*. New York: D. Appleton.

Hines, Thomas. 1999. *The Rise and Fall of the American Teenager*. New York: Avon Books.

Leary, Mark, R., and Sharon E. Dobbins. 1983. "Social Anxiety, Sexual Behavior, and Contraceptive Use." *Journal of Personality and Social Psychology* 45 (6): 1347–54.

Maltby, Richard. 2003. *Hollywood Cinema* (2nd ed.). London: Blackwell.

McMahan, Ian. 2009. *Adolescence*. Boston: Pearson.

Miller, Brent C., and Brad Benson. 1999. "Romantic and Sexual Relationship Development during Adolescence." In *The Development of Romantic Relationships in Adolescence*, edited by Wyndol Furman, B. Bradford Brown, and Candice Feiring, 99–121. Cambridge: Cambridge University Press.

Milner, Murray, Jr. 2004. *Freaks, Geeks, and Cool Kids: American Teenagers, Schools, and the Culture of Consumption*. New York: Routledge.

O'Donnell, Ruth. 2012. "Performing Masculinity: The Star Persona of Tom Cruise." PhD diss., Royal Holloway, University of London.

Peberdy, Donna. 2010. "From Wimp to Wild Man: Bipolar Masculinity and the Paradoxical Performances of Tom Cruise." *Men and Masculinities* 13 (2): 231–54.

Rall, Veronika. 1993. "This Isn't Filmmaking, It's War: A Gendered Gaze on the Tom Cruise Phenomenon." *Visual Anthropology Review* 9, no. 1 (Spring): 92–104.

Shary, Timothy. 2002. *Generation Multiplex: The Image of Youth in Contemporary American Cinema*. Austin: University of Texas Press.

——— . 2005. *Teen Movies. American Youth on Screen*. London: Wallflower.

Speed, Lesley. 2010. "Loose Cannons: White Masculinity and the Vulgar Teen Comedy Film." *Journal of Popular Culture* 43 (4): 820–40.

Studlar, Gaylyn. 2001. "Cruise-ing into the Millennium: Performative Masculinity, Stardom, and the All-American Boy's Body." In *Ladies and Gentlemen, Boys and Girls: Gender in Film at the End of the Twentieth Century*, edited by Murray Pomerance, 171–83. Albany: State University of New York Press.

Traube, Elizabeth G. 1992. *Dreaming Identities: Class, Gender and Generation in 1980s Hollywood Movies*. Boulder, CO: West View Press.

Van Noorden, Tirza H. J., and William M. Bukowski. 2011. "Social Development." In *An Introduction to Developmental Psychology* (3rd ed.), edited by Alan Slater and Gavin Bremner, 577–610. Hoboken, NJ: Wiley.

2

GAZING AT TOM CRUISE

Sean Redmond

When one begins to think about the affective qualities of Tom Cruise's star image, then the significance of gazing at him becomes immediately apparent or *transparent*. As with so many male Hollywood leads, looking at Tom Cruise is a lens-based strategy used in those films he stars in, in advertorial and promotional materials, in magazine and television interviews, and in the paratexts that circulate around his star image. Viewers and readers are asked to gaze at Tom Cruise in the intimate proximity of the close-up; in high-octane action shots; while running, smiling, eating, emoting; in moments of stillness and introspective contemplation; and through ironic or subversive juxtaposition, where the Cruise image is lampooned and resexualized. Gazing at Tom Cruise is very often meant to confirm his status as a heterosexual, Hollywood heartthrob, and a white salvific American hero. And yet, of course, gazing at Tom Cruise also involves a degree of perverse desire, particularly as his star image has shifted, since when looking at Cruise he seems so often to appear as too emotionally excessive, too plastic, and always as potentially queer.

Tom Cruise occupies a vexing space, then, in terms of desire and desirability. On the one hand, he is masculine perfection personified, and yet, on the other, his desirability is liminally oriented, awkwardly fleshed, opening up his star image and media representation to queer longings and gender fluid interpretations. Tom Cruise often occupies what Alex Doty (1993, 21) defines as a queer space in which "already queerly positioned viewers can connect with in various ways, and within which straights can express their queer impulses." When one is asked to gaze at Tom Cruise within a filmic context, there is an inherent tension or struggle over how he is to be desired, even or especially when the regime of looking is constructed within homosocial action films and heterosexual romances.

This liminal gazing is, of course, compounded or affected by the paratexts and commentaries that impose or suggest a queer reading on or over his films. As Gaylyn Studlar (2001) observes, "This can be discerned in the slippage between the construction of his onscreen desirability as both a homoerotic and heteroerotic sign and offscreen fan inscriptions of him as the object of gay desire coupled with media innuendoes to the effect that he is gay." There is nothing straightforward about looking at Tom Cruise.

This chapter will explore the phenomenon of gazing at Tom Cruise, focusing on three films: *Top Gun* (Tony Scott, 1986), *Jerry Maguire* (Cameron Crowe, 1996), and *Born on the Fourth of July* (Oliver Stone, 1989). *Top Gun* offers up hyperbolic images of a hypermasculine and heterosexual Cruise, coupled with highly charged homosocial and homoerotic male relationships. These excessively coded images and encounters are said to ultimately undermine the heterosexual script the film tries to run with. *Jerry Maguire* attempts to "fix" Cruise's desirability and heterosexual orientation within the conventions of the romantic comedy. However, through excessive, racially coded visual gesturing, the film ultimately reconfigures the desire that is on offer. In *Jerry Maguire* the real love story, the real regime of gazing it unleashes, is between two men of different races. *Born on the Fourth of July* offers the viewer a "broken" image of Cruise, whose role as a disabled Vietnam vet is meant to be anything but desirable. However, narratively and contextually speaking, the films draws on the honed and youthful star image of Cruise to haunt the disability representation that follows. What *Born on the Fourth of July* offers the viewer is a perverted form of desiring or gazing at Tom Cruise. These are perversions, in fact, that sit at the queer heart of his star image.

The three films taken together display Cruise at the height of his star power, from the mid-1980s to the mid-1990s, and as such, they collectively work to reveal how in *seeing* Tom Cruise, gender, and sexuality are openly called into question. Across his film career, it will be shown, Cruise is always a star image of gender and sexual ambivalence.

"Take My Breath Away"

In *Top Gun*, Cruise plays Pete "Maverick" Mitchell, an ace fighter pilot who attends the Naval Fighter Weapons School at Naval Air Station Miramar. The film immediately sets up Maverick as an especially skilled and daring pilot, though one who also breaks rules and seems to care more about himself and individual acts of heroism than he does the "team," or squad. Coming out at the time of rampant Reaganism and the virulent forces of neoliberalism, *Top Gun*'s concern with possessive masculine individualism and the need to gather together under the American flag, points to the tension inherent in valorizing the self while needing to foster aggressive nationalist sentiment.

Top Gun's aesthetic very much embodies or translates the hyper-consumption fantasies that emerged during this decade. From the fetishization of war machines and motorcycles, to the picture-postcard sun-drenched beaches and boulevards, to the masculine bodies that are sun kissed, undressed, and adorned with high fashion military iconography, the film is set within a militarized shopping-mall-inspired mise-en-scène. Of course, Cruise is a "perfect fit" for the film, and the character of Maverick, since his star image at this time is connected to new forms of stylized metro-masculinity. Cruise is as much a consumerist dream—here replete with aviator sunglasses, blue eyes, soft voice, and hard body—as he is a serious actor (Simpson 1994). When it comes to looking or gazing at Cruise in the movie, this tension, or layering, is played out. As Ruth O'Donnell (2012, 52–53) suggests, "The homoerotic male display, which characterizes the film, is responsible for defining the persona. Ray-Bans, now in the Aviator style, are worn by Cruise riding a motorbike: the ultimate in consumer desirability. His character embodies the persona's contradictions: a macho Navy pilot flying high-tech fighter planes, yet objectified in a manner typical of Hollywood's representation of women."

Cruise is objectified in the film in terms of how he is gazed at, but this objectification occupies different registers, each depending on who is doing the looking, what the scene involves, and on what Cruise is performing as the looking regime is activated. First, the "objective" camera gazes at Cruise as he maneuvers fighter planes, plays beach volleyball, and looks out over the ocean, although the difference between seeing Cruise in action or inaction creates different moments of desiring spectacle. The film gazes at Cruise through long lenses as well as tight close-ups, and in extended advertorial moments where popular music washes his presence and the high-sheen landscape he moves through. For example, after the tragic death of Goose, for which he feels partly responsible, Maverick, dressed in his leather bomber jacket and wearing the iconic aviator sunglasses, rides his Kawasaki Ninja motorcycle—then the fastest production motorcycle in the world—to the edge of the air force base. As the orange sun sets, and palm trees rush buy, a fighter plane enters the scene as Maverick comes to a halt and stares up in melancholic contemplation. In close-up and reaction shots, the camera catches Cruise's youthful face, and while the iconography suggests a potent hypermasculinity is on display, there is something "bipolar" (Peberdy 2010, 231) about the way he signifies here. Cruise is too soft, too much of a poseur, as I will outline further below, to carry off this type of masculinity while his beauty within this shimmering setting asks of us to (queerly) desire him.

Second, male characters gaze at Cruise in training sessions and in one to ones, locking him/them in an intense stare that "pauses" the narrative and fosters or forces sexual tension to emerge. For example, in the induction for pilots new to Top Gun, the actor is caught in a relay of gazes. Sitting behind him and to his left are Iceman (Val Kilmer) and Hollywood (Whip Hubley), the latter with his arm over the other's shoulder. As the commander, Mike "Viper" Metcalf (Tom Skerritt), details what is required of them, he stares intently at Maverick. Maverick returns the gaze in what appears to be a solo setting because of the shot's framing, which excludes Goose but who we realize later is sitting next to him. This creates the sense that this exchange of looks between Maverick and Iceman is deeply personal. In many of Cruise's films, as Studlar (2001, 177) argues, the "intensity of commitment and feeling is displaced from the heterosexual to the homosocial to the homoerotic." Further, because of the way Viper and Hollywood have been framed together, as if they are a "couple," it feels like a love triangle in the (un)making.

The scene ends with Maverick and Goose getting up first to leave the briefing. As they do so, Iceman makes a derogatory comment about Maverick's chance of being Top Gun, telling him his plaque will be in the "ladies' room." The ambivalence of the scene is explicitly brought to the fore through this revelatory joke: Iceman gazes at Maverick as if he is a woman to be conquered, something Cruise's liminal star image allows to be projected onto or into. Further, in this scene and many others, Maverick returns the gaze, and the coded meaning of this depends not so much on where his gaze falls—on friend, rival, or lover—but in its pansexual inclusivity.

Third, female characters gaze at Cruise in moments of dreamy desirability, seemingly confirming his heterosexual, masculine availability. However, and with specific regard to his main love interest, "Charlie" Blackwood (Kelly McGillis), gender relations and attractions are confused and complicated as binaries fall away. Charlie, a masculinized name, appears as both "beard," or "a heterosexual prop to dispel possible accusations of homosexuality on the part of Maverick" (O'Donnell 2012, 55), and, more complexly, identity transgressor in the film, taking up the position of male, rather than female, suitor. In *Top Gun*, the looking regimes between Charlie and Maverick are relatively equal: they are "both to be looked at." However, there are scenes in which Charlie occupies the masculine position, most notably in the elevator, where, hair tucked up, she is conventionally wearing male clothes (baseball cap, leather bomber jacket) as she converses with Maverick. In this scene, Maverick is still wet from the shower he has just taken and wears just a singlet: a context and aesthetic that is usually associated with female characters. High-key lighting picks out his youthful features more than they do Charlie's, and given she is the instructor, she holds a position of power over him. The dialogue fizzes with sexual innuendo and chemistry, but the role reversals here draw attention to heterosexual performativity and to the liquid ravines of Cruise's star image. The scene ultimately becomes one taken up in paratextual commentary and fanfic to "out" Cruise, most notably in the film *Sleep with Me* (Rory Kelly, 1994), in which Quentin Tarantino as a party guest undertakes a queer reading of the film.

Finally, Cruise's Maverick gazes at himself through reflective surfaces and mirrors, trapped in his own consumerist narcissism, showcasing a virulent form of self-love, while embodying the liminal art of the poseur. Posing

> insists on self-awareness, image, and surface and keeps in place the temporal and material positions of "original" and "copy," and . . . functions within an interaction among creator, spectator, and the object of the gaze—an interaction that is already saturated with implications of power and desire. Importantly, to "strike a pose" is to stop the action of the body, to allow the viewer to become absorbed in visual pleasure and desire, and also to allow the poser the pleasure of inhabiting the object position. (Peraino 2012, 156)

Two key scenes are particularly worth exploring in relation to gazing at Cruise as poseur. First, the beach volleyball scene has become an iconic moment in the Cruise oeuvre. Here, we see Maverick and Goose engage in a match against their squad nemeses', Iceman and Hollywood. We watch a shirtless Maverick in sports-action mode striking poses, his toned and muscular body flexed and stilled. Long shots and close-ups are used to capture the physicality of this body and to texturize his muscle, back, and torso. Iceman and Hollywood, also both shirtless, strike similar poses, and the anthemic soundtrack that scores this scene, "Playing with the Boys" by Kenny Loggins, anchors the display as decidedly masculine, competitive, and homosocial. As O'Donnell (2012, 54) suggests, "Cruise . . . inhabits this exhibitionist space and solicits the male gaze himself." Cruise's on-display body is on one level active here, but the relationship to body building through the poses each man strikes renders the gazing and the activities as objects and subjects of male desire: of existing in, or entering into, a decidedly queer space. As Mark Simpson (1994, 42) suggests, "The male bodybuilder dramatizes in his flesh the insecurity, the uncertainty, the enigma of masculinity. He is living testament, not so much to the capabilities of the male body, its phallic power, its massive irresistible virility . . . but rather to the sacred mystery of sex and gender, the fluidity of the categories male and female, masculine and feminine, hetero and homo and the fabulous, perverse tricks they play." The scene ends with Maverick leaving the game early to rendezvous with Charlie. Given that Charlie occupies a liminal position in the narrative, it can be read that Maverick is leaving this one male arena to be within (in) another. There is an easy and fluid transition here for Cruise's character: the posing found in the game leads to posing in front of Charlie.

The second key scene in which posing takes place happens in the locker room as the Top Gun squad are getting changed. The narrative context is important here: during an earlier combat training sortie, Maverick abandons his wingman, Hollywood, to chase Viper, only to be maneuvered into a position from which he can be shot down from behind. The scene is meant to demonstrate the value of teamwork over individual prowess. In the locker room, Cruise, Goose, Iceman, and Hollywood are all undressed, with only a short towel covering their genital areas. The locker room is steamy, and all the characters strike poses reminiscent of classical Greek male statues, such as the Riace Warriors; Diskobolos, the discus thrower (attributed to Myron ca. 450 BCE); and the Nike of Paionios at Olympia (ca. 420 BCE). These bodies are hypermasculine but are also perfectly sculpted with curves and softness that suggest gender ambivalence. All the characters in this scene are to be wetted, carrying the connotations of sexual arousal. Iceman delivers a speech, outlining why Maverick is "dangerous" and questioning whose side he is on. (As he does so, Maverick "presents" himself to Iceman, to the objective camera), posing in a manner that is usually attributed to female models in highly sexualized contexts. Maverick goes on to promise Goose that he won't make the same mistake again, but here the "mistake" is set within a deeply charged homoerotic "sauna" and the ambiguity leaks its way into Cruise's star representation. The scene ends with a still, medium shot of Maverick in contemplation mood, looking up toward the heavens, his perfectly calved chin reminiscent of gods who were neither male or female, neither straight nor gay.

Taken as a totality, gazing at Tom Cruise in *Top Gun* creates an ambivalence in terms of gender binaries and heterosexual imaginings. Envisioning Cruise results in the blurring of the masculine and feminine, and on how and where desire manifests, creating these queer spaces of connectivity. The film's most famous nondiegetic song is Berlin's "Take My Breath Away." It is used in the film over utopian settings and military machinery and to anchor the love affair between Maverick and Charlie. But more than this, the song defines Cruise's star image, holds his visage in lovingly feminine and queer hands. It his face that is meant to take all our breath away.

Show Me the Money

In *Jerry Maguire*, Tom Cruise plays the film's titular character, a highly successful thirty-five-year-old sports agent working for the proto-competitive Sports Management International. Jerry has a long A-list of male sports stars but realizes that he has lost his way within the capitalist, corporate machine, which no longer cares for its clients or employees but only for profit and gain. In response, he writes and distributes a mission statement based on the ethos of having fewer clients, with each one developing out of or into friendships. Jerry is subsequently fired—by his protégé, Bob Sugar (Jay Mohr)—within a week of writing this mission statement, and he loses all but one of his clients: Arizona Cardinals wide receiver Rod Tidwell (Cuba Gooding Jr.). Rod stays with Jerry not only because he sees and hears in him a certain reflection of his "alienated" self but also because he has few options given that his career seems to be on the wane. Cruise and Rod develop a biracial "buddy" friendship (Fuchs 1993), and by the end of the film, a lucrative contract has been secured.

Jerry Maguire offers us a critical take on consumer capitalism, pairing Jerry and Rod as outsiders, the former because he rejects ethically bankrupt neoliberal capitalism, the latter because as a black American male his access to the American dream is clearly coded by inequality and inequity. Within the film's leanings toward conscious capitalism, there is a recognition of the ferocious nature of individualism and the need for work to have higher purpose, one "that goes beyond making money" (Conscious Capitalism n.d.). Nonetheless, Jerry and Rod's relationship is still a commodified one, driven and shaped by the desire to succeed within capitalism, whether it cares or not.

Cruise is a perfect fit for the role of Jerry Maguire since, as outlined above, his star image sits across these two vectors, in an ambivalent space between hard-bodied hyperindividualism and softhearted collective belonging. The film draws on character echoes and iconic images from *Top Gun* in particular. At the start of the film, Jerry is Maverick, a possessive individual whose plastic personality is all about looking out for number one. The Ray-Bans are carried over from *Top Gun*, as is the potentiality of the homoerotic, with Rod substituting, albeit much more complexly, for Iceman. The locker scene from *Top Gun* is repeated in the sense that one of the more intimate and "baring" encounters between Jerry and Rod happens in this space. Similarly, single mother Dorothy Boyd (Renée Zellweger), Cruise's main love interest in the film, provides the heteronormative space to make safe this latent homoerotism and to romanticize and heterosexualize him. Dorothy is a homespun, sweeter version of *Top Gun*'s Charlie.

With respect to this patriarchal and heterosexual triangle, O'Donnell (2012, 35) suggests that "the business dynamic between Rod Tidwell and Maguire is more complicated: mutual affection appears to circumvent the worst excesses of capitalism, but the relationship is undermined by the profit model. The only reliable bond a man can rely on, so the logic of *Jerry Maguire* goes, is that between husband and wife: the closeness of the two men is undermined by their marriages. The message is that heterosexual romantic bonds will win out." Nonetheless, while Rod's marriage is shown to be happy and explicitly reproductive (his wife gives birth during the film), Jerry's marriage to Dorothy is, at least until the end of the film, outed as unhappy, as a marriage of convenience for him. Their marriage grants him access to Dorothy's son, whom Jerry closely bonds with, and ties him to a patriarchal triangle that seems to exclude women. This triangle is made up of Rod; Ray (Jonathan Lipnicki), Dorothy's son; and Dickie Fox (Jared Jussim), Jerry's mentor in the film whom we see in a series of "memorial" flashbacks. What we have here is Cruise's character craving for, and succeeding in, male-bonded relationships—again, very similar to the squad mentality in *Top Gun*. These friendships, particularly with respect to Rod, are so powerfully constructed that they fill *Jerry Maguire* with semiotic "surplus value," energizing the film. Jerry is happiest, always, when in male company.

There are two gazing key scenes in the film that I would like to now address, each one framing Cruise's star image as an ambivalent one, filling the text with gendered and sexual uncertainty. In addition, racial ambiguity enters the representation, further splitting Cruise's wholesome-white star image.

First, near the beginning of the film, Jerry is courted at his bachelor party—he is set to marry his fiancée, Avery (Kelly Preston), whom he later rejects. He enters the scene like a movie star, high-fiving his excited male work colleagues, who respond to his greeting with exuberant hand claps. He beams his trademark smile and moves like a famed celebrity—like a "Tom Cruise" among them. We see these male colleagues offer him confirming gazes, and as a fat cigar is lit for him and then smoked, the phallocentric energy of the scene is completed. Again, there are echoes of the male camaraderie of *Top Gun* carried forward in this scene but given that this film plays more than ten years after that, and with a turbulent public image, it is Cruise's now slick, hyperreal star image that slickly or sickly greases the scene. The scene feels or reads as reflective and reflexive: the gazes undermine the Cruise image as they simultaneously reveal the emptiness at the heart of *Jerry Maguire*.

At this party, a montage video of Jerry's ex-girlfriends' thoughts on him has been put together. As he watches it, we can see him become uncomfortable as certain truths hit home. Each of the women comment on how "he doesn't do intimacy" and how he doesn't like to be alone. They mimic his trademark greeting gesture, drawing attention to his phony posturing and posing. Cut among these commentaries are shots of Avery preparing to torch his little black book that contains the names of those female conquests. The relay of looks in this scene is very powerful: each of these women stare out of the screen and back at Jerry; Jerry stares hauntingly at the montage as it unfolds and then around at other partygoers to check whether they are watching him watch the video. We see glances of recognition and awkward smiles. Jerry becomes self-aware in the scene and yet only partially so: the intimacy he runs from in the film, the intimacy he fails to feel or transfer out to others, has not to do with his "lack" or in not having yet found someone "right." The intimacy failure has to do with the heterosexual script Cruise is bound to. His character finds plenty of intimacy in the film, but it is with other men—it is with Rod.

Second, Jerry and Rod's friendship develops in the "classic" way of movie biracial buddies: they grow to understand each other; they are placed in similar predicaments; and their friendship is tested, grows, and endures. In many ways, Rod takes on the comedic role that builds from and maintains the racial stereotype of the foil to the white male lead (Ames 1992). There are elements of the "coon" represented, most notably in the hysterical way that Rod deals with crisis, while Jerry is, at least initially, situated within a middle-class milieu that essentially civilizes him (Lasch-Quinn 2006). Nonetheless, there is also a degree of role reversal and of blackface. Jerry is an outsider within the corporate world, loses all his clients except for Rod, on whom he has to now rely, and seems to respond to crisis through excessive performative gestures, not dissimilar to way black males are historically racially fixed (Snead 2016). There are also mirroring scenes (most notably with "show me the money"), where Jerry has to strip away his reserve to embody Rod's desire for Jerry to work for him while revealing the pain of having to do so. Of course, the "show me the money" scene is also the money shot of the film. Cruise, captured in a tight close-up, has to emotionally ejaculate, highlighted in the frenzy of the visible that sees him reach an orgasmic plateau. The film connects sex and money in numerous ways, but what we see and hear in this scene is Cruise's Jerry "coming" for Rod.

This mirroring and excessive gesturing is picked up in the locker room scene. When Jerry tries to convince Rod to "drop the attitude," Rod interprets this suggestion as asking him to "entertain," explicitly picking up on the racial implications of such a request. Jerry then adopts the black entertainer's role, inhabiting the space of the locker room to wildly gesticulate, elasticizing his body to do so. The black–white power dynamic demonstrably shifts in this scene: Rod both interprets how Jerry is "hanging by a thin thread" and laughs at this mimicry. Nonetheless, one can also read this scene as

Jerry's wanting and seeking Rod's affection: Cruise's performance of race and gender here is one designed to capture the gaze of the love interest, and his Jerry is indeed a worthy suitor for Rod. As the scene ends, Rod is seen in long shot for the first time, and we see that he has been naked for its entirety. Cruise has been performing for Rod in an arena where everything is being revealed, or "outed."

The ambivalence in Cruise's star image enables such forms of "passing," which is of course a power granted to white stars in particular (Redmond 2004). However, this passing is here homoerotically charged and moves in and across gendered spaces. When Jerry runs to Dorothy's house at the end of the film to let her and her son know that they "complete" him, there is something both false and queer about the confessional. Set in a highly coded female space, the parlor or lounge, which is full of single women or female divorcées, Jerry seemingly commits to family life and heterosexual love. However, he enters this female space as a man whose life has been built on the strength of male-to-male relationships and whose relationships with women have been shown to be noncommittal and sterile. In accepting Jerry's love soliloquy as truthful, Dorothy, then, will allow Cruise to pass as straight, but the money shot of the film has been shown to exist elsewhere and with someone else.

Just to Be Whole Again

In *Born on the Fourth of July*, Cruise plays Ron Kovic, whose biography the film is built on. Spanning twenty years of Kovic's life, the film creates a chronology that charts his childhood and teen years; his military service, active combat, and paralysis during the Vietnam War; and his transition to anti-war activist. The film's wider set of political contexts addresses nationalism, populism, racism, and the growth of the counterculture movement.

Born on the Fourth of July offers us, then, another political discourse to set Cruise's star image against or into, one that stands in contrast to both the selfish and conscious capitalism found in the other two films analyzed above. More generally, this is a film that disables the Cruise star image found in his preceding film roles and foreshadows the corporate Cruise that follows it in *Jerry Maguire*. What we implicitly see is the different avenues his career takes and how that sits within the contradictory and shifting logics of late American capitalism. Cruise can do this, as I note above, because his star image is built on ambivalence.

In choosing Cruise for the part, Oliver Stone reveals, "I saw this kid who has everything. . . . And I wondered what would happen if tragedy strikes, if fortune denies him. In the film, one thing after another begins to unravel in a man's life. He kills one of his own men and atones by wandering through nine circles of hell. I thought it was an interesting proposition: What would happen to Tom Cruise if something goes wrong?" (Dutka 1989). It is telling that Stone collapses the star Tom Cruise into the character of Kovic, as if he recognizes that when we watch the film it will be Cruise that we are gazing at and connecting with. *Born on the Fourth of July* seems to explicitly make this connection through the lighting and framing techniques that capture Cruise's Kovic before he heads off to fight in Vietnam. He is both glamorized and heroically embodied, his youthfulness carried over from earlier films, particularly the masculine–feminine traces of his role in *Top Gun*, which saturate or punctuate the text with his star impressions. Nonetheless, there are desiring consequences for having these star traces hang over the film, since his perfect if liminal image continues to haunt the narrative long after he has been rendered a paraplegic. One perversely desires Cruise even or especially because his character's body has been damaged and resignified as flaccid.

This star hauntology emerges in a powerful scene that transitions between a romantic dance with his college sweetheart at the prom and an orange dawn on the killing fields of Vietnam. Kovic has not planned on going to the dance, too shy to ask Donna (Kyra Sedgwick) to go with him. However, after a prayer conversation with God, crouched beneath a cross in his bedroom, he runs through the streets in the rain to dance and kiss her as the song "Moon River" plays over the ballroom speakers. This is a classically encoded romantic scene, often found at the end of a romantic comedy, where it confirms the essential worth and power of heterosexual romance. Again, Cruise's androgynous looks create the impression that Kovic is dreamier than Donna. However, just as we are invited to imagine this "happy ending," the film's use of elliptical editing pushes us forward in time to the fiery, smoky landscape of Vietnam. Kovic is not going to be able to consummate his relationship with Donna but will instead be crippled on the battlefield, a message not singularly to do with their relationship but also with the patriarchal script enmeshed in the horrors of war.

This question of Cruise and sex is also one that more generally haunts his star image, as I have been teasing out in this chapter. Cruise generally has bad or unfulfilling heterosexual sex in his films, or his desire to have meaningful sex is thwarted or stands in for desires that belong somewhere else or with someone else, as is the case with both *Top Gun* and *Jerry Maguire*.

For example, in a later scene in *Born on the Fourth of July*, set at the Villa Duce (Village of the Sun), a haven for wounded Vietnam vets, Kovic has simulated sex with Maria, a prostitute (Cordelia González). The scene, set in a nondescript, low-rent hotel room, is bathed in red lighting, suggesting both the illicit nature of the engagement and the violence from which he has returned from, washed, as he is, in metaphorical blood. His long and matted hair and oversize mustache are both signs of giving up and of corporeal resistance to the industrial-military complex that has failed him. As Maria begins to unbuckle his trousers, Kovic tells her, "I can't feel anything, I was paralyzed in the war. . . . It doesn't move, it is no good. . . . Please, no. My spine was severed. I have no movement, no feeling, there is nothing down here at all. Nothing happens." Cruise is rendered a eunuch in this scene, and this positioning works since his star image often feels or reads flaccid in relation to heterosexual encounters. Maria goes on to mount him: she performs her own arousal as if Kovic is penetrating her, and the camera lingers on her breasts and the curves of her body, creating sensorial textures. The camera returns to Cruise, his face wetted on the pillow as tears fall down his cheeks. Kovic is haunted by his past, by his decision to go to war and not stay at home with Dorothy; his broken body stands in not only for the failure of the Vietnam War to make masculine heroes of its young men but of his own monstrous abjection as well. Here, Kovic's abjection is born from Cruise's star image.

Julia Kristeva (1980, 9) argues that "abjection is above all ambiguity. . . . It does not radically cut off the subject from what threatens it—on the contrary, abjection acknowledges it to be in perpetual danger." Further, as Margrit Shildrick (2005, 341–42) suggests, the domain of the abject "is no mere abstraction but a site that is in fact 'densely populated' by all those whose bodies, practices, and desires contest the boundaries of the normative subject. They are the sexual outlaws, the people with disabilities, the racial others, the monsters of every kind, all those who have been denied a place in the symbolic, the domain of the intelligible and fully realized subject in the mode of sexed and gendered self-sufficiency and self-control." Cruise's star image is a site where these nonnormative potentialities emerge, since, to paraphrase Rod, it is always hanging by a thread of ambivalence. The type of perversion found in this film, however, "is not a repudiation or celebration of certain acts but ways of thinking such acts" (MacCormack 2004, 3), which brings them into out into the open. Cruise is a vehicle for thinking about such perversions, undermining normative discourse as he does so.

Perverse desire works in another form in the film, however. This is the desire for the body that is wheelchair bound and unable to run, work, consummate: a form of paraphilia fetishization, then, for the body that shatters boundaries as it lies shattered in a symbolic anti-normalized space. But there is also desire for the Cruise body that is *performing* this disability on screen. That is to say, perverse desire works so well in *Born on the Fourth of July* because Cruise's star ambivalence is already a challenge to embodied norms and normalized sexual practices.

One scene, set on the eve of the Fourth of July, which is also Kovic's birthday, plays out this double dialogue of desire and perversion extremely well. Kovic had earlier been asked to give a speech at the Independence Day parade but is unable to finish it after he hears a crying baby in the crowd and has a flashback to Vietnam, where he and the viewer are returned to the firefight where a family with small children are negligently killed. Kovic's friend Timmy (Frank Whaley) rescues him from the parade and together are now found sitting on the porch, drinking beer. The scene is initially a two-shot, which captures the shared nature of the conversation between them as each reveals his traumatic memories. As the scene progresses and the depths of their despair is agonizingly explored, the camera moves closer in on Kovic's face, even when Timmy is talking. At this stage of the film, Kovic appears somewhere between a clean-cut soldier and a ragged returning vet. His hair has grown and he wears informal civilian clothes, but the clean-shaven, boyish face shines through. There is innocence entangled with experience, beauty with the beast of war. Of course, it is Cruise's star image that allows such opposites to seed and root. Further, we are invited to desire him, to be attracted to the abjection he now embodies. As the camera moves from medium shot to a close-up, Kovic says: "Who gives a fuck now if I was a hero or not. I was paralyzed, castrated that day. Why? It is so, so stupid. I have my dick and my balls now and I think . . . I would give everything I believe in, everything I got, all my values just to have my body back again, just to be whole again. I am not whole and never will be and that is just the way it is." Cruise's face occupies half the screen; the remainder is out of focus dark space, into which fantasies can be projected. However, the dialogue refers us to his body and his flaccid penis, drawing our attention to his sexual immobility, rearing into view his disability, filling the void of the frame with the longing to see his flaccidness. His face is still the chiseled version from *Top Gun*, but its luminance continues to invite us to queerly desire him. We desire him not in spite of his disability but because of it, since his star image has always been an ambivalent one, a perverse one, here magnified in an affective close-up. Cruise will never be whole, ontologically secure, and the answer he gives to his own question rings true across his entire film career. This is a splitting worth having, nonetheless, since it breaks down heteronormative binaries, flooding the films he stars in with possibility and potentiality.

Conclusion

One can chart both the connecting fibers of Cruise's star image across the three films under discussion in this chapter as well as the political contexts his ambivalent representations seems to be speaking to. To take the films in order of their release, we see Cruise starring in the pro-war and hyperindividualist *Top Gun*, then in the anti-war and socially conscious *Born on the Fourth of July*, and finally in the soft capitalism of *Jerry Maguire*. We see the imprints of the Reagan, Bush Sr., and Clinton administrations shaping the different ideologies of the film, alongside the long bow of the failure of the Vietnam War. We can see the way Cruise's star image is fluid enough to move across these different ideological terrains and how his star image also connects and works against the grain of these films. His ambivalent star image often over-determines the way they can be read, a reading that invites gender and sexual uncertainty into the "houses" where they are set. When we gaze at Tom Cruise, a sea of delirious and delicious affects emerges, as desires take flight, bodies break down, and love floats into rainbow-colored homes.

Works Cited

Ames, Christopher. 1992. "Restoring the Black Man's Lethal Weapon Race & Sexuality in Contemporary Cop Films." *Journal of Popular Film and Television* 20 (3): 52–60.

"Conscious Capitalism: A Definition." n.d. Arthur W. Page Center, Pennsylvania State University. Accessed September 1, 2019. https://pagecentertraining.psu.edu/index.php/public-relations-ethics/corporate-social-responsibility/lesson-2-introduction-to-conscious-capitalism/conscious-capitalism-a-definition/.

Doty, Alexander. 1993. *Making Things Perfectly Queer: Interpreting Mass Culture*. Minneapolis: University of Minnesota Press.

Dutka, Elaine. 1989. "The Latest Exorcism of Oliver Stone: With Ron Kovic's 'Born on the Fourth of July,' the Film Maker Returns to Vietnam to Cast out More of the War's Demons." *Los Angeles Times*, December 17, 1989. www.latimes.com/archives/la-xpm-1989-12-17-ca-1635-story.html.

Fuchs, Cynthia J. 1993. "The Buddy Politic." In S. Cohan and I. R. Hark, eds., *Screening the Male*, edited by S. Cohan and I. R. Hark, 194–210. London: Routledge.

Jordan, Chris. 2003. *Movies and the Reagan Presidency: Success and Ethics*. Westport, CT: Praeger.

Kristeva, Julia. 1980. *Desire in Language: A Semiotic Approach to Literature and Art*. New York: Columbia University Press.

Lasch-Quinn, Elisabeth. 2006. "Identity Crisis." *New Humanist*, January–February 2006. https://newhumanist.org.uk/articles/940/identity-crisis.

MacCormack, Patricia. 2004. "Perversion: Transgressive Sexuality and Becoming-Monster." *Thirdspace: A Journal of Feminist Theory & Culture* 3, no. 2 (March). arro.anglia.ac.uk/111399/1/Perversion%20revision.pdf.

O'Donnell, Ruth. 2012. "Performing Masculinity: The Star Persona of Tom Cruise." PhD diss., Royal Holloway, University of London.

Peberdy Donna. 2010. "From Wimps to Wild Men: Bipolar Masculinity and the Paradoxical Performances of Tom Cruise." *Men and Masculinities* 13 (2): 231–54.

Peraino, Judith A. 2012. "Plumbing the Surface of Sound and Vision: David Bowie, Andy Warhol, and the Art of Posing." *Qui Parle: Critical Humanities and Social Sciences* 21 (1): 151–84.

Redmond, Sean. 2004. "*Titanic*: Whiteness on the High Seas of Meaning." In *The Titanic in Myth and Memory: Representations in Visual and Literary Culture*, edited by Tim Bergfelder and Sarah Street, 197–204. London: I.B. Taurus.

Shildrick, Margrit. 2005. "Unreformed Bodies: Normative Anxiety and the Denial of Pleasure." *Women's Studies* 34 (nos. 3–4): 341–42.

Simpson, Mark. 1994. *Male Impersonators: Men Performing Masculinity*. New York: Cassell.

Snead, James. 2016. *White Screens/Black Images: Hollywood from the Dark Side*. London: Routledge.
Studlar, Gaylyn. 2001. "Cruise-ing into the Millennium: Performative Masculinity, Stardom, and the All-American Boy's Body." In *Ladies and Gentlemen, Boys and Girls: Gender in Film at the End of the Twentieth Century*, edited by Murray Pomerance, 171–83. Albany: State University of New York Press.

3

LOSING CRUISE CONTROL

DISENCHANTMENT OF TOM CRUISE'S
STAR IMAGE IN *EYES WIDE SHUT*

Defne Tüzün

Upon its release, Stanley Kubrick's last film, *Eyes Wide Shut* (1999) seems to have caused more unpleasure than pleasure to everyone from the general audience to film critics. Many commentators have considered the film to be too slow, lengthy, boring, and highly pretentious.[1] I argue that the critics' evaluation of the film as unpleasurable is indeed the very effect and response that *Eyes Wide Shut* intends to elicit in its spectators. The film purposely undercuts the spectators' pleasure by frustrating their emotional and erotic investment in the diegesis. The film uses various strategies that draw the spectators' attention away from the narrative and invite them to contemplate their own subject positions. In this sense, *Eyes Wide Shut* is self-reflexive as it forces us, the spectators, to come face-to-face with our voyeuristic desires by putting emphasis on the cinematic techniques employed, specifically and explicitly foregrounding their artificiality and constructedness, thereby calling attention to the language of the cinematic apparatus.

Tom Cruise's star image is a primary means that *Eyes Wide Shut* uses to sabotage its purported eroticism. In the film, Cruise plays Bill Harford, a successful, affluent, handsome New York doctor who is married to a

---

1 Lee Siegel (1999, 76) gives a detailed overview of how critics dismiss the film "for not living up to the claims its publicists had made for it" and find it "a disaster and a titanic error, trite and self-important, one of the worst movies [they] had ever seen."

beautiful, intelligent art curator, Alice (Nicole Kidman). Bill, driven by the fantasy of his wife making love with a naval officer, sets out on a stumbling sexual tour. All his searches for further sexual options to his marriage end up in frustration. All the narration-wise games are staged in order for the viewer to experience the same sort of frustration felt by our protagonist. As the protagonist's sexual desires are rejected, the viewer's voyeuristic/erotic expectations are rebuffed as well.

Eyes Wide Shut invites its spectators to libidinally invest in Cruise's "extraordinary" star image, that of being energetic, youthful, successful, and heroic with "an indefinable something special" (Dargis 2000, 21) that goes beyond his good looks and sexual appeal. However, his star image is incoherent and ambiguous: it is also ordinary in that it embodies an everyman quality and personality, representing the average white male. *Eyes Wide Shut* reinforces this ambiguity, at first highlighting the extraordinariness of Cruise's image but later undermining it by revealing its artificiality and constructedness. In the film, Cruise's character believes that he is special and not at all an "ordinary" man. Cruise's star image of being "an all-American winner" (Hayward 2006, 383) enriches the fictional character he portrays, yet this very character and the psycho-sexual journey he takes on shatter this image. John Ellis (1999) explains the star image as a hybrid notion that involves a person who is simultaneously ordinary and extraordinary, available to be desired but also unattainable. On the one hand, the ordinary raises the feeling of accessibility, but on the other hand, the extraordinary is so gorgeous, marvelous, and remote that it never satisfies this desire for intimacy. *Eyes Wide Shut* uses the lead actor's rather unextraordinary height in such a way as to almost destroy the duality of his star image. According to Krin Gabbard (2001, 22n2), "The vertical measurements of male stars are zealously guarded secrets. . . . In Hollywood . . . the industry has thoroughly mastered the art of disguising the diminutive physical stature of leading men." *Eyes Wide Shut* deliberately chooses not to create a sensory illusion of Cruise being taller; by presenting him in his real-life height, the film shows how Bill Harford attempts, without considering his status, to take a disproportionately larger part in the social game.

Eyes Wide Shut utilizes Cruise's star image in order to heighten its verisimilitude and to authenticate its story. Yet through the course of the film, the sexual frustrations and the symbolic failures experienced by the fictional character of a self-confident doctor cause a disenchantment of Cruise's screen persona, which is inescapably endowed with fantasies and fictions about his sexuality and masculinity. Cruise's former body of work is inevitably inscribed on his actual body and it is almost impossible to separate the two entirely. *Eyes Wide Shut* emphasizes the character's "ordinariness" and "impotency" in both literal, sexual and symbolic terms as it makes the audience contemplate the constructedness of this "extraordinary" image. The star image of Cruise, that is produced through films, advertising, marketing, news releases, interviews, and commentaries is polysemic in the sense that it is saturated by "complexity" and "contradictoriness" (Dyer 1998, 63).[2] Tom Cruise's star image constructed through his films represents success, masculinity, heterosexuality, and virility. As an "idealized heroic, heterosexual and all-American white male" (Redmond 2014, 44), he embodies honesty and integrity. Yet from early in his career, the actor's heterosexual virility has often been questioned.

There has been endless speculation about Cruise's sexual identity and orientation, his marriages, his adoption[3] of two children, and his relationship with his biological daughter. Thus, his normative masculine image is a fragile one, and counterimages are also produced through paratextual media representations. In other words, what this constructed image represents is constantly contested through the media. Just as Tom Cruise does not have control over his constructed image, which is marked by ambiguities, contradictions, and ambivalence, viewers of *Eyes Wide Shut* soon realize that Bill Harford only seems as if he controls the narrative, but he most emphatically does not. Although the course of events seems to be directed by Bill, in fact, what really drives the film's narrative is actually the desire of his wife, Alice, which is played out in a fantasy about a naval officer.

2 For Richard Dyer (1998, 3), the star functions as a "structured polysemy, that is, the finite multiplicity of meanings and affects they embody and the attempt so to structure them that some meanings and affects are foregrounded and others are masked or displaced." Along similar lines, Robert C. Allen (1999, 548) points out that stars function as "complex images containing multiple meanings."
3 Within the heteronormative understanding, adoption may throw into jeopardy man's infertility. Kelly Oliver (1998, 87) remarks on "the debates in the press about Tom Cruise's sperm count," stating that "the centrality of virility to our conception of masculinity makes adoption with its images of infertility a threat to men."

Family Romance

Eyes Wide Shut is structured around the "family romance," which in terms of psychoanalytic theory is the site of Oedipal narrative. The threat of a symbolic breakdown, the threat of castration, forms the narrative of the family romance. In *The Analysis of Film*, Raymond Bellour (2002, 12) offers a brief sketch of the cultural and sexual formations supporting the Oedipus of both psychoanalysis and cinema: "From it psychoanalysis is born . . . using the univocal model of Oedipus and castration to organize conflict and sexual difference around the restricted sense of nuclear family." As far as film theory is concerned, the idea of the Oedipus complex as a story of family and the origins of identity, desire, and (paternal) law that come to counter it has been decisive. As Vicky Lebeau (2001, 82) points out, "An 'Oedipally fueled fantasy' of the heterosexual couple (the first step towards a conjugal family) remains a staple of American cinema." Lebeau further explains that cinema can form or deform this fantasy, but it still remains as a key structure within which the various configurations of fantasy life are performed.

The family romance staged in *Eyes Wide Shut* is both reinforced and authenticated by the fact that the film stars the real-life, then married couple, Cruise and Kidman. Long before the film was made, there was a steady flow of rumors about their rocky relationship, which heightened the verisimilitude of the onscreen couple's marriage problems when the film was released. However, Cruise's role is a significant departure from his established star image, as he had not been associated with family and stability before *Eyes Wide Shut*. Gabbard (2001, 9) includes Cruise in the Hollywood tradition of male stars who are hard to imagine playing "a domesticated man in a stable relationship with a wife and child." Up until this movie, Cruise had not played a married family man. Furthermore, diverging from his previous roles, in *Eyes Wide Shut* Cruise plays a bourgeois character who is wealthy, educated, and cultivated. In a scene that seamlessly crosscuts a typical workday for Dr. Harford with a typical day at home for Alice, the film establishes the stability, indeed the routineness, of the Harfords' family life. Before *Eyes Wide Shut*, only in *The Firm* (Sydney Pollack, 1993) does Cruise portray a newly married man, yet sexuality and marriage are not the focus in the film that centers instead on his job in a law firm, which affords him an affluent lifestyle and turns out to be a front for the mafia. In other cases, such as *Cocktail* (Roger Donaldson, 1988) and *Jerry Maguire* (Cameron Crowe, 1996), marriage occurs only as a narrative solution at the end of the films. Although Cruise is regarded as the epitome of masculinity, the characters he portrays in his films from the 1980s and 1990s are typically boyish and immature, and only through the journeys his character undertakes does he achieve maturity by acquiring qualities such as self-control, integrity, and responsibility. As Gaylyn Studlar (2001, 76) notes, "In many of his vehicles, Cruise's character is depicted as moving from a manly 'boy' who is attractive, muscular ... to a true 'man.' ... His films consistently move his characters from a performance of manliness into 'authentic' manliness." However, at the beginning of *Eyes Wide Shut*, Cruise's Bill Harford is at a place where the actor's other characters usually struggle to arrive throughout the course of the narrative events in his other films.

In *Eyes Wide Shut*, the narrative of family romance is structured around the lack of a sexual relationship, which is substituted with a "Oedipally fueled fantasy." In other words, the lack of a unitary sexual relationship is covered over with a fantasy structure. Like Bill, the narrative of the film is driven by the threat of castration, which Alice's fantasy of the naval officer presents. In the bedroom scene, when Alice begins recounting her sexual attraction for a naval officer in order to challenge Bill's total confidence in her fidelity, the camera cuts to a close-up of Cruise four times. Each close-up punctuates and perpetuates the seriousness in Alice's story and the effect it is having on Bill. This series of close-ups is one of the few instances where *Eyes Wide Shut* provides close-ups of Cruise's face, which is unusual; normally, in his film work his face is often a point of focus. When Alice says, "He glanced at me as he walked past, just a glance, nothing more. And I could hardly move," the camera cuts to Cruise's face, which is motionless, frozen, as if Alice's words are echoed in his facial expression. Alice tells Bill that after her brief encounter with the officer, she and Bill made love in that afternoon; meanwhile, she says, "at no time was he [the officer] ever out of my mind." The camera then cuts to the second close-up of Cruise's face, which fills in the screen with an astonished gaze. His face in the second close-up is almost indistinguishable from the first: he still cannot move, and he keeps staring into space (into "us") without blinking. Alice then says, "I thought that if he wanted me, even if it was only for one night, I was ready to give up everything. You, Helena, my whole fucking future." During Alice's revelation, as the camera cuts to the third close-up of Cruise's face, he looks slightly down. However, when Alice stresses the word "you," he again directs his look toward her, as in the first two close-ups. The last close-up comes after she says, "At that moment my love for you was both tender and sad." Cruise's face is still motionless, yet a look of sadness is discerned, again echoing Alice's words. Kidman, shot in profile as she speaks, delivers a variety of emotions, ranging from passion and lust to gentleness and compassion. Cruise, who unexpectedly finds himself in this unknown territory of victim fantasy, remains silent during her monologue.

Analyzing these series of Cruise's close-ups, Dennis Bingham (2004, 255) characterizes Cruise's response to Alice's story as an "ambiguous" and "essentially unreadable reaction" and observes that "Cruise reacts, but we have no idea how." I disagree with Bingham's account, and would argue that rather than ambiguity, this reaction exhibits how perplexed, confused, and disoriented Cruise is. These analogous close-ups—which stay for a considerable length of time on the screen—expose the materiality of the *moving image* and by doing so disclose the artifice of the Cruise *star image*, thereby reducing him to a mere *plastic image*. Yet at the same time, this reaction is authentic in a filmic universe where Cruise has never been exposed before to the complexities of sexuality that cannot be comprehended in terms of intimacy, commitment, compassion, or care. His response is genuine and authentic in the sense it is marked by the absence of masquerade. In other words, Cruise fails to perform "authentic masculinity" that he is used to executing in his previous films, which as Studlar (2001, 176) argues is itself "a construction, a masquerade." Interestingly, the scene ends with Cruise saying, "I have to go there and show my face" when a call from Marion (Marie Richardson), a patient's daughter, interrupts his silence. In a self-reflexive way Cruise acknowledges that he needs to get over the shock, to put on a mask and be prepared for the coming scene, for the masquerade.

Throughout the episodic narration of *Eyes Wide Shut*, Cruise's face, posture, and actions remind the spectators of the roles that he has acted in before. At Victor Ziegler's (Sydney Pollack) Christmas party in which Bill says he does not know anyone, he runs into an old friend, Nick Nightingale (Todd Field), who dropped out of medical school to become a pianist. Since Cruise's films are dominated by strong male bonds, Cruise seems almost as if he recognizes Nick from his screen past; he could be one of his male friends from an earlier film. Later at the jazz club, when Nick tells him about the secret, exclusive party that he will attend but is reluctant to disclose its location, the peer dynamic between the two becomes evident as their male bonding is marked by not only intimacy and closeness but also by competition and rivalry. Here, Cruise dons the familiar mask of a rival friend, and he says grinningly, "You know there is no way on earth that you are leaving tonight without taking me with you." Furthermore, Bill's relation to Ziegler, a figural father in the film, is again reminiscent of many of Cruise's films that centralize (troubled) father–son dynamic.

Thus, Cruise's performances in these episodes fall within the range that he is typically asked to play. Yet in the scene discussed above, when confronted with Alice's desire, Cruise cannot put on a familiar face; he remains unmasked. This is the moment of his symbolic castration, which is further reiterated later in the film when Cruise is asked to remove the literal mask he put on in the masked orgy scene. Bingham (2004, 256) describes Cruise's performance in *Eyes Wide Shut* as "Brechtian" and offers that he puts on different masks as he plays various roles in each of the episodes: "the face of the hail-fellow (at the party), the face of the ardent lover and the trusting husband, the face of the caring doctor, the face of the husband after he has heard of his wife's desire to be *unfaithful*, the face of the thrill-seeker" (emphasis added). Cruise's facial expressions draw from familiar codes that are reminiscent of his filmic repertoire. Yet again his reaction to Alice's story is unfamiliar and "authentic" since her account is far from conventional; Alice's desire is not to be "unfaithful"; what she offers is a fantasy scenario in which "the most elementary desire" is staged, it is "the desire to reproduce itself as desire (and not to find satisfaction)" (Žižek 2006, 61). This fantasy reveals Alice's capacity to desire; as Slavoj Žižek (2001, 174) firmly states, "Desire, at its most radical, *is* a reflexive 'desire to desire.'" Mark Pizzato (2004, 93) remarks that "such a fantasy appears not to be 'beyond the phallus,' since it involves another man. Yet it actually shows a feminine jouissance beyond the need for either man—beyond the patriarchal orders of romance, husband, and family." This view entails a common misreading of feminine jouissance as something outside of the phallic function. "Such a reading," Žižek (2007, 155) explains, "completely misses Lacan's point, which is that this very position of the Woman as exception ... is a masculine fantasy *par excellence*." It is Bill's "fantasy" of Alice's fantasy that configures such feminine jouissance that is beyond the symbolic order. Bill's "fantasy" discloses the dynamics of how the man is seduced by and entangled in the "mystery" of a woman once he attaches an enigmatic, mysterious jouissance to her.

Bill, on his way to the house of a deceased patient, entrapped in the "fantasy" of feminine jouissance, imagines Alice and the naval officer making love. Soon after he arrives in Marion's apartment, in the room where her father's corpse is lying in the bed, she passionately kisses Bill and declares her love for him. Just as Alice was ready to abandon him and Helena for the naval officer, Marion is willing to leave her fiancé just to live near Bill, even if she could never see Bill again. This apparent congruity between Alice's fantasy and Marion's confession points at Bill's "fantasy" construction of female sexuality, which is uncontrolled, subversive, and dangerous. In his brief analysis of the film, Žižek (2001, 174) comments that "it is only Nicole Kidman's fantasy that truly is a fantasy, while Tom Cruise's fantasy is a reflexive fake, a desperate attempt to artificially recreate/reach the fantasy, . . . a desperate attempt to answer the enigma of the Other's fantasy." It is Bill's fantasy formation that sets up woman as enigmatic and leads him to investigate more about female sexuality hidden behind the seductive, deceptive appearance, which allegedly camouflages secrecy and danger.[4]

Throughout Bill's Oedipal voyage, flashes of the imagined sex between Alice and the naval officer is inserted several times. In these scenes, the naval officer is either in a uniform or his built-up, muscular body is shown naked. The naval officer's hypermasculine image in Bill's fantasy brings to mind Cruise's roles in *Top Gun* (Tony Scott, 1986) and *A Few Good Men* (Rob Reiner, 1992) and as such foregrounds the constructedness of Cruise's masculinity. Alice's portrayal of the naval officer as having the phallus evokes the threat of castration in Bill. Furthermore, Bill envies Ziegler who is supposed to be the real possessor of the phallus, which is in fact "not a real object, but an absent one (a fantasmatic object marked by loss)."[5] In the

---

4 Žižek (2000, 214) elaborates that what is behind the surface occupies the status of a feminine secret, an "Enigma" *only* for whom it is staged, for the Other. "A 'feminine secret' [the Enigma embodied] which eludes the male gaze," he writes, "is constitutive of the phallic spectacle of seduction—the first lesson of feminine seduction is that In-itself is always For-us, for the very other whose grasp it eludes."

5 "For Lacan, the signifier of castration is the phallus, and the Lacanian formulation of the Oedipal scenario is framed in terms of its possession. . . . Phallus is not the symbol of a thing; rather it represents the very fact of symbolization" Robert Stam, Robert Burgoyne, and Sandy Flitterman-Lewis (1992, 133–34).

search of the phallus, Bill shields his vulnerable masculinity with phallic symbols. Throughout the film, he shows his business card several times: to the owner of the costume-rental shop, to the waitress at the coffee shop, and to the receptionist at the hotel. He does not do this for professional reasons but to enjoy the privilege it provides, the information he acquires in exchange. The other signifier, the other phallic symbol that Bill draws on for maintaining his sexual identity, is money, which he doles out excessively. Paying a prostitute he does not actually have sex with reaffirms his alleged privileged subject position.

While wandering through New York streets and preoccupied by imaginings of Alice having sex with the naval officer, Bill is subjected to a series of sexual temptations and propositions. After Marion declares her love for him, he is harassed on the street by college boys who call him a "faggot"; later, is picked up by a "gorgeous" prostitute. In a costume shop, the owner offers Bill his seemingly willing teenage daughter for sex. Coffeehouse waitresses and a gay hotel receptionist also suggest sexual possibilities. However, all these opportunities turn out to be futile. Compared to the serious tone of the images of Alice and the officer, which are shot in black and white with a tint of blue, Bill's sexual opportunities feel theatrical and artificial. By emphasizing Bill's "[in]capacity to fantasize," Žižek (2001, 174) describes the protagonist's encounters as a "window-shopping trip for fantasies: each situation in which he finds himself can be read as a realized fantasy." There is an aspect of parody and foregrounded performativity in each of these scenes. It can be argued that these episodes are staged for the spectators in order to show them the fragility and constructedness of Tom Cruise's star image. Those sexual opportunities are indeed challenges to his perfected, ideal image, which requires constant performance and reaffirmation. Each episode or encounter can be seen as a threat to his ideal, normative image, offering up fantasies of adultery, pedophilia, and homosexuality. Bill's entire journey from the beginning to the end of the film brings the Tom Cruise image to the fore, and the fictional character Cruise is employed to enact undercuts his star image.

Masks and Masquerade

At the center of such a plot, the orgy scene is quite important for the analysis of the film. For this scene, the key point is less the erotic nature of the spectacle than its ritualistic aspect. The spectators may project their erotic expectations onto the orgy rite and indulge themselves with the supposedly sexually charged atmosphere of the scene, yet they are simultaneously jarred by the ironic use of pop songs such as "Strangers in the Night" and "When I Fall in Love." With the display of naked female bodies, the mask-wearing men in velvet cloaks, and the highly stylized manner of implied sexual intercourse, the film constructs a kitschy setting. Moreover, in this orgy sequence, while the protagonist is wandering around, the camera shows various scenes of sexual intercourse, most of which are watched by the curious guests of the party. The potentially voyeuristic spectator of *Eyes Wide Shut* is blocked from viewing the scenes clearly by the bodies of the Peeping Toms present in the film's diegesis.[6] Even though the film's audience can see some of the sexual acts, they are constantly reminded of their spectator role by the presence of these other voyeurs in the scene. Viewers are compelled to think about what they are watching but are never allowed to fully and satisfactorily indulge in voyeuristic pleasure. This ritualism of this mask-and-robe orgy scene purposefully fails to satisfy the spectator's voyeuristic expectations; the audience now experiences what the protagonist, whose erotic expectations are constantly thwarted, does.

The ritualistic tone of this scene may remind the audience of Cruise's involvement in Scientology. Scientology's consciously esoteric rituals and practices are typically viewed as involving a secret society of "elites." Cruise is known for his controlling personality, and his commitment to Scientology fosters his "control freak image" as he often promotes "the efficacy of Scientology as a technique of self-mastery" (King 2015, 18). It is ironic that the scene alluding to Scientology is the one in which the actor must entirely lose his self-control, remaining defenseless and completely exposed. It is noteworthy that when the patriarchs at the party

---

6   In order to deliver an R-rated film, Warner Bros. digitally altered the orgy scene for the film's American release. Besides injecting Peeping Toms into the orgy scene, additional digital figures were added to obscure the camera's view of sex acts. Unfortunately, the addition of these hooded figures works totally against Kubrick's strategy of shattering the voyeuristic illusion by showing the banality and ordinariness of the sexual acts. Instead, shielding the audience with these figures serves only to foster and fuel their voyeuristic expectations, luring them to imagine what they've been forbidden to see.

command him to remove his mask, the film does not provide any close-ups of Cruise's face. When he is unmasked as his character, he is humiliated and emasculated, and Cruise's perfected, normative masculinity breaks down as well. Throughout his journey, he puts on familiar masks borrowed from his screen past, yet here once again the fragility of Cruise's star image is foregrounded. What is played in the orgy scene is the game of "masquerade." The masquerade is staged by the men of power to cover the phallus, which is itself a masquerade. What these extremely powerful men try to mask is their "role" in the social game, another kind of mask. For Bill, though, the masquerade is an attempt to cover up his lack, and his failure is that he thinks he can achieve this through the act of masquerade. But the phallus is not the symbol of a thing; rather, it represents the very fact of symbolization. Hence, a masquerade can be substituted only with another pretense. However, as Bill fails in this game of masquerade, when Cruise's old mask of masculinity falls down, he fails to put on a new one.

In analyzing a film whose own title contains the word *eyes*, thus invoking the concept of the gaze, it is necessary to consider the dynamic between the notions of gaze and desire. In his book *Looking Awry*, Žižek (1993, 114) mentions a Kafka story to articulate the "*antinomy* between eye and gaze." He writes: "In Kafka's parable 'The Door of the Law' the man from the country waiting at the entrance to the court is fascinated by the secret beyond the door he is forbidden to trespass. In the end, . . . [i]ts power is lost when the door keeper tells him that this entrance was, from the very start, meant only for him. . . . The thing that fascinated him was, in a way, gazing back at him all along, addressing him. That is the man's desire was from the very start 'part of the game.'" This parable perfectly defines Bill's situation in the film. Bill can get into the house where the orgy party takes place since he knows the password. But when he is asked what the second password is, he says that he has forgotten it; in fact, a second password does not exist. Then he is faced with the total threat of castration: he is asked to get undressed, "strip!" He is threatened by the fact that the partygoers are going to find out that he does not have the phallus. But the crucial point is that the phallus never belongs to anyone. That there is no second password—that is, no phallus—is known only by the men of power but not by our protagonist. The phallus itself is a masquerade. Toward the end of the film, Ziegler explains that all it was a game, a charade; we can add to Ziegler's words that this social game and "the field of etiquette, social rules and manners" (Žižek 1993, 71) are what constitutes the symbolic order.

This order is an invisible structure that shapes and holds together our intersubjective community and makes up a coherent system out of the outer reality. So the protagonist, from the very beginning, is driven by the threat of castration, which in fact does not exist. This is "the fundamental paradox that, according to Lacan, defines 'symbolic castration,' the 'prohibition of incest': the prohibition of the *jouissance* that is already in itself impossible to attain" (Žižek 1993, 43). As a result, the film's narrative is structured around this impossible lack that the protagonist keeps seeking, which is highlighted by the self-conscious camera movements throughout the orgy scene. The camera, which incessantly wanders around objects and other characters, corresponds to Bill's unyielding search for truth (which presumably lies behind the masks) and calls attention to his "fantasy" of the "mystery" and "danger" that feminine sexuality possesses. Analogous to the use of the camera, the nondiegetic sound is also used to build up suspense, which also goes unfulfilled, sound thus becoming its own lacking absence. In *Eyes Wide Shut*, György Ligeti's piano cycle "Musica ricercata" is used as a leitmotif; a high piano note that plays over and over again as the film unfolds. The piece initially contributes to the purported suspense, while later the same note becomes repetitious, highly dissonant and disturbing, and ultimately yields nothing but turns out to be a joke on the audience as their expectations of suspense become futile.

In this scenario of family romance, Alice delivers a performance of the "feminine masquerade,"[7] an overacted performance of femininity, which

---

7   The concept of the feminine masquerade was first theorized by Joan Riviere (1986) as a kind of reaction formation against the capacity that enables woman to alternate between a feminine position and a masculine position. Riviere suggests that by putting on the masquerade of femininity, the woman is able to ward off the anxiety and the reprisal that can be directed at her by men if she is found to have a "masculine" subject position. As Mary Ann Doane (1991, 25) puts it, "After assuming the position of the subject of discourse rather than its object, the intellectual woman ... felt compelled to compensate for this theft of masculinity by overdoing the gestures of feminine flirtation." Riviere (1986, 38) further points out that in the masquerade, the woman imitates a "genuine womanliness"; in return, the dividing line between genuine womanliness and masquerade gets

denies any claims of an authentic self. Alice's masquerade enables her to keep a distance from her own image, as she is quite aware of self-representation. In the film, whenever Alice is going to wear her feminine masquerade, she takes off her glasses. According to Mary Ann Doane (1992, 236), the figure of women with glasses, a recurrent motif of classical Hollywood cinema, has a cliché meaning in the cinema: "The woman with glasses signifies simultaneously intellectuality and undesirability; but the moment she removes her glasses . . . she is transformed into spectacle, the very picture of desire." In other words, the meaning of women with glasses is overdetermined: they are codified as the owner of the look; they are not the addressee but the holder of the look.

Just after the party scene, from a medium shot, the camera shows a naked Alice in front of the mirror, taking off her earrings. At this moment, wearing only her glasses, she stares at her image on the mirror. Then Bill enters the frame, touches her body, and kisses her neck. While Bill is kissing her and caressing her breasts, Alice finally takes off her glasses, placing her in this self-realized masquerade, flaunting her femininity, where she returns his kiss. At the end of the scene, holding her glasses in her hand, she again gazes at the mirror. The audience, while absorbed into a potentially highly voyeuristic scene, are denied the pleasure of looking. The working mechanisms of voyeurism are hindered by the narcissistic look of the female protagonist. At the very end of the scene, she stares almost directly at the camera, thereby entirely challenging the voyeuristic look's essential requirement from its exhibitionist subject/object: Alice is being indifferent to the camera and therefore to the presence of the audience.[8] Kidman's awareness of the camera and her consciousness of the dynamic between herself and audience debilitates the viewer's voyeuristic fantasy.

Toward the end of the film, when Bill comes back home after that immensely frustrating night, he finds Alice sleeping and giggling in her

---

blurred: "There is [not] any such difference; whether radical or superficial, they are the same thing."

8   Christian Metz (1984, 63) writes: "The cinema's voyeurism must (of necessity) do without any very clear mark of consent on the part of the object. . . . This is the origin in particular of that 'recipe' of the classical cinema which is said that the actor should never look directly at the audience."

dream. She seems to be taking pleasure from whatever she is dreaming about. Bill wakes her up. "I thought you were having a nightmare," he says. Once Alice awakens, her laughter turns to tears and she says, "I had such a horrible dream." Although the exact opposite seems true, she begins to tell him about how terrible her dream was. If we think of this scene in relation to the one that follows, her real designs are revealed. In this next scene, when Alice is helping with Helena's math homework, Bill looks at her, and the camera slowly zooms in on his face, which seems tense and suspicious. Then the camera cuts to the close-up of Alice's smiling face. She is wearing glasses so is not in her feminine masquerade at this time. The voice-over that we hear belongs to the previous scene, in which she recounts her bad dream to Bill: "I was fucking other men, so many, I do not know how many I was with." Before the voice-over ends, the camera once more cuts back to Bill. The smile on his face seems to be more of a smirk. It is clear that in the preceding scene she was not having a nightmare.

Feigning that she was having a bad dream is a way for Alice to meet Bill's expectations—she mimics the role of a vulnerable, weak, helpless female. Our cultural imagination has constructed the female subject as the visible, as spectacle for the male gaze, not as something that itself looks. However, here, Alice, wearing feminine masquerade, experiencing her femininity as role-playing, gains the agency and mobility provided by masquerade and directs a desiring look. While *Eyes Wide Shut* unmasks Cruise's star power by denying him the performances of masculine identity, Kidman attains agency through taking hybrid/various roles, that is, via her ability to masquerade.

Doane (1991, 37) asserts that the concept of masquerade is a powerful strategy against "anything claiming to be a 'female epistemology,' with a theory which valorized closeness, immediacy, or proximity-to-self." For Žižek (2007), masquerade confirms the fact that the woman is more subject than man. The woman is aware that her self-representation is not a mask concealing the inner substance (self), but is the very domain where the symbolic operates. The woman's consciousness of the very *insubstantiality*—the emptiness that is constitutive of subjectivity—makes woman more *reflected*, less immediate to herself, and thus more subject. A man, on the other hand, "stupidly believes that, beyond his symbolic title, there is deep in himself some substantial content, some hidden treasure which makes him worthy of love" (163).[9] In *Eyes Wide Shut* acts of masquerade enable Alice to have a more subject position, as she does not believe she has substantial, inherent worthiness above and beyond the symbolic.

As a master of masquerade, Alice knows that there is nothing beneath the mask. Thus, in the film, while masquerade enables Alice to occupy a stronger subject position, Bill's attempts at masquerade fatally fail as he searches for phallus in the wrong place (i.e., behind and beyond the masquerade); "the phallus is a pure semblance, a mystery which resides in the mask as such" Žižek (2007, 162). Bill's attempt to masquerade (as someone powerful, rich, potent, etc.) completely fails because he thinks having and showing off phallic symbols like business cards and money will suffice to make his act believable. He tries to give "the impression that he really is what he pretends to be," but Bill does not realize that only "'by pretending to be something,' by 'acting as if we were something,' [do] we assume a certain place in the intersubjective symbolic network, and it is this external place that defines our true position" Žižek (1993, 74). Bill's portrayal as someone who is symbolically disempowered destabilizes Cruise's star image, which both despite and because of its differences from the character Bill, substantially contributes to the quality of Cruise's performance.

After his failed attempts at masquerade in this exhausting journey, Bill returns home. As he finds his mask from the party laid out on his pillow

---

9   Žižek (2007, 161) explains:

> True, the so-called "modern man" is also caught in the split between what (it seems to him that) the other (woman or social environment in general) expects from him (to be a strong macho type, etc.), and between what he effectively is in himself (weak, uncertain of himself, etc.). This split, however, is of a fundamentally different nature: the macho image is not experienced as a delusive masquerade but as the ideal-ego one is striving to become. Behind the macho-image of a man there is no "secret," just a weak ordinary person that can never live up to his ideal, whereas the trick of the feminine masquerade is to present itself as a mask that conceals the feminine secret. In other words, in opposition to man, who simply tries to live up to his image—to give the impression that he really is what he pretends to be—woman deceives by means of deception itself; she offers the mask as mask, as false pretence, in order to give rise to the search for the secret behind the mask.

next to his sleeping wife, he collapses and bursts into tears. This scene marks the moment where Bill's tireless search for the truth/depth/substance that is ostensibly lurking behind the seductiveness of the surface, behind the mask, comes to an end. Cruise cannot remain in cruise control, and his tragic cry becomes a manifestation of his hysteria, which "can be glimpsed in moments of incoherence or powerlessness in the male body" (Smith 2004, 52). *Eyes Wide Shut* strips Tom Cruise of his star power and thereby attacks a mode of filmmaking that primarily caters to voyeuristic desires. The film uses the medium (cinema), which itself is based on the voyeuristic and fetishistic pleasures of looking, to evoke visual pleasure but not satisfy it. That is to say, the film, by using means immanent to cinema, severely criticizes a cinema that is fundamentally based on voyeuristic pleasure. The film's criticism of voyeurism is tightly entangled with its deliberate and successful attempt to undermine Cruise's star image. The spectators' erotic and voyeuristic desires are called on intensely; however, because the film does not allow for yielding to those desires, the audience is drawn in by identifying with Bill's frustrations and his failed attempts at masquerade. Bill's troubles with maintaining his masquerade of masculinity not only reveal the impossibility of the masculine ideal but also shatter the fantasies concerning Cruise's masculinity.

Works Cited

Allen, Robert C. 1999. "From Film and History: Theory and Practice: The Role of the Star in Film History [Joan Crawford]." In *Film Theory and Criticism: Introductory Readings*, edited by Leo Braudy and Marshall Cohen, 547–61. Oxford: Oxford University Press.

Bellour, Raymond. 2002. *The Analysis of Film*. Bloomington: Indiana University Press.

Bingham, Dennis. 2004. "Kidman, Cruise, and Kubrick: A Brechtian Pastiche." In *More Than a Method: Trends and Traditions in Contemporary Film Performance*, edited by Cynthia Baron, Diane Carson, and Frank P. Tomasulo, 247–74. Detroit: Wayne State University Press.

Dargis, Manohla. 2000. "Ghost in the Machine." *Sight & Sound* 10, no. 7 (July): 20–23.

Doane, Mary Ann. 1991. *Femmes Fatales*. New York: Routledge.

———. 1992. "Film and the Masquerade: Theorizing the Female Spectator." In *The Sexual Subject: A Screen Reader in Sexuality*, edited by Mandy Merck, 227–43. London: Routledge.

Dyer, Richard. 1998. *Stars*. London: British Film Institute.

Ellis, John. 1999. "From Visible Fictions: Star as a Cinematic Phenomenon." In *Film Theory and Criticism: Introductory Readings*, edited by Leo Braudy and Marshall Cohen, 539–46. Oxford: Oxford University Press.

Gabbard, Krin. 2001. "Someone is Going to Pay: Resurgent White Masculinity in *Ransom*." In *Masculinity: Bodies, Movies, Culture*, edited by Peter Lehman, 7–23. New York: Routledge.

Hayward, Susan. 2006. *Cinema Studies: The Key Concepts*. London: Routledge.

King, Barry. 2015. "Stardom, celebrity and the para-confession." In *The Star and Celebrity Confessional*, edited by Sean Redmond, 7–24. London: Routledge.

Lebeau, Vicky. 2001. *Psychoanalysis and Cinema: The Play of Shadows*. London: Wallflower Press.

Metz, Christian. 1984. *The Imaginary Signifier: Psychoanalysis and the Cinema*. Bloomington: Indiana University Press.

Oliver, Kelly. 1998. *Subjectivity without Subjects*. New York: Rowman & Littlefield.

Pizzato, Mark. 2004. "Beauty's Eye: Erotic Masques of the Death Drive in *Eyes Wide Shut*." In *Lacan and Contemporary Film*, edited by Todd McGowan and Sheila Kunkle, 83–109. New York: Other Press.

Redmond, Sean. 2014. *Celebrity and the Media*. New York: Palgrave Macmillan.

Riviere, Joan. 1986. "Womanliness as a Masquerade." In *Formations of Fantasy*, edited by Victor Burgin, James Donald, and Cora Kaplan, 35–44. London: Routledge.

Siegel, Lee. 1999. "*Eyes Wide Shut*: What the Critics Failed to See in Kubrick's Last Film." *Harper's Magazine*, October 1999.

Smith, Paul. 2004. "Action Movie Hysteria, or Eastwood Bound." In *Stars: The Film Reader*, edited by Lucy Fischer and Marcia Landy, 43–56. London: Routledge.

Stam, Robert, Robert Burgoyne, and Sandy Flitterman-Lewis. 1992. *New Vocabularies in Film Semiotics*. London: Routledge.

Studlar, Gaylyn. 2001. "Cruise-ing into the Millennium: Performative Masculinity Stardom, and the All-American Boy's Body." In *Ladies and Gentlemen, Boys and Girls: Gender in film at the End of the Millennium*, edited by Murray Pomerance, 171–83. Albany: State University of New York Press.

Žižek, Slavoj. 1993. *Looking Awry: An Introduction to Jacques Lacan through Popular Culture*. Cambridge, MA: MIT Press.

———. 1999. *The Indivisible Remainder: On Schelling and Related Matters*. London: Verso.

———. 2000. "Death and the Maiden." In *The Žižek Reader*, edited by Elizabeth Wright and Edmond Wright, 206–22. Oxford: Blackwell.

———. 2001. *The Fright of Real Tears: Krzysztof Kieslowski between Theory and Post-Theory*. London: British Film Institute.

———. 2006. *Parallax View*. Cambridge, MA: MIT Press.

———. 2007. *The Indivisible Remainder: On Schelling and Related Matters*. London: Verso.

4

"NOTHING IS 'IMPOSSIBLE' IF YOU'RE TOM CRUISE"

Scientology, Spiritual Neoliberalism, and the Tom Cruise Closet

Brenda R. Weber and Sasha T. Goldberg

> To go into a state of temporary insanity and to jump around and uncontrollably yell out a lie like "I love Katie Holmes!" while in a public place. Often happens because of self denial or following stupid cults see scientology.
>
> —"Tom Cruise" (n.d.), as defined in Urban Dictionary

Tom Cruise has dominated the ranks of A-list celebrities for nearly four decades, renowned as a virtual superman for whom "nothing is impossible"[1] due to his daring physicality, charming braggadocio, astronomical blockbuster appeal, and perpetual agelessness. His personal life has been equally fascinating to fans and audiences, who are taken with his intense offscreen love affairs with women, rumors of sexual escapades with men, extravagant celebrity marriages, and so far rather spectacular divorces to, respectively, Mimi Rogers (1987–90), Nicole Kidman (1990–2001), and Katie Holmes (2006–12).

Along with these movie star bona fides, Cruise also carries the distinction of being perhaps the world's most famous—and reclusive—Scientologist.

---

1 We owe this chapter's title to Truitt (2018, B-1).

As evidenced by the epigraph that begins this piece from the crowd-sourced Urban Dictionary, Cruise's enthusiastic, even manic, declarations of romantic heterosexual love—particularly as voiced in 2005 for Holmes while jumping on Oprah Winfrey's on-set couch—have been so fanatical that they have also fostered a broader suspicion. The public's sense that the star doth protest too much has branded Cruise's extremism both willful stage management to cover his reputed secret gay life as well as the evidence of his own brainwashing by the "stupid cult" of Scientology.[2] Indeed, the extremes of Cruise's star persona and his Scientology devotion are so interwoven, that they have led Benjamin Wallace (2012) to reflect that there is an "unholy contiguity between Tom Cruise the man, formerly Thomas Mapother of New Jersey, and Tom Cruise the empire, brand, and action hero made flesh.... At the heart of this story, as of all Cruise stories, is the central Cruisean mystery, the conundrum of his thought-policing religion, Scientology, and the degree to which he is in its grip. Is Cruise really the short-circuited Scientology android he appeared to be when he was first courting Holmes? A prevailing unified field theory of the Cruise-iverse ... is that everything flows out of his wacky religion."

Cruise's cumulative movie star persona, from the cocky fighter pilot Maverick (*Top Gun*, Tony Scott, 1986) to the resilient no-holds-barred spy Ethan Hunt (in the *Mission: Impossible* series, 1996–present[3]), seems clearly a product of Hollywood. And it is. But as we will demonstrate in this chapter,

---

[2] We do not intend this chapter to serve as a referendum on the relative goodness or badness of Scientology or to weigh in on the degree of exploitation experienced by its adherents. We also do not take a position in this chapter on whether or not Scientology should count as a legitimate church and therefore merit its tax-exempt status from the US government. But we do take what might be considered a value-neutral position on evidence, situating popular media texts, such as tabloids or YouTube videos, as important to scholarly archives, even that media expressing strong opinions about and against Tom Cruise and Scientology.

[3] The films in the series are: *Mission: Impossible* (Brian De Palma, 1996); *Mission: Impossible II* (John Woo, 2000); *Mission: Impossible III* (J. J. Abrams, 2006); *Mission: Impossible—Ghost Protocol* (Brad Bird, 2011); *Mission: Impossible—Rogue Nation* (Christopher McQuarrie, 2015); *Mission Impossible—Fallout* (Christopher McQuarrie, 2018). As of this writing, two more films are expected, both to star Cruise and be directed by McQuarrie.

Tom Cruise celebrates his love for Katie Holmes on *The Oprah Winfrey Show* in 2005.

the Tom Cruise persona also enacts a logic of the Church of Scientology that preaches a strict and uncompromising adherence to self-improvement ("going up the bridge"), which, in turn, promises superhuman results: freedom from illness, moving matter with the mind, superiority to all others not on the bridge, and most important, the capacity to save, or "clear," the planet.[4]

We contend that a concept of upward aspirationalism endemic to both the Church of Scientology and to entertainment celebrity culture might be considered a recalibrated neoliberal ethos, what Brenda R. Weber (2019) defines in *Latter-Day Screens* as spiritual neoliberalism, where marketplace

---

4 Many sources, both popular and scholarly, attest to the strict rule culture of Scientology. Donald A. Westbrook (2019, 13–14) notes the strong culture of orthodoxy and orthopraxy within Scientology, called "Keeping Scientology Working," or KSW. This concept holds that "Hubbard's technologies are workable only insofar as they are uniformly understood, applied, and perpetuated by members. Any deviation from this self-referential hermeneutic is considered the cause of any perceived failure of 'the tech' as it works to deliver the mental and spiritual gains Hubbard promised."

ideals are supplanted by personal growth regimes that will maximize in divine rewards—in this case, making literal the association between heaven and its (movie) stars. Because it is a hegemonic system, spiritual neoliberalism has direct bearing on notions of normative gender and sexuality, and the Church of Scientology offers no exception. While Scientology does not formally exclude LGBTQ or gender nonnormative people, it does categorize homosexuality as a grievous moral failing. In another enactment of "pray the gay away," the self-improvement apparatus of auditing in service of "going clear" provides a perceived remedy for LGBTQ failings. As such, to go up the bridge as a means of self-improvement is to move mindfully and purposefully away from both queer practices and desires.

We argue here that mediated Scientology, which is to say the religion as conveyed in and through media, is concomitant with Tom Cruise's celebrity persona, or the *idea* of Tom Cruise–ness, particularly since both are tinged with an association of the nonnormative, the excessive, and, increasingly, the queer. Semiotically, the meanings of what both Scientology and Tom Cruise come to represent are fused through a complex network of cross-platform mediation, and it is the amalgamation of the referent (or the actual) with the signified (its many connotations) that fuses in the sign. In the case of Scientology and Cruise, the semiotic meanings behind church and actor enact a management of celebrity that is bound to extreme secrecy and committed to excessive visibility. We call this relation between the sublimated and the sublime the Tom Cruise Closet, arguing that mediated Scientology also resides in a Tom Cruise Closet that is framed by the tension (and attention) of transparency and secrecy. In this, both Cruise and the Church of Scientology follow founder L. Ron Hubbard's mandate to shape publicity so as to never *be* the subject of publicity. As such, "the first objective is 'no story at all'" (*Leah Remini: Scientology and the Aftermath* 2016–19).[5] And while this dynamic might well illustrate one element of Eve Kofosky Sedgwick's (1990) "epistemology of the closet," central to our discussion in this chapter are Scientology's methods that both map and mirror the mediated and queer meanings of the Tom Cruise Closet, particularly as linked to the teleology of spiritual neoliberalism that serves as the binding thread of celebrity and Scientology.

---

5   For more on Hubbard's rules for dealing with the press, see Hubbard (n.d.).

Mediated Meanings

In all cases, we are interested not so much in matter as in meaning, which is to say we examine not the doctrine or history of Scientology or the life history of Cruise but the way each are discursively constructed across various media texts, including documentary, memoir, tabloid, reality television, websites, social media posts, and scholarship. Here it is helpful to move sideways, theoretically speaking, to Richard Dyer's (2003) discussion in *Heavenly Bodies*, which considers the factors that go into creating the phenomenon of the star. Dyer notes that the movie star is a composite that results not just from his or her films but from ancillary promotion in the form of "pin-ups, biographies and coverage in the press" (2). The star's image, he writes, becomes coherent through "what people say or write about him or her" as well as "the way the image is used in other contexts such as advertisements, novels, pop songs, and finally the way the star can become part of the coinage of everyday speech" (3). It is always "extensive, multimedia, intertextual" (3), relying on multiple forms of media for the saturation, intelligibility, and spread of the idea of a celebrity, who is a fusion of person and fable. Dyer suggests in both *Heavenly Bodies* and *Stars* that the concept of the star tells us something more broadly about personhood by making the "deep and constant features of human existence" tangible to audiences (1979, 17). The star, he argues, reifies the saliency of structuring belief systems, sometimes by reinforcing cultural values and other times by violating them. And because of this important cultural work, celebrity is never random or mercurial but historically specific and emblematic of deep cultural investments in notions of selfhood, meaning, and identity, including the anchoring concepts of normative gender and sexuality.

As such, we are interested in the concepts of Tom Cruise and Scientology as they exist, intertwine, and are made intelligible through media representation. Transportable and transmutable, the semiotic fusion of Scientology and Cruise gains fluency, intensity, and volatility through its transmission, functioning much like Dyer's concept of celebrity. In this regard it is media that matters for Scientology as an idea, not the truth or falsity of the church's claims or the orientation of Cruise's sexuality. Even more, we are invested in better understanding how both Scientology and Tom Cruise combine in the mediasphere, so that a person need not be aware of one to be introduced to the other and that to reference one is always a peculiar, even queer, gesture to the other. Here, we deliberately use the term *queer* to stand for nonnormative, as in nonheterosexual and nonprocreative sexual practices and relationships, as well as broader connotations indicating novelty, peculiarity, and atypicality.

For his part, Cruise has never hidden his devout belief in Scientology, having publicly converted when Mimi Rogers introduced him to the religion in 1990 and having renewed the intensity of his devotion following his divorce from Nicole Kidman. But Cruise has also kept his allegiance to Scientology somewhat close to the vest, making his public statements all the more striking. Yet in the broader multimedia discourse that helps make the meanings of Tom Cruise intelligible, it has become increasingly difficult to talk about Cruise without also, and eventually, referencing Cruise's queer relation to Scientology. As one example, a recent Reddit post titled "Is it just me, or is Tom Cruise beginning to look like a middle aged lesbian?" (n.d.) begins by ruminating on men, aging, and appearance through the figure of Tom Cruise. But the thread soon turns to Scientology, suggesting that Cruise's Thetan levels are out of alignment or making jokes about auditing. Perhaps even more surprising on a social media site such as Reddit, renowned for juvenile and often trollish discussion threads, the conversation turns to what reads as sincere ruminations on recent mediated exposés of Scientology, including the HBO documentary *Going Clear: Scientology and the Prison of Belief* (Gibney 2015) and the reality television show *Leah Remini: Scientology and the Aftermath* (2016–19).

Indeed, a broader swath of popular culture ranging from *South Park* (Stone and Parker 2005) to the two-act play *The TomKat Project* (Ogborn 2015) attributes Cruise's successes and sometimes spectacularly erratic behavior to Scientology, as most explicitly and publicly expressed in 2005 when Cruise was doing press for the sci-fi feature film *War of the Worlds* (Steven Spielberg, 2005). In the now infamous couch moment on *The Oprah Winfrey Show* (2005), Cruise jumped on and off Oprah's sofa, affectively alternating between coy, shy, and ecstatic. Declaring "I'm in love" in front of (and for) the mostly female audience, Cruise built a monument to heterosexuality, to Katie Holmes in particular and to women in general. "I've never seen you like this!" Oprah declared, and neither had the public. Days later, Cruise questioned fellow actor Brooke Shields's use of Paxil to treat postpartum depression, vocalizing a resistance that tacitly announced his adherence to Scientology and Hubbard's mandate that psychology and psychopharmaceuticals were to be absolutely avoided. The tacit connection to Scientology emerged into fullness weeks later when Cruise appeared on *Today*. Far more Lestat than Jerry Maguire, Cruise lectured host Matt Lauer about the "pseudo-science" of psychiatry and the absurdity of Brooke Shields turning to pharmaceuticals when she should have sought a cure through exercise and auditing. With narrowed eyes Cruise denied the existence of chemical imbalances, railed against the use of prescription drugs, and added, "Matt. Matt, Matt, you don't even—you're glib. You don't even know what Ritalin is. If you start talking about chemical imbalance, you have to evaluate and read the research papers on how they came up with these theories, Matt, okay? That's what I've done" (*Today* 2005).[6]

If the couch episode was unbelievable, the Lauer episode was *unbelievable*. Cruise on the couch was a performance of a man in ecstasy; Cruise with Lauer seemed less performance than delusion, a man unhinged. Public responses to these episodes were swift, intense, and persistent, causing Cruise's Q-scores and box office appeal to plummet.[7] Though Cruise contextualized, apologized, and insisted "I can create who I am" following these events, time and distance did not alter the sense that Cruise's couch jumping changed everything (Enlow 2015). Until Tom Cruise's publicly professing his Scientology beliefs to Matt Lauer changed everything again. Cruise's behavior in both contexts was seen as so over the top as to be farce, even camp,[8] a suspicion reinforced when reports emerged in 2012

---

6   In taking on Matt Lauer (and criticizing Brooke Shield's use of antidepressants to treat post-partum depression), Cruise matched the FAQ section from the Church of Scientology website nearly word for word. "Scientologists do use prescribed medical drugs when physically ill and also rely on the advice and treatment of medical doctors. Scientologists do not take street drugs or mind-altering psychotropic drugs. They consider drugs cause extremely damaging effects on a person—physically, mentally and spiritually. . . . They are a 'solution' to some other problem, but ultimately prove an even bigger problem" ("What Is Scientology's View on Drugs and Medicine?" n.d.).

7   For more on how these incidents raised the banner of Scientology and stalled Cruise's popularity, see Amy Nicholson (2014, 143–46).

8   The meanings of and theorizations about camp are too numerous to adequately represent in this chapter. In its briefest terms, camp suggests that something or someone is over the top, self-aware, ironic, and infused with a gay sensibility. For more on camp, see Corey K. Creekmur and Alexander Doty (1995).

that the Church of Scientology had auditioned various starlets (including Katie Holmes, Scarlet Johansson, and Nazanin Boniadi) for the role of a lifetime, playing Tom Cruise's beard,[9] here positioned as Cruise's "Scientology soulmate."[10]

Celebrity, Scientology, and the Superstar

To understand the implications of Cruise's star text and its insistent merging with Scientology, we want to provide some background about the church, making connections to celebrity theory. Scientology is a new American religion, established in 1952 by science fiction writer L. Ron Hubbard and based on his earlier work, *Dianetics: The Modern Science of Mental Health* (1950). According to religion scholar Donald A. Westbrook (2019, 13), Dianetics was a "relatively grassroots mental health movement" that Hubbard deliberately transformed into a "hierarchical and corporatized religious organization," which he called the Church of Scientology. Dianetics and Scientology each promise a triumph of rationalism through heightened self-knowledge as the cure for modern ills, including psychological distress, interpersonal conflict, physical disease, national warfare, and global crises. Generating a good deal of controversy in its relatively short history, Scientology at one extreme is critiqued as a fantasy-driven cult designed to brainwash adherents and bilk them financially; at the other extreme, it is credited as being a rational vehicle of human enlightenment that provides the great desirables of life—health, happiness, prosperity, and sublime well-being. Scientology also offers a deliverable that other systems of self-improvement do not: the capacity to act in a godlike capacity to save the world and prevent its total annihilation.

---

9 *Beard* is the slang term for a person who stands in as a heterosexual love interest as a means of covering the partner's homosexuality.

10 The most credible substantiation of this claim comes from Maureen Orth (2012), the *Vanity Fair* special correspondent who reported in chilling detail the processes for finding a new, suitable, and Scientology-approved spouse for Cruise. Such is the power of both Orth and *Vanity Fair* that the story was picked up and repeated through various respected news sources, including ABC News, which reported on Scientology's effort to find Cruise a "drop-dead beautiful true believer to share his life" (Vargas and Davis 2012).

For a group that already sees itself as the supersaviors of the planet, Cruise exists as one of its most exalted members, certainly far superior to those who are still on the bridge, or worse, to those unwilling to take the journey at all. The present leader of the Church, David Miscavige (called COB for chairman of the board) considers Cruise the second-most important person in Scientology, after himself. Others report that Cruise and Miscavige "worship one another," the reflective light from one shining onto the dark spaces of the other (Vargas and Davis 2012). Mediated Scientology suggests that Cruise is treated like a demigod within the religion; his Scientology-provided chaperones twenty-four hours a day ensure that he never crosses a street or opens a door on his own. When former Scientologist and security officer Brendan Tighe appeared on *Today* in 2018, for example, he told reporter Megyn Kelly that Cruise's visits to Scientology campuses require that those working for him must pass inspection on their appearance. In Tighe's case, this meant having cosmetic dentistry, including teeth whitening procedures.

Leah Remini reinforces these claims. On the podcast *The Joe Rogan Experience*, Remini told Rogan that Scientology is very purposeful about recruiting celebrities and treating them as deities. "It's like nothing you could ever imagine. The amount of power they receive from this church is like nothing in Hollywood." Celebrities are afforded absolute deference. In Remini's words, "You don't talk back, like ever. You don't step out of line, you don't give an opinion, you don't make a face, you don't make a gesture, you don't sigh" (Rogan 2017). Remini recalls that she was not allowed to be in any building that Tom Cruise entered, a restriction that was lifted after she gifted a million dollars to the Celebrity Centre. She believes that Cruise stays in Scientology not because of the threats of blackmail regarding rumored gay desires but because the treatment he receives within Scientology could never be approximated outside of the system.

As thus described, celebrity in Scientology functions as a way to instantiate and naturalize distinctions in rank as announced by status. Rather than Cruise's stature being a function of his birth, as it would be with royalty, his kingly treatment is projected as democratic. In other words, Tom Cruise's fame, fortune, and celebrity are positioned as earned through a combination of hard work, persistence, and rigorous self-making, in every way augmented and enhanced by Scientology. In *Celebrity Culture and the American Dream*, Karen Sternheimer (2011, 1) argues that celebrity culture is infused with the ideal of the American experiment, including a belief in meritocratic class mobility, egalitarian access to the dividends of the good life, and the ability to "rise from obscurity to fame and fortune," where impediments imposed by gender, race, or class simply do not exist. Likewise, in the logic of Scientology, all who aspire to success might achieve it, given the right combination of work and determination (and the ability to afford auditing sessions).

While Sternheimer sees the relation between the American dream, celebrity, and American society as more literal, we understand these relations as conceptual. So the aspirational goals of fame and fortune are not something promised only in and through the United States or American culture but instead are something broader, less specific, and more globally desirable and achievable that anchors the upward mobility of celebrity—the promises of Americanness absent the physicality of the nation state. In this, Tom Cruise is both exemplum and emperor, reigning as the boy who took a different, more audacious path that has rewarded him with global celebrity. Cruise credits Scientology for helping him overcome dyslexia and boosting his self-confidence, thus serving as catalyst for his transformation from ordinary to extraordinary. According to Cruise, Scientology's mandates for self-improvement have indeed made him a better man (superior to the man he was before as well as to all other humans). In Cruise's star text, Scientology is the road to success; it has taught him how to transcend his own limitations and rewarded him for his efforts to do so. By 2019, *People* magazine introduced him not as "Tom Cruise, practicing Scientologist" but as "Scientologist Tom Cruise" ("Scientologist Tom Cruise" 2019), thus fusing Scientology and the superstar.

Spiritual Neoliberalism and Scientology

The marquis above the Scientology Center in New York City's Times Square says it succinctly: "You don't have to be a Scientologist. You just have to be curious." Or, put a bit differently, you just have to be open to the idea that you can will yourself to transcend humanity, catapult yourself to a state of the divine, and reside in a place of riches, both tangible and existential. The invitation to be "sci-curious" is not such a hard ask if you consider that a broader ideology of Americanness reinforces this same idea: hard work will be rewarded with material prosperity. Scientology merely ups

Scientology as a state of mind.

the ante on the American dream by also offering spiritual fulfillment as a payoff to meritocratic labor. Along with the middle-class guarantees of the American dream—the house with the white picket fence and the college educations—this version of the dream also suggests that fame will be linked to fortune, celebrity as the rightful dividend to those who toil.[11] This is a palpably desirable notion, that a scientific/religious regime might enact a process of individual improvement so powerful that the enlightened one, the Thetan, could then live in great physical comfort while also eradicating the world of all of its harms. It is also one we characterize as typifying spiritual neoliberalism.

As a term to describe a political economy, neoliberalism stresses the efficiency of privatization, the reliability of financial markets, and the decentralization of government, often announcing itself in cultural terms through practices and policies in the language of markets, efficiency, consumer choice, and individual autonomy to shift risk from systems to persons and to extend this sort of market logic into the realm of social and affective relationships. Under neoliberalism, the individual is the primary unit of agency, and personal choice reigns supreme as the reason one succeeds or fails. Neoliberalism is fueled by governmentality, a concept made salient through Michel Foucault (1975) to indicate the degree to which systems, such as government, religion, and mainstream culture, produce citizens who are best suited to the policies of the state. Within the market-based logic of neoliberalism, governmentality colludes with other hegemonic factors to create the terms for a docile body, willing to write on itself the codes of success that will enable competition within a larger global marketplace. Critical to the idea of governmentality is the regulation of micropractices—self-control, guidance of the family, management of children, supervision of the household, and development of the "self." Neoliberalism and governmentality thrive on the

---

11 In truth, however, fame and fortune have always been intertwined appeals of the American dream as exemplified through the Horatio Alger stories of lifting oneself by his own bootstraps in the *Ragged Dick* series. Paired with his "stories of success," for instance, is a novel actually called *Fame and Fortune; or, The Progress of Richard Hunter* that, like *Ragged Dick*, features a vagabond boy in nineteenth-century America who makes something of himself through hard work and persistence, thus proving the white, straight masculinist promise of American meritocracy.

pedagogies offered in and through the Tom Cruise Closet, particularly as such instruction is often labeled a form of beneficent self-help or, in the words of Oprah Winfrey, learning to "live your best life."

Religion and commerce have long been bedfellows, of course, yet advanced capitalism has shifted these dynamics to new ground so that churches now compete in a crowded field of brand culture. As Sarah Banet-Weiser (2012, 171) writes, even in light of religion's long commodification, "the contemporary political economy of advanced capitalism encourages a shift from commodification to the branding of religion, where brand strategies intersect with consumer activity and content to create a brand culture around religion, and where capitalist business practices merge with religious practices in an unproblematic, normative relationship." In this symbiotic relationship between branding, self-care, and religion, we indicate a phenomenon at work even beyond the neoliberal exploitation of religion under advanced capitalism. Indeed, at stake in the term *spiritual neoliberalism* is less the co-opting of religion and more the establishment of spiritualized goals—such as salvation, peace, transcendence, fulfillment—as achievable through neoliberal methods requiring "free" choice and "open" markets predicated on competition and advancement. This domain in which spiritualism and neoliberalism fuse constitutes what might be viewed as a neoliberalism 2.0, where financial success must be matched and bettered by benchmarks in both self-improvement and spiritual attainment.

Scientology certainly lends itself to this kind of calibrated market logic. According to mediated accounts, the Church of Scientology, as established by Hubbard and now propagated through Miscavige, offers its practitioners a clear and concrete teleology, the "Bridge to Total Freedom," that will, in turn, lead its most faithful to a place of perfection, called "clear." As described by sociologist David V. Barrett (2011, 360), going clear is "the attainment of Man's [sic] dreams through the ages of attaining a new and higher state of existence and freedom from the endless cycle of birth, death, birth. . . . Clear is the total erasure of the reactive mind from which stems all the anxieties and problems the individual has." Scientology.org describes clear as "something far higher and better than a human being" that has long been dreamt of by human society but is only achievable through the Church's procedures that make a person "much more themselves" ("What Is the State of Clear?" n.d.). Scientology can thus be defined as a technology of selfhood, which posits subjectivity as the locus of all power. In this, Scientology is a subtractive technology that undoes the inscriptions, or engrams, encoded on the reactive mind to reveal a truer, stronger, and more powerful essential self. A Scientologist self.

The mechanism for revealing this glorious new self, which is at the same time the true essence of a timeless self, is the audit. An audit is an interview between a PC (a pre-clear) and a trained questioner who takes the PC through a series of previous life moments and challenges as a way of purging the emotional power of traumatic memories. In the audit, the PC holds two devices, which are connected to an E-meter (somewhat like a polygraph machine) that is meant to measure and record the PC's reactive experience. The audit requires long hours on the part of both analyst and analysand. Sessions are typically eight to twelve hours per day for each of the many levels of the Bridge. Each level is similarly subdivided, so that going clear is process of years and lifetimes (particularly since Scientology ascribes to reincarnation). Set up in a pay-to-play structure, auditing courses typically costs several thousand dollars per course (public sources estimate the price tag as between $100,000 and several million dollars, since it is often necessary to redo levels or pay for other people to receive auditing).[12]

Adherents are required to go up both sides of the Bridge in order to go clear and then emerge into OT, or Operating Thetan, where there are further courses for sale that promise continued self-perfection. OT levels provide superhuman powers through a process of "exteriozation," whereby an adherent is able to manipulate MEST (matter, energy, space, and time). At the height of OT, a Thetan is believed to be able to create illusions, build universes, and control others from a distance. Without irony, these capacities—creating illusion, building universes, controlling others from a distance—are also the métier of Hollywood that entrances and entertains through illusion, image, and story.

12 For those who are particularly devout or who might not be able to sustain the high cost of enlightenment, there is the Sea Organization (or Sea Org), an elite group of workers who dress in naval uniforms and who have signed billion-year contracts in perpetual service to the Church. Sea Org members both dispense and receive auditing as part of their compensation from the church. In terms of financial compensation for the labor they provide to run and manage the extensive operation of the church, Sea Org members typically receive room, board, and about $75/week in allowance.

Scientology works through a logic of upward aspirationalism, in both literal and figurative terms. According to former Scientologist and outspoken critic Leah Remini on *Leah Remini: Scientology and the Aftermath* (2016–19), "The promise of Scientology is that you will reach your full potential in all areas of your life. So, you'll be the best mother, you'll be the best group member, you'll be great to animals, you'll take care of the environment. You'll reach the highest potential as a spiritual being. Not only are you fixing yourself, but you are also helping mankind. It offers you a sense of purpose in life." This, then, suggests the parallel truth of neoliberalism: if you succeed, it is to your credit; if you fail, it is your own damn fault. In Remini's words: "If I succeeded, it was because of Scientology. If I failed, it was because I wasn't doing Scientology." Celebrity Scientologists Tom Cruise and John Travolta avow that their successes are a direct consequence of the self-improvement hierarchy of Scientology and so to leave the chain of development the Church mandates would be to consign themselves to failure, which here is taken as equivalent to ignominy.

All major religions might boast famous adherents, of course, but there is something quite singular about Scientology's deliberate cultivation and use of entertainment celebrities. Hubbard certainly wasn't coy about how his religion should identify, cultivate, recruit, and exploit the power of celebrity: "Celebrities are very Special people and have a very distinct line of dissemination. They have comm[unication] lines that others do not have and many medias [*sic*] to get their dissemination through" (Sea Organization Flag Order 3323, May 9, 1973; capitalization in original).[13] Scientology

---

13 "Project Celebrity" was first published in *Ability* newsletter in 1955. The missive lists sixty-three celebrities and asks members to identity a celebrity, whom Hubbard (1955) called "quarry," in order to cultivate that person for church recruitment. "These Celebrities are well guarded, well barricaded, over-worked, aloof quarry. If you bring one of them home you will get a small plaque as your reward. If you want one of these celebrities as your game, write us at once so the notable will be yours to hunt without interference." In the present moment, this regard for celebrities as a tool for heightened church visibility still exists. On *Leah Remini: Scientology and the Aftermath* (2016–19), Mike Rinder remarks, "The exact purpose of the Celebrity Centre is: to help LRH [L. Ron Hubbard] sell and deliver high standard Dianetics and Scientology services to celebrities and thus convert earth's top strata of beings into Scientologists." Hubbard encouraged the

created and maintains several Celebrity Centres internationally, with the primary and most opulent being in Los Angeles. According to Scientology Flag Order 2310, the stated purpose of these Celebrity Centres is to "expand the number of celebrities in Scientology" and, of course, to treat them well within the exclusive domains of the resorts. Celebrities are thus expected to "pay" for good treatment with good deeds, specifically through public relations work on behalf of the church. Former Scientologist Amy Scobee was responsible for cultivating and recruiting celebrities. Her job duties, as described on *Leah Remini: Scientology and the Aftermath* (2016–19) were to "collect celebrities and make them into walking success stories of Scientology." Chief among these, Scobee emphasized, was Tom Cruise.[14]

At present, Cruise has achieved level OT VII, the Ring of Fire, meaning he is past clear, and "more human than human," a level that requires him to clear the planet, through gestures large and small. In a much-circulated and parodied video that Scientology unsuccessfully tried to remove from YouTube, Cruise offers a nine-minute rumination on his role as a Scientologist that is filled with his characteristically Cruisean bravado, eerily aggressive laughter, and intense staring. Dressed in a body-hugging black turtleneck with *Mission: Impossible*–esque music playing in the background, Cruise says he has a higher calling than most people. Reflecting on his singularity, he intones, "When you drive past an accident, it's not like anyone else. As you drive past, you know you have to do something about it because you

> recruitment of midlevel celebrities seemingly about to emerge into super stardom. At present, Scientology stars (besides Cruise) include John Travolta, Kirstie Alley, Nancy Cartwright, Laura Prepon, Jason Lee, Jenna Elfman, Anne Archer, Rebecca Minkoff, Chick Corea, and Elisabeth Moss. Famous now-deceased Scientologists include Gloria Swanson and Isaac Hays. And of course, the list of former Scientologists, typically referred to as SPs for suppressive persons, continues to grow and includes Cruise's ex-wives Katie Holmes and Nicole Kidman.

14 Carole M. Cusack (2009) argues that celebrities such as Tom Cruise, John Travolta, and Kirstie Alley render Scientology familiar and even desirable, thus naturalizing the more obscure and/or outlandish aspects of Scientology through exposure. We argue, by contrast, that celebrity and celebrities serve an ideological function that draws on other epistemological systems related to meritocracy and neoliberalism. Whether this, in turn, makes Scientology more desirable, we do not know, but it certainly makes it more recognizable.

know you're the only one who can help" ("Tom Cruise Scientology Video" 2008). Here, Cruise succinctly articulates a basic premise of both Scientology and celebrity—to be exalted within and through either system is to be perceived as better, stronger, and more capable than all others. It is a position bordering on masculine arrogance that suits itself well to Cruise's much-noted tendency toward cockiness.

But for the celebrity such as Cruise, Scientology offers an important salvo, in that it suggests fame and fortune are the merited reward for dedication and hard work. Religious studies scholar Hugh B. Urban sees the underlying ideologies of both Scientology and celebrity as mutually supportive. In an interview on Beliefnet, Urban explains: "Celebrity is a religion that fits very well with a celebrity kind of personality. It's very individualist. It celebrates your individual identity as ultimately divine. It claims to give you ultimate power over your own mind, self, destiny, so I think it fits well with an actor personality" (Chasan n.d.). Thus, Scientology sanctifies the self, rewarding the enhancement of the individual as the most important precursor to spiritual development and social welfare. Of equal importance, Urban argues that Scientology lets a celebrity off the hook for his or her wealth or success: "These aren't people who need more wealth," he notes, "but what they do need, or often want at least, is some kind of spiritual validation for their wealth and lifestyle, and Scientology is a religion that says it's OK to be wealthy, it's OK to be famous; in fact, that's a sign of your spiritual development." In a modified version of the prosperity gospel, the logic of Scientology holds that fame and fortune are evidence of spiritual devotion. Indeed, according to Hubbard, Scientology is precisely the tool that a human needs in order to access material prosperity. We should perhaps take this idea with a grain of salt, however, since Hubbard also said, "You don't get rich writing science fiction. If you want to get rich, you start a religion."[15]

Conclusion: The Epistemology of the Tom Cruise Closet

As Sedgwick (1990, 5) brilliantly theorizes, the closet as metaphor contains an elaborate architecture of overlap and contradiction, which is bound by the idea of same-sex desire and yet disconnected from it. The closet is animated

---

15 Hubbard is reported to have made this comment in November 1948 at a meeting of the Eastern Science Fiction Association (Engel and Kelley 2015).

by its silences, in turn rendering "ignorance . . . as potent and as multiple a thing . . . as knowledge." In similar fashion, the Tom Cruise Closet is a highly mediated site, ostensibly open, transparent, seemingly straight while also hidden, silenced, and decidedly queer. Yet as Sedgwick also surmises about the closet as metaphor, the strict binaries of in and out, of gay and straight do little to describe the epistemologies of the closet.

One way to evidence this claim as it relates to Tom Cruise and Scientology is through Comedy Central's notorious animated sit-com, *South Park*, which boasts an equally notorious episode, "Trapped in the Closet" (Stone and Parker 2005). In the episode, Stan (one of the boys in the South Park gang) is curious about Scientology and agrees to a free personality test. As expected, the test reveals that he is the perfect candidate for their program, which will remove his negative emotions and improve his life for the low cost of $240. Stan's vacuousness—he has no engrams to eradicate through auditing—inclines the auditor to believe that Stan is L. Ron Hubbard reincarnated. Stan is catapulted to the head of the church, where he is greeted (on bended knee) by cartoon versions of David Miscavige and John Travolta. Once home, Stan is met by a cartoon Tom Cruise, who also falls to a knee. Desperate for Hubbard's praise, Cruise peppers Stan with questions, asking which of his films Hubbard likes best. Flustered, Stan utters the line that crushes Cruise's ego: "You're not, like, as good as Leonardo di Caprio, but you're OK I guess." Stan/Hubbard adds insult to injury: "That Napoleon Dynamite guy" is way better. A crestfallen Cruise bemoans, "I'm nothing! I'm a failure in the eyes of the prophet" and promptly locks himself in Stan's closet, which allows the rest of the episode to work out a running gag, repeated in some variation twenty-two times: "Tom Cruise won't come out of the closet!" Travolta tries to talk Cruise out of the closet but ends up joining Cruise in it, thus leading to a new gag, "Tom Cruise and John Travolta still will not come out of the closet!"[16] The episode ends when Stan refuses to play along with the "big fat global scam" of charging people for enlightenment. Stan exposes Scientology, the church threatens to sue,

---

16 Other popular culture reference points equally, and homophobically, put fellow Scientologists Cruise and Travolta in the celebrity queer closet. Consider, for instance, conservative provocateur Rivera's (2015) controversial Twitter post: "Does Scientology have [a] special program to provide cover for closeted gay super stars?"

and there is an immediate cut to the credits (all of which are listed as either John Smith or Jane Smith to comically avoid liability).

From the outside, this episode seems to reinforce precisely what Sedgwick (1990) decries—the clear binaries of in and out, the unambiguous distinctions between gay and straight. Yet the mediated aftermath tells a different story. Scientologist and South Park voice actor Isaac Hayes resigned in protest, and Cruise reportedly threatened to back out of promotion obligations to *Mission: Impossible III* if Viacom, the parent company to both Comedy Central and Paramount Pictures, rebroadcast the episode. But fans of the show struck back in what was termed "Closetgate,"[17] threatening to boycott *Mission: Impossible III* if the *South Park* episode was not aired again. Fans also posted the episode online, making it virtually impossible for the church or its lawyers to block it from being seen. Far from being trapped in the closet, the episode opened the closet's dark spaces for all to see.

"Trapped in the Closet" and its mediated ripples are important, transgressive even, because they show how fully media have intervened in the logic of Scientology and, in turn, how queerness permeates these spaces, voiding the distinction between in and out. Closetgate also demonstrated that the Hubbard playbook had limited potency in the context of new media. In the 1960s, Hubbard introduced a policy called "fair game" that said the church could and should retaliate through any means possible against those SPs perceived as subverting the mission of Scientology. The goal of fair game is to discredit or destroy opposition, through harassment, legal suits, or harming the reputation of the SP. In *The Road to Total Freedom*, sociologist Roy Wallis (1977) notes, "The Church of Scientology is not known for its willingness to take what it construes as criticism without recourse. Indeed its record of litigation must surely be without parallel in the modern world." For many years, the threat of lawsuits and other "fair game" practices made it treacherous for scholars, journalists, and other SPs to shine a critical light on Scientology, yet new media practices have made it impossible for Scientology to continue in the tight mold Hubbard created, thus upending its own orthodoxies. As the *South Park* episode, Closetgate, and even Geraldo Rivera attest, the mediascape has risen up against the Tom Cruise

---

17 For more on Closetgate, see Usborne (2006), Emerson (2006), Carlson (2006), and Goodman (2006).

Closet, shattering its capacity to dissimulate and creating a new epistemology of the closet.

The mediascape has yet, however, to undo the assurances of spiritual neoliberalism that recompense hard work with rewards, both material and spiritual, bound as they are to the teleologies of both celebrity and Americanness. Indeed, the logic of upward aspirationalism and reward is so fully demonstrated in and through the figure of Tom Cruise, and Cruise, in turn, has been used so fully to evidence Scientology's claims, that we expect their signifiers to be perpetually merged for as long as Cruise can endure as "the most charismatic man on the planet" (Martin 2013). That may be another forty years, or if he is reincarnated as Scientologists believe he has been, Cruise's star may shine forever.

Works Cited

Alger, Horatio, Jr. 1868. *Fame and Fortune; or, The Progress of Richard Hunter*. Boston: Loring.

Banet-Weiser, Sarah. 2012. *Authentic: The Politics of Ambivalence in Brand Culture*. New York: New York University Press.

Barrett, David V. 2011. *A Brief Guide to Secret Religions: A Complete Guide to Hermetic, Pagan and Esoteric Beliefs*. New York: Little, Brown.

Carlson, Erin. 2006. "South Park—Scientology Battle Rages." *Rapid City Journal*, March 17, 2006. rapidcityjournal.com/news/new-south-park--scientology-battle-rages/article_3f6dbf98-80c9-5bf1-8edc-70add5637b7d.html.

Chasan, Alice. n.d. "Mind over Matter: How Scientology's Founder Science-Fiction Writer L. Ron Hubbard Created a Religion of Individualism and Personal Power." Interview with Hugh B. Urban. Beliefnet. www.beliefnet.com/faiths/scientology/mind-over-matter.aspx.

Creekmur, Corey K., and Alexander Doty, eds. 1995. *Gay, Lesbian, and Queer Essays on Popular Culture*. Durham, NC: Duke University Press.

Cusack, Carole M. 2009. "Celebrity, Popular Media, and Scientology: Making Familiar the Unfamiliar." In *Scientology*, edited by James R. Lewis, 389–410. New York: Oxford University Press.

Dyer, Richard. 1979. *Stars*. London: British Film Institute.

———. 2003. *Heavenly Bodies: Film Stars and Society*, 2nd ed. New York: Routledge.

Emerson, Jim. 2006. "Closetgate: Latest Shocking Updates." *Chicago Sun-Times*. March 20, 2006. https://web.archive.org/web/20090830035115/

http://rogerebert.suntimes.com/apps/pbcs.dll/article?AID=%2F20060320
%2FSCANNERS%2F60320007. (URL inactive)

Engel, Pamela, and Michael B. Kelley. 2015. "Neil DeGrasse Tyson: Christians Have No Right to Call Scientologists Crazy." *Business Insider*, April 1, 2015. www.businessinsider.com/neil-degrasse-tyson-defends-scientology-2015-4.

Enlow, Courtney. 2015. "How Tom Cruise Jumping on Oprah's Couch Changed Everything." VH1 News, May 22, 2015. www.vh1.com/news/20262/tom-cruise-oprah-interview-changed-everything/.

Foucault, Michel. 1975. *Discipline and Punish: The Birth of the Prison*. Trans Alan Sheridan. New York: Penguin.

Gibney, Alex, dir. 2015. *Going Clear: Scientology and the Prison of Belief*. HBO Documentary films.

Goodman, Tim. 2016. "Death March with Cocktails: South Park at 10 Trumps Tom Cruise." *San Francisco Chronicle*, July 15, 2006. www.sfgate.com/entertainment/article/Death-March-With-Cocktails-South-Park-at-10-2531583.php%3e.

Hubbard, L. Ron. n.d. "Procedure on Entheta Press." In *Manual of Justice*. Operation Clambake. November 1, 2019. www.xenu.net/archive/go/man_just.htm.

———. 1955. "Project Celebrity." Operation Clambake. November 10, 2019. www.xenu.net/archive/celebrities/1955-ability_project_celebrity.png.

"Is It Just Me or Is Tom Cruise Beginning to Look Like a Middle-Aged Lesbian?" Reddit. Accessed December 12, 2018. www.reddit.com/r/funny/comments/71r085/is_it_just_me_or_is_tom_cruise_beginning_to_look/.

Leah Remini: Scientology and the Aftermath. 2016–19. No Seriously Productions. Intellectual Property Corporation.

Martin, Joe, dir. 2013. *Scientologists at War*. Roast Beef Productions, Channel 4 Television Corporation.

Nicholson, Amy. 2014. *Anatomy of an Actor: Tom Cruise*. New York: Phaidon Press.

Ogborn, Brandon. 2015. *The TomKat Project*. CreateSpace Independent Publishing Platform, Amazon Digital Services.

Oprah Winfrey Show. 2005. "Tom Cruise." Harpo Studios, May 23, 2005.

Orth, Maureen. 2012. "What Katie Didn't Know." *Vanity Fair*, September 26, 2012. www.vanityfair.com/hollywood/2012/10/katie-holmes-divorce-scientology.

Rivera, Geraldo. "Does Scientology have [a] special program to provide cover for closeted gay super stars?" Twitter, May 10, 2015. twitter.com/geraldorivera/status/219598241694613504.

Rogan, Joe. 2017. *The Joe Rogan Experience*. Episode 908, "Leah Remini." Podcast, January 30, 2017. podcasts.joerogan.net/podcasts/leah-remini.

"Scientologist Tom Cruise 'Not Allowed' to Have Relationship with Daughter Siri." 2019. *US Magazine*, July 31, 2019. www.usmagazine.com/celebrity-moms/news/tom-cruise-not-allowed-to-have-relationship-with-daughter-suri/.

Sedgwick, Eve Kofosky. 1990. *Epistemology of the Closet*. Berkeley: University of California Press.

Sternheimer, Karen. 2011. *Celebrity Culture and the American Dream: Stardom and Social Mobility*. New York: Routledge.

Stone, Matt, and Trey Parker, creators. 2005. *South Park*. Season 9, episode 12, "Trapped in the Closet." Comedy Central, November 16, 2005.

Today. 2005. "Matt Lauer Interviews Tom Cruise." NBC, June 23, 2005.

Today. 2018. "Former Scientologist Shares His Story, Interactions with Tom Cruise." NBC, June 27, 2018. www.today.com/video/former-scientologist-shares-his-story-interactions-with-tom-cruise-1265119299851.

"Tom Cruise." n.d. Urban Dictionary. Accessed January 12, 2019. www.urbandictionary.com/define.php?term=tom+cruise.

"Tom Cruise Scientology Video." 2008. YouTube, January 17, 2008. www.youtube.com/watch?v=UFBZ_uAbxS0.

Truitt, Brian. 2018. "Nothing Is 'Impossible' if You're Tom Cruise." *USA Today*, July 24, 2018.

Usborne, David. 2006. "*South Park* Declares War on Tom Cruise." *Independent*, March 19, 2006. www.independent.co.uk/news/media/south-park-declares-war-on-tom-cruise-6106252.html.

Vargas, Elizabeth, and Linsey Davis. 2012. "Maureen Orth on Tom Cruise, Scientology Wife Audition Article." *Good Morning America*. ABC News, September 5, 2012. abcnews.go.com/GMA/video/maureen-orth-tom-cruise-scientology-wife-audition-article-17158290.

Wallace, Benjamin. 2012. "An Inquiry into the Very Public Private Marriage of Katie Holmes and Tom Cruise." *New York Magazine*, July 22, 2012. www.vulture.com/2012/07/katie-holmes-cruise-has-left-the-building.html.

Wallis, Roy. 1977. *The Road to Total Freedom: A Sociological Analysis of Scientology*. New York: Columbia University Press.

Weber, Brenda R. 2019. *Latter-Day Screens: Gender, Sexuality, and Mediated Mormonism*. Durham, NC: Duke University Press.

Westbrook, Donald A. 2019. *Among the Scientologists: History, Theology, and Praxis*. New York: Oxford University Press.

"What Is Scientology's View on Drugs and Medicine?" n.d. Scientology Canada. Accessed January 12, 2019. www.scientology.ca/faq/scientology-attitudes-and-practices/scientology-view-on-drugs-and-medicine.html.

"What Is the State of Clear?" n.d. Scientology. Accessed March 14, 2019. www.scientology.org/faq/clear/what-is-the-state-of-clear.html.

5

SEARCHING FOR THE "DESERT OF THE REAL" IN THE FILMS OF TOM CRUISE

Loraine Haywood

In Joseph Kosinski's American Savior narrative, *Oblivion* (2013), Tom Cruise as Jack Harper / Tech-49 comes face-to-face with his own image (Jack Harper / Tech-52) in the "desert of the real" (Baudrillard 2017, 1). Astronaut Jack Harper is the real subject of which the drone technicians are exact copies or DNA maps. This shock revelation is a confrontation with the Real of death. This encounter can be used to explore theories that Jacques Lacan and Jean Baudrillard considered as maps of human reality. This tearing of the map finds the real territory underneath, and it is that search for realness that typifies Tom Cruise in his performance; as Slavoj Žižek (2003, 63) explains, "Authenticity lies in the act of violent transgression from the Lacanian Real."

Facing death in the performance of ever more dangerous stunts, Tom Cruise screens fables as the star of Savior narratives that reconstitute American greatness. The fable "On Exactitude in Science" by Jorge Luis Borges curiously engages in the same themes of empire, the territory, the map, the city, and the deserts that inform this discussion. The fable traces the development of the disproportionate map, which does not satisfy the pretensions of the Empire. The cartographers made a map where the scale was an exact copy, only "in the Western Deserts there remained piecemeal Ruins of the Map" (Borges and Bioy Casares 1973, 123). The fable conveys the psychoanalytic geography of the Empire that wanted an image to encompass all its territory. As image, Tom Cruise performs as the Empire if we use the fable that was the basis for Baudrillard's enigmatic concept of the "desert of the real." Chris Lukinbeal (2004, 247) explains that "film and television act as maps for the everyday social-cultural and geopolitical imaginaries and realities of everyday life." America in film is analogous to the fable because of the colonizing religious odyssey of its foundation narrative, imperial overreaching, arrogance, and its desert geography that sustains its New World utopia.

Tom Cruise repeatedly, in film, readily sacrifices the body to the belief in the dream of mapping the human odyssey. But the excessive nature of his life is not limited to filmic representation as he presents a transgressive form of "masculinity as performance" (Peberdy 2010, 231). In a search for the "desert of the real" in the films of Tom Cruise, the Real of his desire to fill in the gap, his drive for perfection, is impossible because it is the confrontation with the Lacanian Real of death.

The Reality of the Virtual, Lacan, Baudrillard, and Tom Cruise

Scott Davis, while interviewing Rebecca Ferguson (2018), made the following remark concerning *Mission: Impossible—Fallout* (Christopher McQuarrie, 2018): "When I go to see Tom in these *Mission* movies, I think, How is he going to top himself?" Ferguson replies, "Doesn't topping oneself mean killing yourself off?" Davis replies, "Well, it's a double meaning for Tom." How can we understand this drive or descent into the "desert of the real" that really does not fit the way Baudrillard expands on it? It can only be understood in the Lacanian aspect, particularly in regard to how Lacan is used in film studies.

Films create maps of human reality that can be analyzed by critics. Lacanian psychoanalysis has been used in film studies to understand how film mediates his registers. Both Todd McGowan and Slavoj Žižek have argued for a particular realization, in film and the filmic apparatus, that is the Lacanian Real. Žižek (2002a, 246) describes the Real "as not the 'true reality' behind the virtual simulation, but the void which makes reality incomplete or inconsistent, and the function of every symbolic Matrix is to conceal this inconsistency." Tom Cruise, through his characters, functions as an exception, entering the breakdown of the symbolic order and restoring the inconsistency through sacrifice. His films stage the breaking down of the American dream and its ideas of utopia, which are then restored at the film's conclusion. The filmic images flow like a map of human reality, a timeless image, starring Tom Cruise.

The enigmatic desert prophet of our age, Jean Baudrillard, considered that the Real would disappear as it corresponded with models as simulation (Baudrillard 2017, 2). As he wandered America, he saw this future coding in its psychoanalytic geography as the program of utopia existing within a simulation like the cinema. Encoded into this mythic simulation is an image that captures the mood of America—Tom Cruise. He performs as the double of himself, but he also doubles as the empire—America. The senseless repetition of the iconic simulation of Tom Cruise in cinema is America's map of self-image, its dream of a "Savior" and the fulfillment of the prophetic utopian vision that is the continuation of its founding narrative. His recognizable image screens the continuance of an imaginary wholeness, the "imaginary" as one of Lacan's registers of human reality. An example of this phenomenon can be found in the film *Oblivion*. Jack Harper as the cloned Tech-52 never speaks. Lacan's imaginary stage is without language and is purely the child's recognition of its own image in the mirror. In the closing scene, it is Jack / Tech-52 who stares at Julia across the lake symbolizing the mirror. Through Tom Cruise the audience recognizes America's self-image, that of belief in a psychoanalytic geography of utopia restored to an Edenic wholeness (Haywood 2016, 15).

American cinema functions in this "New World" as a utopian psychological support. The grand biblical narratives that dominate imaginary cinematic history are apocalyptic visions in which America is destroyed (particularly New York City), disrupted, and plagued by social breakdown, alien attack, and corruption in an endless cycle that culminates in restoration by the hero. The importance of Tom Cruise in this imaginary cinematic history of America is a translation of his body as a text, a map, and a story that keeps the illusion of wholeness in America's vision of empire. The sacred film text is Tom Cruise as America playing itself, the utopian vision sustained by the cinematic dream, "invincible, powerful, successful, wealthy and exceptional" (Haywood 2018, 41), living in an excess of its own fantasy that sustains this reality (Žižek 2007, 57).

The Psychoanalytical Geography of an Exactitude in Filmmaking

Tom Cruise and his exactitude in filmmaking inscribe a psychoanalytic geography on the world that dominates the narrative through images and spectacle. Paul Kingsbury (2009, 489) describes the link between psychoanalysis and geography as "an abiding interest in the worldly." He further claims that an "indelible 'o' that is inscribed between 'psych' and 'analysis' is the mark of an orb—an earth writing or 'geo-graphia'" (489). Film is a medium of earth writing, and world creation that uses the landscape as the place and setting for its characters in a simulation of reality. For an audience, cinema is an encounter with this psychoanalytic geography.

In the films of Tom Cruise, and the characters he portrays, is a type of world creation that transgresses and surpasses normal interaction in the relationships of power. He embodies the geography or terrain in the geopolitical sphere, the signs, and formulas for American consciousness as a simulacrum of himself and repetition as a substitute for any real depth of self-reflection. For example, characters such as Jack Reacher and Ethan Hunt operate outside the usual constraints, allowing their superior physical strength, abilities, and strategic thinking to achieve maximum effectiveness. The *Jack Reacher* and *Mission: Impossible* films are an example of a world created for Tom Cruise where he embodies the American consciousness confronted by the effects of the gaps in the symbolic order, its utopian vision, which is interrupted by the Real. This narcissism is miraculously materialized through a mythical transformation in cinema; as Baudrillard claims, all America is cinematic (Baudrillard 1988, 56).

In *Oblivion*, overlaying the Borges fable is an interesting engagement with the psychoanalytic geography of the American "desert of the real." Jack Harper / Tech-49, a fragment of the last vestiges of the empire overtaken by an alien invasion, comes face-to-face with the Real of his death. This is not limited to this one scene: Tom Cruise as Jack Harper also confronts the psychoanalytic geography of New York City. In flashback scenes are the memory of "Earth before the war." This relates the filmic text within the context of 9/11 and the irruption of the Real of death. The camera places the audience on the Empire State Building viewing platform, staring into the void where the Twin Towers once stood (Haywood 2018, 35). As an allegory of the destroyed empire of America, the ruins of the Empire State Building stand in for the Twin Towers on 9/11. This "ruined abstraction [testifies] to a pride equal to the empire" (Baudrillard 2012) and confronts us with a dimension of human experience that is the Lacanian Real.

Lacanian Film Theory What Is the Real?

Lacanian psychoanalysis "confronts individuals with the most radical dimensions of human existence" (Žižek 2007). Lacan considers that human reality involves three interconnected levels: the Imaginary, the Symbolic, and the Real. McGowan (2007, 3) explains these levels in the following terms: "Whereas the imaginary is the order of what we see, Lacan considers in the child's recognition in the mirror as an illusion of mastery over the image, the symbolic as the structure supporting and regulating the visible world. . . . The Lacanian real is the incompleteness or gap in the symbolic order."

In regard to the Real, Žižek (2007, 65) warns that "if there is a notion of the real it is extremely complex. . . . It cannot be comprehended to make an ALL out of it." In film, the Real is most often perceived in its effects, a traumatic irruption to the flow of normal everyday life. Dylan Evans (2010, 159) claims that for Lacan "at first the real is simply opposed to the realm of the image, which seems to locate it in the realm of being, beyond appearances." However, for Evans, the term has ambiguity; it develops and shifts over time but maintains a traumatic quality. He also claims that Lacan makes the Real a site of "radical indeterminacy . . . and in hallucinations and traumatic dreams. The real is both inside and outside" (160). Sean Sheehan (2012, 25) proposes that "the Real is the change in perspective that produces a different way of looking and experiencing reality."

As a traditional film theorist, Laura Mulvey (1989, 14–26) argues that Lacan's Imaginary is cinema's appeal, the mastery over the image and the masculine gaze that engages the spectator in the fascination with images. McGowan (2003, 29) claims that spectators engage with the object of film itself as a returning gaze; the film looks at you, involving the spectator in the image. For McGowan, this transforms the experience of film spectatorship, which can involve a "traumatic encounter with the Real . . . the failure of mastery. . . . It is what spectators desire when they go to the movies" (2). In *The Perverts Guide to Cinema* (Sophie Fiennes, 2006), Žižek asserts that "it is only in cinema that we get the crucial dimensions we are not ready to confront in our reality." In *Oblivion*, audiences can confront the Real of death by choosing to see the conclusion of the film as an irruption of the Real and not a "happy ending." The image of Tom Cruise as Jack Harper / Tech-52 is the illusion of wholeness and is the miracle return through DNA cloning. What intrudes and disrupts this fantasy construction is the Lacanian Real registered as a gap, an absence. Through the setting of the film in New York

City and the constant referral to the space where the Twin Towers of the World Trade Center once stood, absence is a recurring theme that confronts the audience. In the ending of the film, the impossible confrontation with the Real of death is the realization that Jack Harper is dead and the clone is only a copy.

Baudrillard argues that images are situated in a hyperreality and ignores what Žižek terms as the "reality of the virtual" (Stolze 2016, 95). Counterarguing that Baudrillard does not acknowledge a preexistent world as a material reality, Ted Stolze writes: "The material world has not disappeared but has remained causally effective, however much it has become increasingly mediated through technological, cultural, and conceptual means" (95). Rather than a disappearance of the Real, as Baudrillard argues, in the films of Tom Cruise it is the fable that finds applicability. In some sense, Cruise is exceeding the limits of filmmaking, and this is a dangerous encounter.

Tom Cruise: Screening the Real as Savior

In the fantasy life of Tom Cruise, it is as if the Real announces itself in his dream to make films (Žižek, 2007, 57). Jack Harper's search for the "desert of the real" brings an authenticity to Cruise's performance that extends to all those involved in the production. The level of this perfection in the cinematic image—that is, the map that encompasses the territory of America—is his exactitude in the science of film. What is achieved is a "desert of the real," the confrontation with the impossible, the Real of death.

By placing himself in this impossible position, in film and in real life, Cruise suspends his place in the symbolic order while simultaneously upholding and supporting its continuance. For example, in the *Mission: Impossible* films, *War of the Worlds*, *Jack Reacher*, and *Oblivion*, the ideology of the exceptional hero is maintained while he operates outside the social and cultural worlds that he "sets right." Gaylyn Studlar (2001, 176) suggests that in the films of Tom Cruise "he is overconfident, displaying a stubborn disobedience to patriarchal rules." It is his disobedience to the rules in the narrative of film and the risk-taking in his filmmaking that underscores an obsession with the Real. He cannot be reduced to ideological control because he possesses "what is in the subject more than the subject. . . . All mastery is constrained and haunted by this little piece of the Real that has the ability to completely topple authority" (McGowan and Kunkle 2004, 157–58).

In the films of Tom Cruise, real and metaphoric barriers exist to his assimilation into forms of the symbolic order, whether this is fatherhood, marriage, or home, as mirrored in his real life. His characters often exist outside of the rules and laws of which the film's symbolic order is constituted. Tom Cruise as Jack Reacher and Ethan Hunt goes beyond the boundaries of the laws and rules of society to ensure the continuing safety of America and its utopian vision. In *Jack Reacher: Never Go Back* (Edward Zwick, 2016), his knowledge of the military and its organization allows him to break Maj. Susan Turner (Cobie Smulders) out of a military prison and expose a conspiracy from within its ranks. Ethan Hunt transgresses borders and the sovereignty of other nations in order to protect an idealized America from any terrorist organization. The endings of Cruise films highlight his characters' leaving humanity with the Real returned to its place, usually after a confrontation with death. To complicate this situation, he faces death even while doing his own stunts, such as hanging out of helicopters with the real risk of falling. That dimension of fear is real both inside and outside of the script's text. It was revealed in an interview with Simon Pegg (2018), who plays Benji Dunn in the *Mission: Impossible* films, that in his line "I find it's best not to look," there is "a meta thing going on." This is a reflection of the fear shared by the cast and crew while witnessing Tom Cruise performing his own stunts. Cruise is the fantasy that supports his own reality (Žižek 2007, 57). But this is situated in the blurring of his characters with his real life, which supports the smooth running of the system, or the film, signaling a return to its functioning. We can all rest easy knowing that Tom Cruise as Ethan Hunt can save us from destruction.

Mission: Impossible

The ethos in the *Mission: Impossible* films is that Ethan Hunt must forsake social and cultural realities in the symbolic order of marriage and "real" life and continuously confront an ominous evil agent who is often aided from within Hunt's own government. He embodies the American political configurations of "a state of exception" against terrorism. Tom Cruise as Ethan Hunt confronts "living in the Real," the constant threat of an irruption from within and without America, as he "saves the world" through an Odyssean style of wily intelligence, physical stamina, and his cunning.

In the latest *Mission: Impossible* film in the franchise, *Fallout*, Ethan Hunt experiences "the Real that announces itself in" a dream in which he encounters "the traumatic Real" (Žižek 2007, 57). Ethan dreams that he and his ex-wife, Julia (Michelle Monaghan), are on an idyllic beach where Solomon Lane (Sean Harris), a terrorist he captured at the end of the previous film, is performing their marriage. Ethan is aware of the oddness of the dream. The words Lane uses in the ceremony reflect the cost, for Julia, of being married to Ethan Hunt—not the typical ideal usually espoused at weddings. It suggests the conflation of marriage and funeral rites, which is a theme in Greek tragedy (as seen in female characters like Polyxena and Iphigenia, for example). As Julia looks adoringly at the man who could get her killed, a nuclear explosion wipes away everything with a flash of light. Ethan awakens from his dream to a knock on the door[1] that delivers him his next task: life, as a mission impossible, resumes.

Žižek (2007, 57–58) would claim, in a Lacanian-style reanalysis of Freud's study of the Dream of the Burning Child, that Ethan wakes to avoid the Real of his desire. This desire is to have a relationship with Julia, which is impossible as it will get her killed. Perhaps this is the Real mission that is impossible in the films: to restore Ethan to the social and cultural life of America. The psychoanalytic geography of the picturesque mountain and riverside wedding scene interrupted by a nuclear blast acts as a prophecy of an approaching threat that Ethan must counter as a heroic odyssey. The knock on the door breaks the encounter with the Real of the traumatic event announced in his dream, and he awakens into the resumption of life. The mission is delivered in a hollowed-out copy of Homer's *The Odyssey*,

---

1 De Quincey (1823) claims that a peculiar effect is achieved in Shakespeare's play *Macbeth*. During the episodes before, during, and immediately after the shocking murder of Duncan, the audience enters a time of suspended judgment and moral dislocation. It is not until the knocking at the gate, when normal daylight life suddenly returns, that the full horror of what has happened breaks in on them. In *Fallout*, Ethan wakes from a nightmare to a knocking at the door, thus replicating the sensation of a traumatic displacement, followed by the resumption of his mission. It is not until the end of the film that the full horror of the dream is realized and breaks in on Ethan and his team.

objectively linking the art of film as a story of human odyssey. The Greek-style heroic journey of Ethan and his team allows the latent return of the Real in the symbolic structure. Ethan stays outside of marriage and family, which gives him free rein as a killing machine (not unlike Achilles). But Ethan's desire is also America's desire to wipe out all threats anywhere in the world anytime. There are no sovereign borders that cannot be penetrated.

War of the Worlds and *Oblivion*

Tom Cruise's characters in the post-9/11 science fiction films *War of the Worlds* and *Oblivion* have an encounter with the Real that involves the geographical landscape of destruction as a symptom of 9/11. Both films attempt to create narratives of male heroism and the restoration of the world through the family.

In *War of the Worlds*, Cruise's Ray on an ordinary workday, like many New Yorkers on September 11, finds himself and his children in a fight for survival in the aftermath of a strange, severe lightning storm. Leaving his daughter, Rachel (Dakota Fanning), with her brother, Robbie (Justin Chatwin), Ray goes out on the streets where people have gathered around a crater. The crater irrupts to reveal the Real of alien terror underneath, and the war on the streets begins. Ray, covered in ash, calls to mind the iconic images of survivors immediately following the 9/11 terrorist attacks. Ruined buildings, such as the church in the town square, become a metaphor for God's indifference and the crumbling symbolic order faced with an irruption of the Real, aligning with the Real of 9/11. This is the destruction of an idealized vision of American exceptionalism as a righteous nation protected by God. Tom Cruise as Ray stands in for the failure of the empire, as both imaginary and symbolic father, an acknowledgment that America had failed to protect its citizens on 9/11.

It has been argued that the ending of *War of the Worlds* allows for Ray's redemption as a worthy father figure for his children (Gunn 2008; Redmond 2006). Ray's lack of parenting skills, as evidenced by the open contempt Robbie displays for him and by his lack of knowledge concerning the needs of Rachel, is established early in the film. Žižek (n.d.), McGowan (2003, 37–39), and Gunn (2008) have all observed that Steven Spielberg's key films involve problems with fathers. Concerning the father in *War of the Worlds*, Gunn (2008, 9) argues that "unless one separates the imaginary father as an image, and the symbolic father as a function, it is easy to get the two confused." The claim is that the imaginary father has been redeemed in the eyes of the family, and the symbolic father becomes a redemption of American "hyper-masculine strength" (Redmond 2006, 293). Gunn (2008, 21) argues that the spectator is forced to see "Ray as the only figure of hope." However, it is also possible to see Ray as a figure of pathetic human struggle and despair when faced with an overwhelming and catastrophic event that mirrors the events of 9/11. Ray is "the real father . . . the biological father" (Evans 2010, 160), and at the end of the film he is left standing in the street. He holds on to Robbie, but outside of this image of reconciliation is the Real of destitution. Ray will be emptied of his symbolic identification, and he will disappear in his imaginary role, and as such, he is situated outside the symbolic order, replaced by Tim (David Alan Basche), his ex-wife's (Miranda Otto) new husband.

The territory of the inside of the house, a map of the social order that embodies family life is an unlikely return for his struggle to survive. This is the safety and structure denied to him in the "desert of the real." At the end of *War of the Worlds*, Ray is in the street, his symbolic identification drained of all relevance to a symbolic order. But he performs, or acts, to perpetuate its functioning; the family will survive without him. The children are returned to their mother, Mary Ann, immaculately conceived by Spielberg in her perfect, pregnant image of motherhood, and their caretaker father, Tim, a biblical Joseph. Ray's functioning in the final moments is to disappear into the "desert of the real," reduced to his DNA as a biological marker, to be the symbolic dead father and the imaginary father as a simulation.

Oblivion, like *War of the Worlds*, uses the iconic image of Tom Cruise as America in order to explore 9/11. Tom Cruise is Jack Harper / Tech-49, a cloned copy for which there is no original (he has become hyperreal). He embodies and personifies the psychoanalytic geography of America in its journey through trauma (this has included Vietnam in his past films). This transference of the trauma, of 9/11, onto Tom Cruise in *Oblivion* and *War of the Worlds*, is highlighted by the setting within the geographical boundaries of New York City and its ruined architecture. In *Oblivion*, Jack Harper is a remnant in America's search for DNA after 9/11 at the World Trade Center Twin Towers' site. The geospatial universe of the film, in the dream sequences and flashbacks, relay the absence of the Twin Towers, which is the subtext of the film *Oblivion* (Haywood 2018, 35).

The Desert of the Real—*Oblivion*

In *Oblivion*, Jack Harper has dreams and flashbacks of meeting a mystery woman in New York City. As they walk on the viewing deck of the Empire State Building, he sees the observation binoculars, "the object standing in for absence" (McGowan 2007, 71), which links the absence of the astronaut, Jack Harper, and the Twin Towers of the World Trade Center. The spectator encounters the Real of Jack's desire for Julia (Olga Kurylenko) in his dreams, the reawakening of memory (replayed as repetition and flashbacks), the gaze, and traumatic irruptions of the Real. The literal setting of the "desert of the real" is a key moment as a revelation that is a shock to the spectator.

The film appropriates an alien invasion story set on an apocalyptic Earth as a screen for the subtext of 9/11. The alien known as Sally (Melissa Leo) constructs a symbolic order onto the existing geography of America, creating a hyperreality of the map and the territory that she assigns to her clones. This is laid out in geographical space with a male and female clone assigned in towers. Tower 49 is where Jack Harper and Victoria Olsen (Andrea Riseborough) are stationed. This geographical area is in the ruins of New York City, where the authentic Jack Harper was a resident. Jack's psychoanalytic geography, contained in his memory, "the memory of a once proper humanity" (Colebrook 2016, 148), is awakened, reconnecting him to the symbolic order, the fragments of his humanity that establish a link to Earth before the war, a subtext of pre-9/11. Jack Harper / Tech-49 has nostalgic dreams and flashbacks in which he is on the viewing platform at the Empire State Building, looking out over Manhattan. This aspect looks out over the void where the Twin Towers once stood. The absence of the Twin Towers aligns with the absence of the real Jack Harper who exists only in DNA and memory.

Sally's DNA mapping of Jack and her cover story of a Scav, or scavenger, invasion cannot overcome the Real of desire that exists in the fragments of Jack's / Tech-49's humanity. Tech-49's full memories are reawakened by an encounter with the observation binoculars and Julia's retelling of their engagement on the ruins of the Empire State Building, seen as a flashback in color as opposed to earlier flashbacks, which were filmed in black and white. Returning to the Sky Tower, Jack / Tech-49 tries to save Victoria, but she reports to Sally, who releases Drone 109 in the dock. This drone's purpose is to eliminate the off-mission clones, and Victoria is turned to ash by the drone's weapon. Jack and Julia escape, and Sally attempts to destroy them by sending even more drones. They are literally pushed through the geographical boundary separating Jack / Tech-49 and Julia from the Real. They now enter the gap into Tech-52's territory, where Jack / Tech-49 confronts the "desert of the real." After their bubble ship crashes, Jack makes his way on foot over the sand dunes. He hears a drone signal and in the distance spies the disabled drone that tried to bring them down. Another technician, Tech-52, has landed with a bubble ship and is trying to repair the drone. As Jack / Tech-49 confronts the repairman, he shockingly comes face-to-face with his own likeness.

The Real of Jack's desire for Julia is exchanged for the Real of death as Jack Harper / Tech-52 experiences the same flashbacks of Julia and the Empire State Building. Coming face-to-face with his own image, Jack Harper's constructed humanity is as the tearing of the map of his symbolic identity. In this cinematic imagery are Jean Baudrillard's theories of America as a simulation, the Borges fable of the territory, and the Lacanian Real, which are all entangled in the literal "desert of the real." The psychological engagement with Jack / Tech-49 as he comes face-to-face with Tech 52 is an encounter with the Real of his own death. He says to Julia, "I am not him!" He is not the authentic subject but a DNA copy of Jack Harper, husband of Julia; that is, he is not Tech-49 but merely clone 49. Jack comes face-to-face with the Real outside the constructed digital world of Sally. Kosinski's reveal in the desert breaks through the dominant fiction of a constructed symbolic order, a world that the alien Sally had created for Jack.

Joseph Kosinski uses the incredible versatility and exactitude in Tom Cruise's performance to create a world that while reflecting absence allows his image to dominate and fill the screen. Tom Cruise reflecting himself as absent in the filmic medium seems ultimately to be impossible, but the off-screen death of the original Jack Harper and the clone's filling in for the original subject intersect with the way the actor in the filmic medium is subsumed into created worlds.

Tom Cruise as Jack Harper, Tech-49, follows the Savior narrative in the American empire, which adheres to blowing things up as a solution to world politics. To justify destruction, the narrative follows Tech-49 as he goes on a suicide mission to blow up the alien space station known as the Tet. He meets Sally, the Other as a galactic predator. He blows her up, killing himself and Malcolm Beech (Morgan Freeman) and thereby saving the world—again! Following Jack / Tech-49 as the embodiment of the Real of the American apocalypse, as destroyed territory, is the embodiment of the American dream of itself, crumbling and "falling into ruins" (Baudrillard 2017, 1). Like the Twin Towers themselves, Jack Harper is only found in the remnants of dust, DNA, and memory in the "desert of the real itself" (1).

The Psychoanalytic Geography and 9/11: Searching for the "Desert of the Real"

Baudrillard (2017, 2) considered that the Real would be simulated to correspond with a model, but the Real irrupted on 9/11, specifically in the model of disaster film, and shredded the filmic map, the cinematic history, that had been more real than the territory. The Twin Towers were the myth of empire, a fable that skillful cartographers had mapped out in the psychoanalytic landscape of images, a technological exchange in the exactitude of human reality, a "window on the world" (Natali 2001, 107).

Through the science fiction genre, Tom Cruise readily embodies the traumatized American landscape that cannot assimilate 9/11 into a narrative that would give it closure. It is only through the timeless image of cinema that America manages to temporarily, through the consumption of film, have closure. However, that closure needs to be repeated because it remains an open wound. In *Oblivion*, it is possible to enjoy a "happy ending" because Eden is restored, thus suturing the wounded American landscape after an alien terrorist attack. Tom Cruise is at the center of this restoration, but as an image of American success outside of film, he is overshadowed by his unsuccessful marriages and his religious fundamentalism.

The missing Twin Towers remain in the imaginary spaces of film and never stop being imagined (Baudrillard 2012, 36). After 9/11, cinema was searching for the "desert of the real" or realness rather than the master narratives that were designed to screen trauma. Terence McSweeney (2017) and E. Ann Kaplan (2003) consider that cinema was caught in Freud's repetition compulsion where 9/11 underscored American films. However disturbing the narrative of heroes and unprovoked attack with America as victim, the attempts at narrative closure are derailed where the Lacanian Real and the gaze persists in the filmic medium itself. Judith Greenberg (2003, 24) explains: "September 11 blew apart... our psychological unity.... Internally, it tore many of us into fragments." The unresolved trauma of 9/11 cannot be integrated into the symbolic order of American exceptionalism and invincibility, and it can admit neither to vulnerability nor its sense of abandonment by God. The crumbling of America's foundational narrative, the map of the territory of religious freedom as utopia is torn away, and the gaps in that ideal landscape irrupt in film despite its attempts at completeness in narrative and in image. Enter Tom Cruise, a Savior to restore the illusion of wholeness and restitution, the fantasy to screen the audience from the Real.

The ability of film to make and preserve memory leads to a confused perspective between historical events and cinematic history, as described by critics such as Žižek (2002b). In *Welcome to the Desert of the Real*, he claims that the citizens of America in New York on 9/11 were "introduced to the 'desert of the real'—for us, corrupted by Hollywood, the landscape and shots of the collapsing towers could not but be reminiscent of the most breathtaking scenes in big catastrophe productions" (15). If the "desert of the real" was corrupted by Hollywood in the 9/11 event, then the real must be discernible for audiences. This belies the claims of Baudrillard that the real has disappeared.

In the films of Tom Cruise, it is the nostalgic making, unmaking, and then remaking of America in a self-assuring cinematic journey. Through his characters, he is entangled with the "desert of the real," and his sacrifice aligns with the religious functioning of utopia, a "nostalgia for Eden" (Eliade 1961, 207) in the constant creation of "something more real" (Cioran 1992, 287).

Conclusion

Tom Cruise is like the skilled cartographers of Borges fable, mapping out with exactitude the science of the technology of film. He is a vehicle through which we can traverse the psychoanalytic geography of America. But this is Baudrillard's America, through which the cinematic landscape of senseless repetition searches for the realness, the fragments of the "desert of the real" that he considered would be lost in simulation. America reconstitutes utopia through film by staging its failure or breakdown and then restoring the imaginary illusion of wholeness (McGowan 2007, 16), of plenitude without lack, and the symbolic order of moral law and rules. Tom Cruise in his films is in a metaphorical and filmic "desert of the real." The fable by Borges, appropriated by Baudrillard, is an insistence that the real persists regardless of Baudrillard's enigmatic claims of simulation. The real persists, as Žižek

(2003, 62) explains, "in the image beyond the image." When discussing the stunts performed by Cruise on *Mission: Impossible—Fallout*, Simon Pegg (2018) in an interview confessed, "You hope you don't get the call.... There's always a slight sense of doom on set." The Real intrudes and disrupts even the process of making the film as Tom Cruise searches for the "desert of the real." He confronts death, the ultimate performance of the Savior narrative as he is obsessed by his own fantasy constructions that overtake him.

For Žižek, fantasy is more fully tied to reality and structures our reality. Donna Peberdy (2010, 250) claims that "Cruise's performances, both on-screen and offscreen, foreground a concern with distinguishing the real from the unreal, or acting from not acting." In terms of the Borges fable, the map of film that exactly covers the territory has become indistinguishable from understanding Tom Cruise and his performance. To find the "desert of the real" in the films of Tom Cruise requires what intrudes and disrupts the imaginary and symbolic narrative. The Real interrupts the notions of the return to the symbolic order, an order that wants resolution. The Real interrupts the resolution of Ray as the redeemed father in *War of the Worlds*. Similarly, Jack Harper is dead, which is revealed in the "desert of the real" as the clones Tech-49 and Tech-52 face off. The ending of *Oblivion* is perhaps the most disturbing moment of the film, as the returning husband is actually Tech-52, merely a reflected absence of the real Jack Harper (Haywood 2018, 44). In *Mission: Impossible—Fallout*, Ethan's desire for a marriage with Julia, perhaps the only truly impossible mission in the franchise, is to restore himself to a life of social norms and rules. This reflects the real Tom Cruise, unable to live as anything other than an exception to the rule.

Žižek and McGowan claim that an encounter with the Real is the attraction of cinema, but overwhelmed by the fantasy of making film, Tom Cruise exceeds this encounter as he is more fully the territory in film. Borges's fable and Baudrillard's adaption illustrate where the real irrupts. The prophetic future captures the entanglement that film has produced in its image of human reality, Baudrillard (2017, 1) states: "Today it is the territory whose shreds slowly rot across the extent of the map. It is the real and not the map, whose vestiges persist here and there." Tom Cruise persists as the real image of an anticipated Savior, as he sacrifices his own body in attempts to prolong the American dream through film. In the perfection of his performance, he searches for the "desert of the real."

Works Cited

Baudrillard, Jean. 1988. *America*. Translated by Chris Turner. London: Verso.

———. 2012. *The Spirit of Terrorism and Other Essays*. Translated by Chris Turner. London: Verso.

———. 2017. *Simulacra and Simulation*. Translated by Sheila Faria Glaser. Ann Arbor: University of Michigan Press.

Borges, Jorge Luis, and Adolfo Bioy Casares. 1973. *Extraordinary Tales*. Edited by Anthony Kerrigan. 1st British ed. London: Souvenir Press.

Cioran, Dima. 1992. "The Ethnographer as Geologist: Tocqueville, Lévi-Strauss, Baudrillard and the American Dilemma." *Social Science Information* 31 (2): 267–92.

Colebrook, Claire. 2016. "Time That Is Intolerant." In *Memory in the Twenty-First Century: New Critical Perspectives from the Arts, Humanities, and Sciences*, edited by Sebastian Groes, 147–58. London: Palgrave Macmillan.

De Quincey, Thomas. 1823. "On the Knocking at the Gate in *Macbeth*." *London Magazine*, October 1823.

Eliade, Mircea. 1961. *The Sacred and the Profane: The Nature of Religion*. New York: Harper & Brothers.

Evans, Dylan. 2010. *An Introductory Dictionary of Lacanian Psychoanalysis*. London: Routledge.

Ferguson, Rebecca. 2018. "Mission Impossible Fallout Cast Interviews—Henry Cavill, Simon Pegg, Vanessa Kirby." HeyUGuys interview with Scott Davis. YouTube, July 16, 2018. www.youtube.com/watch?v=EaNehFjKOdQ.

Greenberg, Judith. 2003. "Wounded New York." In *Trauma at Home after 9/11*, edited by Judith Greenberg, 21–35. Lincoln: University of Nebraska Press.

Gunn, Joshua. 2008. "Father Trouble: Staging Sovereignty in Spielberg's War of the Worlds." *Critical Studies in Media Communication* 25 (1): 1–27.

Haywood, Loraine. 2016. "Nostalgia for Eden: Joseph Kosinski's *Oblivion*, an Apocalyptic Genesis." *SeaChanges* 7: 1–19.

———. 2018. "Reflecting Absence, Mediating the Real: *Oblivion* as a Requiem for 9/11." *Performance of the Real Working Papers* 1 (2): 26–46.

Kaplan, E. Ann. 2003. "A Camera and a Catastrophe: Reflections on Trauma and the Twin Towers." In *Trauma at Home: After 9/11*, edited by Judith Greenberg, 95–103. Lincoln: University of Nebraska Press.

Kingsbury, Paul Thomas. 2009. "Psychoanalytic Theory/Psychoanalytic Geographies." In *International Encyclopedia of Human Geography*, edited by Rob Kitchin and Nigel Thrift, 487–94. Amsterdam: Elsevier Science.

Lukinbeal, Chris. 2004. "The Map That Precedes the Territory: An Introduction to Essays in Cinematic Geography." *GeoJournal* 59 (4): 247.

McGowan, Todd. 2003. "Looking for the Gaze: Lacanian Film Theory and Its Vicissitudes." *Society for Cinema & Media Studies* 42 (3): 27–47.

———. 2007. *The Real Gaze: Film Theory after Lacan*. SUNY Series in Psychoanalysis and Culture. Albany: State University of New York Press, 2007.

McGowan, Todd, and Sheila Kunkle. 2004. *Lacan and Contemporary Film*. New York: Other Press.

McSweeney, Terence. 2017. "Introduction: American Cinema in the Shadow of 9/11." In *American Cinema in the Shadow of 9/11*, edited by Terence McSweeney, 1–20. Edinburgh: Edinburgh University Press.

Mulvey, Laura. 1989. *Visual and Other Pleasures*. Basingstoke, UK: Macmillan.

Natali, Maurizia. 2001. "The Sublime Excess of the American Landscape: Dances with Wolves and Sunchaser as Healing Landscapes." *Cinemas* 12 (1): 105–25.

Peberdy, Donna. 2010. "From Wimps to Wild Men: Bipolar Masculinity and the Paradoxical Performances of Tom Cruise." *Men and Masculinities* 13 (2): 231–54.

Pegg, Simon. 2018. "Mission Impossible Fallout Cast Interviews—Henry Cavill, Simon Pegg, Vanessa Kirby." HeyUGuys interview with Scott Davis. YouTube, July 16, 2018. www.youtube.com/watch?v=EaNehFjKOdQ.

Redmond, Sean. 2017. "Nowhere Left to Zone in Children of Men (2006)." In *American Cinema in the Shadow of 9/11*, edited by Terence McSweeney, 291–306. Edinburgh: Edinburgh University Press.

Sheehan, Sean. 2012. *Zizek: A Guide for the Perplexed*. London: Bloomsbury. eBook.

Stolze, Ted. 2016. "Contradictions of Hyperreality: Baudrillard, Zizek, and Virtual Dialectics." *International Journal of Zizek Studies* 10 (1): 88–100.

Studlar, Gaylyn. 2001. "Cruising into the Millennium: Performative Masculinity, Stardom, and the All-American Boy's Body." In *Ladies and Gentlemen, Boys and Girls: Gender in Film at the End of the Twentieth Century*, edited by Murray Pomerance, 171–83. Albany: State University of New York University Press.

Žižek, Slavoj. 2002a. "The Matrix or, the Two Sides of Perversion." In *The Matrix and Philosophy: Welcome to the Desert of the Real*, edited by William Irwin, 240–66. Chicago: Open Court.

———. 2002b. *Welcome to the Desert of the Real*. New York Verso, 2002.
———. 2003. *The Puppet and the Dwarf: The Perverse Core of Christianity*. Cambridge, MA: MIT Press.
———. 2007. *How to Read Lacan*. New York: W. W. Norton.
———. n.d. "The Perverts Guide to Family." Lacan.com. Accessed November 3, 2018. www.lacan.com/zizfamily.htm.

II

Genre Cruise

6

THE AMERICAN EVERYMAN GOES IRISH

Gender, Genre, and Ethnicity in *Far and Away*

Carlos Menéndez-Otero

Ron Howard and Bob Dolman wrote the first draft of *Far and Away* (Ron Howard, 1992) around 1982. Preproduction, however, was not to start until 1989 because no one was willing to finance an Irish-emigration-cum-western epic right after the commercial failure of *Heaven's Gate* (Michael Cimino, 1981). The involvement of Brian Grazer and, later, Tom Cruise, along with the success of *Dances with Wolves* (Kevin Costner, 1990) and a rise in the interest in Irishness in the United States, gave the project the final push it needed, and filming eventually commenced in May 1991.

After premiering at Cannes, the film was released commercially on May 22, 1992, in the United States, where it would end up making $58.8 million—an unexpectedly disappointing box office result for a $60 million production that had scored very well with test audiences (Gerosa 1992; Box Office Mojo n.d. b). Despite faring better abroad ($78.9 million), *Far and Away* was labeled a flop, even more so because the previous Tom Cruise–Nicole Kidman film, the similarly budgeted *Days of Thunder* (Tony Scott, 1990), had taken in $82.6 million in the United States and $75.2 million overseas and barely made a profit (Box Office Mojo n.d. a).

The reviews were mixed at best and scathing at worst, with most praise given to the 65 mm cinematography and most scorn given to the script, which was considered old fashioned, shallow, hackneyed, and fully reliant on film cliché, implausible coincidence, and two-dimensional characters. Unfavorable comparisons were made between Howard and David Lean and John Ford because of Howard's (failed) attempt to build an

Irish-emigration-cum-western-cum-boxing-film epic that could compare to *Ryan's Daughter* (David Lean, 1970) and *The Quiet Man* (John Ford, 1952). Comparisons, also unfavorable, with 1930s melodrama and rom-com were made as well (see, e.g., Ebert 1992; Hinson 1992; Kelly 1992; Mars-Jones 1992; McCarthy 1992).

Critics were in general slightly more lenient toward Cruise and his costar and then wife, Kidman, and some found their performances and Irish accents passable or even good,[1] even though it was often remarked that the scale of the project called for a different type of male star. For instance, Todd McCarthy (1992) of *Variety* praised Cruise's "physicality" but contended that the "script would have perfectly suited Tyrone Power or Errol Flynn in the 1930s"—two examples, in turn, of the "larger-than-life Hollywood movie star" that Hal Hinson (1992) of the *Washington Post* believed Cruise, "lightweight" and "paltry," could not match. Writing in the British *Independent* newspaper, Adam Mars-Jones (1992) argued that the overall believability of the film suffered because of uncalled-for references to the Cruise persona, on the one hand, and Howard's inability to grasp the limitations of that persona, on the other. Mars-Jones illustrated his point with three scenes from the film: First, in the chamber pot scene in the Christie mansion, Shannon (Nicole Kidman) "peeks . . . with a sort of shy greed that has more to do with Tom Cruise's status as a pin-up than with anything in 19th-century Ireland." Next, in the scene in which Joseph (Tom Cruise) instructs Shannon on how to wash and hang clothes, he draws the pegs as if he were "a cowboy at high noon," hoping that his natural charm may help make up for the bland script. Finally, Mars-Jones argued that breaking in a wild steed by punching it, as Cruise does at the start of the final race, is something that only Clint Eastwood and Sean Connery could get away with. Therefore, with the scene the film "asks more of Tom Cruise than he can deliver," as "his charisma is too neutral, too eager to please." In other words, for these critics, Cruise was a soft male star and, consequently, unsuitable for an epic period film.

---

1 Just to give an example, in an otherwise negative review for the *Washington Post*, John F. Kelly felt that, surprisingly, Cruise and Kidman were "almost entirely credible in their roles. He's comfortable with his spud farmer accent; she's . . . believable as a naive heiress" (Kelly 1992).

Joseph (Tom Cruise) about to break in the wild steed in *Far and Away*.

The Cruise Star Persona in the 1980s

Critical opinion notwithstanding, and despite the relative flop of *Days of Thunder*, Cruise was undoubtedly a major and highly bankable star by 1992. Since his breakout in *Risky Business* (Paul Brickman, 1983), he had starred in the highest-grossing films of 1986 and 1988 (*Top Gun* [Tony Scott, 1986] and *Rain Man* [Barry Levinson, 1988]), had only one massive commercial failure (*Legend* [Ridley Scott, 1985]), and even managed to gain artistic respectability for *Risky Business*, *The Color of Money* (Martin Scorsese, 1986), *Rain Man*, and *Born on the Fourth of July* (Oliver Stone, 1989). Furthermore, over the latter half of the 1980s, all his films but *The Color of Money* had made at least $160 million from budgets of $15 million to $25 million, showing that audiences were more than happy to pay to see him in different roles across genres.

This phenomenal success was disconcerting to many critics, even more so because the Cruise persona had little in common with either of the overmasculine, laconic masculinities that dominated screens during the Reagan era through the genre of action cinema: the hypermuscular, heavily armored heroes of Sylvester Stallone and Arnold Schwarzenegger, or the flawed, ironic ones of Harrison Ford and Mel Gibson (Jeffords 1993b; Bou and Pérez 2000, 58–77; Deleyto 2003, 54–69, 163–70). What is more, being athletic rather than muscular, and being delicate featured, more articulate, younger, and shorter than the alpha males of 1980s mainstream cinema, the Cruise persona soon began to be associated with a soft, bland—even homosexual or feminine—masculinity. Over the 1980s, this association would be accentuated by the tendency of his characters to solve conflicts through (feminine) verbosity and technical skill rather than (masculine) physical confrontation, as well as the preeminence of homosocial/homoerotic over heterosexual bonds in most of his films. Also contributing to this was his recurrent romantic pairing, onscreen and off, with taller, seemingly older and wiser, mother-like women—a type Nicole Kidman, whom Cruise married in January 1990, clearly fit both in real life and in the films they made together (Studlar 2001).

Despite the differences, Cruise's characters in his most successful films of the 1980s share some fundamental traits with those of the stars above him. Out of them all emerges a clear picture of the contemporary ideal American everyman: middle class, urban, and nonethnic white; radically individualistic; often rebellious; strong willed and idealistic; and endowed with superior mental and physical attributes. If properly channeled and allowed to develop, these attributes will lead to personal and material success or allow the hero to save the world from different forms of destruction and chaos caused or unleashed by nontraditional families, working and/or feminist women, liberal politicians, government officials and regulations, communists, nonwhites, or sexual minorities—in short, anything the Republican Party disliked at the time (Jeffords 1993b; Deleyto 2003, 54–69, 163–70).

Unlike many other stars, Cruise seemed able to be equally successful regardless of genre. Still, by 1992, his films—mostly A-class vehicles built around his persona—were in themselves "like a film genre such as the Western, the musical or the gangster film" (Dyer 1998, 62), so his involvement in a project was able to set a rather clear-cut horizon of expectations for the film.

In his review of *Days of Thunder*, Roger Ebert (1990) first attempted to establish what viewers had come to expect from a Cruise film over the 1980s—that is, the narrative features that helped define the actor as a distinctive brand within the US film market. Building on Joseph Campbell, Christopher Vogler, and Robert McKee, among others, Ebert proposed that at least *Top Gun*, *The Color of Money*, *Cocktail* (Roger Donaldson, 1988), and *Days of Thunder* shared a narrative structure made up of nine elements: (1) the Cruise character, "a young and naïve but naturally talented kid who could be the best, if ever he could tame his rambunctious spirit"; (2) the Mentor, "an older man who has done it himself and has been there before and knows talent when he sees it, and who has faith in the kid"; (3) the Superior

Woman, "usually older, taller and more mature than the Cruise character, who functions as a Mentor for his spirit"; (4) the Craft he "must master"; (5) the Arena where he is "tested"; (6) the Arcana, "the specialized knowledge and lore that the movie knows all about"; (7) the Trail, "a journey to visit the principal places where the masters of the craft test one another"; (8) the Proto-Enemy, who "provides the hero with an opponent to practice on" at the beginning but ends up being best friends with him; and (9) the Eventual Enemy, "a real bad guy who turns up in the closing reels to provide the hero with a test of his skill, his learning ability, his love, his craft and his knowledge of the Arena and the Arcana."

Ebert aptly called this formula the "Cruise Picture" and warned that, as of 1990, although "still effective," some elements were "beginning to wear out their welcome." The same can be said of the more extreme variants of the muscular, armed masculinity of the Reagan era, which were at the time starting to be replaced with the gentler, self-reflective, protective, and family-oriented model of American manhood first glimpsed in *Die Hard* (John McTiernan, 1988) (Jeffords 1993a). It is often overlooked, though, that the masculinity of the *Die Hard* saga hero, John McClane (Bruce Willis), is also defined by his being a working-class American of Irish descent and, more important, that the "big switch" in cinematic masculinity largely intersects with the US surge in interest in Irishness that also facilitated the production of *Far and Away*. This surge, however, was not as rooted in the actual Ireland as it was in the tradition of representation of Ireland and the Irish in American popular culture, especially film (Rains 2007, 69–70).

Irishness and US Cinema

According to the US Census (2018), about 32.3 million American citizens claim to be of Irish descent. Diane Negra and Stephanie Rains, among others, have discussed whether and how many of these actually have grounds for the claim and why, after decades of decline, this interest showed signs of resurgence in the 1970s, gained momentum over the 1980s, and has continued blossoming since the early 1990s. As Ron Howard himself acknowledged in the making-of book of *Far and Away*, "Bob and I chose to tell a story about Irish immigrants. A lot of Americans—this is true of me—are of a very mixed heritage. That's the melting pot. But if there's any bit of Irish, it often seems to move to the top of the list when you ask people what they're made of. I felt that making a film about Irish immigrants becoming Irish Americans has something a lot of people would relate to—whether they are Irish or not" (Howard and Dolman 1992, 43).

Among the many factors contributing to this interest in Irishness seem to be the Northern Ireland conflict, the impact of globalization on identity, and especially the black, LGBT, and women's liberation movements, born out of resentment toward a white, male, heterosexual establishment that Irish-Americans have been perceived as part of since the 1940s. Feeling as disenfranchised and discriminated against as the minority protesters, mixed-white Americans have been increasingly choosing Irish as their primary ethnic affiliation to claim "ethnic victimhood and exclusion, based upon the historical experience of both Ireland's colonization and the discrimination experienced by earlier generations of Irish Catholics in the United States," while simultaneously maintaining "the inherent privileges of whiteness" (Rains 2007, 8). That is, Irishness would allow them to claim an innocent, blue-collar whiteness untainted by imperialism (Negra 2006) and patriarchy, arguing that their traditional values are not oppressive but oppressed.

Although *Far and Away* is set between 1892 and 1893, the biggest influx of Irish immigrants actually arrived in America in the mid-nineteenth century, fleeing from the dire poverty and starvation caused by successive severe potato crop failures between 1845 and 1849 and a land system that made the vast majority of the population dependent on the crop for survival. These largely Catholic, illiterate, unskilled, and traumatized migrants were met with resentment and prejudice; throughout the second half of the nineteenth century, the stereotypical Irish "Paddy" and "Bridget" became frequent objects of scorn in American theaters, the popular press, and eventually early cinema. That scorn notwithstanding, a counternarrative of Ireland and the Irish developed in parallel within the Irish-American community. This counternarrative reframed the male emigrants as political exiles who would return one day to free their homeland from British rule and save their relatives from eviction. Ireland itself was, in turn, either personified in the female figures of Mother Ireland and her daughter Erin or romanticized to become a premodern, idyllic rural space that the Irish had been forced to leave to gain political freedom and make progress in life (Miller 1985; Kearney 1997, 87–97).

Up to 1929, about "500 American films were made which had identifiable Irish themes or prominent Irish characters" (Rockett 2009, 18). As filmmaking began to turn into an industry in the late 1900s, several production companies set themselves on luring the Irish-American viewer into cinemas with feature films built on the community's self-idealization. Kalem Film went further and sent a crew to shoot on location in the west of Ireland. The strategy paid off: *The Lad from Old Ireland* (Sidney Olcott, 1910), in which an Irish laborer has to leave for New York and then returns momentarily to Ireland to save his loved ones from eviction and marry his sweetheart, became the first in a string of successful Irish-themed films by Kalem, mostly historical-cum-emigration melodramas with overt Irish Catholic (and American) nationalist subtexts. These films offered "a new and unique cinematic mythology for the Irish in America—a grand narrative of exile and return; of moving forward into the New World without abandoning the Old; of the creation of a trans-Atlantic hyphenated culture, capable of changing the destinies of both host and native lands" (Flynn 2014, 18).

Ruth Barton (2009, 3) points out that "from the early history of Hollywood through to the present day . . . representations of the Irish and Irish-Americans on screen were formulated . . . as part of an on-going negotiation between those texts and their audiences." The first great change in these audiences was due to the outbreak of World War I. While nationalists in Ireland saw the war as an opportunity to gain independence from Great Britain, things were neither clear nor easy for the diaspora, torn between their loyalty to the Irish cause and the official US support for Great Britain, and fearful of being maligned as un-American (Barrett 2012, 239–79). Then, during the interwar years, the violence of the War of Independence and the Civil War, the poverty and oppression of postindependence Ireland, and the gradual decrease in the numbers of first-generation emigrants severed quite a few emotional links with the Auld Sod. Unsurprisingly, a few more were severed on account of the official neutrality of the Irish Free State in World War II.

As a result, from the mid-1910s to World War II, Irish-themed cinema largely abandoned Ireland to focus on the social climbing of the Irish in urban America through blue- and white-collar work, politics and trade unionism, the police and armed forces, boxing and showbiz, interethnic and interclass marriage, and the church and organized crime. On their way up, the cinematic Irish usually have to confront WASP prejudice, opposition from older, first-generation immigrant relatives, competition from other ethnic minorities, and their own inner tendencies toward alienation and self-destruction, often expressed in alcoholism and violence (Shannon 2010). Once they get to the top, the traditional, communal values of the ethnic neighborhood usually act as an antidote to the alienating excesses of WASP individualism, although occasionally they have to be reminded of the importance of sticking to these values by visiting Irish relatives or newly arrived immigrants.

Actors like Pat O'Brien, Spencer Tracy, Bing Crosby, and especially James Cagney[2] first turned the Irish-American man into a model of contemporary American urban manhood: an ideal everyman that the filmmaker John Ford would project into the mythical past of the nation in his many westerns. Although the WASP nation-building myth had erased almost every trace of the Irish presence in the historical Wild West by the early twentieth century (Dungan 2006; Quintelli-Neary 2008), Ford's films like *The Iron Horse* (1924), *Fort Apache* (1948) and *She Wore a Yellow Ribbon* (1949) would reclaim a place for the community in the frontier epic through railway surveyors, construction workers, cavalry soldiers, and especially the communal rituals they brought along with them from Ireland. It is through these rituals (e.g., donnybrooks), notably absent from *Far and Away*, that Irish and WASP peoples bond with each other and start building a shared sense of community, and that the frontier myth opens up to other immigrant minorities and, eventually, Native Americans.

Ford's westerns notwithstanding, by the early 1940s, the second-generation, urban Irish American "Jimmy" was the dominant male Irish type in US film.[3] The real Ireland, with which a rising number of Irish-Americans

---

2 James Cagney was the quintessential cinematic Irish-American for much of Hollywood's Golden Era and his most successful fast-speaking, hot-blooded and often family-bound Irish-American gangsters (*The Public Enemy* [William Wellman, 1931], *Angels with Dirty Faces* [Michael Curtiz, 1938], *White Heat* [Raoul Walsh, 1949]), policemen (*G-Men* [William Keighley, 1935]), boxers (*Winner Take All* [Roy del Ruth, 1932], *The Irish In Us* [Lloyd Bacon, 1935], *City for Conquest* [Anatole Livak, 1940]), soldiers (*The Fighting 69th* [William Keighley, 1940]), and entertainers (*Yankee Doodle Dandy* [Michael Curtiz, 1942]) largely shaped the representation of Irishness in US cinema.

3 Coined by Peter Quinn, it takes "his collective name from Cagney's on-screen characters" (Rains 2007, 150).

had not ever had firsthand experience, was largely forgotten, and to an extent, so was the romanticized Ireland of first-generation immigrants and silent film. Nevertheless, in spite of widespread resentment toward Ireland for its wartime neutrality and outrage at the spiral of violence in Northern Ireland, the largely middle-class, suburban Irish America of the postwar years was to start turning again to the fictional Ireland to seek solace. Idealized as a premodern paradise, Ireland was to become a perfect refuge against the traumas of the war, the feelings of guilt and ethnic betrayal brought about by their own assimilation and prosperity, and their inability to adapt to a rapidly changing world where they were being quickly outnumbered by other minorities and increasingly regarded as part of the WASP establishment. The monumental success of *The Quiet Man*, in which a traumatized Irish-American boxer returns to his native Irish village in search of peace, both reflected and fueled these processes, contributing like no other factor to shaping the Irish-American tourist experience in Ireland as a restorative return to the maternal home.

Far and Away as a (White Revisionist) Generic Hybrid

As *The Lad from Old Ireland* and *The Quiet Man* show, cinematic journeys between Ireland and the United States (or vice versa) have been largely modeled on the romantic opposition between a rural, premodern, communal space almost invariably identified with Ireland, and an urban, (post-)modern, individualistic one almost invariably identified with the United States (Gibbons 1987; McLoone 2000, 53–54).

The first two acts of *Far and Away* are a (sometimes parodic) mash-up of the conventions of classic Irish emigration melodramas sprinkled with elements from the Cruise Picture. The film opens in the rural west of Ireland in 1892 and soon moves to the urban Irish neighborhoods of Boston. Joe Donnelly (Niall Toibin) dies of injuries suffered at an anti-landlord demonstration, and the local landlord's agents, led by the Enemy, Stephen Chase (Thomas Gibson), burn down the family cottage.[4] Soon after, Joe's youngest son, Joseph, sets off in search of revenge against the landlord, Daniel Christie

---

4   Unlike Tom "Iceman" Kazansky (Val Kilmer) in *Top Gun* and Rowdy Burns (Michael Rooker) in *Days of Thunder*, Stephen Chase is not a Proto-Enemy but a rather conventional antagonist who comes in the way of Joseph throughout the

(Robert Prosky). After a series of misadventures, however, Joseph ends up fleeing to America with the Superior Woman—Shannon, the fiery colleen daughter of Christie—in search of what he will not ever have in Ireland: land ownership.

Upon arrival in Boston, Joseph and Shannon get robbed and have to seek the protection of a ward boss, Mike Kelly (Colm Meaney), a sort of dark Mentor who puts them up in a room in a brothel and gets them jobs at a chicken factory. Joseph soon becomes a prize fighter, which gives him money and popularity. Out of jealousy, Shannon asks Kelly for a job in the burly-cue without knowing it is a cover-up for prostitution. In the middle of a fight with an Italian heavyweight, Joseph notices that she is being molested and gets distracted. As a result, he loses the fight, and they are both thrown to the streets. Hungry and cold, they break into a well-off family's house at Christmas and realize they are in love. The owners return unexpectedly and wound Shannon badly. Joseph, knowing that the Christies are looking for Shannon in Boston, painfully takes her to them to save her life.

Rather than solving the narrative conflict the way Irish assimilation melodramas conventionally do (i.e., by reintegrating the hero into the community), the third act of *Far and Away* takes the action to the Wild West and calls on the frontier western (sub)genre to attempt an ending more in line with the WASP individualism of the Cruise Picture.

Set months later, the act begins with Joseph working on the transcontinental railroad. After his father reminds him in a dream of his wish to have his own land, he quits and joins the wagon train going to the Cherokee Strip Land Race (the Trail). Among the thousands of people waiting to take part in the race are the Christies and Stephen, to whom Shannon is now unhappily engaged. Although Joseph has to get by with an unbroken horse, with a bit of help from Shannon he manages to use his horse-riding and fighting skills (the Craft) to beat the Enemy in a one-to-one confrontation at the Arena of the Cherokee Strip Land Race.[5] Nevertheless, as Mark C. Anderson notes,

---

whole film and makes unnecessary the introduction of an Eventual Enemy in the final reels.

5 *Ben-Hur* (William Wyler, 1959), *Cimarron* (Anthony Mann, 1960), and *The Road Warrior* (George Miller, 1981) were used as reference for designing the sequence, as "conceptually, there isn't much difference among Roman charioteers, futuristic nomads and Oklahoma land racers. They're each trying to reach specific

before he can claim his plot of land and consummate with Shannon, Joseph has to renounce his Irishness and turn into a WASP pioneer—something the film symbolically conveys by making him die momentarily in the final sequence (Anderson 2007, 45–50).

In classic Irish-themed films, the land usually proves to be a nonviable "way of life for the Irishman," and the colonial subject can reclaim his "masculinity through the trope of exile into the American Dream," often realized in the ethnic neighborhood (Ging 2013, 42). By contrast, in *Far and Away*, *Quiet Man*-like, neither the city nor prizefighting is able to make the dream come true, so the Irish hero has to fall back on the land to try to regain the masculinity taken away by colonialism. However, unlike Sean Thornton and other cinematic Irish(-Americans) disillusioned with urban America, Joseph does not return to Ireland to take his ancestral land back from the English colonizer; instead, he goes farther west and crosses the colonial divide to claim as his "by destiny" a piece of Native ancestral land.

From the beginning of the narrative, we are made to root for Joseph and Shannon because he is played by film star Tom Cruise, an embodiment of ideal Americanness with whom we readily identify; she is his (at the time) beloved wife, Nicole Kidman; and they are both young, attractive, entrepreneurial, naïve, oppressed, and in love. Besides, we approach *Far and Away* expecting it to play out both as a Cruise Picture and a reenactment of the Cruise-Kidman real-life love story with a happy ending.

Throughout the first and second acts, Joseph and Shannon are robbed, cheated, exploited, discriminated against, thrown to the streets, wounded, and separated from each other. Consequently, when we get to the third act, we inevitably feel that after everything they have been through, it is only fair that they get their dream plot of land and be reunited. As some of our initial expectations of the film are fulfilled, we inevitably forget that the land the US government was "giving away for free" had been forcibly seized from Native Americans a few years prior, that these characters are tainted with imperialism, and that the film is a piece of historical whitewashing primarily addressed to those millions of mixed-white Americans who, by the early

---

goals, while hopefully staying alive" (Howard and Dolman 1992, 131). The same can be said of the F-14 and NASCAR pilots in *Top Gun* and *Days of Thunder*, respectively.

1990s, were using Irishness to keep the status quo by claiming victimhood and innocence of past white oppression.

We may argue whether Joseph, Shannon, and the real-life settlers who participated in the race knew to whom the land belonged originally. Maybe many did not and were, as Howard claims, "innocent about the inner workings of the system." In the making-of book of the film, however, the filmmaker admits that he did know that the Oklahoma Land Runs (i.e., the Arcana of this Cruise film), in which some of his own ancestors took part, were "a fiasco in many ways—a publicity stunt, backed by government and railroad companies, to lure settlers west onto land that was taken from Native Americans." Regardless, he wanted to capture in *Far and Away* the "hope-driven innocence [of the settlers], to celebrate the little dreams of the everyday man and woman setting out in the world" (Howard and Dolman 1992, xi).

Intent on creating this "little creation myth for America, free of such inconvenient original sins as genocide and slavery" (Mars-Jones 1992), Howard echoes a recurring trope in Anglo-American colonial literature, especially about Ireland: the colonized land as previously uninhabited, virgin territory (see, e.g., Hadfield and McVeagh 1994). He reaffirms his vision with an insert of some Native Americans peacefully watching the race, as if it were a spectacle that has nothing to do with them and not the poignant culmination of the process of dispossession, extermination, and forced migration they went through in the nineteenth century—a process of which many Irish immigrants, in spite of the obvious similarities with the Cromwellian conquest of Ireland, were an integral part (see, e.g., Quintelli-Neary 2008, 1–32).

Native Americans are, therefore, almost wiped out of history in *Far and Away*, and so are African-Americans, Jews, Chinese or, for that matter, non-WASP, non-Irish European immigrants. As Mars-Jones (1992) put it, "The America of *Far and Away* may be a place of opportunity, but it is perversely homogenous"—an idyllic rural Irish melting pot that, much like the Ireland of *The Quiet Man*, subsumes "Catholic and Protestant; landlord and tenant; even nationalist and unionist . . . in [a] lush (and literally) green wilderness" (Rockett 2009, 38–39) but allows no one else in. However oppressed and innocent the Irish may seem in *Far and Away*, the film ultimately comes ideologically closer to the pre-1950s WASP supremacist western than to John Ford, whose sense of Irishness would take him

Three Native Americans watch the Cherokee Strip Land Race.

from recognition to sympathy "for a host of socially (and geographically) marginalized Others, among them various tribes of Native Americans, Mexicans and Mexican-Americans, women and African-Americans, Slavs and Poles, Swedes and Germans, poor whites and Southerners" (Ramirez-Berg 2001, 76).

As in his major films of the 1980s, then, the Cruise persona ultimately performs in *Far and Away* the ideological function of preserving a white status quo that considers itself under threat by marginalized Others who are (almost) left out of the mise-en-scène (Dyer 1998, 27). Taken together, all these films present America as a land of opportunity where anyone can succeed regardless of social background, provided that they have the necessary skills and are willing to work to their full potential. However, whereas the entrepreneurial success stories at the core of most Cruise films of the 1980s rely on the nonethnicity of his persona to conceal the prevalence of poverty and inequality among minority groups during the Reagan era, *Far and Away* ethnicizes him to conceal the violent history of the West and deny the existence of white privilege in America.

Conclusion: Joseph Donnelly and the Limits of the Cruise Persona

The number of meanings a star can embody at a given time is limited (Dyer 1998, 3), especially when they fall into the "star-as-professional" mode of stardom, which relies on an appearance of a degree of overlap between the star's public image and their film roles (Geraghty 2000).

By the early 1990s, though Cruise had yet not embarked on the *Mission: Impossible* and *Jack Reacher* sagas, the Cruise Picture, along with his already well-known insistence on doing his own stunts, ensured that the primary mode of articulation of the Cruise persona was the star as professional. At the same time, though, the mildly disappointing box office performance of *Days of Thunder* may have been taken by Cruise as an indication that it was time to tweak his persona. It should be noted, then, that it was the star himself who called Howard to express interest in playing Joseph after Kidman, who was already cast in the project as Shannon, let him read the script in late 1990 (Gerosa 1992). That *Far and Away* could be a much bolder, riskier step than the actor had anticipated did not go unnoticed in the media and, for instance, upon the film's release, *Entertainment Weekly* stressed that it was "his first period piece . . . his first attempt at a foreign accent . . . and riskiest of all, his first all-out love story" (Gerosa 1992).

The meanings a star embodies "develop or change over time," although box office failure is likely when a role is perceived to be inconsistent with the "structured polysemy" of the star and fails to "permit recognition and identification" (Dyer 1998, 63–64, 98). When a film role involves so many "firsts" as Joseph did for Cruise, rather than just selecting "certain images" of the star to try to achieve the desired "fit" between character and persona (127–29), on many occasions, it will either have to deviate from the structured polysemy of the star or add brand new traits to it. As a consequence, the risk of inconsistencies in plot, character, and star image will increase dramatically, and so will that of critical and commercial failure.

As Barton (2006, 227) argues, "Irishness remains the most commercial of identities, appealing not only to the Irish-American population who, in any case, themselves boast multiple hyphenated ethnic allegiances, but to the wider American and non-American cinema viewer." Accordingly, representations of Irish masculinity were abundant in popular film and television during the 1990s. These representations were, however, largely dependent on Irish-born and Irish-American actors whose personas were also largely built on their Irish ethnicity (e.g., Liam Neeson, Aidan Quinn, Gabriel Byrne, and Edward Burns) (Rains 2007, 177–78). It should also be noted that in the absence of distinctive racial features, accent was, and still is, one of the strongest signifiers of Irishness on screen (Barton 2006, 7–10).

Although Tom Cruise is a mixed-white American and does have Irish ancestry, as the Irish Family History Centre proudly certified in 2013

(McGreevy 2013), in the early 1990s his persona bore hardly any trace of ethnicity. If anything, the Cruise persona embodied a sort of flexible American whiteness with whom millions of viewers could easily identify, allowing him in the 1980s to play successfully an array of contemporary, urban characters of different descent—German (*Taps* [Harold Becker, 1981]), Serbian (*All the Right Moves* [Michael Chapman, 1983]), Italian (*The Color of Money*), Slavic (*Born of the Fourth of July*), Irish (*Cocktail*), WASP (*The Outsiders* [Francis Ford Coppola, 1983], *Risky Business*, *Rain Man*, *Top Gun*, *Days of Thunder*), and even some with no identifiable ancestry (*Endless Love* [Franco Zeffirelli, 1981], *Losin' It* [Curtis Hanson, 1983])—without ever alienating audiences. Even though by the 1990s more and more of these audiences were embracing, in Negra's words, "the Irish in them," the likelihood of a seamless fit between the largely nonethnic Cruise persona and a markedly ethnic film role was at best remote.

Universal and the actor's publicists could have reduced the risk of *Far and Away* being deemed incongruous with his image by adding his Irish ancestry to his persona traits. Also, the actor could have offset the deviation by using his acting skills to impersonate rather than just personify (King 1985) the character of Joseph Donnelly, which would have mainly involved mastering the Irish accent.[6] Not only was neither done, but the writers widened the rift between persona and character by coating the latter in an aura of hard masculinity coherent with the western and period film genres yet completely at odds with Cruise's soft, contemporary, urban male star image.

Even though *Far and Away* ultimately manages to establish some degree of continuity with the Cruise persona via the conventions of the Cruise Picture and a rather gratuitous display of his seminaked body and physical ability, this is often achieved, as said above, at the expense of historical accuracy and generic congruence. All in all, from the initial chamber pot peek to the final transformation from Irish emigrant to WASP pioneer, *Far and Away* and Tom Cruise demand of each other more than either can possibly deliver.

---

6 Despite the efforts of dialect coach Tim Monich, who was hired to teach Cruise and Kidman to speak in an Irish accent, and an Irish couple who were hired to stay with them (Gerosa 1992), the actor's *Oirish* accent is considered to this day one of the worst examples of its kind, especially in the British Isles.

Works Cited

Anderson, Mark C. 2007. *Cowboy Imperialism and Hollywood Film*. New York: Peter Lang.
Barrett, James R. 2012. *The Irish Way: Becoming American in the Multi-Ethnic City*. New York: Penguin.
Barton, Ruth. 2006. *Acting Irish in Hollywood: From Fitzgerald to Farrell*. Dublin: Irish Academic Press.
———. 2009. "Introduction." In *Screening Irish-America*, edited by Ruth Barton, 1–14. Dublin: Irish Academic Press.
Bou, Núria, and Xavier Pérez. 2000. *El tiempo del héroe: Épica y masculinidad en el cine de Hollywood*. Barcelona: Paidós.
Box Office Mojo. n.d. a. "Days of Thunder." Accessed February 17, 2019. www.boxofficemojo.com/movies/?id=daysofthunder.htm.
———. n.d. b. "Far and Away." Accessed February 17, 2019. www.boxofficemojo.com/movies/?id=farandaway.htm.
Deleyto, Celestino. 2003. *Ángeles y demonios: Representación e ideología en el cine contemporáneo de Hollywood*. Barcelona: Paidós.
Dungan, Myles. 2006. *How the Irish Won the West*. Dublin: New Island.
Dyer, Richard. 1998. *Stars*. London: British Film Institute.
Ebert, Roger. 1990. "Days of Thunder." RogerEbert.com, June 27, 1990. www.rogerebert.com/reviews/days-of-thunder-1990.
———. 1992. "Far and Away." RogerEbert.com, May 22, 1992. www.rogerebert.com/reviews/far-and-away-1992.
Flynn, Peter. 2014. "*Come Back to Erin*: Themes of Exile and Return in the 'O'Kalem' Films." In *Cinematic Homecomings: Exile and Return in Transnational Cinema*, edited by Rebecca Prime, 15–33. London: Bloomsbury.
Geraghty, Christine. 2000. "Re-examining Stardom: Questions of Texts, Bodies and Performances." In *Reinventing Film Studies*, edited by Christine Gledhill and Linda Williams, 183–202. London: Arnold.
Gerosa, Melina. 1992. "Tom Cruise and Nicole Kidman Star in 'Far and Away.'" *Entertainment Weekly*, May 22, 1992. ew.com/article/1992/05/22/tom-cruise-and-nicole-kidman-star-far-and-away/.
Gibbons, Luke. 1987. "Romanticism, Realism and Irish Cinema." In *Cinema and Ireland*, by Kevin Rockett, Luke Gibbons, and John Hill, 194–257. London: Croom Helm.
Ging, Debbie. 2013. *Men and Masculinities in Irish Cinema*. London: Palgrave.

Hadfield, Andrew, and John McVeagh. 1994. *Strangers to That Land. British Perceptions of Ireland from the Reformation to the Famine*. Lanham: Rowman & Littlefield.

Hinson, Hal. 1992. "Far and Away." *Washington Post*, May 22, 1992. www.washingtonpost.com/wp-srv/style/longterm/movies/videos/farandawaypg13hinson_a0a776.htm.

Howard, Ron, and Bob Dolman. 1992. Far and Away: *The Illustrated Story of a Journey from Ireland to America in the 1890s*. London: Boxtree.

Jeffords, Susan. 1993a. "The Big Switch: Hollywood Masculinity in the Nineties." In *Film Theory Goes to the Movies*, edited by Jim Collins, Hilary Radner, and Ava P. Collins, 196–208. New York: Routledge.

———. 1993b. *Hard Bodies: Hollywood Masculinity in the Reagan Era*. New Brunswick, NJ: Rutgers University Press.

Kearney, Richard. 1997. *Postnationalist Ireland: Politics, Culture, Philosophy*. London: Routledge.

Kelly, John F. 1992. "Far and Away." *Washington Post*, May 22, 1992. www.washingtonpost.com/wp-srv/style/longterm/movies/videos/farandawaypg13kelly_a09f1c.htm.

King, Barry. 1985. "Articulating Stardom." *Screen* 26 (5): 27–50.

Mars-Jones, Adam. 1992. "Accent on the ridiculous: Legs and Co—Tom Cruise in Ron Howard's 'Far and Away'—Jim Jarmusch's 'Night on Earth' Reviewed." *Independent*, July 31, 1992. www.independent.co.uk/arts-entertainment/film-accent-on-the-ridiculous-legs-and-co-tom-cruise-in-ron-howards-far-and-away-jim-jarmuschs-night-1536636.html.

McCarthy, Todd. 1992. "Far and Away." *Variety*, May 11, 1992. variety.com/1992/film/reviews/far-and-away-2-1200429747/.

McGreevy, Ronan. 2013. "Tom Cruise's Irish Ancestry Stretches Back to the Time of Strongbow." *Irish Times*, April 3, 2013. www.irishtimes.com/culture/film/tom-cruise-s-irish-ancestry-stretches-back-to-the-time-of-strongbow-1.1347399.

McLoone, Martin. 2000. *Irish Film: The Emergence of a Contemporary Cinema*. London: British Film Institute.

Miller, Kerby A. 1985. *Emigrants and Exiles: Ireland and the Irish Exodus to North America*. Oxford: Oxford University Press.

Negra, Diane. 2006. "Irishness, Innocence, and American Identity Politics before and after September 11." In *The Irish in Us: Irishness, Performativity and Popular Culture*, edited by Diane Negra, 354–71. Durham, NC: Duke University Press.

Quintelli-Neary, Marguerite. 2008. *The Irish-American Myth of the Frontier West*. Dublin: Academica Press.

Rains, Stephanie. 2007. *The Irish-American in Popular Culture, 1945–2000*. Dublin: Irish Academic Press.

Ramirez-Berg, Charles. 2001. "The Margin as Center: The Multicultural Dynamics of John Ford's Westerns." In *John Ford Made Westerns: Filming the Legend in the Sound Era*, edited by Gaylyn Studlar and Matthew Bernstein, 75–101. Bloomington: University of Indiana Press.

Rockett, Kevin. 2009. "The Irish Migrant and Film." In *Screening Irish America*, edited by Ruth Barton, 17–44. Dublin: Irish Academic Press.

Shannon, Christopher. 2010. *Bowery to Broadway. The American Irish in Classic Hollywood Cinema*. Scranton, PA: University of Scranton Press.

Studlar, Gaylyn. 2001. "Cruise-ing into the Millennium: Performative Masculinity Stardom, and the All-American Boy's Body." In *Ladies and Gentlemen, Boys and Girls: Gender in Film at the End of the Millennium*, edited by Murray Pomerance, 171–83. Albany: State University of New York Press.

US Census Bureau. 2018. "Irish-American Heritage Month and St. Patrick's Day: March 2018." Press Release No. CB18-FF.02, February 6, 2018. www.census.gov/newsroom/facts-for-features/2018/irish-american-month.html.

7

CRUISING THE VAMPIRE

Hollywood Gothic, Star Branding, and *Interview with the Vampire* (1994)

Sorcha Ní Fhlainn

In early 1993, Neil Jordan's *Interview with the Vampire* was greenlit for production after seventeen years of languishing in "development hell" (Jordan 1994). Part of its advancement in production was due to the casting of Tom Cruise, a financially sound yet controversial decision that garnered significant media commentary and fan backlash, particularly in the aftermath of its announcement. As Neil Jordan (1994) later described in his director's commentary on the film, "all hell broke loose" once Cruise's casting was confirmed. Anne Rice, the novel's author, was particularly critical of this decision, decrying Cruise as totally unsuitable to play her "Brat Prince" Lestat in interviews with Movieline (Frankel 1994) and the *Los Angeles Times* (Dutka 1993). Cruise had openly campaigned for the role (against pundit front-runner Daniel Day Lewis), dyeing both his head and body hair blond and visibly losing weight to match Rice's description of Lestat in her popular Vampire Chronicles series, in order to convince Jordan and producer David Geffen of his serious intent to claim the role of, if not outright embody, Lestat. Despite the outcries in both the burgeoning culture of internet fandom and more traditional media commentary, filming commenced in late 1993 with Cruise as its star.

Cast alongside Cruise was the then upcoming star Brad Pitt as the suffering, "whining" Louis de Pointe du Lac, Lestat's creation and depressed immortal companion whose intimate interview discloses their decadent adventures. While Pitt's casting did not garner much commentary by comparison, Cruise's association with the project was described by many critics as wholly unsuitable for this celebrated Gothic text, largely due to a significant clash of styles: Cruise's established screen persona in popular journalism as an all-American boy next door based on his earlier starring roles in *Risky Business* (Paul Brickman, 1983), *Top Gun* (Tony Scott, 1986), and *Rain Man* (Barry Levinson, 1988) branded him as too clean cut and threatened to flatten Rice's edgy material into something bland, if not wholly anesthetized, by his established screen credits. This chapter will explore the casting controversy and the "suitability" of Cruise for the role, framed by the reinvigoration of Hollywood Gothic in the early 1990s. The difficulty of adapting *Interview with the Vampire* to the screen will also be considered, particularly due to its "problematic" queer tinge, which Cruise's casting, I will argue, *attempts* to quell but consequently raises new forms of reading his shimmering queer star persona and foray into Gothic cinema. The final section of the chapter will explore the queer readings of the film, brokered by Cruise's casting whereby his inclusion can be read as an attempt to "straighten" the narrative and/or dampen the queer edginess so established in Rice's literary Vampire Chronicles. Rather than fully eclipse the source novel's celebrated queer Gothic narrative in this long-awaited film adaptation, his casting conversely also furthers the queer potential of the Cruise brand. As *the* casting controversy in his significant screen career to date, Cruise's turn as Lestat still commands fascination as a constellation between his star image, the queering power of Rice's source material, and Hollywood's reinvigoration of adapting Gothic literature for the screen.

New Hollywood Gothic in the Early 1990s

Cruise's casting as Lestat occurred at a particularly important juncture in Hollywood Gothic culture in the early 1990s; Gothic and horror cinema had come back into fashion. It was also a pivotal moment in Cruise's career to campaign for the part, thus enabling him to openly contest his typecasting in Hollywood, shifting away from his established screen presence as a heartthrob-turned-serious-actor and in so doing garnering a significantly darker edge. Cruise had played serious parts before, including *Born on the Fourth of July* (Oliver Stone, 1989), establishing a cinematic trademark of meshing emotional complexity and contestations of masculinity (O'Donnell

2015, 56) with American charm and ideals. This style, along with his transgeneric and box office appeal made Cruise a screen and tabloid star.

Hollywood underwent a serious revision in its attitude to Gothic and horror cinema in the early 1990s, thanks largely to two significant Oscar wins, in 1991 and 1992, respectively. Rob Reiner's *Misery* (1990), an adaptation of Stephen King's 1987 novel, secured an Oscar win for Kathy Bates in her chilling and deranged performance as Annie Wilkes, a nurse and popular-fiction fan who imprisons and forces her charge, Paul Sheldon (James Caan), to resurrect her favorite literary character in his romance series. Wilkes's deranged demands as Sheldon's most ardent fan and "Constant Reader" (an affectionate term King uses for his own most devoted readers) situates the imprisoned author as Scheherazade (of *The Arabian Nights*), expanding his "Misery Chastain" narrative each day to bargain for his life and to sate the literary desires of his captor. Bates's Best Actress win that award season broke the mold in terms of the Academy's notorious derision of Gothic and horror titles, and it bestowed a renewed perception of quality in Gothic-horror hybrid titles, which had previously only been greeted with derision or dismissal. Following the 1980s established motif of "bleed-'em-dry" sequels and direct-to-video titles, varying in aesthetics, production value, and budgets, horror was easy to cast aside as an inferior cultural product. *Misery*, though certainly a Stephen King horror-thriller hybrid, recuperated the Gothic and horror genres in the eyes of the conservative Academy as a worthy artistic endeavor.

This recuperation was not a mere historical blip either: twelve months later in March 1992, *The Silence of the Lambs* (Jonathan Demme, 1991) won the top five Academy Awards,[1] and in its wake launched a strong trend of revisiting Gothic and horror novels ripe for (re)adaptation. As noted by Stacey Abbott (2010, 29), these high-caliber industry successes saw "the main studios returning to classic horror tales taken from literature, comics, folklore, and film history, but now reinvented through the lens of the high concept movie." As Cruise himself was no stranger to starring in high-concept films such as *Top Gun* and *Days of Thunder* (Tony Scott, 1990),

---

1 In a ceremony held on March 30, 1992, *The Silence of the Lambs* won the "big five" awards of 1991: Best Actor (Anthony Hopkins), Best Actress (Jodie Foster), Best Screenplay (Ted Tally), Best Director (Jonathan Demme), and Best Picture (for producers Ron Bozman, Kenneth Utt, and Edward Saxton).

which deliberately sought to capitalize on his box office draw, once horror had cracked the mainstream of commercial and Academy adulation, Cruise's attachment to high-concept horror appears on the surface as a natural confluence. Within a brief few years following the success of *The Silence of the Lambs*, Francis Ford Coppola's visually lush reinterpretation of *Bram Stoker's Dracula* (1992), Kenneth Branagh's homoerotically charged *Mary Shelley's Frankenstein* (1994), Mike Nichols's *Wolf* (1994), and Stephen Frears's *Mary Reilly* (1996) all boasted significant all-star casts (Anthony Hopkins, Robert De Niro, and Julia Roberts among them) alongside a host of rising youthful stars in these reinvigorated treatments of classic Gothic tales. It is only because of this shift in industry perception and accolades that Hollywood A-list stars were now keen to be featured in lavish Gothic fantasies playing archetypes, including the vampire, the galvanized corpse, the lupine creature, and the horrid double.

The Academy also recognized the work of Irish director Neil Jordan, whose Oscar-winning screenplay for *The Crying Game* (1992) meditated on guilt and desire and included overt queer dynamics and discourse, which was also largely overlooked by mainstream Hollywood until the early 1990s.[2] Queer cinema emerged from 1970s and 1980s arthouses and, like the horror genre, its financial lifeblood circulated thanks to the local video store, film clubs, and fan cultures. While the Academy's recognition of a genre or art form typically *follows* a trend, rather than incepting it, both horror and queer cinema's separate and belated legitimation, and the long-overdue recognition of queer representations onscreen beyond melodramatic illness (thanks in large part to the industry's new emerging voices and prominent stars), gave studios the confidence and financial savvy to greenlight edgier and more mature projects.

Cruise's foray into the Gothic (a mode with which he would never be associated up to this point) may not have been as surprising in hindsight as it was when first announced in late 1993, but it nonetheless generated a powerful ripple effect in the media. There was something altogether different about his participation in this Hollywood Gothic movement that seemed, to those who query his screen versatility, to be *too* clean, *too* nice, and *too* mainstream to be sullied by the darkness of blood, murder, and mayhem.

---

2   Jordan won the Oscar for Best Original Screenplay for *The Crying Game* at the Sixty-Fifth Academy Awards on March 29, 1993.

De Niro, Hopkins, and Jack Nicholson had previously played madmen or troubled anti-heroes and won Academy recognition and critical acclaim for such triumphs,[3] but Cruise embodied a largely wholesome and charming, if not overtly *corporate*, aspect of the American dream that would read as out of place in, if not wholly contrary to, this mode in media commentary.[4] While Jordan's own films were seen as far removed from Hollywood circles and studio money and its conservative conventions, his association with *Interview with the Vampire* enabled him to mesh these two seemingly irreconcilable worlds at precisely the right moment in Hollywood culture; following his own Oscar win, Jordan became bankable and could make an ideologically independent film (with an openly gay film producer and financier, David Geffen, who was determined to film the "unfilmable" script Rice had adapted from her novel) with a strong cast to serve an existing fan base precisely when the Gothic was back in vogue.

3   All three actors won Academy Awards for complex and dark performances. For De Niro, his iconic performances in both *The Godfather: Part II* (Francis Ford Coppola, 1974), and *Raging Bull* (Martin Scorsese, 1980) won awards, but equally his dazzling descent into madness in *Taxi Driver* (Martin Scorsese, 1976) and *The King of Comedy* (Martin Scorsese, 1982) informs the "troubled psyche" aspect of his screen legacy. Hopkins won his award for his hypnotic, vampiric performance as the psychotic Dr Hannibal Lecter in *The Silence of the Lambs*. Nicholson won two Academy Awards for playing men afflicted with mental illness and emotional problems in *One Flew over the Cuckoo's Nest* (Milos Forman, 1975) and *As Good as It Gets* (James L. Brooks, 1997).

4   Cruise certainly played a few serious roles prior to *Interview with the Vampire*, most notably in *Rain Man* as Charlie Babbitt, the cold yuppie-turned-caring sibling for his autistic brother, Raymond (Dustin Hoffman). In *Born on the Fourth of July*, Cruise played Vietnam veteran Ron Kovic in a stellar performance based on Kovic's biographical journey from ultra-patriot to paralyzed anti-war protester. This highly emotional and physically demanding performance includes nightmarish sequences of terror and suffering but always positions Kovic as a victim of this torment; such moments do not transform the overall aesthetics and mood of the film beyond war drama. Cruise's role as a vampire challenges his screen legacy by foregrounding Gothic supernatural abilities and a penchant for killing and gleefully casts off any semblance of a loose moral code that typically demarcates Cruise's other screen characters up to this point.

Interview with the Vampire (adapted by Anne Rice from her 1976 novel and polished by Jordan without a screen credit) concerns the exploits of two immortals, Lestat (Cruise) and Louis (Pitt), as recounted by Louis to a human interviewer, Malloy (Christian Slater). The vampiric duo's relationship through eternity is marred with guilt and emotional turmoil. Lestat delights in the power and cruelty of undeath, believing vampirism to be a powerful and pleasurable ascension, while Louis, beset with human grief, cannot bear its sins and his vampiric thirst. Starving himself in penance, Louis rejects the immortal pleasures Lestat attempts to bestow. Upon wishing to break free from both Lestat's cruelties and his own personal despair, Louis ventures to Europe to find vampire elders who can ease his burden and explain the origins of their kind; the Parisian vampire coven he encounters, led by vampire elder Armand (Antonio Banderas), discover Louis's transgressions of their ancient vampiric laws—the creation of a vampire child, Claudia (Kirsten Dunst) and her attempted murder of Lestat to flee his abuse—and they burn Claudia in retribution. Killing the coven in revenge and rejecting Armand's advances, Louis eventually returns to America and finds some solace in the power of storytelling, the ability to recapture memories and magic through cinema, and he briefly reunites with Lestat. Now living in ruins and arrested in his own terror of being temporally dislocated in contemporary times, Lestat finds the confidence to venture out again in modern-day America only at the film's conclusion, after witnessing Louis's own assimilation with contemporary culture and technology. Louis, having confessed his life story on tape to Malloy, deems his "interview" a failure since he cannot pass on the tale without giving humans the desire to experience vampirism for themselves; the telling of the tale is another form of infection. As a recorded disclosure, Louis's interview reinvigorates vampirism though the power of postmodern storytelling in its alignment with undead subjectivity—privileging an unknown, marginal voice with rich interiority and secret complex histories—and in so doing, he literally revives Lestat, and vampirism itself, for this new age (for more on this, see Ní Fhlainn 2019).

Vampirism and Star Image

The Gothic prides itself on its ability to horrify, to complicate and destroy rigid categories and binaries, and to amplify, as Jerrold Hogle (2002, 12) observes, "threats of and longings for gender-crossing, homosexuality, or bisexuality, racial mixture, class fluidity, the child in the adult, timeless timeliness and simultaneous evolution and devolution . . . : all these motifs, as possibly evil *and* desirable, circulate through Gothic works across the whole history of the form." Hogle's succinct cataloging of the Gothic's central preoccupation to provoke and to trouble desire with danger certainly applies to Rice's novel and Jordan's film adaptation, evident from its opening moments with Lestat and Louis's orgasmic swoons and bloody kisses.

In its opening ten minutes, Cruise's first appearance is built up to unveil him as a Gothic spectacle: established by having Lestat's back to camera to build anticipation for his entry into Louis's narrative as his vampire sire, the scene soon climaxes with Lestat spectacularly emerging from the shadows, hissing and pouncing as a Gothic predator. It is an extraordinary moment of entry into the narrative and hinges on the desire to see Cruise transformed into a member of the chic undead. Cast against type, Cruise transgresses the perceived homogeneity of his "safer" and established screen credits from the offset of Jordan's film, which, alongside his rigorously guarded persona, only adds to the mystique. Moreover, his performance as Lestat adds a new and threatening dimension to Cruise's screen evolution. Cruise's screen fluidity is often swallowed up by limited perceptions of his ability, and he is evidently honing his craft and challenging these criticisms in using his onscreen charm to convey an alluring sense of menace. Consequently, while this is not Cruise's first foray into playing characters with troubled histories, Lestat nonetheless breaks many of Cruise's established screen norms simultaneously, thus contributing to its status as a signal film in his career to date.[5] What is particularly worthy of note in his performance are his

---

5   Beyond *Mission: Impossible* (Brian De Palma, 1996) and *Jerry Maguire* (Cameron Crowe, 1996), Cruise followed up this breaking with star convention again by the end of the decade in roles wherein he deliberately sought to diversify and challenge his typified casting. Both Stanley Kubrick's *Eyes Wide Shut* (1999) and Paul Thomas Anderson's *Magnolia* (1999) presented Cruise as troubled and emasculated by the desires and perceived failures of others, hysterically reacting to his loss of status. In Kubrick's last film, Cruise's Dr. William Harford narcissistically wallows in the imagined horror of his wife's sexual abandonment and attends an orgy on his dreamy sexual odyssey in this meditation on marriage and desire; in Anderson's epic, Cruise's scene-stealing performance centers on his hysterical denigration of women as a foul-mouthed pickup artist, before eventually finding emotional

gleeful displays of violence, made all the more unsettling with a cruel glint in his eyes during moments of suggested sexual desire.

Cruise's appeal, then, initially disguises his hidden Gothic potential as his iconic features are playfully twisted, particularly during moments of violent sport. An early scene in *Interview*, in which he bites a prostitute's breast and drains her flowing blood into a glass to tempt Louis to drink human blood, plays with Cruise's established screen seductions only to revel in its spiral here into vampiric depravity. Completing this display of brutal indifference to her suffering, Lestat disposes of her in a coffin as she begs for her life and quips with evident disdain, "It's your coffin, my love. Enjoy it! Most of us never get to know what it feels like." The unfolding realization that Lestat's sadism trades on a pleasurable incredulity and tension in Cruise's casting deliberately produces readings that are simultaneously disturbing and blackly humorous.

Upon its release, Roger Ebert (2009) made a similar observation, noting that Cruise's acting ability is extraordinary, and yet "this is an actor who is so clean cut in his everyday image that whenever he does something like this, we're almost saying he can't do it, and then he pulls it off." Cruise's "audacious" turn, as Peter Travers (1994) observed in *Rolling Stone*, signals a courageous decision to play with established modes of stardom and image: "Give Cruise credit for guts.... He broke ranks with the bland before in *Risky Business*, *Rain Man* and *Born on the Fourth of July*, but *Interview* is a real bust-out. Any star willing to kill women, children and pets onscreen is not that worried about protecting his image. Besides, Cruise's fratboy charm fits in with Jordan's concept." Janet Maslin (1994) also found promise and menace in his performance, expressing genuine surprise at the shattering of his star conventions:

> Talk about risky business: here is the most clean-cut of American movie stars, decked out in ruffles and long blond wig, gliding insinuatingly through a tale in which he spiritually seduces another foppish, pretty young man. And here is the surprise: Mr. Cruise is flabbergastingly right for this role. The vampire Lestat, the most commanding and teasingly

---

redemption at the conclusion of both films. While both parts earned Cruise critical praise (including his third Oscar nomination for his supporting role as Frank T. J. Mackey in *Magnolia*), such departures were arguably *less* controversial following the brouhaha over his casting as Lestat a few years earlier, wherein he established his ability to successfully transcend his screen persona as a dramatic actor.

malicious of Ms. Rice's creations, brings out in Mr. Cruise a fiery, mature sexual magnetism he has not previously displayed on screen.

In hindsight, it is evident that in the popular imagination Tom Cruise, the screen actor, had been consumed by Tom Cruise, the Hollywood star, as evidenced in Maslin's "surprise[d]" response. Drawing on Dyer's (1986, 2–3) distinction of the creation of stardom and public and private selves, Cruise's unsuitability for the role was sustained in commentary by the intertextual perception of Cruise's actual acting abilities (Can he *really* do this? Can he portray a serious and beloved Gothic character onscreen?); his private life (What's he *really* like? What does this choice reveal about Cruise privately?); and his carefully crafted career and image (Why is he *really* doing this?). This casting decision all at once provoked these queries and relied on his established commodity as a box office draw but brought with it all the baggage of star persona and screen branding. It was too Hollywood for some horror fans (who distrusted this production "compromise") and a strange generic direction in Cruise's established mold—starring in melodramas, coming of age films, biopics, or high concept pleasures—for others.

These tensions are not new, even for Cruise: they surface on occasion around his casting in prestige films or when working with "quality" directors such as Barry Levinson or Stanley Kubrick, whereby Cruise's persona is deemed incompatible with serious casting, only to later achieve acclaim for his technical excellence as an actor. However, this split between star image and artistic excellence is "artificial as certain directors with an understanding of the persona have exploited it for their own artistic ends." (O'Donnell 2015, 29). In *Interview with the Vampire*, Jordan channels Cruise's film star persona to truly align the screen metaphors of vampirism and stardom. Cruise's mesmeric performance draws on the vampire's established ability to fascinate and enthrall[6] and firmly holds audience attention while onscreen. Rice's own vampires in her novels also become stars in their own right—none more so than Lestat[7]—and so Cruise's casting is actually *remarkably* apt, despite her initial public derision of it.

---

6 The most influential example of this mesmeric quality typically associated with vampires originates with Lord Ruthven in John Polidori's *The Vampyre* (1819).

7 In Rice's series, spanning thirteen installments, Lestat ascends the ranks in the vampire kingdom from brat outsider to noble prince and holy vessel. He becomes infamous among humans and vampires alike, a vampire celebrity par excellence.

Rice openly declared that she had no such desire to see her novel's eventual screen adaptation sacrificed at the altar of Cruise's stardom or screen vanity. She vented to the *Los Angeles Times*:

> I was particularly stunned by the casting of Cruise, who is no more my Vampire Lestat than Edward G. Robinson is Rhett Butler. I told Jordan that myself. . . . I'm puzzled why Cruise would want to take on the role. He's a cute kid, on top of the world and on his way to becoming a great actor, but I'm not sure he knows what he's getting into. I'm tempted to call up (CAA chief) Mike Ovitz and tell him that everyone will be gunning for his client. Cruise should do himself and everyone else a service and withdraw. (Dutka 1993)

This biting comment certainly leaves no room for charity, nor any belief that Cruise could overcome the author's evident frustration with his charm and talent. Rice herself also stirred up considerable bad blood with this soundbite, leaving David Geffen no choice but to rush to Cruise's defense. Geffen dismissed Rice's concerns outright and, in mild hubris, responded by predicting that Cruise would secure an Academy Award nomination for his performance. While Rice would eventually retract her remarks and declare Cruise's turn as brilliant, Geffen's prediction did not transpire for Cruise during the 1995 Academy Award season. Just prior to its release date at the end of 1994, Rice publicly retracted her criticisms online, and in a paid advertisement in *Daily Variety* on September 23, 1994, she hailed Cruise's performance as "flawless," thoroughly revising her stance and criticizing other media outlets that still echoed her earlier sentiments about Cruise's ill-suited casting. This volte-face only added additional fuel to the ongoing media fire that Cruise's performance would be divisive. Unlike many of his screen contemporaries in the 1990s, including Tom Hanks, Holly Hunter, and George Clooney, Cruise did not begin his screen career in either Gothic or horror titles,[8] and so his turn as Lestat was not born of regression to earlier, "cheaper" forms of film production, or of a need to revive his career,

---

8   Tom Hanks had a bit part in *He Knows You're Alone* (Armand Mastroianni, 1980), and Holly Hunter had a small part in *The Burning* (Tony Maylam, 1981), while George Clooney starred in the comedy-horror *Return of the Killer Tomatoes!* (John De Bello, 1988).

but rather a deliberate, clever, "actorly" choice. As a marketing move, it was a masterstroke: Cruise's involvement buoyed up extensive commentary and film coverage in the media and trade papers and built up further anticipation. In turn, it gave Gothic and horror films further industrial legitimacy (once it did not stray too far into distaste and schlock) and conversely also opened up concerns that horror would be subject to industry-led dilution and too much mainstream attention, or so the online fandoms debated. Through the haze of his star persona, Cruise suffered from the vocal criticisms that he was not capable as an actor, and that commentary, he admits, wounded him: "I remember being so surprised by the controversy . . . I remember being very hurt, actually . . . Image is something that is created by the press, by different audiences on particular movies. All actors go up against this. . . . I feel for actors, because I know they hear all the time how they can't do it: 'well, you don't look the role.' There's not a lot of imagination" (Sischy 1994, 104).

Nonetheless, those who decried Cruise's casting at the time did have a legitimate point in their assessment of his star turns and credits. Bookending *Interview with the Vampire*, Cruise, led all-star casts in *A Few Good Men* (Rob Reiner, 1992) and John Grisham's *The Firm* (Sydney Pollack, 1993), films notable for the pursuit of justice—it is a common theme in his filmography, whether he represents the establishment or acts to individually expose its nefarious infiltration or corruption in the paranoid 1990s—only to immediately return to his other established adrenaline-fueled screen stunts in *Mission: Impossible* (Brian De Palma, 1996) and as a romantic lead in the melodrama *Jerry Maguire* (Cameron Crowe, 1996). In the years since Jordan's film, this only amplifies the signal nature of Cruise's Gothic turn in this "feminizing" part as a vampiric dandy, as he quickly returned to spectacle-led cinema that overtly emphasized his masculinity (though critically he continues to embody a subtle sexual fluidity by displaying his toned physique) and showcased his physical prowess. Though Cruise's queer/ed performance emphasized the slippages of his sexuality onscreen, Lestat's muted appetites nonetheless retain identifiably queer pleasures.

Reading Cruise's stardom intertextually and through Dyer's (2006, 5) prism of multiple strands of imagery, public and private collage, and image manufacture, his turn in Gothic cinema was so singular in his career in the mid-1990s that it became a postmodern punch line in the Steve Martin–Eddie Murphy vehicle *Bowfinger* (Frank Oz, 1999) by the end of the decade. *Bowfinger* is a witty comedy concerning budget filmmakers trying to make it big in Hollywood, a "fake it till you make it" extended joke that laughs at Tinseltown media personas such as Cruise's while also envying their fame and exceptional lifestyles. Bobby Bowfinger (Steve Martin) tries to convince Jiff Ramsey (Eddie Murphy) to impersonate his famous twin brother, Kitt (also played by Murphy), in his budget film project that (he believes) will assure his ascension into the Hollywood filmmaking elite. This is also achieved by surreptitiously filming Kitt Ramsey without his consent. Film star Kitt is deliberately written with Cruise's tabloid persona in mind (including his involvement with a new age religion and its gurus, here renamed "Mind Head"), but it is a seemingly throwaway line trying to get around the issue of filming and consent that produces its best (and the only direct) reference to Cruise: "Did you know that Tom Cruise didn't know he was in that vampire movie until two years later?" This superb line not only jibes at the persona of Cruise being prodded and mocked in the film via the unhinged diegetic screen career of Kitt but also laughs at the screen incongruity of Cruise playing a vampire as well as the comedic notion that Cruise in fact acts *exactly* like Lestat off-camera and was simply filmed without his consent. Vampirism and stardom are both equally at a remove from the everyday and draw on their powers of fascination for sustenance. Jordan (2001) also admitted in a retrospective interview that the metaphorical similarities between stardom, celebrity, and vampirism, particularly concerning Cruise, swam in his imagination during the filming process:

> The world of a vampire is not that different from the world of a Hollywood star. . . . You're kept from the daylight, you know, from the harsh daylight. You live in a strange kind of seclusion. Every time you emerge, a tremendous kind of ripple runs through people. . . . Lestat would enter a room and [it was like] an invisible-stone-had-dropped-into-a-pool kind of thing. It was an interesting metaphor on the kind of star–vampire, vampire–star . . . and as well as that, they are eternally youthful, or they're condemned to be eternally youthful.

The mysterious tabloid persona of Cruise, always at a remove from our world, is endowed with spectacular fascination; filtered through a Gothic lens by Jordan and via comedic interpretation and satirical commentary in *Bowfinger*, both point to the reflexive nature of Cruise's stardom and its inherent commercial and critical contradictions.

Queer Texts and Straight(er) Images

In many ways, *Interview with the Vampire* is not a typical "Tom Cruise film." Indeed, this role alone contests the media-led and limited concept that there is one specific type of Tom Cruise vehicle. Despite his top billing, Cruise is only part of its sumptuous spectacle, albeit the driving force for many to explore the film beyond its hard-core Gothic fandom. Evidence of the anticipation built to see the film was confirmed by its significant opening weekend, "racking up more than $36 million in ticket sales . . . the biggest opening ever for an R-rated film" (Pizzello 1995, 43). Despite his above-the-title top billing, Cruise is missing for forty minutes onscreen, leaving Pitt to carry the emotional and narrative weight of its somber and pensive tone. Cruise also quite brilliantly steals the best moments, bursting through windows in displays of supernatural physicality and debating immortal philosophy in fits of rage and sardonic humor, all enlivened by Lestat's delight and sheer audacity in embracing his immortality. His overt opulence and taste for the finer things is also emphasized throughout, queering Cruise's iconic features (including his million-dollar smile, now twisted into a malicious grin) and making strange his "magic face" (46). Cruise is costumed in silks, satins, and crushed velvets, and he appears distinctly ethereal and uncanny thanks to Stan Winston's eerie makeup of alabaster skin and delicate tracing of his facial veins, giving him a marble coloring yet paper-thin delicate complexion. Furthermore, Philippe Rousselot's cinematography, which accentuated Cruise's atypical gaunt appearance through precise shadowing, draws out his cheekbones and the glint in his eyes to amplify his exceptional role here from "those he's played in the past" (46).

While shying away from overt homosexual couplings onscreen (and Rice's novels are infamous for their overt and descriptive homoerotic acts), the film nonetheless oozes with sexual suggestion and polyerotic coupling from an early sequence in which Louis recalls his first encounters with Lestat. On the docks of the Mississippi, itself a liminal space of sexual impropriety and clandestine acts, it is suggested that Louis is beginning to have oral sex performed on him offscreen by a prostitute before he is attacked by her opportunistic pimp, only to be saved by Lestat's intervention in killing both malefactors. Elegantly emerging from the shadows, Lestat hisses as he comes into view, unveiling Cruise's vampiric face as an announcement of his Gothic transformation. Lestat, fulfilling Louis's death wish, scoops him up and vertically carries him heavenward in a dizzying display of oral penetration and sexual ecstasy, captured through Pitt's half-opened eyes and parted lips in surrender and Cruise's fixated stare to camera as Lestat drinks deep from Louis's throat. There is a distinctive emphasis on Lestat's bloodied lips, slick and shiny, as he asks Louis, "Do you still want death, or have you tasted it enough?" Typically read as the first invitation to a desired queer penetration (and certainly amplified by vampirism's HIV+ / AIDS cultural associations since the 1980s onscreen), sexual invitations with vampires remain tinged with the death drive in cinema. This coupling is then soon repeated when Lestat returns to Louis the following night, caressing the folds of fabric that surround his sickbed and beckoning him out to the cemetery to be turned. There, in the dying light of sunset, Lestat forcefully lies on top of him, draining Louis fatally on this second occasion and offering his bleeding wrist from which to suckle. Louis greedily feeds until Lestat spasms away in self-preservation, the experience of being fully turned leaving both of them gasping in the throes of their reciprocal orgasmic feeding and subsequent *petites morts*. For Louis and Lestat, their cohabitation as vampire sire and progeny soon fuel murmurs on the plantation, which can only be temporarily nullified by their aping of domestication until suspicion becomes too great and the estate is destroyed. In order to emotionally entrap Louis in this curated fantasy of familial bliss, Lestat manipulates him with the creation of a vampire child. This is perhaps the most Gothic creation of all in this film, for Claudia's own vampirism, arresting her in a doll-like body, complete with camp fussiness, is twisted into an effective expression of corrupted innocence and stunted rage. In their final scene together, upon Louis's return to America in the late 1980s, Lestat muses on their homoerotic magnetism: "No one could refuse me, not even you, Louis. . . . Yes, you tried, and the more you tried, the more I wanted you." Once again, Jordan's own constellation of Lestat's queer desire for Louis's affections and Cruise's own stardom is evident in their final scene together: the metaphors of stardom and vampirism merge in a manner that seems at once both enviable and damning, drawing affirmation from and being drained by the gaze of others.

Numerous reviews mulled over Cruise's queered turn onscreen, especially given its seemingly dynamic and overt content overall (in contrast with the audience-led queer readings of the volleyball scenes in *Top Gun*, for example, which entered mainstream critique on Tony Scott's film years after its release). In effect, the film serves Jordan's vision above fan expectations or audience demands; it hints at, suggests, and occasionally lingers on moments of arousal and sexual suggestion but rarely provides any overt climaxes, particularly with Cruise, beyond its opening act. As Harry M. Benshoff (1997, 272) notes, it "draws the spectator close to a frightening queer sexuality, then, in backing away from it, once again reasserts 'normality' (i.e. heterosexual values)." Benshoff is referring here to a particular scene in which Louis and Armand are in an intimate embrace and read as coded to kiss. The proxemics and sustained intent of both actors, and its tight framing, provokes a palpable frisson that threatens to fully indulge in a moment of homoerotic tenderness; instead, the kiss seems delayed at first, and then goes unrealized as both Louis and Armand withdraw from their tête-à-tête without any release, instead reveling in the pleasures of denying its fruition.

While Benshoff highlights this particular moment of sexual denial among many as causing an audience to stir as though they are awaiting a moment of horror rather than intimacy, Jordan's film is full of such dynamic turns in its framing of characters who are made culturally queer but are captured in its cinematography as isolated in the frame, reasserting their bewildered "normality" through spatial separation. Jordan wishes to deny an overtly sexual climax in favor of muted suggestion and a lingering feeling of want. Normality here is not heterosexuality but rather palpable isolation—a desire for fulfilment that, like vampirism, cannot ever be truly sated—and speaks metatextually to the mirage of celebrity and immortality and its true cost.

Jordan's camera deliberately keeps its two male leads physically devoid of any suggested sexual contact beyond Louis's transformation and the onset of his vampiric gloom. Beyond its opening scenes in which Lestat and Louis share their dark blood ritual and kill an innocent barmaid and suckle from her together—a visual homosocial triangle literalized in the film wherein the barmaid functions as a physical blood conduit to slake both vampire's thirsts simultaneously, and is promptly discarded once she is dead—they rarely share the same cinematic frame. Rather, Lestat and Louis are more often captured as two separate narrative lives in a homosocial contestation of power but distinctly lack erotic feeling; as a quarreling duo bound together in a disintegrating marriage of convenience, no tenderness remains in their exchanges or intimate desire in their touch. This feeds into the singular place Jordan's film occupies within the Hollywood Gothic movement: Rice's script is deliberately more heterosexualized and drained of any *overt* queer displays or physical intimacies than readily found in her novel (but crucially it retains its queer dynamics in its vampiric domestication) for the sake of widespread box office appeal and to quell any distinct commercial unease.[9]

Rice had rewritten the script in a desperate effort to secure a screen adaptation, transforming the role of Louis into a female character, before abandoning these changes and returning to its original vision when she realized its unique characteristics were being compromised for the sake of reactionary homophobia. For Rice's script to remain relatively faithful to its source material and to survive its adaptation to the screen largely unscathed, Louis, then, is explicitly heterosexualized in his grief by losing a wife and child rather than openly mourning the passing of his dead brother. Lestat's appetite for young fops and innocents is used against him in a deliberate ruse by Claudia to murder him, but this is emphasized more as a ploy than an overt queer commentary: she poisons two young boys with laudanum and encourages Lestat to drink their dead blood to firmly put him "in his coffin," but this is as far as the film goes in referencing Lestat's particular penchants. Lestat's murder of Widow St. Clair's companion, a gilded youth with whom he shares a suggested embrace before draining him, emphasizes his hunger for good sport over sexual conquest, but the resultant embrace and kill is kept offscreen and only signaled by Lestat scraping the companion's wincing face with his deadly pointed silver thimble, a displaced small phallic point, which brims with malicious intent.

Like many moments in Jordan's film, the queer nature of the original material shines through as an amplified pleasure of queer edge-walking by creating a delicate frisson. Jordan walks a careful line between adapting celebrated material and star power, between initial commercial reluctance and Gothic screen renaissance, and manages a gaze that aids the film's central performances (especially Cruise's) while sustaining a subtle queer tinge to satisfy Rice and her ardent fandoms. What is most remarkable about this

---

9   At the time, Hollywood representations of gay or queer cultures in mainstream cinema were distinctly muted, or drained of mature sexual content, in comparison with art house cinema.

balance is that it truly succeeds: Jordan's adaptation cleverly uses the power of Cruise's stardom for production and commercial ends *and* nurtures a nuanced and mature performance from the actor; he adapts a difficult novel to the screen at precisely the right cultural and commercial moment in the Hollywood Gothic movement, a feat that was unthinkable before it, and now replete with A-list talent, and delicately counterbalances, with panache and to eventual acclaim, tabloid media criticism and commercial conservatism, which at various points threatened to derail the project.

Conclusion: A Playful Gaze

Cruise's ability to play up rebellion and maverick behavior typically courts a slippery heterosexual iconography, and thus, it was feared, such a powerful screen legacy would simply "straighten" Rice's celebrated text, transforming this charged and rebellious tale of homoerotic immortality in favor of chasing an established fan base and mainstream audience, all at the direct expense of the tale's dramatic queer drive. Cruise's association with the project threatened to but ultimately did not obliterate all that was deemed important about it in the first place. Jordan's commitment to Cruise's casting as Lestat was steadfast and revealed a particular quiet power in his direction that was able to utilize and channel Cruise's star power as a direct extension of the vampiric metaphor onscreen and to playfully imbue Cruise's "fratboy" charm, as Travers's identifies, into a courting of the queer gaze that is not fully and explicitly realized. Cruise's presence cues up a series of contradictions, as Gaylyn Studlar (2001, 180–81) observes: "The film assimilates homosexuality into the existing phallocentric discourse by making Lestat triumphantly phallic as well as 'effeminate.' Lestat may be feminized through his 'homosexual' signs of behavior and manner, but he is phallic in his powers . . . no less so at the end of the film than in the beginning." Cruise's association with the queer gaze/culture has been identified by Ruth O'Donnell (2015, 55) as an awkward reconciliation "of two seeming ideological oppositions of heroic masculinity and vulnerable, yet sexually exhibitionist, boyishness." In *Interview*, this exhibitionism is relayed away from displays of his gaunt frame in favor of orally focused eroticism, transformation, and Gothic excess. Yet, privately, Cruise fervently polices his own sexuality in the media (he won defamation lawsuits against the British tabloids, for example) (Studlar 2001, 175). While *Interview with a Vampire* was read in part as a "coming out" declaration (or as wish fulfillment of such to escape a perceived closeting by Hollywood conservatism), a close analysis of the film's composition complicates this reading, insofar as the incongruity onscreen is not that vampires are polysexual, and have been historically aligned with sexual othering including queered identities (Ní Fhlainn 2019, 69–97), but rather that Cruise's casting as an undead dandy distinctly bristled with his established filmography up to that point. Cruise's presence does not fully straighten Jordan's film, nor does the film fully queer Cruise's star brand: Jordan's film assimilates both heteronormative and queer gazes; delights in slippages, innuendo, and masquerades (what the vampire does best); and serves his own sublime vision of Rice's celebrated novel. The contestation of its queer power and the reach of stardom has become its own reward in *Interview with the Vampire*, affirming its status as a signal film in 1990s vampire cinema and celebrates the Gothic potential of Tom Cruise.

Works Cited

Abbott, Stacey. 2010. "High Concept Thrills and Chills: The Horror Blockbuster." In *Horror Zone*, edited by Ian Conrich, 27–44. London: I. B. Tauris.

Benshoff, Harry M. 1997. *Monsters in the Closet: Homosexuality and the Horror Film*. Manchester: Manchester University Press.

Dutka, Elaine. 1993. "A Look inside Hollywood and the Movies: *Interview with the Vampire*'s Picky Creator." *Los Angeles Times*, August 22, 1993. https://www.latimes.com/archives/la-xpm-1993-08-22-ca-26172-story.html.

Dyer, Richard. 2006. *Heavenly Bodies: Film Stars and Society*. 2nd ed. London: Routledge.

Ebert, Roger. 2009. "Siskel & Ebert: *Interview with the Vampire*." YouTube, July 1, 2009. www.youtube.com/watch?v=yrVq6uLbQgs.

Frankel, Martha. 1994. "Anne Rice: Interview with the Author of *Interview with the Vampire*." Movieline, January 1, 1994. movieline.com/1994/01/01/interview-with-the-author-of-interview-with-the-vampire/.

Hogle, Jerrold. 2002. "Introduction: The Gothic in Western Culture." In *The Cambridge Companion to Gothic Fiction*, edited by Jerrold Hogle, 1–20. Cambridge: Cambridge University Press.

Jordan, Neil. 1994. Director's commentary, in *Interview with the Vampire*. Directed by Neil Jordan. Geffen Films, Blu-ray.

———. 2001. Interview, in *Interview with the Vampire: In the Shadow of the Vampire*. Directed by J. M. Kenny. Warner Bros., DVD.

Maslin, Janet. "Film Review: 'Interview with the Vampire'; Rapture and Terror, Bound by Blood." *New York Times*, November 11, 1994. www.nytimes.com/1994/11/11/movies/film-review-interview-with-the-vampire-rapture-and-terror-bound-by-blood.html.

Ní Fhlainn, Sorcha. 2019. *Postmodern Vampires: Film, Fiction, and Popular Culture*. London: Palgrave Macmillan.

O'Donnell, Ruth. 2015. *Tom Cruise: Performing Masculinity in Post-Vietnam Hollywood*. London: I. B. Tauris.

Pizzello, Stephen. 1995. "Interview with the Vampire Taps New Vein." *American Cinematographer* 76, no. 1 (January): 43–52.

Sischy, Ingrid. 1994. "The Interview, the Vampire, the Actor." *Interview Magazine*, November 1994, 104, 127.

Studlar, Gaylyn. 2001. "Cruise-ing into the Millennium: Performative Masculinity, Stardom, and the All-American Boy's Body." In *Ladies and Gentlemen, Boys and Girls: Gender in Film at the End of the Twentieth Century*, edited by Murray Pomerance, 171–83. Albany: State University of New York Press.

Travers, Peter. 1994. Review of *Interview with the Vampire*. *Rolling Stone*, November 11, 1994. www.rollingstone.com/movies/movie-reviews/interview-with-the-vampire 190514/.

8

CRUISING INTO THE FUTURE

The Redemption of "Authentic" Masculinity in the Science Fiction Films of Tom Cruise

Linda Wight

In 2005, Tom Cruise was widely criticized for his increasingly erratic behavior. For many, Cruise's over-the-top declaration of love for Katie Holmes on *The Oprah Winfrey Show* and his public attacks on the psychiatry profession suggested masculinity in crisis. Media commentators condemned Cruise's behavior as being inconsistent with his star image, which had previously been marked by self-control and privacy (Hellmore 2005). Furthermore, Cruise's declaration of love was so "excessive in its affect, it came over as stage-managed" (O'Donnell 2016, 426). Thus, Cruise's masculine persona, which had traded on "sincerity and authenticity" (426), was revealed as a performance and, moreover, as a performance that was now failing to approximate the masculine ideal with which Cruise had long been associated (DeAngelis 2010, 42). Recently, however, popular opinion of Cruise has shifted toward a celebration of the authenticity of his filmic performances, in particular the stunts he performed for *Mission: Impossible—Rogue Nation* (Christopher McQuarrie, 2015) (O'Donnell 2016, 426). This chapter will argue that Cruise's science fiction films—*Vanilla Sky* (Cameron Crowe, 2001), *Minority Report* (Steven Spielberg, 2002), *War of the Worlds* (Steven Spielberg, 2005), *Oblivion* (Joseph Kosinski, 2013), and *Edge of Tomorrow* (Doug Liman, 2014)—similarly chart the movement of the male protagonist from crisis to redemption through his performance of a heroic masculinity built on a newfound awareness of his authentic self and the real state of his world.

In much science fiction, the "natural" or "authentic" man is positioned in opposition to the artifice of technology (Ryan and Kellner 2004, 49); films set in the near future, like Cruise's science fiction, often explore concerns about the repercussions of new developments in science and technology for men. Since the 1970s, many science fiction films have featured a "recurring motif of . . . a dehumanized, dystopian future where individual liberty and freedom of thought have been suppressed by technology" (Chapman and Cull 2013, 5). Many contemporary science fiction films, such as *Moon* (Duncan Jones, 2009) and *Source Code* (Duncan Jones, 2011), articulate "anxieties about the ramifications of a high-tech age for 'ordinary' men" (Rehling 2010, 116); in a technologically advanced future, these films suggest, the "authentic" masculinity of such "ordinary" men is under threat.

Such concerns are evident in Cruise's science fiction films, which depict near-future societies in which technology (human or alien) creates a barrier to self-knowledge and subjects the protagonists to control and abuse. These films, and twenty-first century science fiction films more broadly, engage with a popular narrative of masculinity crisis. In 1990, Robert Bly's *Iron John: A Book about Men* responded to the perceived erosion of men's rights and privileges following the second-wave feminist movement. Bly argued that men's insecurities and grief in reaction to the feminization of society could only be overcome by reclaiming an imagined original, authentic masculinity (Rehling 2010, 24). Cruise's science fiction protagonists are all initially marked by ignorance, loss, and/or trauma, tapping into the white man-as-victim narrative popularized by Bly and found in such films as *Falling Down* (Joel Schumacher, 1993) and *Fight Club* (David Fincher, 1999).

The Cruise protagonists are also marked by personal inadequacies that they must overcome in order to prove their worth. This is most evident in the four films released after 9/11, an event that raised fears that "the nation and its men had gone 'soft'" (Faludi 2008, 8). The US administration and media responded by constructing a "triumphant masculine narrative," of the "idealized male hero" (Bjerre 2012, 241) who would track down the terrorists and protect the vulnerable. Sarah Godfrey and Hannah Hamad (2012, 157) argue that "the return of formerly outmoded masculine traits of protectionism and violent vigilantism" were negotiated through a rhetoric of "protective paternalism" in action films such as *Taken* (Pierre Morel, 2008) and *Die Hard 4.0: Hacker Underworld* (Len Wiseman, 2007). This rhetoric is also evident in Cruise's post-9/11 science fiction films in which the protagonist's shift from inadequate victim to "real man" is achieved largely through his use of violence to protect a vulnerable woman or child.

Each protagonist of these Cruise films combines the violence of the warrior with the sensitivity and emotional articulacy long associated with Cruise. Godfrey and Hamad (2012, 159) note "the tearful introspection that characterized Tom Cruise's eponymous *Jerry Maguire*," singling this film out as a "cultural touchstone of the late 1980s and 1990s." Ruth O'Donnell (2015, 4) similarly emphasizes the significance of Cruise in modern culture, arguing "his screen persona can be understood as an expression of preoccupations regarding masculinity in late twentieth- and early twenty-first-century America." Cruise's filmography reveals a recurring concern with masculinity in process or crisis. O'Donnell (2015) notes the positioning of Cruise's characters as trainees in films such as *Top Gun* (Tony Scott, 1986) and *The Last Samurai* (Edward Zwick, 2003), and other films focusing on the Cruise protagonist in a period of crisis, including *Rain Man* (Barry Levinson, 1988) and *Jerry Maguire* (Cameron Crowe, 1996) (34–35). Thus, "Cruise's films are preoccupied with . . . a very real fear of failure" (60) and feature tests of masculinity (57) by which his protagonists prove their worth, "moving from a manly 'boy' . . . to a true 'man'" (Studlar 2001, 176). This narrative of masculine redemption is reflective of a broader trend in Hollywood film offering reassurance that the "real" man, the man who understands himself and his world, and proves his worth through heroic protection of others, will experience redemption and reward, even in a technologically advanced future.

Masculinity in Crisis

In *Contemporary Hollywood Masculinities*, Susanne Kord and Elisabeth Krimmer (2011, 2) argue that "the most potent hero in today's cinema is not the steady fighter, but the man who has undergone castration and still emerges as the guy with the biggest stick." This trend reflects the "triumphant masculinist narrative of 9/11" (Bjerre 2012, 241) through the repeated depiction of "seemingly defeated protagonists [who] rise from the ashes and convert their setbacks into ever-greater glory" (Kord and Krimmer 2011, 1–2). In each of his science fiction films, Cruise's protagonist begins metaphorically castrated. In *Vanilla Sky*, Cruise plays the immature David Aames Jr. who, despite his wealth, position, and playboy lifestyle, is tormented by the fear that he will never live up to his father, even though David Aames Sr.

has been dead for ten years. An adaptation of Alejandro Amenábar's 1997 film *Abre los ojos*, *Vanilla Sky* was shot prior to 9/11, responding to concerns about masculinity that had circulated in American culture since at least the 1990s. Gaylyn Studlar (2001, 176) defines the "manly boy" of the Cruise oeuvre as typically "inauthentic, greedy, narcissistic, self-absorbed, selfish, lacking in self-control, and/or 'dangerous' to others," an apt description of David, who reacts to his insecurity by indulging his selfish desires, blowing off his responsibilities as owner of his father's publishing house, and using his friend, Julianna (Cameron Diaz), for sex. David proclaims that he is "living the dream," but the dream sequence that opens the film, showing David running panicked through an empty Times Square, exposes the loneliness of his superficial life.

O'Donnell (2015, 168) observes that Cruise's filmography took "a darker turn" after 9/11: "*Minority Report* deals with the trauma of loss and preordained guilt . . . [and] *War of the Worlds* deals with attack on home soil," as do *Oblivion* and *Edge of Tomorrow*. Cruise's John Anderton, the protagonist police chief of *Minority Report*, released the year after the 9/11 attacks, seeks, like *Vanilla Sky*'s David, to hide his loneliness and trauma behind a successful veneer. Anderton is the admired leader of the Precrime unit, which in 2054 uses the psychic visions experienced by three "precogs" to arrest people before they commit murder. Anderton is fixated, however, on his grief for his son, Sean (Dominic Scott Kay and Tyler Patrick Jones), who was abducted from his care six years earlier. Tormented by guilt, Anderton seeks redemption through his job but is so consumed by his loss that his concern for others' welfare is "detached" (132). He describes the precogs as "pattern recognition filters," advising, "It's better if you don't think of them as human."

Oblivion and *Edge of Tomorrow* similarly feature protagonists marked by inadequacy. *Oblivion* is set in 2077, sixty years after an alien attack on Earth. Most of the human population are now supposedly living on Saturn's moon, Titan, where they have been transported by a space station known as the Tet. Cruise plays Jack Harper, a technician stationed on Earth to protect the fusion energy generators that are draining the planet's oceans in order to power the human colonies on Titan. Jack works to secure the future of humanity by repairing the aging drones that assist him and his partner, Victoria (Andrea Riseborough), to secure the area. However, Jack later discovers that the Tet is an alien spaceship and that he has been assisting the

In *Minority Report*, Precrime leader John Anderton (Cruise) is haunted by the loss of his son.

aliens to strip Earth of its remaining resources and that the "alien scavengers" whom his drones have been hunting down are human refugees.

Jack's characterization taps into the white man–as–victim narrative; in contrast, Cruise's Maj. William Cage in *Edge of Tomorrow* is critiqued for his cowardly victimization of others. As media spokesperson for the United Defense Force, Cage inspires civilians to join the fight against the alien Mimics who are conquering Europe. Cage is aware that soldiers sent to the front are "cannon fodder in an unwinnable war" (O'Donnell 2015, 53), and his willingness to expose others to death and trauma while avoiding such risk himself is condemned. Disgusted by Cage's cowardice, his general has him demoted and transferred to an infantry company about to embark on a major military assault. Cage joins J-squad, whose skill and bravery stand in stark contrast to his own terrified bumbling. Thus, Cage is metaphorically castrated, with his high public profile and rank stripped away to reveal another of Cruise's self-absorbed "manly boy[s]" (Studlar, 176).

War of the World's Ray Ferrier is another Cruise protagonist in the "manly boy" mold. Ray's insecurity is fed by the middle-class affluence of his ex-wife, Mary Ann's (Miranda Otto), new husband Tim (David Alan Basche), whose expensive coat contrasts sharply with Ray's own dirty jeans and old sweater. Ray mocks Tim's new car—"Hey, this is one safe-looking new vehicle you've got yourself here"—implying that Tim lacks masculinity in comparison to Ray, who indulges in risk-taking behavior in his Mustang. However, Ray's car is positioned as evidence of his immaturity and selfishness, which has a negative impact on his children, sixteen-year-old Robbie (Justin Chatwin) and ten-year-old Rachel (Dakota Fanning). Arriving home late to find his children waiting, Ray is indifferent to Rachel's concern that there is nothing to eat, offhandedly telling her, "You know—order," before retreating to his bedroom, shutting the door on the unwanted adult responsibility his children represent. Critics have noted the "inadequate father" (Hamad 2011, 241) and "imperiled family" (Gordon 1008, 260) are recurring themes in Spielberg's films, as evident in both *Minority Report* and *War of the Worlds*. These tropes reflect a broader cultural concern with absent fathers, as emphasized by President Clinton's 1995 address to the nation in which he identified "the growing absence of fathers from their children's homes" as "the single biggest problem in our society" (qtd. in Kord and Krimmer 2011, 37). Echoing Bly's concern that the absence of fathers has resulted in the feminization of American men (and, by extension, the nation), Clinton presented an idealized image of father as protector and guide (38). Both *War of the Worlds* and *Minority Report* present protagonists who are metaphorically castrated by their failure in this role.

Escalation of Crisis

In each of Cruise's science fiction films, however, the protagonist's insecurities and traumas remain relatively hidden behind a façade of competence and success until a moment of extreme crisis strips it away, much as 9/11 escalated fears of the emasculation of the American nation and the 2005 "jumping the couch" episode reduced Cruise to a figure of public ridicule. In *Vanilla Sky*, a car accident leaves David with significant facial disfiguration and debilitating headaches. David's injury is a direct result of his selfish immaturity. The night before the accident he met Sofia (Penélope Cruz), whom he describes as "the last semi-guileless girl in New York City," suggesting he craves something genuine in his life. But when he leaves Sofia's apartment he gets into "fuck buddy" Julianna's car in response to her implied offer of sex. Upset by David's careless use of her, Julianna drives the car off a bridge, killing herself. Following the accident, David fixates on Sofia to avoid dealing with his trauma or acknowledging his responsibility. This avoidance is signaled by the prosthetic mask David wears; as in another Cruise film, *Eyes Wide Shut* (Stanley Kubrick, 1999), "use of the mask suggests a fear of exposure" (O'Donnell 2015, 40) and also a reluctance to face the reality of his life or critically examine his own identity.

David's avoidance culminates in his choice of a virtual reality existence offered by Life Extension, which keeps its clients' bodies in cryonic suspension while inserting their minds into a perfect dream life. David lives an idealized life with Sofia, his injuries miraculously healed. As David's fears and guilt return to haunt him, however, his dream life turns into a nightmare. Tormented by visions of his disfigured face, David wakes up to find Julianna in his bed. Terrified and confused, he suffocates her and finds himself imprisoned, his face again disfigured and hidden behind the prosthetic mask. The bars on the prison window signify that David is entrapped in a nightmare of his own making, while the mask indicates he is still unwilling to face the truth about himself and his life. The mask is particularly significant given that Cruise's star image has long centered on his youthful, athletic body and trademark cocky smile. In *Vanilla Sky*, the mask and David's body trauma strip away these signifiers of desire, heightening the sense of masculinity in crisis.

Minority Report's Anderton is similarly plunged into his own living nightmare when the precogs predict he will kill Leo Crow (Mike Binder), turning Anderton into a fugitive from the justice system which has provided the only meaning in his life since Sean's disappearance, for which he feels responsible. Hunted by his former colleagues, Anderton's persecution by the same men who earlier idealized him resonates with media attacks on Cruise's star image; even prior to the 2005 crisis, Cruise expressed a sense of persecution in the face of allegations of homosexuality and impotence, which threatened to undermine his status as (heterosexual) male idol (King 2011, 19). Just as Cruise has always vehemently rejected such claims, Anderton determines to prove his innocence. In the process, however, he discovers grief has blinded him to the truth about Precrime. When he visits Dr. Iris Hineman (Lois Smith), the cocreator of Precrime, she informs him that the precogs do not always agree; in some cases, a minority report is produced that casts doubt on the guilt of the accused. This revelation shakes Anderton's faith in both Precrime and his father figure, Lamar Burgess (Max von Sydow), who has hidden the existence of the minority reports. Anderton also learns that the precogs were the children of drug-addicted mothers, casting a critical light on his own utilitarian treatment of them. At this point, however, Anderton still primarily sees Agatha (Samantha Morton), the most powerful precog, as a data repository: "She's got information inside her. . . . I need you to hack into her." Focused on his own concerns, Anderton is blind to the meaning of the vision of the drowning woman that Agatha repeatedly shows him, a vision he will need to understand if he is to uncover the truth about Precrime.

In *Oblivion*, Jack's life is similarly plunged into crisis when he realizes the extent of his ignorance. Not only has he been working as "Tech-49" for the alien invaders, he is also a clone of astronaut Jack Harper, one of thousands produced and programmed by the aliens. Science fiction film has long explored dystopian visions of future societies in which technology is used to produce and police the undifferentiated masses. From *THX 1138* (George Lucas, 1971) to *Moon*, science fiction filmmakers have explored fears that technology will erase individual subjectivity. Not only has alien technology constructed Jack and thousands identical to him, it has also sought to regulate his thoughts, feelings, and behaviors through programmed "memories," making him a compliant employee. His compliance has further been ensured by the warnings his flyer emits to avoid dangerous "radiation zones," preventing Jack from encountering another clone—until he crashes his flyer and inadvertently comes face-to-face with "himself." Throughout his career, Cruise has repeatedly been cast in the role of "everyman," and his casting as clone—literally everyman—draws attention to the potential for this persona to undermine the masculine exceptionalism with which Cruise has also long been associated. As Barry King (2011, 21) observes, "As star, Cruise would not wish to claim he is just an 'average Joe.'" Thus, after this encounter, the rest of the clones are sidelined in order to allow Jack/Cruise to redeem his masculinity by demonstrating his exceptional capacity for heroism.

Whereas Jack's discovery that he is a clone undermines his previously secure sense of self, the alien crisis in *War of the Worlds* heightens Ray's awareness of his inadequacy as a father and forces him to confront its potentially lethal consequences, just as the events of 9/11 spurred elements of the US media to interrogate the potentially lethal consequences of the nation's perceived masculine inadequacies. Kord and Krimmer (2011, 52) observe that the "inept, neglectful, emotionally crippled, or unreliable father" is a recurring character type in post-9/11 science fiction disaster films including *Signs* (M. Night Shyamalon, 2002) and *The Day after Tomorrow* (Roland Emmerich, 2004), reflecting a heightened tendency to conflate the crisis of masculinity with a crisis of fatherhood. This conflation has also been evident in post-2005 media claims that Cruise is "less than a 'real' man, being sterile or impotent; that the baby he fathered with Katie Holmes was actually an *in vitro* infusion" (King 2011, 19). In *War of the Worlds*, Ray's paternal inadequacy is emphasized when he reacts to Rachel's screams by telling her to shut up and then later makes her a peanut butter sandwich, unaware she is allergic. When Robbie attempts to join the military, Rachel clings to him, crying, "Who will take care of me if you go?" A long shot of Robbie holding Rachel, with Ray standing apart, emphasizes Ray's distance from his children.

As in *War of the Worlds*, the alien conflict in *Edge of Tomorrow* confronts the Cruise protagonist with the potentially lethal consequences of his inadequacies. Dropped into the battle front, Cage staggers to his feet as experienced soldiers around him are crushed, shot, and engulfed in flames, before he himself is killed. As he dies, however, Cage detonates a Claymore mine that also kills an Alpha, a superior breed of Mimic, whose blood traps Cage in a time loop where, each time he is killed, he reawakens on the Heathrow tarmac, forced to relive the events of the day. Realizing there is no escape, even in death, the last vestige of Cage's arrogance is stripped away as he is confronted with the fear that he and humanity are doomed, no matter what he does.

Redemption of the Authentic Male Hero

Cage's complacency is shattered by his exposure to the brutal reality of war, just as the unprecedented attacks of 9/11 exposed Americans to unfamiliar feelings of shock, despair, fear, and vulnerability. Following the attacks, however, the US administration and media sought to restore America's "narrative of strength" (Bjerre 2012, 242) through the valorization of the idealized male hero. One month after 9/11, Peggy Noonan (qtd. in Faludi 2008, 4) wrote in the *Wall Street Journal*, "From the ashes of September 11, arise the manly virtues"; Cruise's science fiction films similarly reassure audiences that the crisis that exposes a man's weakness can also serve as catalyst for his redemption. The possibility of redemption is given weight not only by Cruise's frequent casting as a "regular guy" who proves his masculine worth but also by the redemption of Cruise's own star image in recent years. Cruise's commitment to performing his own stunts has been repeatedly cited as evidence of his professional focus, exceptional physicality, and commitment to authenticity, offering a counternarrative to earlier accusations of artificiality and loss of self-control. Mirroring the redemption of Cruise's star image, in each of his science fiction films crisis gives the protagonist newfound knowledge of his "authentic" self and the real state of his world, allowing him to lay claim to a heroic identity centered on the protection of women and children from an unprecedented, technologically enhanced threat.

In *Vanilla Sky*, the focus on saving others, which became the dominant masculine ideal post-9/11, is downplayed, but the care for others, self-awareness, and choice of an authentic life that underpin David's redemption aligns this film with Cruise's post-9/11 productions. Studlar (2001, 176) observes that Cruise's films "consistently move his characters from [an unstable] ... performance of manliness into 'authentic' manliness through the incorporation of qualities—gentleness, self-control, compassion—that might be regarded as 'feminine.' In this respect, Cruise straddles 'hard' and 'soft' modes of masculinity." In *Vanilla Sky*, David reclaims his self-control when he realizes that in order to escape his nightmare he must face the fears and memories he has repressed. David also demonstrates compassion when he finally takes responsibility for his mistreatment of Julianna and Sofia. He then chooses an authentic life, opting to return to the real world, even though 150 years have passed and everyone he knew is dead. In order to wake up, however, David must jump from a tall building, a terrifying prospect given his fear of heights. David's plunge emphasizes the heroism of his choice to step out from behind the mask and expose himself both to his own self-critique and the challenges of the real world.

Redemption in *Minority Report* similarly involves the Cruise protagonist taking control of his self-destructive emotions, just as Cruise would later need to demonstrate physical and mental self-control through his film stunts in order to counter his perceived loss of control epitomized by the jumping-the-couch incident. In *Minority Report*, Anderton's sorrow and desire for revenge have left him vulnerable to manipulation by Burgess, who, afraid Anderton will expose the truth about Precrime and Burgess's murder of Agatha's mother, creates a scenario to make Anderton believe Leo Crow took Sean. Burgess hopes Anderton will be imprisoned for killing Crow; indeed, this is the future the precogs foresee. However, like *Vanilla Sky*'s David, Anderton has a choice, although it requires a heroic struggle to overcome the painful emotions that have dominated his life. Instead of killing Crow, Anderton reads him his rights, rejecting the identity of murderer that Precrime technology has projected, to claim his "authentic" identity as an officer of the law. Once again, self-control is positioned as a central feature of mature masculinity, moving a character marked by Cruise's "typical vulnerability" (O'Donnell 2015, 16) from a "small fellow... getting dumped on" (Leonard Quart and Albert Auster, cited in O'Donnell 2015, 19) to a position of self-definition and authority.

Crow, however, shoots himself, and Anderton and Agatha flee to his ex-wife Lara's house where Anderton realizes that Agatha, like Sean, was an innocent child snatched from her mother. To redeem himself for his failings as a father, Anderton must save Agatha from the half-life of the precogs and secure justice for her mother's murder. Faludi (2008, 13) notes a cultural "fixation on restoring an invincible manhood by saving little girls" following 9/11. Although physically a woman, Agatha is framed as a vulnerable abused child, with Anderton practically carrying her as she struggles to cope with the stimulus of the real world. Before Anderton can avenge her, however, he is imprisoned; held in restraints, with his head shaved, "he resembles a foetus *in utero*" (O'Donnell 2015, 132). This imagery emphasizes Anderton's rebirth as male hero. Once freed, Anderton makes Burgess's crime public and confronts him, risking his own life (the precogs have predicted Burgess will kill Anderton) to ensure Precrime will be shut down and the precogs freed. *Minority Report* rewards Anderton's heroism by reuniting him with Lara (Kathryn Morris), whose pregnant figure "bodes new life and the promise of his reinstatement as a father" (141). Cruise's positioning as the good and competent father has become increasingly significant as age has threatened to make his earlier star persona, "predicated on his youth" (165) untenable. Although O'Donnell claimed in 2015 that "Cruise's ageing appearance is threatening to close down his casting opportunities" (166), his shift in the previous decade toward a persona invested in a more mature father role reinforces Cruise's ongoing relevance in the twenty-first century.

As with *Minority Report*, *War of the Worlds* focuses on the redemption of the father, which Ray achieves through a movement from self-interest to protection of his children, a shift that begins when Ray, Robbie, and Rachel first flee the tripods: "Gripping Rachel's hand, Ray strides purposefully to the only functioning vehicle in the vicinity... a Plymouth Voyager people-carrier, reminiscent of Tim's higher-end safe-looking new vehicle... [connoting] safety, family, and mature, responsible driving" (Hamad 2011, 245). Significantly, the car works only because Ray earlier suggested the mechanic swap the solenoid that had been burned out by the electromagnetic pulse emitted by the tripods. His automotive expertise allows Ray to remove his children from immediate danger, evoking the mechanical competence with which Cruise has long been associated. O'Donnell (2015, 37) notes that Cruise is "known to own motorbikes, fast cars and a plane (as well as a licence to fly it)." However, it is only when Robbie leaves to join the military that Ray has the space to fully develop as a father, at which time his "worthiness as a father and credentials as a hero" must be affirmed through "his successful enactment of action-oriented protectionism" (Hamad 2011, 248). Ray kills Harlan Ogilvy (Tim Robbins), whose crazed desire to fight the aliens from the basement in which Ray and Rachel are hiding puts Rachel's life in danger. In the following scene, Ray allows himself to be taken by the tripod that has captured Rachel, risking his own life to kill the alien and save his daughter. In science fiction disaster films such as *War of the Worlds*, "the child's survival . . . is symbolically linked with the nation's survival" (Kord and Krimmer 2011, 52), and the idea that "if the crisis is to be solved at all, it has to be done by Father" (38) is reinforced by Ray's discovery of the aliens' weakness, both when he detonates the grenade to destroy the tripod and, later, when he alerts the military that the tripods' shields are down. Ray's actions typify the framing of Cruise's star image. While Cruise has built his reputation around his ability to play an ordinary, everyday guy often struggling to make his way in the world, his star image also rests on his perceived exceptionality—his Hollywood smile, talent, and physical prowess positioning him as a masculine ideal. The ideal of the male hero as an everyday guy who proves his exceptionalism by saving others is reinforced by the conclusion of *War of the Worlds*, where Robbie's embrace and Mary Ann's whispered thanks affirm Ray's successful performance of both a heroic masculine identity and mature fatherhood.

Redemption of the male protagonist in both *Oblivion* and *Edge of Tomorrow* again requires his commitment to self-sacrifice and the protection of others, a choice that relies on the hero's newfound awareness of his authentic self and the real state of his world. In *Oblivion*, Jack's natural curiosity about his world and willingness to break the rules by collecting artifacts from humanity's past escalates into full-blown rebellion once he discovers the truth about the Tet. Both his early minor disobedience and subsequent fight to destroy the Tet are inspired by fragmented memories of his wife, Julia (Olga Kurylenko), memories that the aliens have sought to wipe from the clones. The original Jack's love for Julia was so integral to his identity, however, that it cannot be completely erased. Thus, when Jack finds mementoes of his past with Julia, these repressed memories resurface, feeding Jack's desire to discover the truth of the woman's identity and, by extension, his own. Once Jack meets Julia, who has been held in a stasis chamber on a drifting spacecraft for the past sixty years, his memories flood back, heralding a return of his authentic self. Jack recognizes that, as a clone, he is not the man whom Julia married, but Julia insists: "These memories are yours, Jack. They're ours. They are you."

Jack's memories instigate his movement from ignorance to knowledge, oppression to freedom, and artifice to nature. Asserting his right to self-definition, Jack rejects the control of the Tet and achieves redemption by sacrificing himself to save the human survivors, including Julia who, unbeknownst to him, is pregnant with his child. His sacrifice aligns him with the original, "authentic" Jack who, sixty years prior, saved Julia and the rest of his crew by ejecting the pod in which they slept, leaving himself and Victoria to be captured by the Tet. This time, Jack returns to the Tet armed with a bomb. Although he (Tech-49) dies in the explosion, the narrative insists that Jack's heroism is rewarded by allowing one of his clones (Tech-52) "a happy ending with his wife and child" (O'Donnell 2015, 170), reminiscent of *Minority Report* and *War of the Worlds*. Once again, masculinity is imbricated with fatherhood, with the fate of humanity resting on the heroic violence of the good father, further emphasizing the increasing significance of this ideal to the Cruise star image in the twenty-first century.

Like Jack, *Edge of Tomorrow*'s Cage is redeemed through his willingness to sacrifice himself to save both the woman he loves and the human race. Early in the film, movement toward a heroic masculine ideal is thematized by a speech Sergeant Farrell (Bill Paxton) delivers to the newly demoted Cage: "Battle is the great redeemer. The fiery crucible in which true heroes are forged." Farrell valorizes a militarized masculinity that became a dominant narrative post-9/11 (Michael 2011, 74). In battle, Farrell suggests, Cage will be "baptized, born again"; however, he must first endure countless deaths in order to move beyond his habitual self-interest and develop the skills he needs to play his heroic role. Initially he resists when Rita Vratasky (Emily Blunt), who previously had and lost the power

In *Edge of Tomorrow*, Cage (Cruise) redeems himself by demonstrating characteristics of both "hard" and "soft" masculinity.

to reboot each time she was killed, tells him, "I need your help winning the war." Reluctantly allowing her to train him, Cage develops feelings for her, which inspire his heroism and signal "a real maturation of the persona" (O'Donnell 2015, 53) through his development of the characteristics of "soft masculinity"—gentleness, love, compassion—for which Cruise has become known (Studlar 2001, 176). Initially, though, his growing feelings impede his mission. Unable to figure out a scenario where Vratasky lives beyond a farmhouse where they encounter a host of Mimics, Cage is unwilling to go on and kill the Omega, knowing that Vratasky will never be resurrected if he is successful. Emotionally exhausted, Cage determines on the next reboot to undertake his task alone. This time he succeeds in getting to the dam where the Omega is supposedly hiding, his military prowess demonstrating the characteristics of "hard masculinity" needed to narratively balance out his softer side. He discovers, however, that the visions were a trap and narrowly escapes the waiting Alpha by once again taking his own life.

Cage's real test of heroism comes when he receives a blood transfusion, eliminating his ability to reboot. His decision to face the Omega, despite knowing he will have to die to defeat it, signals his final step in the movement from Farrell's "parasitic scum" to "true hero." As in *Oblivion*, however, the film reassures audiences that heroic sacrifice must be rewarded, just as Cruise's own "heroic" stunts have been rewarded with renewed public respect. As Cage dies, the Omega's blood seeps into his wound, restoring his power to reboot, and he reawakens at the start of the previous day, though this time before his meeting with Brigham, to find the world celebrating the inexplicable demise of the Mimics. Thus, the film concludes with the reward of the male protagonist who, knowing the real state of the world and aware of the cost to himself, has redeemed himself through heroic self-sacrifice.

Conclusion

Despite the genre's potential to critically interrogate dominant gender ideologies by imagining alternative social structures and gender roles, Hollywood science fiction films, especially those set on a near-future Earth, often respond to contemporary concerns by valorizing a conservative heroic masculine identity that reassures audiences of the enduring power and position of the "authentic" white man, even in a threatening, technologically advanced future. Identified by Sean Redmond (2006, 32) as "an archetypal white American hero," Cruise has long been a cultural touchstone of masculinity, his films and star persona articulating both concerns about masculinity in crisis and a masculine ideal to which viewers and fans are encouraged to aspire. His science fiction films respond in particular to the post-9/11 escalation of anxieties about the feminization of the American nation through the recurring trope of the inadequate, ignorant, traumatized man redeemed through a heroic performance made possible by his newfound self-awareness, understanding of his world, and concern for the protection of others congruent with the post-9/11 narrative of "protective paternalism" (Godfrey and Hamad 2012, 160). Both the rewards enjoyed by Cruise's protagonists at the end of his science fiction films, and the resurrection of his own public image, provide reassurance that moments of extreme crisis can provide the impetus for men to recognize their failings and develop a successful and admired "authentic" masculine identity, a heroic identity capable of protecting the vulnerable and ensuring the security of the American nation into the future.

Works Cited

Bjerre, Thomas Ærvold. 2012. "Post-9/11 Literary Masculinities in Kalfus, DeLillo, and Hamid." *Orbis Litterarum* 67 (3): 241–66.

Bly, Robert. 1990. *Iron John: A Book about Men*. Shaftesbury, UK: Element Books.

Chapman, James, and Nicholas J. Cull. 2013. *Projecting Tomorrow: Science Fiction and Popular Cinema*. London: I. B. Tauris.

DeAngelis, Michael. 2010. "Tom Cruise, the Couch Incident, and the Limits of Public Elation." *The Velvet Light Trap* 65 (1): 42–43.

Faludi, Susan. 2008. *The Terror Dream: Fear and Fantasy in Post-9/11 America*. Melbourne: Scribe.

Godfrey, Sarah, and Hannah Hamad. 2012. "Save the Cheerleader, Save the Males: Resurgent Protective Paternalism in Popular Film and Television after 9/11." In *The Handbook of Gender, Sex and Media*, edited by Karen Ross, 157–73. Malden, MA: Wiley-Blackwell.

Gordon, Andrew M. 2008. *Empire of Dreams: The Science Fiction and Fantasy Films of Steven Spielberg*. Lanham, MD: Rowman & Littlefield.

Hamad, Hannah. 2011. "Extreme Parenting: Recuperating Fatherhood in Steven Spielberg's *War of the Worlds* (2005)." In *Feminism at the Movies: Understanding Gender in Contemporary Popular Cinema*, edited by Hilary Radner and Rebecca Stringer, 241–53. New York: Routledge.

Hellmore, Edward. 2005. "What's Eating Tom Cruise?" *Guardian*, June 6, 2005. www.theguardian.com/world/2005/jun/05/usa.film.

King, Barry. 2011. "Stardom, Celebrity and the Para-confession." In *The Star and Celebrity Confessional*, edited by Sean Redmond, 7–24. London: Routledge.

Kord, Susanne, and Elisabeth Krimmer. 2011. *Contemporary Hollywood Masculinities: Gender, Genre, and Politics*. New York: Palgrave Macmillan.

Michael, Magali Cornier. 2011. "Don DeLillo's *Falling Man*: Countering Post-9/11 Narratives of Heroic Masculinity." In *Portraying 9/11: Essays on Representations in Comics, Literature, Film and Theatre*, edited by Véronique Bragard, Christophe Dony, and Warren Rosenberg, 73–88. Jefferson, NC: McFarland.

O'Donnell, Ruth. 2015. *Tom Cruise: Performing Masculinity in Post Vietnam Hollywood*. London: I. B. Tauris.

———. 2016. "Mission: Impossible? The Rehabilitation of Tom Cruise." *Celebrity Studies* 7 (3): 425–28.

Redmond, Sean. 2006. "Intimate Fame Everywhere." In *Framing Celebrity: New Directions in Celebrity Culture*, edited by Su Holmes and Sean Redmond, 27–44. London: Routledge.

Rehling, Nicola. 2010. *Extra-Ordinary Men: White Heterosexual Masculinity in Contemporary Popular Culture*. Plymouth, UK: Lexington.

Ryan, Michael, and Douglas Kellner. 2004. "Technophobia/Dystopia." In *Liquid Metal: The Science Fiction Film Reader*, edited by Sean Redmond, 48–56. London: Wallflower.

Studlar, Gaylyn. 2001. "Cruise-ing into the Millennium: Performative Masculinity, Stardom, and the All-American Boy's Body." In *Ladies and Gentlemen, Boys and Girls: Gender in Film at the End of the Twentieth Century*, edited by Murray Pomerance, 171–83. Albany: State University of New York Press.

9

CRUISING THE CLOSED WORLD

The Cold War and the Cyborg in *Top Gun*, *Mission: Impossible*, and *Minority Report*

Alex Wade

"The Closed World" of Tom Cruise

Cruise's cinematic acting career spans nearly four decades. His earliest films from the 1980s are a Lydian stone for Generation X youth, and *Risky Business* (Paul Brickman, 1983) was the first film where Cruise was cast in the lead role of particular note as a coming-of-age drama in a decade that is often seen as been defined by the genre. The promise and optimism offered in these films is mirrored by the increase in living standards that was seen throughout the Cold War (Piketty 2014, 78), a period that ran from 1948 until 1991 and is often marked by high-stakes nuclear-laden tension between NATO and the Warsaw Pact nations, particularly the Soviet Union. The potential for nuclear war between these enemies, enabled by unprecedented inventions and discoveries in science and technology, became the overriding discourse of the time, and it played out on both movie and TV screens in genres as diverse as *Dr. Strangelove* (Stanley Kubrick, 1964) and *Threads* (Mick Jackson, 1984). The encompassing of the globe in war machines is a feature of what Paul N. Edwards (1996, 307) terms "the closed world," an existence marked by "displays of technology, particularly military and other high technology." As *Risky Business* shows, one of the unintended positive consequences of these technologies was a concomitant rise in living standards for the civilian population (Oldenziel and Zachmann 2009, 7). Following the post–World War renewal of social contracts between citizens and the state, the US and European middle class reaped the benefits of massive state spending. While threatened on the one hand by nuclear annihilation found in the warfare state (Edgerton 2006), they were also, on the other hand, protected by the burgeoning welfare state (Zimmern 1934), which in continental Europe and the Soviet Union, at least, ensured affordable health care, housing, and education for all.

Edwards's (1996, 273) central argument in *The Closed World* is that Cold War technologies' key aim is to progressively assimilate humans into technological—and especially computer—loops with recourse to "artificial intelligence, man-computer symbiosis and human information processing . . . to integrate humans fully into command and control." Edwards uses the tensions evident between machines and humans, especially in their fused identities, and the increasing militarization of the world and its percolation into everyday civilian life through the globalization of warfare to show how these discourses are also deployed in the science fiction of the 1970s and 1980s. In the narrative form, as with those seen in the hypermilitarized spaces of the Cold War, such as the submarine, missile silo, and war room, the closed world "is a world radically divided against itself. It is consumed and defined by total apocalyptic conflict" (307). Even if this marks much science fiction cinema of the time, from *Red Dawn* (John Milius, 1984) to *Rocky IV* (Sylvester Stallone, 1985), the three films starring Tom Cruise selected for this chapter—*Top Gun* (Tony Scott, 1986), *Mission Impossible* (Brian De Palma, 1996), and *Minority Report* (Steven Spielberg, 2002)—chart how this closed world is deployed in the immediate aftermath of the Cold War and its potential legacy. As the chapter will show, the tensions of the spaces and times of the closed world are contingent on the integration of Cruise as a cyborg into these closed worlds, with the technology used both as a means to contain, limit, and destroy these worlds and also to construct the discourses that permit an understanding of them.

If *Risky Business* shows the indirect benefits of high technology, then the relationship between Cruise and high technology in its military (or paramilitary) forms can be seen throughout subsequent films. *Top Gun*, *Mission: Impossible*, and *Minority Report* are cases in point, drawing on the real-world hardware of the US Navy, the fictional software of US intelligence's NOC (nonofficial cover) list, and the theoretical wetware (Riskin 2007, 97) of the Precrime initiative. The films themselves are guided by directors whose use of set pieces and special effects are typical of Hollywood's fascination with technological visual excess, and to this is added Cruise's own professional penchant for action/thriller cinema, a genre that has traditionally been associated with imbuing its protagonists with star power, from Amy Adams to Billy Zane. If the dynamics of coming-of-age films of the 1980s refracted threat through increased living standards provided by an ethos of protection, then science fiction films, with their commentary on the spaces and times of possible worlds are active in the construction of experiences, given that closed world dramas do not "passively 'reflect' political and social 'realities.' They *are* political and social realities" (Edwards 1996, 306). This chapter will show that the Cold War chronology of Cruise's films suggests that the idea of the closed world is not fully realized until *Minority Report*. As a film set fifty years in the future and with a narrative that questions the challenges of predestination, it provides a *possible* closed world outcome, which may be presaged by the films before it, but does not announce it as inevitable. Indeed, both *Top Gun* and to a lesser extent *Mission: Impossible*, in spite of their inspiration in the pastel skies and mean streets of the Cold War, betray a greater degree of human agency than is implied by the high-budget, high-tech, high-concept thrillers, which ordinarily pit closed world protagonists and "their own rationality, their reflexes and their technical expertise against a dominating system and its technology from within" (311). Instead, all three films betray evidence of being part of the magic and wonder of a green world, itself marked by "openness and humility" (312) even if Cruise is revealed as increasingly part of a cyborg discourse, which is eventually and ultimately triumphant.

To become the cyborg of the closed world involves a "strategic blurring of boundaries," defined by a discourse of "disassembly, engineering and reconstruction" (2). For viewers of Cruise's films and his wider position in society, this ambiguity has a familiar ring. His rejection of mainstream science in favor of the Church of Scientology has led Cruise into controversial positions with regard to the treatment of mental health; haziness around his sexual orientation is of constant fascination to the paparazzi and couch commentators, reaching its apogee with the now infamous "couch jumping" interview on *The Oprah Winfrey Show* in 2005 and criticizing Brooke Shields's use of paroxetine for postpartum depression in the same year. This haziness is in keeping with Cruise's on screen characters. Within the films presented in this chapter, the emergence of the cyborg is complex, gradual, and in endless flux. The prominence of military and high technology is evident with its integration focused on the emergence of technologies that are temporarily or permanently forged onto the body, from the oxygen mask of *Top Gun* to the implanted eyes of *Minority Report*. In this regard, work from Freund (2004, 273) is instructive in showing how the "seams in the cyborg" permit a crossing of boundaries between the spaces and times, or rhythms, of technology, the body, and the wider social and natural world. With the locus of attention on the individual body traveling through the closed world, a wider awareness of the effects of technology, especially in the simultaneous distancing and projection of space and time is shown through the writing of Paul Virilio (2008), whose work reveals inextricable links between cinema and war in the twentieth century. With Tom Cruise's screen personas as the cyborgian vehicle of these ideas, his position as one of their strongest, most visible yet most nebulous advocates continues well into the twenty-first century.

Hardware

Released in 1986, *Top Gun* features Cruise as Lieutenant Pete "Maverick" Mitchell, who attends Fighter Weapons School, a US Naval advanced training academy for the best pilots. Set during the mid-1980s, a period of considerable tension between West and East, Maverick and his compatriots battle, to greater or lesser success, enemy pilots of an unknown designation but who are assumed to be to be Soviet / communist by their appearance and the aircraft they fly. At first blush, the film appears to be synonymous with Cruise's familiarity with the closed world. The opening credits fade into the spherical, pointed nose of the Grumann F-14, the US Navy's fighter aircraft, silhouetted against the setting sun over the Indian Ocean. For the viewer, this has two effects. First, it hones the gaze onto the preeminence of the projection and distancing of power during the Cold War. Maritime technologies are traditionally associated with moving military might into other areas away from the home country; empires throughout history are founded on this idea (Virilio 2008, 134). Here, the relative slowness of the ship is contrasted to the aircraft, which transforms from a stationary object to a supersonic vehicle as it leaves its mobile base. Second, the aircrew on the flight deck of the aircraft carrier are seen in purely a support role. They are instrumental to the service of machines and specifically the star cyborg of Cruise. By pointing and guiding aircraft for takeoff, their sphere of operations is guided not by the circadian rhythms of night and day, moon and tide, but instead by "pure war" (112), which infuses all spaces and times of the contemporary world, insisting that the rhythms of humans follow those of machines and specifically, war machines, in what Freund (2004, 274) terms the "technological habitus." This is where the cadence of machines permeates the seams in the cyborg to further inculcate the individual human being toward being machine-like in its responses and outputs, thus becoming more closely integrated to the closed world. Just as the worker body wakes up before the alarm clock, so the military body follows the vagaries of the spaces and times of pure warfare.

In the positioning of aircraft in the first instance, by the director of the film, Tony Scott, and, in the second, by the marshalers of the aircraft, or "rampies," the opening credits of *Top Gun* actually acts in placing humans front and center, with individuals directing the hardware through the hazardous but navigable space and time of aerial and oceanic warfare. While the notable omission of the star vehicle of Cruise from the opening scene suggests that the star of the show is an aviation vehicle in the guise of an F-14 aircraft—especially so given that *Top Gun* was tacitly supported and vetted by the US Navy (Paris 1995, 205)—the opening credits instruct the opposite. The eponymous *Top Gun* fighter school's aim is to teach pilots the lost art of aerial dogfighting, which was so important to wars throughout the first half of the twentieth century. Dogfighting is a technique, so embedded in the—masculine—body that extreme technologies threaten its existence. Aircraft able to withstand gravitational forces beyond the scope of the human body mean that pilots conduct warfare at beyond visual range, their targets only perceived as a smudge on the cathode ray tube of the radar scope.

The threats and their manifestations in aviation suggest that the "techniques of the body" (Mauss 1973, 70) are in peril from technologies of projection and distancing. This is especially evident in how visual depictions are used with the characters, betraying this closing of the world. Before Maverick can see the enemy MiG planes, they are identified at distance on the radar scope by the navigator ("Talk to me, Goose," Maverick says to his navigator). Although one step removed from the pilot, the navigator Goose (Anthony Edwards) is still in the same arena as Maverick. However, the darkened, fuggy war room of the aircraft carrier located two hundred miles away is the archetypical closed world of the Cold War. It has a plan view of the engagement, with the personnel located there able to provide a running commentary on the theater of drama and war for both the pilots and the viewer while being inured from any threat of destruction. Meanwhile, Cruise, who starts the film with his face visible inside the aircraft, attaches the cyborgian prosthetic of the oxygen supply as he engages the enemy MiG, his face and vision rippling in response to the G-forces of close quarters engagement, mirroring the sheen of the MiG pilots' mask, which remains closed and reflective of the technology of the cockpit in all its appearances within the film. With the body visibly under strain, the viewer's gaze strains to see anything but the pilot, inert at speed and increasingly integrated, via the umbilical cord of the flight suit, into the technological habitus of the machine.

For a film so renowned for its cinematic aerobatics, it is the power of the still image that scores itself into the opening scene. As Peter Adey (2010, 87) notes, military aerial photography has been used as a weapon throughout its history and in its execution "opened up the world to a distanciated gaze by telescoping these distances for the imposition and projection of power and reach." In defiance of the closing of the world by technology throughout *Top Gun*, Maverick and his comrades maintain a jocular, joking, jockeying distance from the stricture of military service, with games and competitions infusing the narrative from unauthorized flybys to the playful homosociality that runs throughout the film, a theme brilliantly sent up in Rory Kelly's *Sleep with Me* (1994). In an aerobatic display of playfulness, as Maverick and Goose outwit the MiG aircraft, Maverick inverts the F-14 while Goose takes a canopy-to-canopy Polaroid photograph. The mastery of the human over hardware is evident here. Maverick can bend the aircraft to his whim, and although he is not able to deploy ordnance to defeat the enemy, the weapon of the photograph, of the collection of knowledge and intelligence, is expedient. Irrespective of what happens in the war room or on the radar scope, the projection of the lens, at close quarters, is paramount; as Goose says to Charlie (Kelly McGillis) later, "I have a great Polaroid of it."

Ultimately, Maverick's wingman Cougar (Bill Cortell) is spooked by the technologies of projection and distancing exuded by the still image of the photograph. His closeness to the enemy is contrasted, through a picture in the cockpit, to the distance from his young family. The technology of the photograph acts as a figurative medium of the open, green domestic world to the closed, gray military world of the cockpit. It projects and intensifies the emotional response of the character through illustration of the distance, both geographical and psychological, that is demanded by military hardware. Cougar's response rejects the technological habitus, and in his panic, he is unable to bring the aircraft safely back to base. Maverick, again displaying his mastery of the machine, guides his stricken comrade back to the aircraft carrier. This presages the demands that the machine makes on the body and the human later in the film, where Maverick's aircraft is caught in wake turbulence, killing Goose and leaving Maverick with doubts about his ability to ably control the machine. The ambivalence at the core of Cruise as action hero and as matinee idol is silhouetted here. In the cyborgian opposition between the softness of the flesh and the hardness of the machine, even if the posthuman element of the cyborg fails, the human is able to rectify and redeem an ailing situation, so converting loss into a win and following a binary program that repeats itself and casts stardust onto Cruise's persona of an individual able to achieve the impossible.

The failure is caused as much by the human breakdown in the mastery of technology as the technology itself. Yet it is indicative of the way in which *Top Gun*, through the vehicle of Cruise, resists a closing of the world. To negotiate the labyrinth of self-questioning, Maverick repositions himself away from open skies and closed cockpits and toward the green world. When visiting Viper (Tom Skerritt) on a Sunday to discuss his future as a pilot in the navy, nature is illuminated by a bright sun in the form of hanging baskets, pine trees, and children playing around Viper's neighborhood. Maverick asks Viper about his father and is told that such information could end Viper's career. Nevertheless, Viper continues to disclose the classified material, a key theme of green world dramas where cosmic order is restored by "surpassing rationality, conventions, authority, technology" (Edwards 1996, 310). The disclosure encourages Maverick to continue as a pilot, and he ultimately graduates from the Top Gun Academy.

The tendency toward green world drama plays out fully in the final scenes of the film, where a clearly psychologically distressed Maverick, his condition physiologically betrayed by sweat on his masked face and the clutching of Goose's dog tags, enters a mêlée against a squadron of enemy MiGs. Cruise and the other characters draw on the transcendence of the green world, where magical and mystical powers guide the brothers in arms through the struggle of war. Maverick, Iceman (Tom Kazansky), and their comrades repeatedly draw on appeals to a higher force—"Goddamnit! Oh my God! Jesus Christ!"—with Maverick experiencing a moment reminiscent of the trench scene of *Star Wars*, the cinematic paragon of the green world drama (332), as Maverick, grasping the dog tag, recalling the opening scene of *Top Gun*, pleads, "Talk to me, Goose." Following the mystical appeal, the pilots defeat their nemesis and the playful celebrations can begin with Maverick flying by the control tower of the aircraft carrier. Even if Maverick will never be able to profess complete mastery over machines in the future—a narrative that remains open for the *Top Gun: Maverick* (Joseph Kosinski, 2020) sequel—Cruise's position as protector and agent in the Cold War and protagonist of the green world archetype remains assured, in spite of flirtations with closed world, cyborgian discourses throughout the film.

Software

Mission: Impossible evinces a very different world to the rose-cirrus skies of *Top Gun*. Based on the 1960s TV series of the same name, this film, which started an extended franchise, focuses on the Impossible Mission Force (IMF), an elite group of agents charged with protecting the West's way of life, which is under threat from increasingly fractured Eastern powers, who are as motivated by money as by ideology of the failed Soviet Union. With much of the film set in Europe, the Cold War as a reckoning with the dissolution of previous certainties built on a bipolar world and social contract is tangible. The opening scene, set in Kiev, is an elaborate film within a film, its form and content a search for identity. Jack Harmon (Emilio Estevez), an IMF agent, watches a traditional Cold War spy operation set in an Eastern bloc hotel unfold on a black-and-white television screen. The boxy functionality of the TV screen contrasts with a shiny computer, its own screen bristling with multicolored data. The contrast between the two screen-based technologies transitions *Mission: Impossible* from its origins as a Cold War television series to the sheen of the cinema. While this seems to be an upgrade, it is the appearance of the computer that is most revealing, as it shows the struggle between the two preeminent entertainment media of the early and mid-twentieth century with the computer, the exemplar technology of the late twentieth century. As the viewer is introduced to Cruise, here playing IMF agent Ethan Hunt, it becomes apparent that not everything is as it appears. Cruise's face, possibly his most valuable asset in his repertoire of star power, is hidden behind a mask. The mask, a recurring leitmotif for subterfuge and tension throughout the *Mission: Impossible* series of films, shows Cruise as becoming more immersed within the themes of the closed world, his identity reliant on technology. As Cruise removes his mask, vacuum packed to his face, the stage that is set for the sting operation also falls away as the stereotypical cinematic narratives of Western agents pitting their guile and industrial technologies (sedatives, poison) against the wile and resilience of Eastern agents physically falls apart. The TV set is replaced by the special effects of the cinema, most evidently manifest in the use of the computer, which is connected to a database that permits Harmon to access information immediately and effortlessly. From here, the computer and its software perform a recurring, starring role throughout the film.

For Edwards (1996, 13), the closed world is most emphatically realized in the division between East and West, epitomized by the Cold War, a space and time of high drama, where the "stage was a globe as a whole, truly a world divided against itself like never before." With the falling away of this world in the opening scene, two questions are raised: Where does this leave the IMF warriors of the Cold War? And, ultimately, who (or what) replaces it? At the end of the film, Jim Phelps (Jon Voight), questions Cruise's position within this new discourse, as the mastery of hardware is replaced by the requirement for someone (or something) more malleable, more postmodern. Dismal in his reflection, Phelps tells Hunt, there is "no more Cold War. No more secrets that you keep from yourself. . . . Then you realize it's over. You are an obsolete piece of hardware, not worth upgrading, a lousy marriage and $62,000 a year." The fall of the Berlin Wall, as powerful as it was, was achieved without any recourse to war between West and East. The decades of expenditure net result a spectrum of overnight-obsolete weapons and techniques, intelligence and knowledge, and tactics and strategies that would never be used in anger other than in the first Persian Gulf War in 1991. The computer, both as hardware and more pertinently as software, replaces the dangerous human work that Phelps, Hunt, and the IMF undertake. If the art of dogfighting in *Top Gun* was under threat in the post–World War II paradigm from the appearance of technologies that pushed the body beyond acceptable limits, then the craft of spying was under a similar threat from rewriteable floppy disks and depthless databases. The memory that Phelps recants to Hunt is of the body of the spy, sneaking and invisible in hostile locales. Yet this is a body rendered out of commission by the technological memory of software that never forgets but, equally, can be programmed to never remember, thus carrying none of unbearable existential heaviness of war won but never fought.

For Paul Virilio (2008, 55), the computers of the Cold War were employed for purposes of "exocolonisation" with the aim to adventure beyond the confines of the closed world and reach toward the hopes and dreams of stellar travel, epitomized by the space race of the 1960s to 1980s. As the Cold War came to a close, computer technologies, miniaturized to perfection through reiteration and Moore's Law, turned inward to explore interior worlds of DNA, nanotechnologies, and microbiology. These are processes termed "endocolonisation" (55).[1] *Mission: Impossible*, along with its contemporaries *GoldenEye* (Martin Campbell, 1995) and *Enemy of the State* (Tony Scott, 1998), brings the turn inward to bear on those working in intelligence agencies. Instead of being tasked to keep the civilian population safe, they take Phelps's crisis to its lowest common denominator, "creating a closed world which is radically divided against itself. Turned inexorably inward without frontiers or escape" (12). This is a central element of the plot of *Mission: Impossible*, the search for a disloyal spy in the multinational IMF team, aptly termed a "mole hunt" for such is the myopia and insularity of these animals of endocolonization.

The alarming transition from Cold War othering to 1990s insularity, from exocolonization to endocolonization, and from green world to closed world is spotlighted in the meeting between Hunt and Eugene Kittridge (Henry Czerny) at the Akvarium restaurant in Prague. Initially surprised at Kittridge's location in the Czech capital ("You're in Prague?"), Hunt deduces quickly that the loss of his team was not purely due to operational failings but instead to the presence of an additional IMF team at the embassy that evening. All those involved in the operation worked under different identities and are also present in the Akvarium later that night. Even Alexander Golitsyn (Marcel Iures), whose Slavic origin would have seen him cited as the enemy just seven years before is "one of ours with the real NOC list safe at Langley." The scene indicates that all the identities of the team are malleable and fluid, emulating the theme of betrayal throughout the film's narrative, in which the world divides and turns on itself, placing Cruise in

---

1   An early turn toward endocolonization can be seen in Joe Dante's *Innerspace* (1987).

a losing position as a mole digs a tunnel ("It's deep inside, and like you said, you survived").

As Stephen Mulhall (2006, 104) observes, the menace of the closed world hangs over the scene. The greens and blues of the seawater appear as banks of servers or monitors, overseeing the division of the world around it. Yet the camera, with a diagonal zoom to Kittridge's face draws the viewer's attention to the threat posed by the green world to this closed world. Even in its suspended state as a simulacrum of nature, the maritime predators offer a counterdiscourse to the closed world of moles, Langley, and masks. The only way in which Hunt can escape from the dichotomy between two worlds of clashing identities is to physically destroy it with a plastic explosive in the guise of chewing gum. As the zero-nutritional-value food counts down to zero hour and explodes, Hunt is off and sprinting through the water, his black-and-white tuxedo the embodiment of the debonair, masculine Western star-spy, most famously seen in the James Bond franchise but modernized in *Mission: Impossible* and the *Bourne* (2002–16) series, with any relationship to the green world, in its simulated form or not, utterly destroyed, left gasping for water on the cobbled streets of the Eastern bloc.

It is in the transition to the central scene of the film that the viewer sees Cruise voyage fully for the first time into the closed world. The discussion that takes place between the disavowed IMF agents, Hunt, Claire Phelps (Emmanuelle Béart), Luther Stickell (Ving Rhames), and Franz Krieger (Jean Reno), occurs on a train, its closed compartment demonstrating unity of place as closed world transfer between locations takes place in sealed vehicles (Edwards 1996, 310) and is followed by the donning of disguises as the team travels to Langley in a fire truck, their identities and faces almost completely hidden from view. The conversation on the train focuses on the mother of all hacks: the acquisition of the second part of the NOC list, a literal search for identity in the ultimate closed world of the US intelligence headquarters that houses the machines and people who spent the twentieth century building the closed world of the Cold War, their simulations and theorizing folding the world back on itself infinite times in the search for a future that may or may not come to pass. Once inside Langley, the male members of the team move through the nested, vertical enclosures of conduits and air pipes, the world around them constricted.

When Cruise emerges through the hole in the ceiling, being lowered into the closed world of computers and servers, he appears as a cyborg.

Highly augmented with eyeglasses, a torch, and communication radio attached to his head, it is the temperature gauge strapped to his wrist that reveals the real weakness in the closed world: the human. If the temperature of the room changes too drastically, as might occur with a physiologically and psychologically stressed human hung by a trapeze, then the countermeasures are triggered and the mission fails. While Mulhall (2006, 106) sees this as an inherently human trait, the hanging of Cruise emblematic of an "embodied mind" can be seen as the beginning of the embodiment of Cruise as a cyborg subject "for whom experience and knowledge are built bit by bit, as it were, from pure information" (Edwards 1996, 237). With acquisition of information held on the software of the CD-ROM central to a contorted plot that mirrors the closed world in its structure, infinitely folded back upon itself, second-guessing its own future, it is Cruise, two-thirds of the way through the opening film in the franchise that would most categorically define his superstar status and acting career, that can be seen in the same light as the information on his red liquid crystal display, screening the dangers of being human in a post–Cold War but endlessly closing world.

Wetware

Based on Philip K. Dick's short story of the same name, *Minority Report* envisions a world where a pilot program run in Washington, DC, known as Precrime, is effectively able to nullify violent crime by being able to visualize it before it happens. This is permitted through the joint precognition of three siblings who, with special abilities, can provide images and insight into crimes that result in death before they happen. The world that *Minority Report* was released into was very different to the evil other seen in *Top Gun* and the enemy within of *Mission: Impossible*. The commercial failure of *Spy Game* (2001), showed how far from the Cold War the West's imagination had moved, its suffusion of European spy thriller and bureaucratic exposition of no interest to audiences who wondered where the next attack could originate from and how—if at all—it could be halted. As America turned inward, a prophylactic response to a modern world of mass transit and mass media turned against itself, its surveillance turned outward: attempting to prevent attacks from citizens of the world—of America—became a key strategy of the post-2001 closed world. The words of Paul Virilio (2008, 51), writing in 1984, are chilling in their prescience "with the transportation revolution, this neighbor will become a 'spectre' that one will see again only accidentally, the foreigner will remain hidden among us." This spectral world, set fifty years hence, in 2054, is ambivalently illuminated by its director, Steven Spielberg, and is consistent with the cultural capstones of a world where the threat arises not from military or intelligence agencies but from within civilian society itself. The specter moves all around Washington, DC, haunting an environment that has been "replaced progressively by what is suspect and poses a threat [and] thus signals less the decline of defense than the absence of allies, the discrediting of civic alliance" (169). For those who live in Washington, DC, where the pilot program for the Precrime initiative takes place, there are no neighbors or allies among the population, only foreigners who must be rooted out precognitively. Using precognition might lead one to believe that this is a trajectory of legislation that is executed without any thought, but that would be a mistake, as there is plenty of intent on the side of the lawmakers of the Precrime initiative. Indeed, while everyone is potentially a felon, *Minority Report* closes the civic alliance between the rule of law and due process even further. In Washington, DC, there are not even any suspects, as the citizen is guilty before the fact, folding the future into the time *before* the present. Prior to John Anderton (Cruise) pursuing a felon, legal oversight is provided by judges who remotely pass judgment on the veracity of the visual and sonic insight provided by the visions of the "precogs"—three empathic, somnambulant siblings who can see, or at least feel, the ruptures in the fabric of time caused by a future murder.

With hyperactive intensity, Anderton dashes around a "world literally bleached of any color to leave behind a cold palette of metallic blues and greys" (Muir 2012, 273). The specters of foreignness and crime not yet committed makes this a translucent world, where evil, unlawfulness, and dissent are revealed, reviled, and redacted before it has time to make itself known to the population. Technology throws such blanket floodlighting on everyday life that it is humans who "have become mere shadows, ghosts in the machine" (274). This is seen in how the body is positioned within this Precrime, postlaw society. In the earlier Tom Cruise films, the cyborg is emergent, proliferating as spaces close in, but remains at arm's length, a means by which to compare, contrast, and identify with the human condition. In *Minority Report*, the world is so closed in that the entire body is part of a printed circuit in the technological habitus, ambiently refracted in shimmering pools of data capital. Rather than having any autonomy over its direction through time and space, its futures closed off by precognition, the cyborg body is a vehicle for security, surveillance, and advertising. As Anderton travels through the translucent corridors and stairways, similar to those of Langley but all pervasive here, he is assailed by images encouraging consumption, targeted advertising based on unique identifiers that are tailored to his social-economic status, the ubiquity of the Cold War's commitment to raising living standards portrayed as a tunnel vision of commerce, "as if the consumption of space and time follows upon and repeats the consumption of raw materials" (Virilio 2008, 109). Again, the closing of the world is pronounced. Even in consumption, where choice (and content) is ostensibly king, alternatives are rooted out before they have chance to percolate, meaning that in a neat commentary on the predestination of buying habits from the mailshot to the cold call, Anderton is encouraged to purchase a Lexus, a car he already drives. No time can be wasted in the search for sales, or for the pursuit of the translucency of truth.

If *Mission: Impossible* folded the spaces of the closed world infinitely back on itself, then *Minority Report* closes off the dimension of time. Anderton is the vehicle of time in this narrative. His cyborgian presence is assured by his proclivity for seeing the future as a set of images and then being able to manipulate it via gesture control, before actively preventing it from occurring through intervention in a potential crime of passion by Howard Marks (Arye Gross). Just as Anderton shifts visual and sonic perception with the assistance of computers and the wetware of the precogs, the viewer is provided with commentary by Anderton's coworkers as he races against the "time horizon" of the crime. The time horizon is an imminently closing world, the trajectory of time managed by John Anderton like a train heading toward a tunnel, each additional possibility a branch line progressively closing off as zero hour approaches. Unlike the water imagery that pervades the film, such as the precogs' bath of suspended animation, Anderton's flashbacks to his son's disappearance and the murder of Anne Lively (Jessica Harper), time is not perceived as a flow that is subject to the rhythms of the natural as well as the technical world. Instead, it is seen as a point—in time—which is programmed in at the locus of departure and—like the train—follows this track to its destination. About his wife, Marks says, "I wasn't going to kill her," yet he is guilty before the fact. That the Precrime team is tasked with preventing this destination relates to Virilio's (2008, 57) thesis in *Negative Horizon* that "the project of a rigorous management of

Time, following that of space, tends to become that of *a prevention of the moment*" (emphasis in original). In doing so, it places *Minority Report* on the continuum of the closed world narratives that become more and more prevalent in Cruise's high-concept, high-technology thrillers.

In common with the content, the structure of the film indicates that Washington, DC, is a world that interminably closes in on a single point in time. When Anderton, in keeping with the film's tagline "Everybody runs," races to find the truth about the Precrime program, he encounters the program's cocreator, Dr. Iris Hineman (Lois Smith), as the mistress of a green world that has turned against outsiders. This is not a *Midsummer Night's Dream*, a venue for reflection or redemption. Mutated plants attack Anderton, preventing him from accessing the property and physically turning their heads toward him as he asks about the "lead" precog, Agatha (Samantha Morton). Anderton finds some semblance of truth here, but this is a green world that has been contaminated by the closed world. Sentient plants in a translucent greenhouse join sentient machines in a translucent society, which, much like the Akvarium in Prague, is an artificial home for natural life-forms. In *Minority Report*'s future, both the environment and the living beings, in common with the humans who tend to them, are products of a simulation, with their tactile affection for Hineman as unsettling as their hostility toward Anderton.

The negation of the green world is compounded by the cloying feeling of the film closing around one point in time in its dénouement: the murdering of Leo Crow (Mike Binder) is Anderton's ultimate fate which was itself programmed by Lamar Burgess (Max von Sydow), the architect of the Precrime initiative. Given that it is Agatha who instructs Anderton that there is always a choice and that nothing is predestined, the only truly natural beings within *Minority Report* are the precogs. This is illuminated by the way in which they interact with the closed world around them. In spite of their extra-human, even posthuman abilities, the precogs are able to pass through the society of 2054 without being seen as guilty, as they alone can see the future, or being sold to, as their bodies sit outside the circuits of consumption that drive commerce. They alone are able to travel unencumbered through the closed world of technology, whereas Cruise must use a backstreet body augmenter to begin his trip back toward the green world; his eyeballs are replaced so that he is able to evade the surveillance-consumption state, the ocular augmentation of humans key to evading a world overseen by machines. This journey, toward Anderton's semi-green world house on the lake still exudes the blanche of metallic blues and grays and remains ambiguous in its ending: only the precogs end up in a green world, reading books in a cottage on a lake cut off from digital technology. For Anderton, reunited with his wife, Lara Anderton (Kathryn Morris), the viewer is presented a different type of closed world, one suspended in the green world of Lara's womb, pregnant with the question, Will this future be better than the other one?

Conclusion: Time's Up

This is the question that Cruise, through the characters in his films, continues to ask as the first quarter of the twenty-first century draws to a close. Following Cruise's science fiction corpus, the relationship between the spiraling of time and space, the cyborg body, and the subsequent closing of the world becomes more evident. *Edge of Tomorrow* (Doug Liman, 2014) traps the aptly named soldier-cyborg Cage (Cruise) in a spiral of time from which there is no immediate escape. In *Mission: Impossible—Fallout* (Christopher McQuarrie, 2018), Cruise's Ethan Hunt isn't even a victim of circumstance as he becomes the vehicle for the potential destruction of the world when he sets the nuclear clock to countdown in his battle with August Walker (Henry Cavill). Even thirty years after its cessation, the legacy of the Cold War's most notorious and terrifying technology is set toward fusion, not to threaten the world but in the paradoxes created by the folding of space and time upon itself to save it.

Cruise as an actor, as a star, and as the embodiment of the cyborg remains constant through all this. In his stunts, which are tantamount to almost deliberate acts of self-harm that other actors would never contemplate, he places himself into dangerous situations for the sheer entertainment of viewers. They watch, agape at the foolhardiness of his actions, which become more outlandish as he grows older: his waning body paradoxically waxing his star attraction as millions of people wince at him laughing about breaking his ankle on the set of *Mission: Impossible—Fallout*. For this cyborg, age is just a number, merely information, his star power the closed world transfer between the screen, the talk-show couch, and commercial—if not critical—adulation. For the audience, safely ensconced in consumption of the cinematic gaze of idolatry, of popcorn and nachos, are themselves products of the Cold War, and they can relate to Cruise's one mission, one that he has accepted without compromise: to take his audience on a journey through the potential brutal effects of the closed world that was constructed during the excesses of the Cold War and beyond. What Cruise achieves in his flirtation and—always—ultimate triumph over the closed world is to ensure that the Cold War that is experienced is the domestic bliss of the golden opportunities seen in the coming of age of *Risky Business* and not the predestined future bleakness of time never realized in *Minority Report*. When his rear admiral superior (Ed Harris) tells Maverick (Cruise) in *Top Gun: Maverick*, "The end is inevitable, Maverick, your kind is headed for extinction," he is partly correct given Hollywood's shift from star power to brand identity. Yet it will not be the cyborg that fails, the spirit willing but the flesh weak. Instead, it will end with the closed world itself, the environment that breathes life into the cyborg driven to extinction by Cruise's never-ending losses and victories in and over infinitely folding spaces and times.

Works Cited

Adey, Peter. 2010. *Aerial Life: Spaces, Mobilities, Effects*. Chichester, UK: Wiley Blackwell.
Edwards, Paul N. 1996. *The Closed World: Computers and Discourse in Cold War America*. Cambridge, MA: MIT Press.
Freund, P. E. S. 2004. "Civilised Bodies Redux: Seams in the Cyborg." *Social Theory and Health* 2 (3): 273–89.
Mauss, Marcel. 1973. "Techniques of the Body." *Economy and Society* 2 (1): 70–88.
Mulhall, Stephen. 2006. "The Impersonation of Personality: Film as Philosophy in *Mission: Impossible*." *Journal of Aesthetics and Art Criticism* 64, no. 1 (Winter): 97–110.
Muir, Lorna. 2012. "Control Space? Cinematic Representations of Surveillance Space between Discipline and Control." *Surveillance and Society* 9 (3): 263–79.
Oldenziel, Ruth, and Karin Zachmann. 2009. "Kitchens as Technology and Politics," in *Cold War Kitchen: Americanization, Technology and European Users*, edited by Ruth Oldenziel, and Karin Zachmann, 1–29. Cambridge, MA: MIT Press.
Paris, Michael. 1995. *From the Wright Brothers to Top Gun*. Manchester, UK: Manchester University Press.

Piketty, Thomas. 2014. *Capital in the Twenty-First Century*. Cambridge, MA: Belknap Press.

Riskin, Jessica. 2007. "Eighteenth Century Wetware." In *The Artificial and the Natural*, edited by Bernadette Bensaude-Vincent and William R. Newman, 97–125. Cambridge, MA: MIT Press.

Virilio, Paul. 2008. *Negative Horizon*. London: Continuum. Originally published in 1984.

Zimmern, Alfred. 1934. *Quo Vadimus? A Public Lecture Delivered on 5 February 1934*. London: Oxford University Press.

10

CRUISING STARDOM IN HOLLYWOOD FRANCHISING

Tom Cruise as Franchise Star in the *Mission: Impossible* and *Dark Universe* Storyworlds

Tara Lomax

The idea of a "franchise star" reflects creative and industrial shifts in how the interplay of stardom, intellectual property (IP), and narrative is negotiated in contemporary Hollywood. As Derek Johnson (2008, 216) identifies, the star system and franchising are "two modes of Hollywood product differentiation" that sometimes work in contestation. The Hollywood star system, Paul McDonald (2001, 1) explains, constitutes "the standard mechanisms used by the film industry to construct and promote the images of leading performers." Such mechanisms—like public persona management, contract negotiations, character typing, and genre branding—leverage stars as marketing drawcards; in many cases, the star persona embodies enough signifying force that it compensates for—or even impedes—the development of a narrative world. As McDonald (2012, 169) also states, "The actor uses the voice and body to give material substance to [a character's] actions and characteristics, so acting contributes to the making of the narrative world and the creation of story." Like the star system, Hollywood franchising leverages the marketability of recognizable icons; however, the difference between the two systems is that stardom's iconicity centers on the bodily spectacle and narrational significance of human persona (Dyer 1998, 12), and the franchise system leverages the iconicity of IP and story brands—like "Star Wars" and "Marvel"—that are "extended in an ongoing fashion" (Johnson

2013, 28). This process of extension is enabled by synergistic branding strategies and broader convergence practices in the media culture landscape. As such, Daniel Herbert (2018, 86) notes that franchises are "cultural texts whose intertextual linkages have been made by industrial design, with the aim to expand and spread that same property as far and wide as possible." Stardom and franchising are therefore both effective industrial systems with comparable marketing objectives suited to different modes of production. Sometimes these systems converge, but they do not always easily coalesce. Focusing on producer and actor Tom Cruise as a case study, this chapter examines the negotiation of stardom and franchising as it relates to storyworld design and industrial synergy.

In the franchise era of the early twenty-first century, the star brand is no longer of central importance to Hollywood's marketing strategy or creative development. In this context, "a character such as Spider-Man or a concept such as Star Wars was more important than any one actor" (Block and Wilson 2010, 813). This is reinforced by Kristen Thompson (2007, 6) who recognizes that "today the franchise is often the star" and by Johnson (2008, 217) who determines that in the franchise system "star and celebrity persona arguably take a back seat." This tension between stars and franchise brands stems from a shift in the ways in which the contemporary Hollywood industry is organized by mega-conglomerate business practices that facilitate media synergy. Geoff King (2003, 68) explains that "stars occupy a distinctive position in this industrial context.... [They] establish brand images of their own, based on an identifiable persona on-screen and off, effectively converting themselves into their own franchise properties." To be sure, this process of star branding is not at all new in Hollywood but underpins the very nature of the star text since its classical formulation in the studio system. However, the intensification of media convergence and IP synergy in contemporary Hollywood complicates the way that stardom functions in relation to franchise production and expansive storyworld design: star brands must work to support franchise storyworld development, not supplant it. Cruise is a compelling case study for further examining this convergence because he exemplifies different articulations of compatibility—or "star fit"—between stars and franchise storyworlds. Cruise has been involved with several cross-media franchise properties, but the most compelling of these are *Mission Impossible* (1996–), which is based on the espionage television series that ran between 1966 and 1973 (Bruce Geller, producer, CBS) and 1988 to 1990

(Bruce Geller, producer, ABC), and *The Mummy* (Alex Kurtzman, 2017),[1] touted to launch the *Dark Universe* franchise based on the Universal Monsters IP of the classical Hollywood era but failed after commercial and critical disappointment (Liptak 2017). Where Cruise's stardom works in perfect "fit" with the narrative world of the *Mission: Impossible* franchise—including congruous genre compatibility and character typing—by contrast, Cruise's role in *The Mummy* (2017) signals a problematic or discordant fit between stardom and storyworld development.

The concept of storyworlds is not necessarily unique to franchise production, since the textual representation of "characters, situations, and events" is an essential principle of narratology more generally (Herman 2009, 17). David Herman explains that in storyworld design, narratives become blueprints for developing world creation, and this process involves the construction of medium-specific textual cues "to build up representations of the worlds evoked by narratives" (105–6). He adds that understandings of storyworlds represented by any specific medium need to also "take into account complexities in the design of the blueprint itself—complexities creating additional layers of mediation in the relationship between narrative and storyworld" (107). Herman is referring here to formal aesthetic components of a medium, and it is inarguable that the function of stars as semiotics cues within narratives is a fundamental component of Hollywood cinema. Thus, positioning—or "fitting" (Dyer 1998, 129)—stars within a storyworld requires careful mediation in narrative design and marketing. Storyworld development refers to the way story and plot unfold across a series of texts (as with traditional narratological analysis), but in the context of franchise production it also refers specifically to the development stage of production during which world-building design, narrative conceptualization, and thematic essence is developed and shaped in accordance with production procedures, licensing conditions, and marketing strategy. In this way, storyworld development represents and translates IP branding

---

1 Cruise has also starred in other film examples associated with franchise properties and adaptations, including *War of the Worlds* (Steven Spielberg, 2005), *Jack Reacher* (Christopher McQuarrie, 2012) and *Jack Reacher: Never Go Back* (Edward Zwick, 2016), *Edge of Tomorrow* (Doug Liman, 2014) and its sequel *Live Die Repeat and Repeat* (Doug Liman, forthcoming), and *Top Gun: Maverick* (Joseph Kosinski, 2020).

into narratological terms—as transmedia developer and producer Jeff Gomez (2019) explains, "the process of transmedia development ... put[s] the intellectual property—the storyworld—über-alles." Gomez builds on this point to explain that stars should "behave in honor of their character. ... While they're playing these characters, they're in deference to them," which is, Gomez adds, "the way a fine actor can contribute to the storyworld communication of the franchise and benefit from doing so" (Skype communication with author, February 9, 2019). In this way, the cultural (and marketing) iconicity of storyworld development and IP branding decenters stardom, but this also means that the franchise star needs to be carefully positioned and accounted for within storyworld development. This is especially true for Cruise, because as an A-list star his iconicity demands careful negotiation within franchise production. As such, this chapter will argue that franchise stardom constitutes its own set of implications for narrative design, marketing strategy, and generic conventions.

Franchise Stardom: Where Stars, Intellectual Property, and Storyworlds Converge

The franchise star is a convergence of stardom, IP synergy, and story branding and can be contextualized by the textual, industrial, and cultural intersections of media convergence. Understanding franchise stardom as a convergence of these systems accounts for the contestation between old and new narrational and marketing systems emerging within the synergistic industrial landscape of early twenty-first-century Hollywood. In his seminal account of media convergence, Henry Jenkins (2006, 18) contends that "convergence requires media companies to rethink old assumptions about what it means to consume media, assumptions that shape both programming and marketing decisions." Media convergence, Jenkins explains, "alters the relationship between existing technologies, industries, markets, genres, and audiences" (15). This means that the conditions for media production and engagement are in disruption and transition, in which various creative and industrial systems—like stardom, genre, and media synergy—are not only in transformation but are also converging in sometimes congruous, but often contested, ways. In considering the role of stardom within media convergence, Graeme Turner (2013, 36) considers that "the celebrity, of course, is a very useful (perhaps the best!) way of connecting these cross media processes. They become a vehicle for transferring product from one format to the next, a fundamental part of the process of content streaming. In one sense this is not new. . . . What does seem new, however, is the importance of the celebrity as a *branding* mechanism for media products that has assisted their fluent translation across media formats and systems of delivery." This articulation of stardom as a branding mechanism represents the crux of franchise stardom as a concept that converges multiple self-contained marketing and creative systems: star-driven marketing, media franchising, and narrative/genre formula. Media convergence thus leverages already existing relations between media, texts, and marketing but reconfigures how these strategies are applied in the context of shifting industrial systems (like franchise production).

Cruise exists within the era of media convergence because he remains one of the few 1980s high-concept stars (Wyatt 1994) still working as an active star in the contemporary franchise era. As such, his star brand still carries marketing weight as a high-profile A-lister and is constituted by various depictions and representations—in publicity, promotion, and performance—which function as a marketing drawcard in and of itself. In this traditional stardom model, star iconicity "enters into subsidiary forms of circulation, and then feeds back into future performances" (Ellis 1982, 91). As McDonald (2012, 169–70) explains, "Stars contribute to the representation of the story world, yet at the same time they are visible as known onscreen identities and therefore are on show. It is this tension, the tension between story and show . . . that forms the basic contradiction of film star acting." This is the way that Cruise functions in the *Mission: Impossible* franchise, which works successfully as a star vehicle since it doubles down on Cruise's star brand for narrative and genre significance. This is in contrast with Cruise's function in *The Mummy*, which stifled and detracted from the narrative development and potential longevity of the *Dark Universe* franchise. Gomez considers the impact of Cruise's stardom on the storyworld development of the *Dark Universe* franchise, explaining how star branding "trampled on any world-building that was there because everything had to be turned into the service of Cruise. . . . The result is that we're only getting aspects of what we love about Cruise with a kind of monster movie over it and it just doesn't work" (Skype communication with author, February 9, 2019). Thus, in *The Mummy*, Cruise's iconic star brand obscured storyworld development, and neither the star system nor the franchise system could function effectively.

As a production executive, a trademark, and a brand, Cruise has surpassed the designation of movie actor: the name constitutes a brand characterized by a hybridity of action genre and spectacle, star persona, and legal-industrial proprietary with an iconicity akin to some of Hollywood's most recognizable franchise properties. Focusing on this question of stars as franchises in relation to the cross-media synergies of Will Smith, King (2003, 68) contends that star brands are a "sometimes elusive franchise." However, Johnson (2008, 217) suggests that "in treating stardom and franchising synonymously, [King] does not speak to how stars might approach participation in franchises that exceed their own star texts." Johnson addresses this gap with a case study on how British thespian Ian McKellen negotiates the ideological tensions between his star performance and character-based branding in the *X-Men* franchise. Johnson maintains that despite tension between stardom and character branding, stars still play an important role in franchise production. He argues that "actors' abilities to subsume franchise characters within their star texts remain strained; at the same time, the persistence of stardom, however marginalized in franchise systems, keeps branded intellectual property open to alternative meaning management" (229). This alternative meaning management can relate to a variety of factors, like the contested inflection of a star's ideological, economic, or aesthetic brand in dialogue with an established character property. Indeed, in the case of Cruise, there is always the risk that the controversies of his "private" life—his failed romantic relationships, provocative statements on depression, and his connection to Scientology (and its related ideologies)—will influence how meaning management occurs in his performance of preestablished franchise characters. It is these risks that make the strategies and processes of creative development so important for managing franchise stardom. As such, the convergence of stardom and storyworld development enables an understanding of the franchise star as an inflection of character, genre, and world-building in dialogue with publicity, promotion, and star persona.

In his analysis of stars and franchises, Johnson examines the dynamic between star and character-based brand but does not similarly account for the relationship between stars and franchise storyworlds. As Peter von Stackleberg (2018, 234) signals, contemporary franchise production has driven a "shift from character-based to storyworld-based transmedia." Where Johnson reflects on the impact of preestablished franchise characters that exists before and outside of any single actor's performance, this chapter considers the role of a high-profile star playing an original character within preestablished storyworld properties. In *Mission: Impossible*, Cruise plays Ethan Hunt, and in *The Mummy* he plays Nick Morton: both these characters were conceived of for Cruise to perform within already established storyworld properties. Therefore, with Cruise as a case study, this chapter presents different critical insight to Johnson's analysis of stars who perform preestablished character brands in franchises. As a franchise star, moreover, Cruise is defined not merely by the franchises he is associated with, like *Top Gun, Mission: Impossible, Jack Reacher*, and *Dark Universe*, but also through his executive authority as an actor-producer, the recognizability of his name as a trademark, and the semiotic significance of his stardom both on- and offscreen. From here this chapter will consider three articulations of Cruise as franchise star: as actor-producer, as trademark, and a brand-world. In reinforcing this chapter's focus on storyworld development, the latter of these sections is a primary interest and will further consider the dynamic between stardom and storyworld development in the *Mission: Impossible* and *Dark Universe* franchises.

Executive Stardom: Cruise as Actor-Producer

The significance of Cruise's franchise stardom is industrially reinforced by the star's dual role as actor-producer. In 1993, Cruise established the independent production company Cruise/Wagner Productions with his casting agent Paula Wagner. Cruise/Wagner would go on to produce the first three *Mission: Impossible* installments, plus many more Cruise-headed movies. Although the company ceased to operate as Cruise/Wagner Productions after Wagner left in 2008, Cruise retained producer credit across the entire the *Mission: Impossible* franchise. This affords Cruise executive authority over the storyworld and the function of his franchise stardom in relation to the *Mission: Impossible* brand. P. David Marshall (1997, 94) describes the important interplay between the star brand and corporate organization using Cruise as case study: "The agency that represents Tom Cruise, along with the corporation and production company that has produced the film, attempts to promote an organized conception of Tom Cruise that is connected with the specific release of the film. Cruise, then, is both contained by the package of the film and is the package that works to draw the attention of the press to consider the film significant or of interest." Marshall's case study does not explicitly address Cruise's role as producer, but it goes to follow that as a cofounder, co-owner, and producer of a company that produces movies in which Cruise stars—and in partnership with his own acting agent no less—Cruise's franchise stardom is facilitated by the executive authority afforded to him as actor-producer.

As executive star, Cruise challenges the traditional power dynamic between actor and production company and its negotiation by the actor's agent. As cofounder, co-owner, and executive producer of a production company with his acting agent, Cruise disrupts Richard Dyer's (1998, 7) contention that "a star cannot become a crucial decision-maker (and remain a star)." If this is the case for the traditional conceptualization of stardom, then executive stardom articulates a process of industrial revisionism as it occupies a complex position between decision making, negotiation, and performing contracted labor. King (2003, 69) notes how "stars have gained a great deal more control over their destiny since the classical studio system.... Many stars have established their own companies... [in] an attempt to gain greater control over the kinds of projects with which the star is involved, whether *as* star or in the arena of producing or directing." However, as King explains, such independent studios cannot exist without the resources and infrastructure of larger studios (69)—indeed, Cruise/Wagner began with an exclusive distribution agreement with Paramount Pictures and then MGM. While star-owned studios may provide stars with executive control, this does not grant executive autonomy—thus, executive stardom is not a complete break away from the star system but a disruptive revision of star function within the contemporary entertainment industry.

Stardom as IP: Tom Cruise™

The notion of franchise stardom constitutes potential intersections between stardom and IP, in which Pallotta (2018) identifies that "blockbusters are less about star power these days and more about the power of intellectual property." Thus, both the *Mission: Impossible* and *Dark Universe* franchises demonstrate that the creative manifestation of IP, in the form of storyworld development, must also consider the function of stardom. However, this is not to ignore the already present intersection between star naming and legal ownership in the form of trademark law. According to Jacqueline D. Lipton

(2010, 145), celebrities "have the most commercially valuable personal names because they trade on their names for their livelihood." However, trademark law does not protect a celebrity's name because of its iconicity but because they represent the source of a service of property that is distinct from its competitors (146). For example, Lipton explains, "Audiences may go to see a movie because Julia Roberts is in it, or they may associate a certain quality of performance with Ms Roberts. However, they are unlikely to think that Ms Roberts is the source of the movie in a trademark sense. The movie studio that produced the film is more likely to be regarded as the source of the movie" (147). This clarification takes on further significance in the case of Cruise because his dual role as actor-producer means his trademark not only acknowledges his iconicity as a celebrity but also that he himself constitutes the source and production of his performance as a trademarked property.

Cruise's function as a franchise star is therefore protected by IP law. In 2006, Cruise initiated a legal dispute over the unauthorized use of his name in the domain www.tomcruise.com, in which the World Intellectual Property Organization (WIPO) Arbitration and Mediation Center (2006) sided in favor of Cruise's ownership of "Tom Cruise." The case report states that in initiating such legal proceedings, Cruise "asserts ownership of common law trademark and service mark rights in the term 'Tom Cruise.'" Moreover, Cruise's case claims that "the public has come to recognize and associate the name 'Tom Cruise' as a symbol that identifies and distinguishes the entertainment services provides exclusively by him, and that through long and continuous use, international recognition and extensive advertising and promotion, TOM CRUISE has acquired distinctiveness and secondary meaning as a trademark and service mark" (WIPO 2006).

The case report for this proceeding establishes the global awareness of Cruise's name (international recognition), the consistent longevity of his star image (long and continuous use), and the creative-cultural distinctiveness of his performance (exclusive entertainment service). The precedent of this case is more than a domain name dispute but authorizes "Tom Cruise" as an entertainment property through legal procedure. Reinforcing the legal articulation of Cruise—as a property that can be protected and authorized by law—Cruise is also notable for refusing to license his physical likeness for use in video games and comic books (Official Playstation 2002, 93; Totilo 2006). In addition to the way that domain name trademark procedures give proprietorship to Cruise's name, the licensing restrictions of Cruise's likeness rights impacts the ways that his franchise stardom can extend across cross-media storyworlds.

Stardom Brand-Worlds: Cruise and Storyworlds

There is an already present similarity between the semiotic construction of stardom and storyworlds, both in and out of the franchise system. Dyer (1998, 34) describes stardom as "a complex configuration of visual, verbal and aural signs . . . [that] manifest not only in films but in all kinds of media texts." Correspondingly, Herman (2009, 106) explains that storyworlds are "global mental representations enabling interpreters to frame inferences about the situations, characters, and occurrences." Building on Herman's narratological principles, Marie-Laure Ryan and Jan-Thon Noël (2014, 2–3) contends that storyworlds are "representations that transcend media" whereby "different media converge around [a story]world by presenting different aspects of it." Therefore, the convergence of stardom and storyworlds also implicates strategies and forms like cross-platform synergy, seriality, and transmedia storytelling. The latter is a strategy of narrative dispersal seminally defined by Jenkins (2006, 95–96) to be a "more integrated approach to franchise development" whereby "story unfolds across multiple platforms, with each text making a distinctive and valuable contribution to the whole." Sean Redmond (2014, 77) identifies that stars are already inherently transmedial as a unified construct dispersed across media: "Transmedia celebrities are fictive constructs whose images and stories get dispersed systematically across print, press, television, music, game, and virtual sites and networks. We understand celebrities as the sum parts of these textual fragments; as unified storied beings who grant and award us pleasure through the way we can see them [across multiple platforms]." Similarly, McDonald (2013, 8) notes how cross-media expansion has always been fundamental to the construction of stardom: "film stardom is a multiple-media system. The visibility of film stars extends way beyond the films they appear in to various forms of broadcast, print and online media, involving coverage not only the star's on-screen existence but also his or her off-screen life." Indeed, the idea of stars as transmedial is not new. However, understanding stardom as a form of transmedia semiotics that constitutes a unified star image or texts is different to understanding how transmedial stars are negotiated and managed within franchise storyworlds that are also transmedial by design.

Stars and transmedia narratives both transgress the boundaries of self-contained single texts and mediums to build enriched imaginary worlds that can support multiple characters and stories. As Redmond (2014, 80) explains, "Celebrities exist in complex fictional worlds with numerous other characters and their interrelating stories. These worlds will be comprised of different settings, environments, encounters that are both public and private, with self-contained and inter-diegetic story lines that weave seamlessly together." However, as Cruise's involvement in *The Mummy* reveals, the convergence of stardom and franchise storyworlds is not always seamless; moreover, an enriched imaginary world should not necessarily support the transmedial star brand of a high-profile star. I contend that a primary component of this tension between stars and storyworlds is the consistency of branding as a semiotic strategy (and sometimes obstacle) for effective meaning management in franchise development. More than just a corporate marketing strategy, Carlos A Scolari (2015, 155) asserts that branding is "the most perfect synthesis of the material and the symbolic worlds." Scolari conceptualizes storyworlds as "narrative brand-worlds," which he describes as "a radically different phenomenon [to traditional product branding], where *fiction becomes the brand*" (159–60; emphasis in original). However, the star brand is itself a work of narrative world making because, as Redmond (2014, 81) further states, "the world of the celebrity is a fascinating fiction." I suggest that the notion of the stardom brand-world, therefore, conceptualizes how the franchise star inflects semiotic significance as a narrative brand. In considering stars as agents of serial form, Dyer (1998, 98) suggests that "[stars] and milieu, rather than plot, are the [serial] form's anchors. Because stars are always appearing in different stories and settings, *they* must stay broadly the same in order to permit recognition and identification." This incidentally describes the semiotic significance of the star brand-world but raises a potential problem for a franchise star involved with different storyworlds. For example, in the *Mission: Impossible* franchise, Cruise's brand-world is effective because the franchise is intricately intertwined with Cruise's star brand, but when this star brand supplants storyworld development in the *Dark Universe* franchise, *The Mummy* emerges as merely a variation of *Mission: Impossible*. If the narrative brand-world is a nexus of characters, settings, values, and situations that is constituted through the organized procedures of IP synergy and promotional branding, then the stardom brand-world mediates the semiotic dynamic between stars and storyworlds.

Mission: Impossible: The Tom Cruise Franchise

With a total global box office gross of $3.57 billion (Box Office Mojo 2019) and its six-installments (and counting) longevity,[2] the *Mission: Impossible* franchise is inarguably one of the most successful action franchises. Recognized by the informal moniker "the Tom Cruise franchise" (Brueggemann 2018), media business reporter Frank Pallotta (2018) describes *Mission: Impossible* as a "rare blockbuster franchise sold on a star, not a brand." Moreover, Pallotta adds, "Cruise bucks the franchise trend as the face of the 'Mission: Impossible' movies." Such a claim is made more significant by the fact that the *Mission: Impossible* brand was not conceived of in 1996 with Tom Cruise, but the franchise's iconicity exceeds Cruise's involvement with the original television series and its prior association with actor Peter Graves as Impossible Mission Force (IMF) team leader Jim Phelps. Nonetheless, as franchise star with the executive and trademark authority of an actor-producer, Cruise's name (and face) has become synonymous with the franchise. In this regard, Cruise heightens the high-concept function of stardom, in which the conventions of character, genre, and visual spectacle are serviced by star persona as a presold formulation. As Justin Wyatt (1994, 55) explains, the star persona "often overwhelms the character being portrayed so that the character is identified more strongly with the star than as an integral part of a unique story." In this way, the core narrative and stylistic characteristics of the *Mission: Impossible* franchise—its "storyworld essence," to draw from Gomez (2018, 209)—are intertwined with Cruise's stardom. Cruise himself identifies the essence of *Mission: Impossible* as "the team, the action, the suspense" (Cruise and McQuarrie 2018). Indeed,

---

2 The *Mission: Impossible* franchise is made up of *Mission: Impossible* (Brian De Palma, 1996), *Mission: Impossible II* (John Woo, 2000), *Mission: Impossible III* (J. J. Abrams, 2006), *Mission: Impossible—Ghost Protocol* (Brad Bird, 2011), *Mission: Impossible—Rogue Nation* (Christopher McQuarrie, 2015), and *Mission: Impossible—Fallout* (Christopher McQuarrie, 2018), with two more announced in January 2019.

these characteristics marry well with Cruise's star brand: a strong association with the action genre, the physicality of his stunt work (and excessive running), and his creative authority in the production process.

In positioning Cruise as the "face" of the *Mission: Impossible* franchise, the theme of disguised identity—a core element of the franchise and its espionage action genre—provides a space through which to assert Cruise's franchise stardom. Like the film series, the original television series follows a group of elite secret agents known as the IMF; IMF leader Jim Phelps (Peter Graves) is the only character to feature in both television iterations and the 1996 movie adaptation (played by Jon Voight). In the first movie *Mission: Impossible*, however, Phelps is exposed as a villainous double agent, making way for Ethan Hunt—and Cruise—to emerge as the hero and future IMF team leader. In the film's climax, Hunt masquerades as "Jim Phelps" to expose Phelps villainous wife. Hunt removes his prosthetic mask to reveal the iconic face of Tom Cruise in a moment that characteristically launches the *Mission: Impossible* franchise and its storyworld: this is Cruise tearing off the mask of Phelps as the iconic "face" of the franchise's past and calling the shots as the franchise's future star.

The theme of disguise takes on a different dimension for the franchise with the cross-media tie-ins for the film series, in which Cruise's refusal to license his physical likeness in comic book and video game iterations puts legal constraints on how Cruise's brand-world can work to propel the *Mission: Impossible* storyworld across media. Several attempts have been made to produce video games based on the *Mission: Impossible* IP, including the Nintendo 64 game *Mission: Impossible* (Infogames 1998) the multiconsole game *Mission: Impossible: Operation Surma* (Paradigm Entertainment 2003), and the mobile phone games *Mission: Impossible 3* (Gameloft 2006) and *Mission: Impossible–Rogue Nation* (Glu 2015).[3] In trying to skirt the licensing limitations of not using Cruise's physical likeness, many of these games depict Hunt with no semblance to Cruise. There are multiple risks in portraying Hunt without likeness to Cruise: this can blur Cruise's connection with the franchise's storyworld essence—and thus not consistently or authentically brand the storyworld; or, worse, it can represent a world

---

3   Other video games in the *Mission: Impossible* franchise include the game *Mission: Impossible* (Konami 1990) based on the 1988 television revival, and the game on Nintendo Game Boy (Rebellion Developments 2000).

in which Cruise is not even essential. Indeed, a review of the mobile game *M:I-3* suggests that "Cruise is hardly missed" (Buchanan 2006). In slight narrative contrast, the *Rogue Nation* mobile game is set in the same storyworld continuity, but instead of portraying Hunt without Cruise's likeness, players are tasked with an IMF mission to find Hunt after he goes rogue. With this game, there is perhaps an attempt to represent the significance of Hunt within this narrative world without distancing from Cruise; in leveraging a narrative opportunity facilitated by the events of the 2015 movie, in which Hunt becomes a fugitive, this game works to navigate licensing limitations while also transmedially enriching the storyworld. The 2015 comic book one-shot, *Torn Asunder* (Kussman 2015), also explores this aspect of the storyworld as it follows Hunt during his six months tracking down the Syndicate in the movie, *Rogue Nation* (Watercutter 2015). Most significantly, this comic book depicts Hunt using Cruise's likeness.[4] The specific circumstances of this licensing permission have not been made public, but this comic book signals a shift in how Cruise's franchise stardom, and his iconic association with the storyworld brand, is deliberately articulated across different media.

As the *Mission: Impossible* series has progressed, the franchise has worked to mythologize Cruise's franchise stardom and reinforce his narrative association with the property. To be sure, Cruise's function as executive producer is also crucial to this process of self-mythologizing. This is articulated in *Mission: Impossible—Fallout* (Christopher McQuarrie, 2018), where Hunt's new mission is delivered via a tape recording hidden inside the book cover of Homer's *Odyssey*. In the home release commentary, director Christopher McQuarrie reveals that this book title was deliberately chosen to represent the "epicness of the franchise" (Cruise and McQuarrie 2018). Moreover, this sentiment also underpins Hunt's—or Cruise himself (by now this distinction is surely blurred)—opening scene in *Mission: Impossible—Rogue Nation* (Christopher McQuarrie, 2015). Hunt enters a record store in London and is greeted by the store clerk. Hunt and the clerk exchange a conversation about music, which is presumably identification

---

4 Another *Mission: Impossible* comic book tie-in was published by Marvel Comics in 1996, which served as a prequel to the first 1996 movie. However, this comic book also met the same licensing restrictions with portraying Hunt with Cruise's likeness. Published copies of this comic book are now considered rare.

Ethan Hunt illustrated with Cruise's likeness in the *Mission: Impossible* comic book one-shot, *Torn Asunder* (2015).

protocol, and the clerk hands Hunt a vinyl record with his mission recording. The background music becomes suddenly more dramatic as she admiringly says, "It really is you," and, with presumably deliberate synchronicity, the onscreen intertitles credit Cruise as executive producer. The shot holds on a close-up of Cruise facing away and, as he turns to match her eyeline, she adds, "I've heard stories—they can't all be true."

In the film commentary, McQuarrie explains that this shot was about "playing with the idea of the myth of this character, taking Ethan Hunt and recontextualizing him in a more mythic way" (Cruise and McQuarrie 2015). To be sure, this mythologizing in *Mission: Impossible* is not confined to the characterization of Hunt but is a process of representing the "myth of Tom Cruise" as franchise star. As the *Mission: Impossible* series continues across multiple iterations, Cruise's franchise stardom intensifies the consistency of his image as executive star and celebrity trademark to strive for mythic significance.

Dark Universe: "A New World of Gods and Monsters" . . . and Tom Cruise?

There are various factors involved in the failure of the *Dark Universe* franchise: a shift in genre from its horror source to action adventure, superficial storyworld development, and a clouded publicity campaign that confused genre, franchising, and stardom. These factors all intersect with the tensions between stardom and storyworld development. In a private conversation about the *Dark Universe* franchise's narrational impediments, Gomez contends that in *The Mummy* "the star of the movie—the monster—played a secondary role to Cruise. And that's not the building block for a shared universe franchise—that's a star vehicle and no matter how you slice it, it becomes muddled because cosmology and everything else becomes wayside" (Skype communication with author, February 9, 2019). The publicity and promotional campaign surrounding the release of *The Mummy* demonstrates the clash of marketing strategies underpinning the franchise: between stardom and storyworld development. The *Dark Universe* was inarguably driven by storyworld in its publicity, promotion, and paratextual content—such as posters, a promotional video, the interactive website Welcome to Prodigium, and associated press material—all welcoming audiences to "a new world of gods and monsters" (a reference to *Bride of Frankenstein* [James Whale, 1935]). Moreover, this shared universe storyworld strategy works in tension with other publicity strategies that emphasized Cruise as lead star. The poster illustrates this tension between the Cruise and the *Dark Universe*'s storyworld: the tag line "Welcome to a new world of gods and monsters" is almost quelled in the poster canvas by Tom Cruise's name, which is more prominent in font and style than the storyworld branding. Indeed, the inconsistent marketing approach to *The Mummy*—that is, star focused mixed with storyworld focused—further reflects this process of contested negotiation between Cruise's authority and the *Dark Universe* storyworld.

Despite not holding an official producer credit on *The Mummy*, Cruise still maintained creative authority befitting his executive stardom reputation established with Cruise/Wagner's production of *Mission: Impossible*. According to a 2017 *Variety* exclusive, Universal "contractually guaranteed Cruise control of most aspects of the project, from script approval to post-production decisions. He also had a great deal of input on the film's marketing and release strategy." In this way, "the reboot of 'The Mummy' was supposed to be the start of a mega-franchise for Universal Pictures. But instead, it's become a textbook case of a movie star run amok" (Setoodeh and Lang 2017). This describes the legal and executive authority that Cruise secured but also has creative implications. Gomez (2019) describes that "there was a moral to the story of *The Mummy* (2017), such as it was,

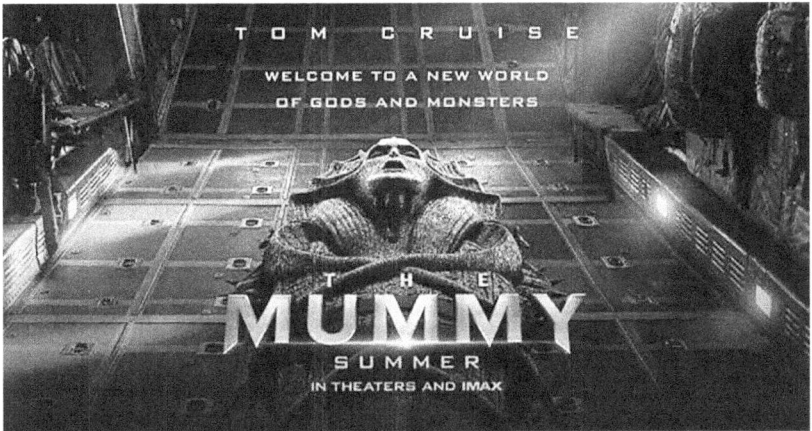

Promotional poster advertising *The Mummy*.

but that was entirely related to the Tom Cruise character, not the Mummy creature, and in no way was it applicable to the entire 'Dark Universe.'" Gomez and his development team, Starlight Runner Entertainment, met with the *Dark Universe* producers to explore the potentiality of working together on storyworld development, but the collaboration did not eventuate. However, Gomez's insights are informative. He explains that the producers of *Dark Universe*

> had a very specific approach in mind that was quite two-dimensional in its thinking—they were scriptwriters, not world-designers. So, for example, in the early meetings with the 'Dark Universe' producers we sat down, and they asked, 'So what do you think you can contribute?' We said, 'Well of course a cosmology.' . . . [They] were very overwhelmed by that kind of thinking and that kind of storyworld design, and said they'll get to that when they need to. That was a fundamental difference in development approach and within ten minutes we were already at an impasse.

This suggests that the *Dark Universe* creators had an outdated and simplified high-concept strategy in mind, which relies on "surface-level imagery, the transmission of narrative information [that] frequently relies upon pre-sold properties, and familiar star images" (Johnson 2008, 216). In setting itself such a limited scope, the *Dark Universe* creators underestimated the complexity of their own IP and the potential to extend the storyworld beyond the star and genre branding systems.

Universal Studios' conception of the *Dark Universe* franchise was founded on an ambitious premise: even before incorporating Cruise into its strategy, this project encountered the marketing challenge of the source material's horror genre. As Universal chairman Donna Langley has admitted, "The horror genre has a ceiling—it's not particularly global" (qtd. in McClintock and Masters 2014). It is for this reason, Langley reveals, Universal decided to translate the source material's horror genre into action adventure, and thus Cruise's iconicity as action genre star performed a crucial role in driving this genre shift. According to McDonald (2013, 31), "Generic conventions contribute to the formation of strongly identifiable and saleable star identities, and the importance of genre has therefore been in evidence amongst the highest echelons of the talent hierarchy." This suggests that employing Cruise as a strategy to help enforce genre branding also afforded his star brand a higher level of creative authority that arguably upstaged the Universal Monsters IP and the development of the *Dark Universe* storyworld. However, this prioritization of star-driven genre branding over well-developed storyworld design has industrial implications: storyworlds are protected by IP law, but genre is not (Altman 1999, 115). Therefore, investing in Cruise as a genre star was at the expense of exploiting Universal's character and storyworld properties. In setting a star brand up against storyworld development, *Dark Universe* demonstrates the continuing impact of stardom in contemporary Hollywood production, the complexity of franchise narrative, and the importance of a marketing strategy that understands the difference between star and story branding.

Conclusion

Contextualizing stardom within media convergence, this chapter has considered franchise stardom as a collision of celebrity, IP synergy, and storyworld branding; in doing so, it has contributed to an understanding of how the star system functions in relation to the franchise system. The Hollywood franchise system is IP driven and storyworld focused, and so it relies less on star-vehicle marketing systems. However, star brands still play an important role within the franchise system, since preestablished cultural familiarity with franchise IP intensifies fan scrutiny toward the casting "fit" of stars—this is evidenced by ongoing online debates surrounding the casting of Batman and James Bond, for example. Such scrutiny, Johnson (2008, 215) notes, is driven by the fact that, like stars, "franchise characters are household names." However, preestablished character branding is not the only crucial convention of the franchise system that impacts the function of stars: the franchise star must also work in relation to storyworld development and IP branding. While scholars King and McDonald have considered how stardom can function as a franchise property in itself, and Johnson has explored the dynamic between stardom and franchising as a site of ideologically contested character branding, I have been compelled by how Cruise articulates a complex interplay of stardom, legal-industrial proprietary, and storyworld development. Cruise's role in the highly successful and ongoing *Mission: Impossible* franchise demonstrates that stardom can still exist and function effectively within the franchise model, albeit with an alternative marketing strategy that mythologizes the star as a brand-world. Similarly, the contestation of Cruise as franchise star in *The Mummy* reflects a need to reconceptualize the star system in the context of storyworld development.

Works Cited

Altman, Rick. 1999. *Film/Genre*. London: British Film Institute.

Block, Alex Ben, and Lucy Autrey Wilson, eds. 2010. *George Lucas's Blockbusting: A Decade-by-Decade Survey of Timeless Movies Including Untold Secrets of Their Financial Success*. New York: HarperCollins Publishers.

Box Office Mojo. 2019. "Franchise: 'Mission: Impossible.'" IMDbPro. Last updated April 7, 2019. www.boxofficemojo.com/franchise/fr3678899973/?ref_=bo_frs_table_24.

Brueggemann, Tom. 2018. "With 'Mission: Impossible—Fallout,' the Tom Cruise Franchise Could Be Bigger than James Bond in North America." Indiewire, July 26, 2018. www.indiewire.com/2018/07/mission-impossible-fallout-tom-cruise-franchise-james-bond-1201987208/.

Buchanan, Levi. 2006. "Mission: Impossible III." IGN, May 6, 2006. https://www.ign.com/articles/2006/05/05/mission-impossible-iii.

Cruise, Tom, and Christopher McQuarrie. 2015. "Commentary." *Mission: Impossible—Rogue Nation*. Paramount. DVD.

———. 2018. "Commentary." *Mission: Impossible—Fallout*. Paramount. DVD.

Dyer, Richard. 1998. *Stars*. London: British Film Institute.
Ellis, John. 1982. *Visible Fictions: Cinema, Television, Video*. New York: Routledge.
Gameloft. 2006. *Mission: Impossible 3*. Wireless Mobile.
Glu. 2015. *Mission: Impossible—Rogue Nation*. Apple iOS/Android.
Gomez, Jeff. 2018. "Transmedia Developer: Success at Multiplatform Narrative Requires a Journey to the Heart of Story." In *The Routledge Companion to Transmedia Studies*, edited by Matthew Freeman and Renira Rampazzo Gambarato, 207–13. New York: Routledge University Press.
Gomez, Jeff. 2019. "Talking Franchises: The World of Transmedia Development with Jeff Gomez." Interview with Tara Lomax. *Assembled Illusions*, March 1, 2019. assembledillusions.wordpress.com/2019/03/01/talking-franchises-jeff-gomez/.
Herbert, David. 2018. *Film Remakes and Franchises*. New Brunswick, NJ: Rutgers University Press.
Herman, David. 2009. *Basic Elements of Narrative*. Malden, MA: John Wiley.
Infogames. 1998. *Mission: Impossible*. Ocean Software. Nintendo 64 and PlayStation.
Jenkins, Henry. 2006. *Convergence Culture: Where Old and New Media Collide*. New York: New York University Press.
Johnson, Derek. 2008. "A Knight of the Realm vs. the Master of Magnetism: Sexuality, Stardom, and Character Branding." *Popular Communication* 6 (4): 214–30.
———. 2013. *Media Franchising: Creative License and Collaboration in the Culture Industries*. New York: New York University Press.
King, Geoff. 2003. "Stardom in the Willennium." In *Contemporary Hollywood Stardom*, edited by Thomas Austin and Martin Barker, 62–73. London: Arnold.
Konami. 1990. *Mission: Impossible*. Ultra Games. Nintendo Entertainment System.
Kussman, Dylan. 2015. "Torn Asunder." *Mission: Impossible—Rogue Nation*. Paramount Movies, December 15, 2015. issuu.com/paramountmovies/docs/mirn_torn_asunder/2.
Liptak, Andrew. 2017. "The Dark Universe Architects Have Abandoned the Project." *Verge*, November 8, 2017. www.theverge.com/2017/11/8/16610248/universal-dark-universe-monsterverse-alex-kurtzman-chris-morgan.
Lipton, Jacqueline D. 2010. *Internet Domain Names, Trademarks and Free Speech*. Cheltenham, UK: Edward Elgar, 2010.
Marshall, P. David. 1997. *Celebrity and Power: Fame in Contemporary Culture*. Minneapolis: University of Minnesota Press.

McClintock, Pamela, and Kim Masters. 2014. "Executive Roundtable." *Hollywood Reporter*, November 12, 2014. www.hollywoodreporter.com/news/executive-roundtable-6-studio-heads-748102.

McDonald, Paul. 2001. *The Star System: Hollywood's Production of Popular Identities*. London: Wallflower Press, 2001.

———. 2012. "Story and Show: The Basic Contradiction of Film Star Acting." *Theorizing Film Acting*, edited by Aaron Taylor, 169–184. New York: Routledge, 2012.

———. 2013. *Hollywood Stardom*. Malden, MA: John Wiley.

Official PlayStation. 2002. "Minority Report: Based on the Tom Cruise Movie . . . Minus Tom Cruise," *Official PlayStation Magazine* 63, December 1, 2002, 92.

Pallotta, Frank. 2018. "'Mission: Impossible': The Rare Blockbuster Franchise Sold on a Star, Not a Brand." CNN Money, July 28, 2018. money.cnn.com/2018/07/27/media/mission-impossible-fallout-box-office-analysis/index.html.

Paradigm Entertainment. 2003. *Mission: Impossible: Operation Surma*. Atari. Xbox, Playstation2, and GameCube.

Rebellion Developments. 2000. *Mission: Impossible*. Infogames. Game Boy Color.

Redmond, Sean. 2014. *Celebrity and the Media*. London: Palgrave Macmillan.

Ryan, Marie-Laure, and Jan-Noel Thon. 2014. "Introduction." In *Storyworlds Across Media: Towards a Media-Conscious Narratology*, edited by Marie-Laure Ryan and Jan-Noel Thon, 1–22. Lincoln: University of Nebraska Press.

Scolari, Carlos A. 2015. "Transmedia Storytelling: Brands, Narratives and Storyworlds." In *Handbook of Brand Semiotics*, edited by George Rossolatos, 151–69. Kassel, Germany: Kassel University Press.

Setoodeh, Ramin, and Brent Lang. 2017. "Inside 'The Mummy's' Troubles: Tom Cruise Had Excessive Control (EXCLUSIVE)." *Variety*, June 14, 2017. variety.com/2017/film/news/the-mummy-meltdown-tom-cruise-1202465742/.

Thompson, Kristen. 2007. *The Frodo Franchise: The Lord of the Rings and Modern Hollywood*. Berkeley: University of California Press.

Totilo, Stephen. 2006. "Video Games Are One 'Mission' Tom Cruise Won't Accept." MTV. April 26, 2006. www.mtv.com/news/1529606/video-games-are-one-mission-tom-cruise-wont-accept/.

Turner, Graeme. 2013. *Understanding Celebrity*. London: Sage.

Von Stackelberg, Peter. 2018. "Transmedia Franchising: Driving Factors, Storyworld Development, and Creative Process." In *The Routledge Companion to Transmedia Studies*, edited by Matthew Freeman and Renira Rampazzo Gambarato, 233–42. New York: Routledge University Press.

Watercutter, Angela. 2015. "New Mission: Impossible Comic Reveals How Ethan Went Rogue," Wired, December 17, 2015. www.wired.com/2015/12/mission-impossible-rogue-nation-comic/.

Wolfman, Marv. 1996. *Mission: Impossible #1*. Marvel Comics, May 1996.

World Intellectual Property Organization Arbitration and Mediation Center. 2006. *Tom Cruise v. Network Operations Center / Alberta Hot Rods*. Case No. D2006-0560. www.wipo.int/amc/en/domains/decisions/html/2006/d2006-0560.html.

Wyatt, Justin. 1994. *High Concept: Movies and Marketing in Hollywood*. Austin: University of Texas.

III
Aging Cruise

11

TOM CRUISE AS FATHER AND SON

Adam Daniel

In a career spanning almost forty years, it is unsurprising that Tom Cruise has played a variety of characters with distinct familial identities, chief among them sons and fathers. By examining the choice of roles he has undertaken, his oeuvre can arguably be read as both a reflection of his personal reckoning with his complicated familial dynamics and as a cultivated staging of performative sonhood and fatherhood. In this chapter, I will examine this fatherhood and sonhood in both a literal and figurative sense through an analysis of Cruise's various portrayals of characters who are sons or fathers and his own familial relationships as both a son and a father. In doing so, I will argue that Cruise's complex performances of masculinity, both in front of the camera and in the world outside of the cinema, have been shaped by what appear to be complicated relationships with his own father and daughter Suri.

It must first be acknowledged that in any examination of the personal life of a celebrity one must account for the constructed or restricted nature of the star's personal disclosures. Much of Cruise's biography, and the dynamics of his family relationships, is known to the public only through revelations that are crafted by either the media or the star himself for the purpose of constructing a celebrity persona, one that is necessarily distinct from the "real" Tom Cruise. Olivier Driessens (2015) makes a distinction between three facets of celebrity personas: the public persona, the constructed private persona, and the "real" private persona. The public persona is that which is known in the public sphere, which for actors includes their performances. "Real life," however, involves a bifurcation between the constructed private persona—in Driessens's words, "the 'private' persona as the celebrities and their entourage want us to see them, within the limits of manageability"—and the "real" private persona, that which is generally known only in private settings but that is occasionally revealed through breaches of privacy (through tabloid sources or paparazzi intrusion) (201–2). I readily recognize that much of the premise of this chapter is based on knowledge primarily of Cruise's public persona and his constructed private persona, but there are still valuable observations to be made.

The analysis offered in this chapter borrows from the "star as auteur" framework, and so it must also be acknowledged that all filmmaking is a collaborative enterprise and that the representations discussed are unquestionably also shaped by the work of the writers, directors, editors, cinematographers, and all others who have contributed to the scenes or films referenced. However, it also should be noted that Cruise's star power has a significant impact on the film itself, both in terms of his influence over these elements of production, and his customary role as the film's protagonist. Cruise has also acted as a producer on a substantial number of his films since *Mission: Impossible* (Brian De Palma, 1996), which has given him the capacity to craft both the narratives of these films and his role within them.

The concept of the star as auteur was arguably first advanced by Patrick McGilligan (1975) in his study of James Cagney. The model McGilligan advances is one in which "under certain circumstances, an actor may influence a film as much as a writer, director or producer; some actors are more influential than others; and there are certain rare few performers whose acting capabilities and screen personas are so powerful that they embody and define the very essence of their films" (99). While auteur theory has typically made reference to filmmakers whose works have defined aesthetic styles or consistent recurring themes, this term has been revised by modern theorists such as Richard Dyer and John Ellis to accommodate a broader range of influences in the production process. In this expanded understanding, which accounts for shifting methods of production and varying modes of reception, auteur theory does not limit itself to the work of the director, and instead attends to where the work of any individual has certain ideological consistencies. As Dyer (1979, 174) contends, "It is certainly possible to establish, as 'auteur theory' enjoins us, continuities, contradictions, and transformations either in the totality of a star's image or in discrete elements such as dress or performance style, roles, publicity, iconography."

To understand the forces at play that have molded both Tom Cruise the man and Tom Cruise the performer, it is important to begin with Cruise's father, Thomas Cruise Mapother III. Mapother III's career aspirations as an inventor and engineer led to a peripatetic way of life for his family. His son, born Thomas Cruise Mapother IV on July 3, 1962, experienced an ever-present sense of domestic instability in the first twelve years of his life, changing schools fifteen times within this period (Nicholson 2014, 7). This constant uprooting ended only when the elder Mapother abandoned the family in Ottawa, Canada, when his son was twelve years old. He refused to pay child support and as a result lost contact with his children until many years later (7).

The difficult relationship that resulted from this abandonment and its influence on Cruise's performances have been previously investigated; however, less scholarly attention has been paid to Cruise's own fatherhood of three children and how this parental role may have shaped the dynamics of his filmography (Morton 2008; Nicholson 2014). Cruise has been married three times: first to Mimi Rogers in 1976 (divorced in 1990), followed by Nicole Kidman in 1990 (divorced in 2001) and Katie Holmes in 2006 (divorced in 2012). Cruise and Kidman adopted two children during their marriage, Isabella in 1993 and Connor in 1995 (Cusack 2009, 400). Cruise and Holmes had a biological child, Suri, in April 2006. This chapter will analyze several of Cruise's performances in light of both his troubled relationship with his father and his complex, and in some aspects, difficult relationships with his children, both adopted and biological, in an attempt to chart the influence of each on the actor's choice of roles and the dynamics of his performances.

Cruise as Son

In the earliest stages of his career, Cruise's choice of roles could be interpreted as an expression of antipathy toward fathers. After the early success of *Risky Business* (Paul Brickman, 1983) and *All The Right Moves* (Michael Chapman, 1983), Cruise's newfound star status provided him with an opportunity to be more judicious about his choice of roles. It is notable that this greater creative freedom coincided with the choice of several film roles where the father–son dynamics were more reflective of the complexities of his own. In *Top Gun* (Tony Scott, 1986), for example, the talented but troubled fighter pilot Maverick, played by Cruise, is haunted by his father's premature death, while in *The Color of Money* (Martin Scorsese, 1986) Newman's pool hustler mentor discards any pretense of a paternalistic concern in his shift to an antagonist and competitor.

Amy Nicholson (2014, 15) contends that there was a notable shift as Cruise's career developed, to a more explicit integration of Cruise's fractured relationship with his father into the preproduction process: "Father issues haunt his films—additions he's had written into scripts. In Cruise's films, fathers disappear but leave a legacy that strangles their sons." The films she points to as examples of this shift include *Rain Man* (Barry Levinson, 1988), *Days of Thunder* (Tony Scott, 1990), *A Few Good Men* (Rob Reiner, 1992), *Magnolia* (Paul Thomas Anderson, 1999), and *Vanilla Sky* (Cameron Crowe, 2001). Within these films there is a clear through-line of filial angst and paternal estrangement. In *Vanilla Sky*, David Aames's cavalier behavior and careless treatment of others is established as partly a result of the premature death of his parents in a car crash when he was a child. Similarly, in *Rain Man*, Charlie Babbitt's falling out with his father prevented him from knowing of the existence of his autistic brother, Raymond (Dustin Hoffman), while in *A Few Good Men*, naval lawyer Daniel Kaffee lives in the shadow of his former attorney-general father.

In later films, the father figure is no longer merely absent but is also untrustworthy, deviously working against Cruise's protagonists. *The Firm* (Sydney Pollack, 1993), *Mission: Impossible*, and *Minority Report* (Steven Spielberg, 2002), for example, each present Cruise's protagonist with an ally who will later be revealed to be an enemy, despite their apparent guise of fatherly concern.

The trauma that Cruise admittedly suffered through the absence of his father and the frayed relationship that persisted into adulthood filters through in many of his performances, but it is in *Magnolia* that Cruise most brilliantly synthesizes his personal history with his onscreen character. Following a meeting with Cruise on the set of *Eyes Wide Shut* (Stanley Kubrick, 1999), Paul Thomas Anderson set about crafting a character specifically for the actor in his follow-up to *Boogie Nights* (1997). The character of Frank T. J. Mackey, a misogynistic self-help guru, shares little superficial resonances with Cruise; however parts of *Magnolia*'s narrative hew very close to Cruise's own emotional arc in relation to his father.

The *Magnolia* collaboration was shaped by a shared loss of a parent to cancer by both filmmaker and actor. Anderson's father, Ernie Anderson, had died in 1997, and while Anderson did not suffer the same distant relationship as Cruise, he understood how to translate the pathos and pain of losing a parent into an unforgettable character. However, the tension in their disparate histories was also evident in the differences between the original screenplay and Cruise's performance (Nicholson 2014, 113).

Cruise has spoken of how he didn't know what would happen when he arrived at the set to play the crucial scene in which his character confronts his estranged father: "In the script, it said 'He gets to the door and he breaks down.... And I said, 'Look, I don't feel that'" (120). Instead, Cruise plays the scene with a coiled tension, and yet his bravado gradually wanes with the understanding that he is saying goodbye to his father; in the scene's final moments, he appears to struggle between buckling with grief and striking with anger.

Anderson's screenplay establishes a partial reconciliation between Big Earl (Jason Robards) and Frank, with the father telling his son: "You are not what you think you are." The scene as it exists in the film features no such redemption and offers only a glimmer of resolution and peace in the conflict between father and son. More prominent than forgiveness is resentment and anger, as Frank tells the dying Earl: "I want you to know that I hate your fucking guts. You can just fucking die, you fuck. And I hope it hurts, I fucking hope it hurts." This rage dissipates somewhat as the scene progresses, until Frank finally acquiesces to his anguish, yet even in his final moments with his father, an anger emerges as he pleads: "Don't go away, you fucking asshole, don't go away, you fucking asshole."

At the time of release of *Magnolia*, Cruise was surprisingly candid about his last moments with his actual father, admitting that he had only seen him twice since his parent's divorce when he was twelve years old: once when Cruise was fifteen, to see a film at a drive-in, and for the final time in his early twenties, when he visited his dying father. Cruise revealed that his father had never seen any of his films. In Cruise's description of his last visit with his father, there is the suggestion that the meeting was more forgiving than that of Frank and Earl in *Magnolia*: "I spent some time with him ... we talked. I think he made so many mistakes that it ate him alive. Even when I went to see him and he didn't want to discuss what had occurred in the past. I said, whatever you want Dad. But I held his hand and I told him I loved him, that I was going to miss him. He said when he got out of the hospital we'd go have a steak and a beer and talk about it then. He died before we could do that" (qtd. in Nicholson 2014, 113). In an interview with *GQ* in

Cruise as Frank T. J. Mackey in *Magnolia*.

1992, Cruise also revealed some insight into how he dealt with the consequences of their strained relationship, describing his decision to forgive the elder Mapother: "When people can't forgive someone, my question is, 'What have you done in your life that you can't forgive this other person?' The things you've got to take responsibility for in your life, it makes forgiveness quite easy. And it also bought me a lot of understanding about him and the pain he was in" (Mansfield 1992).

Ultimately, it is Cruise's vulnerability that underpins the power of his performance as Mackey. While in early scenes in the film Frank struts and poses with hyperbolic machismo, it becomes evident that Mackey is a persona designed to shield his secret pain from others. Analyzing Cruise's performances in terms of masculinity, Donna Peberdy and Gaylyn Studlar each discuss what they describe as a "bipolar masculinity" operating in both Cruise's films and his celebrity persona. Studlar (2001, 174–76), in her study of how Cruise is often rendered the object of a "polymorphous gaze that cuts across the desiring possibilities of male and female, gay and straight spectatorship," contends that Cruise often straddles hard and soft modes of masculinity. She argues that "his films consistently move his characters from a performance of manliness into 'authentic' manliness," yet this authenticity is also a performance: "a construction, a masquerade" (176).

Peberdy (2010, 241) draws a link between Cruise's alternation between hypermasculinity and hypomasculinity in *Magnolia* to the offscreen enactment of his persona in his infamous television appearances of the mid-2000s. She makes specific note of the excessiveness and theatricality of Cruise's performance as Frank and contends that the role encapsulates the "bipolar nature of masculinity," replicating the reverberations between "wild man" and "wimp" that underpin the norms of modern masculinity. However, she also notes that "movement too far in either direction can undermine [the norm]" (231). It is apt to note that it is within a performance that most closely resembles Cruise's autobiographical relationship with his father that these reverberations between "wild man" and "wimp" emerge so prominently.

Cruise and Representations of Fatherhood

Cruise's performance in *Magnolia*, and to a lesser extent his role in *Vanilla Sky*, marks a turning point in the actor's choice of roles. After 2001, Cruise began to choose characters who are less overtly sons in a father–son dynamic, and he began to take on roles where fatherhood was central to the protagonist. In 2002's *Minority Report*, the actor's first collaboration with Steven Spielberg, Cruise's John Anderton is an officer in the Precrime department, a special operations unit that uses the psychic abilities of three "precogs" to predict and prevent crimes before they occur. The character of Anderton is burdened with a personal trauma that is not entirely necessary to the plot: the disappearance of his six-year-old son from a public swimming pool. While this loss underpins Anderton's impassioned commitment to his job, its main purpose within the narrative is to establish conflict between Anderton and his estranged wife, Lara (Kathryn Morris), which is resolved at the film's conclusion with the revelation that they are reconciled and Lara is pregnant with another child.

In 2005, at forty-three years of age, Cruise was almost the same age his father had been when he left the family. He reunited with Spielberg to remake *War of the Worlds* (2005), an alien invasion story that centers around a flawed dad attempting to transport his children to safety. The role of the flawed father was a deliberate construction by Cruise, in collaboration with Spielberg and screenwriter David Koepp. In discussing their approach to the film, Koepp said, "Tom takes being a dad very seriously. So do I. So does Steven." They each decided, however, to make a film that is "about the times we failed hopelessly as a parent." Koepp describes how they wanted to write a movie that was explicitly "about a bad father, who's bitter, whose life had not gone where he wanted" (qtd. in Nicholson 2014, 131). To develop the character of Ray Ferrier, Koepp took aspects of Cruise's previous performances and refashioned them as flaws so that in *War of the Worlds* Cruise's Ray Ferrier has a cockiness that is narcissistic rather than charming and uses humor as a defense mechanism for his inability to connect with his children.

The struggle to connect between father and son is demonstrated in an early scene where they engage in an awkward game of catch. Ray's son, Robbie (Justin Chatwin), establishes the dynamics of their relationship when he walks into the backyard and puts on a Boston Red Sox cap, a clear act of oppositional defiance to his father, who sports a New York Yankees cap, the Red Sox hated rivals. "Is that how it's going to be?" asks Ray. As father and son throw the baseball back and forth, the tension escalates. In a conversation about homework, Ray nags his son: "Just do your report. I don't send you to school so you can flunk out." Robbie's reply is a well-placed jab at Ray's insufficiencies as a father: "You don't pay for it. Tim does." This is a reference to Robbie's stepfather, a man whose domestic competence is placed as counterpoint to Ray's inadequacies in an earlier scene. Ray aggressively rockets the ball back at Robbie, stinging his hand. Father and son bicker for a few moments more, and then Robbie refuses to catch a thrown ball, letting it smash through the rear window of his father's house. As Robbie stalks away, Ray's deflated body is framed through the smashed glass, the broken window a symbol of their shattered domestic relations. Nicholson notes that this baseball scene was a deliberate "echo" of a real moment Cruise shared with his father after he announced that he was leaving the family (15).

There are moments within the film where the limits of flawed fatherhood are examined. As Nicholson notes, "Ray doesn't fight, he hides.... The best he can do is the bare minimum: keep his children alive." To do so, he must go so far as to kill another survivor, Harlan (Tim Robbins), who is jeopardizing their safety by drawing attention to their hiding space. Nicholson notes that although the death largely takes place offscreen, it is still "shocking," and it is likely that Ray's relationship with his daughter, Rachel (Dakota Fanning), will forever be haunted by her witnessing of this "monstrous act" (140).

Flawed fatherhood is, however, largely viewed through a sympathetic lens that the narrative replicates. Hannah Hamad (2011, 250) agrees, arguing that *War of the Worlds* is one of many films that "recuperate failing fatherhood through enactment of paternal protectiveness in extreme circumstances, whereupon the reconstitution of a normative familial unit is not the point of the protagonist's narrative journey, so much as the revalidation of his initially derogated fatherhood." In her postfeminist reading of the film as one of many recurrent depictions of "extreme parenting" by father figures, Hamad contends that the redemption of deficient fathers serves to deflect feminist critiques of masculinity; the fathers of these films compensate for their domestic failings by successfully fulfilling the role of father-protector and demonstrating growth in terms of parenting proficiency and maturity.

Noting that narratives focused on male parenting have become a "prominent feature" of contemporary cinema, Yvonne Tasker (2008, 176) examines how representations of fatherhood often pivot around the insufficiencies described above. Tasker contends that "male parents are frequently presented as *failing* their children" (180) but that in overcoming these insufficiencies, both male parents and their children are transformed. We can return here to the conclusion of *War of the Worlds*, where Ray reunites his daughter with her mother and stepfather. Robbie is revealed to have survived the alien attack, and father and son embrace for the first time in the film. Hamad identifies that this is not only a recuperation of their relationship but also Ferrier's "paternal self-worth" (248). *War of the Worlds* marks the most recent time in which Cruise probed the notion of paternal amour propre with this level of intensity.

Staging Fatherhood

For all the talk of Cruise's interest in telling stories of fatherhood at the time of *War of the Worlds*, it is noticeable that his subsequent choice of films reflects an ambivalence to the notion. The roots of this ambivalence can perhaps be traced back as far as his performance as the eponymous Jerry Maguire. Nicholson (2014) notes that in *Jerry Maguire* (Cameron Crowe, 1996), Cruise's Maguire appears to love his erstwhile love interest Dorothy's son, Ray, more than he loves Dorothy herself. However, she also argues that even that intimacy is strained and awkward. In the scenes between Ray and Jerry, she contends that "Cruise subtly hints that he's not ready to accept even a child's guileless adoration. He steamrolls over him without making eye contact when the boy tries to talk about his dead father, and when the boy first moves in to give him a kiss, Maguire ever so slightly recoils" (93). This inability to perform a simple gesture of intimacy between a "father" and a "son" reemerges in this latter period of Cruise's career through what appears to be a concerted effort to play characters who are not burdened by familial bonds.

Theorizing Cruise's parental roles benefits from an examination of Cruise's own complicated fatherhood. Hamad (2010) argues that in the contemporary postfeminist era, there have been concerted attempts to reframe celebrity fatherhood in Hollywood as having undergone an evolution. In her analysis, she points to the normalization in tabloids of stories in which "divorced dads don't disappear," "kids now don't hurt sex appeal," and "staying at home with the kids is cool" (Bradley Jacobs cited in Hamad 2010, 152). Importantly, she identifies that the "surface appearance of increased gender egalitarianism in parenting and childcare" is countered by a "disingenuously depoliticized shift in the cultural logic of gender roles and parenthood" (153). In Hamad's exploration of "Hollywood dads," Cruise, Russell Crowe, Eddie Murphy, and Mel Gibson are each posited as representative of the failure to achieve the expectations appropriate to the public performance of postfeminist masculinity through their various transgressions, public and private (159). In Hamad's analysis, their carefully cultivated paternal personas were excavated by the damning revelations of their various scandals. Cruise was an ideal example. In the mid-2000s, much of the extra-filmic discourse around Cruise focused on his fatherhood of his adopted children, Isabella and Connor and, later, after his marriage to Holmes, his fatherhood of Suri. Hamad cites a *Daily Telegraph* promotional interview from 2003 in which Cruise is reported as expressing that his children are "the main priority in his life. . . . 'My schedule goes around my kids' he says simply" (John Hisock cited in Hamad 2010, 161).

However, in the following years, Cruise became embroiled in several public relations debacles, culminating in the annus horribilis for Cruise's public image in 2005, a year that included his awkward interview on *Today* with Matt Lauer, his condescending criticisms of Brooke Shields's use of medication for postpartum depression, and of course the infamous couch dance on *The Oprah Winfrey Show*. Each of these no doubt contributed to what could be seen as the nadir of Cruise's career, as Paramount Pictures parted ways with his Cruise/Wagner production company after a fourteen-year relationship.

The birth of Cruise's daughter, Suri, in 2006 exacerbated the tensions around her father's public image; widespread rumors surfaced that Cruise, under the influence of the Church of Scientology, had placed bizarre conditions on Katie Holmes during the pregnancy and delivery of the baby, such as banning epidurals, medication, and medical testing on the newborn infant and demanding a calm and silent delivery (Cusack 2009, 401; see also Di Palma 2018). While his divorce from Kidman had been publicly handled to portray him as a hands-on sensitive, involved parent, this persona quickly unraveled under the burden of the intense media scrutiny around his relationship to Holmes and their new child. Hamad (2010, 162) contends that, at this time, the discursive function of fatherhood in terms of the cultural logic of Cruise's persona "shifted away from stability and maturity and towards associations characterized instead by power, control and a paternalistic comportment long since outmoded by conceptualizations of ideal fatherhood [in a postfeminist sense]." In a *Vanity Fair* cover story in 2006, Cruise attempted to recover some lost ground; the article goes to great lengths to portray the domestic bliss of Cruise and Holmes's life as new parents, including descriptions of Isabella and Connor's contentment with their roles as siblings to Suri. Cruise is even quoted as saying that "having children is a new beginning" (Sarkin 2006).

Cruise and Holmes' marriage lasted less than six years, and rumors proliferated that it was the role of Scientology in the life of their daughter, Suri, that was the final provocation leading to their divorce in 2012. Zimmerman (2019), for example, reported that Holmes was worried that Cruise was going to send their daughter to Sea Org, an elite training division of the Church, and later stated that Holmes had stipulated in the divorce settlement that Suri would have no ongoing relationship with the Church of Scientology. In the years since the divorce, tabloid news sources have reported an estrangement between Cruise and his daughter, with one magazine alleging Cruise hadn't seen his daughter in person for almost four years. While Cruise reportedly has strong relationships with Isabella and Connor due to their continued membership of the church, there are many claims that he has little to no presence in his younger daughter's life, although both Cruise and Holmes have both been guarded when asked about the situation.

Given that Hamad's (2013, 109) central contention in her analysis of fatherhood in contemporary cinema is that early twenty-first-century Hollywood has produced a proliferation of films that "discursively prioritize fatherhood" in terms of representation, narrative, characterization, and marketing in order to "perpetuate extant discourses of fatherhood," it is perhaps unusual that Cruise's choice of roles of in the last ten years seems to contradict this trend. While Hamad's observations are astute, it is interesting to compare Cruise's choice of roles to an actor of similar age and status, such as Brad Pitt. In the last ten years, Pitt, who is a year younger than Cruise, has acted in several films in which fatherhood has been central to the narrative (e.g., *Moneyball* [Bennett Miller, 2011], *The Tree of Life* [Terrence Malick, 2011], and *World War Z* [Marc Forster, 2013]) while Cruise appears to be more interested in film narratives where children play a peripheral role at best.

Conclusion

Examining the roles Cruise has taken instead this decade reveals two common patterns: that despite being in his fifties, Cruise is defiantly crafting himself back into an action star, and that, partly due to this pursuit, his characters are more stoic and less vulnerable. Michael DeAngelis (2010, 42–43) identifies this lack of vulnerability as a "very familiar component of Cruise's star persona," a quality that can lead to Cruise appearing "underdeveloped" and "static." Films such as *Knight and Day* (James Mangold, 2010), *Edge of Tomorrow* (Doug Liman, 2014), and *Jack Reacher* (Christopher McQuarrie, 2012), and *Jack Reacher: Never Go Back* (Edward Zwick, 2016) allow Cruise to demonstrate his heroism and physical prowess but leave little space for the complexities of grounded emotional drama.

A determination to steer clear of the vulnerability presented by familial ties can be evidenced in Cruise's continued development of the *Mission: Impossible* franchise (1996–2018). As a producer of the series, Cruise has played a pivotal role in shaping the central character, Ethan Hunt, and his familial dynamics. In *Mission: Impossible III* (J. J. Abrams, 2006), viewers were introduced to newly retired Hunt's fiancée Julia Meade (Michelle Monaghan). In the film, Julia is abducted by arms dealer Owen Davian (Philip Seymour Hoffman) and used to blackmail Hunt into obtaining the mysterious and illicit "rabbit's foot" for Davian. The film concludes with Hunt and Meade reunited and the couple leaving on their honeymoon. In the next film in the series, *Mission: Impossible—Ghost Protocol* (Brad Bird, 2011), it is discussed that in the interstice between the two films Julia had been murdered by a hit squad; however, this is later revealed to be false—Hunt only fabricated her murder in order to set her up with a new life and new identity, separate from him. *Ghost Protocol* concludes with

Ethan surveying Julia in her new life: he and Julia make eye contact with each other at a distance before Hunt heads out on his next mission. She returns in the latest installment, *Mission: Impossible—Fallout* (Christopher McQuarrie, 2018), again as a villain's target, but also to formally acknowledge the end of their relationship. This unconventional character arc arguably reveals Cruise's antipathy toward investing these films with even the veneer of domesticity.

More recently, *American Made* (Doug Liman, 2017) provides another example of Cruise choosing roles that represent fatherhood in overtly simplistic dimensions. The film tells the story of Barry Seal, a former TWA pilot who allegedly flew missions for the CIA and smuggled drugs for the Medellín cartel in the 1980s. Seal is married and over the course of the film has three children with his wife, Lucy (Sarah Wright), whom he initially tries to shield from knowledge of his ill-gotten gains. As Seal's criminal exploits expand, the family become inordinately wealthy, and the family home is shown to transform from dilapidated wreck to a gaudy mansion. The effects of this transformation are echoed in Seal's relationship with his onscreen children, whom he spoils with lavish purchases but with whom he seems to have no discernible relationship outside of the signifiers of fatherhood. Although the film does not present itself as anything but a heavily fictionalized account of a true crime story, it is notable as an example of how Cruise reconciles the portrayal of paternalistic characters with his apparent disinterest in narratives of fatherhood by outwardly signifying the importance of fatherhood while steering clear of any level of emotional depth or recognizable pathos.

Through this chapter's exploration of the evolution of filial and paternalistic roles in Cruise's filmography, it becomes evident that Cruise's initial urges to reckon with his own familial dynamics through his choice of roles has, over the course of his career, morphed into either a cultivated staging of fatherhood with little to no exploration of its full dimensions or the complete absence of children within his films. Much of this is no doubt effected by Cruise's attempted reinvention as an action star and his apparent lack of interest in dramatic roles that are grounded in real life, yet it could also be argued that the complex performance of masculinity by Cruise, both in real life and in front of the camera, has been undoubtedly influenced and shaped by the complexities of his truncated relationship with his own father and daughter.

Works Cited

Cusack, Carole M. 2009. "Celebrity, the Popular Media and Scientology: Making the Familiar Unfamiliar." In *Scientology*, edited by James R. Lewis, 389–410. Oxford: Oxford University Press.

DeAngelis, Michael. 2010. "Tom Cruise, the Couch Incident, and the limits of public elation." *The Velvet Light Trap* 65 (1): 42–43.

Di Palma, Tania. 2018. "15 Strict Scientology Pregnancy Rules Tom Cruise Made Katie Holmes Follow." The Richest, June 2, 2018. www.therichest.com/lifestyles/15-pregnancy-rules-tom-cruise-made-katie-holmes-follow/.

Driessens, Olivier. 2015. "Expanding Celebrity Studies' Research Agenda: Theoretical Opportunities and Methodological Challenges in Interviewing Celebrities." *Celebrity Studies* 6 (2): 192–205.

Dyer, Richard. 1979. *Stars*. London: British Film Institute, 1979.

Hamad, Hannah. 2010. "'Hollywood's Hot Dads': Tabloid, Reality and Scandal Discourses of Celebrity Post-feminist Fatherhood." *Celebrity Studies* 1 (2): 151–69.

———. 2011. "Extreme Parenting: Recuperating Fatherhood in Steven Spielberg's *War of the Worlds*." In *Feminism at the Movies: Understanding Gender in Contemporary Popular Cinema*, edited by Hillary Radner and Rebecca Stringer, 241–53. London: Routledge.

———. 2013. "Hollywood Fatherhood: Paternal Postfeminism in Contemporary Popular Cinema." In *Postfeminism and Contemporary Hollywood Cinema*, edited by Joel Gwynne and Nadine Muller, 99–115. London: Palgrave Macmillan.

Mansfield, Stephanie. 1992. "Tom Cruise from the Neck Up." *GQ*, December 1992.

McGilligan, Patrick. 1975. *Cagney, the Actor as Auteur*. South Brunswick, NJ: A. S. Barnes.

Morton, Andrew. 2008. *Tom Cruise: An Unauthorized Biography*. London: St. Martin's Press.

Nicholson, Amy. 2014. *Tom Cruise: Anatomy of an Actor*. London: Phaidon.

Peberdy, Donna. 2010. "From Wimps to Wild Men: Bipolar Masculinity and the Paradoxical Performances of Tom Cruise." *Men and Masculinities* 13 (2): 231–54.

Sarkin, Jane. 2006. "Someone Wanted to See Me?" *Vanity Fair*, October 2006. archive.vanityfair.com/article/2006/10/someone-wanted-to-see-me.

Studlar, Gaylyn. 2001. "Cruise-ing into the Millennium: Performative Masculinity Stardom, and the All-American Boy's Body." In *Ladies and Gentlemen, Boys and Girls: Gender in Film at the End of the Twentieth Century*, edited by Murray Pomerance, 171–83. Albany: State University of New York Press.

Tasker, Yvonne. 2008. "Practically Perfect People: Postfeminism, Masculinity and Male Parenting in Contemporary Cinema." In *A Family Affair: Cinema Calls Home*, edited by Murray Pomerance, 175–88. London: Wallflower.

Zimmerman, Amy. 2017. "Tom Cruise's Strange Hold over Katie Holmes: From Scientology Minders to the 'Dating Ban.'" Daily Beast, August 8, 2017. www.thedailybeast.com/katie-holmes-long-road-to-freedom-from-tom-cruise?ref=scroll.

12

"HOW AM I SUPPOSED TO DO THIS?"

The Impossibility of Tom Cruise's Masculine Performance in the Face of His Aging Star Body

Ruth O'Donnell

Tom Cruise remains one of the major stars of the late twentieth and early twenty-first century, both in terms of box office success and industrial power. Now enjoying his fourth decade of stardom, his star persona remains bound up with notions of boyish youthfulness and energy. As Lisa Purse (2017) has noted in her writing on the star, the popular press has commented at length on Cruise's apparent ability to withstand the effects of aging, well into his forties, a narrative that has been by turns pejorative and admiring (e.g., *Daily Mail* Reporter 2010). Much of this scrutiny has been in relation to Cruise's continuing commitment to doing his own stunts, a choice that shores up a narrative of authenticity around his stardom but is now questioned in terms of its age appropriateness for the star. Purse (2017) states that "the flexible relationship that Tom Cruise seems to have to the biological reality of his own aging frequently generates incredulity, derision or anxious attempts to recognize the aging-as-decline narrative onto his body" (175). While Purse pursues a line of inquiry regarding the aging bodies of Hollywood's action stars, I argue that this anxiety in the case of Cruise stems less from his aging per se than from the growing disconnect between his chronological age and his star persona, which is predicated on notions of boyishness and his positioning as a figural son (symbolized at the familial or social level). If the Cruise star image suffers from arrested development, his aging body can only draw attention to this lack: while he may grow older, he will never ascend to the role of patriarch.

The *Mission: Impossible* series, in which Cruise plays IMF (Impossible Mission Force) agent Ethan Hunt, provides a useful case study for charting these challenges to the star persona as the actor ages. His star image is closely aligned with the franchise, which has shaped and showcased persona traits already in circulation in Cruise's other films. Based on the 1960s US TV program, it is a series that has spanned over twenty years, from the first movie's release in 1996 to the most recent, *Mission: Impossible—Fallout* (Christopher McQuarrie), in 2018. Two more episodes were in preproduction at the time of writing. Over time, the films have had to work increasingly hard to reproduce and sustain traits central to Cruise's star persona in the face of his aging. His positioning vis-à-vis Oedipal threat means that the later films must work to disavow the star's real age, instead choosing to represent him in the narrative as a younger man. I shall explore to what extent the narrative "labor" of the franchise has been successful in its re/iteration of Cruise as the figural son, as well as its necessary limitations.

Tom Cruise's Boyish Persona

Tom Cruise came to stardom in the mid-1980s with the film *Top Gun* (Tony Scott, 1986). His star image successfully undertook the ideological work described by Richard Dyer ([1979] 1998, 31) in relation to film stars to apparently resolve the social contradictions of the society that produced them, such as Marilyn Monroe's negotiation of changing sexual mores in 1950s America. Cruise's persona embodies certain paradoxes of gender inscription that appear to be resolved in his film roles, yet give voice to underlying contemporary Western anxieties about what it is to be a man.

The nascent Cruise star image, typified by *Top Gun*, is one predicated on visual spectacle in which the star is rendered, according to Gaylyn Studlar (2001, 171), as "the object of a polymorphous gaze that cuts across the desiring possibilities of male and female, gay and straight spectatorship." This presentation of the star body as erotic object is established in Cruise's earlier films, such as *Risky Business* (Paul Brickman, 1983), *Top Gun*, and *Cocktail* (Roger Donaldson, 1988), which create set pieces of sexualized spectacle, such as the iconic performance of the young Cruise sliding into the suburban house hallway wearing shirt, underpants, and socks in *Risky*

Business. Equally famous are the beach volleyball and locker room scenes in *Top Gun*, which Stella Bruzzi (2013, 11) notes for their "spectacular superfluidity" with little action "bar posturing and men putting themselves on display." The elaborate stunts that characterize the *Mission: Impossible* series mark a shift in the persona, with screen representations moving away from the positioning of the Cruise body as an overt sexual object. Nonetheless, the star remains—alone—in this performative space, with stunt making replacing erotic spectacle as the explicit motivation for looking at the male star body.

Theatricality underpins the Cruise star image, both in terms of the figurative placement of the star—often on stage or a similarly coded space—and a sense of excessive performance. As Studlar (2001, 175) notes, "The male body in performative mode draws attention to the construction of masculinity as a masquerade that attempts to create a set of readable signs signifying 'manliness' and to display these signs as a coherent subjectivity." This is the key to the Cruise persona: his performances, while projecting an idealized version of masculinity, in their embodiment draw attention to the performer's lack. If his star image is based on the idea of "marked" performances of manhood, within the citation is the potential for masculine failure. Furthermore, within his films, the Cruise character's demonstrations of masculinity are for an audience of men, with him craving acceptance from and admission into their circle. Writing on the subject of male display, Michael Kimmel (2005, 33) suggests: "We test ourselves, perform heroic feats, take enormous risks, all because we want other men to grant us our manhood. Masculinity as a homosocial enactment is fraught with danger, with the risk of failure, and with intense competition."

Cruise's citations of masculine aptitude speak to psychodynamic preoccupations, for in their demonstration for an adult male audience, they re-create the boy's original performance for the benefit of his father. For he is "the first man who evaluates the boy's masculine performance, the first pair of eyes before whom he tries to prove himself. Those eyes will follow him for the rest of his life" (34). Role-play is central to Cruise's films, as though he is trying on the guise of being a grown man but falls short in his performance. The Cruise character is afraid of being exposed and humiliated as a fraud. The star's films are replete with depictions of male competition, surveillance, and evaluation by older men as well as a fear of unmasking. Films such as *Vanilla Sky* (Cameron Crowe, 2001) and *Eyes Wide Shut* (Stanley

Kubrick, 1999), as well as the *Mission: Impossible* series, employ literal masks to explore this preoccupation.

In choosing to *play* at being a man, the Cruise character can avoid the father's ire, as he does not pose any real challenge to the patriarch as a rival. This is a compromise formation of sorts. He challenges authority, much as a teenager might, but never overthrows it. He is active, though rarely aggressive. (The action set pieces of his films have, however, become more violent in recent years.) Aggression is often manifested in impulsive explosions of anger. Physical activity is not productive as much as childish: running, jumping, climbing, are all activities that feature in the *Mission: Impossible* series. Various commentators have noted Cruise's propensity for running in his films. A number of online video montages of the star's running highlights exist, with titles such as "Every Tom Cruise Run. Ever" (Burger Fiction 2016). Running symbolizes the Cruise character's preferred response to the threat of the figural father, which is to escape. In *Mission: Impossible* (Brian De Palma, 1996), following a sequence in which his team has been killed on a mission in Prague, Hunt meets with IMF director Kittridge (Henry Czerny) to debrief. Sitting together in a restaurant, Kittridge accuses him of being an IMF mole and explains that the whole mission, which resulted in these deaths, was nothing but a "mole hunt." A series of low and angled close-ups show the instability of Hunt's state as he grows enraged. Incapable of confronting Kittridge directly, and threatened with capture, Hunt chooses to run. He sets off an explosive, destroying the restaurant's huge fish tank, jumping through the shattering glass of the restaurant front, and fleeing into the night. If the Cruise persona's modus operandi is to retreat from paternal threat rather than confront it, then it follows that he is incapable of protecting others. Indeed, he appears to be the one in need of protection, which is often offered by his female protagonist. In his films, women are typically positioned as mother figures, more dominant than the Cruise character, more capable (often taller), who are more likely to rescue him from danger than be rescued. In his inability to defend women—a pattern that is repeated throughout the *Mission: Impossible* series—the character "fails" in his performance of manhood. (For a fuller analysis of Cruise's performances of masculinity, see O'Donnell 2015.)

The central traits of Cruise's persona that address and attempt to ameliorate the attendant anxieties of this immature masculinity find expression in the first *Mission: Impossible* film, with subsequent invocations and repositioning by later films in the franchise. These elements are an Oedipal struggle between the Cruise character and a punishing father figure; exhibitionist stunts, which indicate his positioning as object of a scrutinizing male gaze; a childish excess of purposeless activity (i.e., play); role-playing of an adult masculinity—and the gap between that performance and a more childish sense of self; the centrality of an equally immature group of male peers, to whom he demonstrates a homoeroticized commitment; and female protagonists positioned as "archetypal" mothers, who demonstrate power over the Cruise character, often protecting him from harm, yet whom he fails to protect from suffering in turn. As Cruise the actor ages, each of these traits becomes more difficult to justify. The films' narratives and their supporting mise-en-scène present different solutions to this problem.

Oedipal Conflict

Mission: Impossible was released in 1996, when its star was thirty-four. Tom Cruise plays IMF agent Ethan Hunt, who is framed by his team leader Jim Phelps (Jon Voight) for the murder of his IMF peers while on a covert operation. Voight's casting as the vengeful patriarch is noteworthy, given his early role as a hustler in *Midnight Cowboy* (John Schlesinger, 1969), a film that explores issues of extra-normative sexuality and male sexual objectification, traits closely associated with the Cruise star image. Voight was only fifty-eight when he starred in *Mission: Impossible*, and Cruise was fifty-six at the time of *Mission: Impossible—Fallout*, yet their visual coding, through costume and manner, as father and son are quite distinct. In *Mission: Impossible* Voight's appearance references the original TV series of the 1960s: he sports Brylcreemed hair, heavy glasses, a suit, and beige Macintosh coat. The thirty-something Cruise wears jeans, a leather jacket, and boots (when not donning quasi-military wardrobe to undertake an operation), a look that changes little in the next twenty years of the franchise.

Mission: Impossible establishes its preoccupation with Oedipal concerns early in the narrative: Jim Phelps is the figural father to a group of young IMF agents, which includes his much younger wife, Claire (Emmanuelle Béart), and protégé, Hunt. Hunt's desire for his boss's wife is established in the opening scene. The film opens with the title "KIEV" before revealing a technician perched in front of a surveillance monitor. The man, IMF agent Jack (Emilio Estevez), monitors an interaction in a hotel room. A woman (who is later revealed as IMF operative Claire) lies draped on a bed, wearing a dress, stockings, and suspender belt, her upper body covered in blood. She is both the object, and the victim of, the male gaze. A partially dressed man, in a visible panic, opens the door to an older, mustached figure (whom we later discover is Ethan Hunt in disguise), who quickly reads the situation. He approaches the girl on the bed, opening her eyelids to check for signs of life. Claire has been drugged to "play dead," using her body as leverage to extract a name from the stooge. The hotel room, where she lies dead, is in reality a set. Jack and the rest of the team are set up only feet away from this staged drama. Finally uttering the name of the contact, the target is drugged and falls unconscious. Hunt peels off his mask—a key motif of the *Mission: Impossible* films—and rushes over to Claire's side to rouse her, his hand lingering on her cheek as she awakens. This opening scene sets out several of *Mission: Impossible*'s narrative tropes, employing traits that underpin Cruise's star persona. The scenario is a performance, complete with stage set, actors, and disguises. Hunt performs an assertive masculinity: he hits the "fall guy" in a staged moment of dominance, which Jack, in observing the interaction, shows his approval of by laughing. But Hunt is quickly separated from this show of dominance by the peeling off of the mask, thus separating his self from the performance.

Jack is the stand-in for the all-seeing father: Jim Phelps. Phelps is positioned behind a computer monitor at several key points in the film. An early scene opens with him on a flight, playing a video he has been handed by an air stewardess. The opening credits flash up "for Jim Phelps' eyes only"—an allusion to his control of the male gaze and possession of the mother. Later on, when the IMF agents are in situ performing a mission in Prague to recover one-half of the "NOC list" (the CIA "nonofficial" cover list of US operatives), it is Phelps who watches each of their video feeds at the "Crow's nest" base and gives instructions to them via their earpieces, sending them to their deaths. The most visceral of these murders is that of Jack, who as the IT specialist has his station sitting on the top of a lift cubicle. When his computer instructions are overridden by Phelps and the lift hurtles toward the top of the lift shaft, a metal pylon snaps out just in time to impale Jack through the eye, in a gory reenactment of Oedipal aggression.

Jim Phelps is the first in a succession of punishing patriarchs that Hunt is pitted against in the *Mission: Impossible* series, and whom he must struggle against despite terrible odds. As the star Cruise ages, the antagonists Hunt faces become progressively younger relative to our hero, yet the overarching father–son dynamic is preserved. This constellation is shored up by the presence of a paternal figure in the role of IMF commander, who is often equally punishing in his actions toward Hunt as the villain. Anthony Hopkins plays Mission Commander Swanbeck in *Mission: Impossible II* (John Woo, 2000), juxtaposed with the young antagonist Sean Ambrose (Dougray Scott). Laurence Fishburne is cast as IMF head Theodore Brassel in *Mission: Impossible III* (J. J. Abrams, 2006), who cuts an imposing figure, though he and Cruise are close to the same age. The film's villain, Owen Davian, an arms dealer, is played by Philip Seymour Hoffman, three years younger than Cruise, but also coded to appear older, or more "adult," than the youthful Hunt.

The fourth film in the franchise, *Mission: Impossible—Ghost Protocol* (Brad Bird, 2011), presents a rare benign paternal figure in the form of IMF secretary, played by Tom Wilkinson. He is assassinated early in the film and thus can provide no protective fatherly function for the figural son, Hunt. Hunt's antagonist in this film, Kurt Hendricks (Michael Nyqvist), a Russian nuclear strategist gone rogue, is also peers in age with Hunt. In *Mission: Impossible—Rogue Nation* (Christopher McQuarrie, 2015), Alex Baldwin plays CIA director Alan Hunley. Like Fishburne, Baldwin is similar in age to Tom Cruise but also coded as a paternal figure, and a punitive one at that. Hunley persuades a US Senate committee to disband the IMF, forcing Hunt and his team to pursue "the Syndicate," an international terrorist consortium, without the assistance or protection of the US government. Hunley, however, is eventually persuaded of Hunt's cause and becomes secretary of the IMF when the unit is reinstated at the film's close. In *Mission: Impossible—Fallout*, the latest film in the franchise, Hunley is killed by CIA assassin August Walker (Henry Cavill). We later learn that Walker is working for antagonist Solomon Lane (Sean Harris), former MI6 agent and leader of "the Apostles," a terrorist group that has formed from the ashes of the Syndicate. Here, for the first time in the series, the mission commander is a woman, Erica Sloane, played by Angela Bassett.

The most sinister of the IMF chiefs is Commander Swanbeck, played by Anthony Hopkins, who appears in *Mission: Impossible II*. In the film, Hunt is tasked to thwart the designs of Sean Ambrose, a rogue agent who has stolen the deadly chimera virus developed by Biocyte Pharmaceuticals, which he threatens to unleash on the public unless his financial demands are met. Ambrose is both mission target and sexual rival for Nyah (Thandie Newton). Hunt, having recently entered into an affair with her, is forced to persuade her to resume sexual relations with Ambrose. Yet it is Mission Commander Swanbeck who harnesses the terrifying power of the patriarch, not Ambrose. Swanbeck comes across as malevolent during their meeting in what appears to be a wine cellar in Seville. The dark mise-en-scène recalls Hopkins's role as Hannibal Lector in *The Silence of the Lambs* (Jonathan Demme, 1991). This air of threat is reinforced by his sharing of disturbing black-and-white photos of a pilot's corpse with Hunt, which Swanbeck quips was "stuffed into a suitcase" by Ambrose. It serves as an indication of the danger Nyah will be put in by returning to Ambrose—and which Hunt is powerless to protect her from.

In *Mission: Impossible III*, Hunt is pitted against arms dealer Owen Davian, who is coded in such a manner—the heaviness of the actor's frame, the waxen skin, his dress—as to appear older than the hero. Davian's heavy-set gait and slow walk suggest he is less physically able than the nimble Hunt, but when physically confronted by Davian in a medical surgery near the close of the film, Hunt is powerless to defend himself: Davian has implanted an explosive pellet in the hero's brain, which causes him disabling pain, allowing Davian to physically overcome him. (Hunt is finally able to defeat Davian by pushing him outside, into the path of an oncoming bus.) This physical dominance is also shored up by Davian's self-possession and menace relative to Hunt's panic and uncertainty.

Solomon Lane, the villain of the latter two films, *Mission: Impossible—Rogue Nation* and *Mission: Impossible—Fallout*, is also visually inscripted to appear older than Hunt. In *Rogue Nation*, Lane wears shortly cropped silver hair and heavy rimmed glasses, with a uniform of black turtleneck and tailored coat. He is visually matched to MI6 handler Atlee (Simon McBurney), who also sports silver hair and tortoiseshell glasses. Although ostensibly on the right side as an MI6 operative, Atlee coerces his agent, Isla Faust (Rebecca Ferguson), into returning to the field where she is working under cover with Lane, in spite of her having already fulfilled her mission by providing him with a data file stolen from Hunt. (We later learn that Atlee was responsible for the creation of the Syndicate, before Lane went rogue and turned the group against MI6, further linking the two men.) Lane's visual coding changes in the next film, *Fallout*, reflecting his status as captive of the IMF. In this film, he appears disheveled in stark juxtaposition with his former clean-cut image. Both his unkempt appearance and beard age him. The figural fathers in the universe of *Mission: Impossible* appear limitless in their power, their marshaling of resources beyond the capacity of any government, as well as their talents for deception and secrecy, fooling all but Hunt and his loyal team. Narratives of "disavowal" or abandonment by the IMF predominate, with Hunt and his peers on the margins of their nation(s) and society. Hunt is unable to overcome the father directly so must resort to subterfuge and complexly orchestrated role-plays, burglaries, and associated strategy, where the objective is to avoid getting caught.

Cruise as Exhibitionist: The "Stunt" Space

In common with all the *Mission: Impossible* films is the presence of centerpiece stunts designed to showcase the star's physical athleticism and agility. In the first *Mission: Impossible*, Hunt must break into IMF Headquarters in Langley to steal the NOC list, crawling through a series of narrow air vents, before being lowered down into a secure vault on a wire and harness. Variations of this scenario play out across the subsequent films, with a greater level of self-referencing of this narrative trope with each iteration. In *Mission: Impossible II* Ambrose notes that Hunt will "no doubt engage in some acrobatic insanity before he'll risk harming a hair on a security guard's head." This exhibitionist space of stunt making is reserved for Ethan Hunt alone—with his IMF teammates relegated to the role of audience members. In the rare instance that another agent undertakes a physically risky exploit, his lack of skill (and it is always a he) is foregrounded. In *Rogue Nation*, IMF agent William Brandt (Jeremy Renner) is tasked with crawling through a narrow heating vent to deactivate a security system, while team members Hunt and Jane Carter (Paula Patton) target an Indian tycoon at a glitzy function. Brandt must don a magnetic suit that is steered by a small robot on wheels, allowing his body to hover above the ground. To access the heating vent, he must throw himself into a fan turbine tunnel, which IMF teammate Benji (Simon Pegg) assures him will cut out before he is impaled on the fan drive implement. Brandt awaits instructions to jump, lunging deeply in a comedy attempt to warm up for the task, walking to the edge of the airshaft before turning away in fear, which serves to remind the audience of Hunt's bravery relative to Brandt.

If Hunt were to find his equivalent in the superhero universe (and there are stunts in *Mission: Impossible* that border on the fantastic), his capacities most closely resemble those of Spider-Man. Both are able to climb buildings, and run, jump, and swing through the air at great heights. Owen Gleiberman (2018, 18), discussing the "ritualised stunt fever that [Tom Cruise] enacts as Ethan Hunt," suggests the star has the capacity to "put you up on that building right along with him, making you feel like an all-too-mortal wriggling Spiderman." Spider-Man's alter ego is the adolescent Peter Parker, and it is telling that Hunt is placed in this boyish sphere. The *Mission: Impossible* films all feature set pieces that involve Cruise hanging off buildings (or other surfaces) at great height: a dizzying rock face in the Utah Desert in *Mission: Impossible II*; the eighty-eight-story Jinmao Tower in Shanghai in *Mission: Impossible III*; the Burj Khalifa building in Dubai—currently the highest in the world—in *Ghost Protocol*; a military aircraft as it takes off in *Fallout*. Such is their ubiquity in the *Mission: Impossible* universe that "IMDbrief" (2018) created a video collage of series highlights, asking viewers "What's your favorite stunt? A death-defying dangle or *Fallout*'s building to building leap that snapped Cruise's ankle?"[1]

The use of the term "dangling" is not insignificant, given the frequency with which Hunt undertakes stunts that require the use of a wire and harness, suggesting simultaneous freedom of movement and restriction. In relation to this, Hunt is often associated with physical restraint, which is another psychosexual trope suggesting infantile constraint and ensuing trauma. In some instances, the restraint is more overt and may include Hunt being physically bound. The opening scene of *Mission: Impossible III* (which is later shown to be a flash-forward to a later scene) shows Hunt shackled in what appears to be an antique dentist's chair. Davian points a gun at Hunt's wife, threatening to pull the trigger once he reaches the count of ten, in a bid to extort the location of the "rabbit's foot" from him. Hunt tries all manner of responses: pleading, bargaining, shouting, and eventually an energetic but frustrated struggle against his bindings, but he is helpless in the face of the destructive patriarch. The scene ends when Davian pulls the trigger.

Depictions of physical restraint run throughout the *Mission: Impossible* films, becoming more sinister as the series progresses, with a greater emphasis on total entrapment. In the opening of *Rogue Nation*, Hunt finds

---

1 The commentator was referring to the accident that occurred on the set of *Fallout*, sustained by Cruise while performing a building-to-building leap.

his way to a London music store, where he converses with the young female sales assistant who hands him a record to play in a private booth. Putting the record on the turnstile and placing his palm on the vinyl, he opens a computer file that tells him about the Syndicate: a worldwide terrorist organization that Hunt and his disavowed IMF agents must bring down. But it is a trap: the audio announces that this *is* the Syndicate speaking and they now know his identity. Poisonous gas pours in from the vents, and Hunt bangs his hands against the door in an increasingly frenzied attempt to escape the booth's confines. Through the glass he sees an older man (later identified as Solomon Lane) pointing a gun at the sales assistant's head, then pulling the trigger, just as Hunt slips from consciousness.

Rogue Nation closes with Lane entrapped in the same way Hunt had previously been incarcerated. Hunt and his team lure Lane into the London sewers, where he finds himself trapped in an enclosed space, revealed to be a glass box, and surrounded. It is a moment of theater in which Lane—unwillingly—ends up in the performative space associated with Hunt. In a direct mirroring of the earlier scene, the box fills with gas and Lane slumps unconscious. Hunt chooses not to kill Lane, but instead delivers him to the authorities. It is a move that, in the following film *Fallout*, CIA operative August Walker criticizes Hunt for, implying he was not man enough to kill Lane (we later discover Walker is working for Lane). Once again, Cruise fails to overthrow the father.

Parallel treatment of protagonist and antagonist continues in the second of the two films (*Fallout*) with Lane as villain. Lane spends much of the movie restrained or enclosed in a small space: he nearly drowns in the back of a police van transporting him through Paris, when it crashes into the Seine, for example. This parallels the near drowning of Hunt in *Rogue Nation* when he breaks into an underwater security unit to override a database. Overall, Lane's placement within a mise-en-scène of restraint usually reserved for Hunt (and Cruise more generally) is indicative of the pair's changing fortunes.

Role-Play and Masks: Performing Masculinity

In spite of the terrifying figural fathers that Hunt must defeat, nevertheless there is the sense that the *Mission: Impossible* universe is characterized by make-believe and play. (The nomenclature "Impossible Mission Force" is certainly tongue in cheek.) The use of disguises and especially masks emphasizes the films' performative aspects. In *Fallout*, incoming CIA director Erica Sloane dismisses the IMF as "like Halloween. A bunch of grown men in rubber masks playing trick or treat," suggesting both childishness and a fantasized mastery. (Note that this judgment comes from an older woman—the archetypal mother.) This is highlighted by Benji's enthusiastic question in *Rogue Nation*: "Will I get to wear a mask?" The notion of play is supported by the imaginary rehearsing of set piece scenarios, often featuring highly risky and increasingly fanciful solutions centering around stealing a "MacGuffin." This is a motif that runs throughout the series, with Hunt often explaining to his team how the perfect heist will be accomplished. That these scenarios border on the comic becomes evident in a scene in *Rogue Nation* in which Benji imagines himself, in disguise, walking through a series of identification devices on his way to stealing a protected data file. The third identification test measures gait: in the fantasy scenario, the computer declares Benji's walk "unauthorized." Cue flashing red lights and a painful tasering. This failure of "performance" draws attention to the increasingly self-reflexive and pastiche nature of theatrical set pieces in the *Mission: Impossible* world.

Benji's enthusiasm for dressing up signals a shift in how masks are utilized by the films. As Stephen Mulhall (2006, 102) indicates, in *Mission: Impossible* only Hunt uses masks to disguise himself. Additionally in these scenarios, Hunt is engaged in the impersonation of more dominant men, such as IMF leader Jim Phelps, thus the disguise signals a performance of masculine mastery. The use of masks in the later films (from *Mission: Impossible III* onward) in a greater number of contexts, settings, and characters, focuses less on Hunt's performance of dominant masculinity than on *Mission: Impossible*'s theatrical deceptions. Emphasis is now on pulling off a stunt without being caught, which also underlines the collaborative work of the IMF team. This reflects the growing importance of the male-dominated or entirely male team in the series. It is always Hunt's primary and most supportive audience. That the IMF team (with the exception of Ving Rhames's Luther Stickell) is increasingly younger than Hunt, marks an important part in this denial of the star's aging body: he relates to them as a peer, not as a leader.

Hunt's Vulnerable Women

If Cruise's exhibitionist performances and impossible stunts as Hunt are designed to be admired by other men in the films, and constitute a form of play-acting with few consequences, the women in the *Mission: Impossible* universe remain vulnerable, both to injury and death. Hunt's women protect *him* from harm rather than the other way round. In *Mission: Impossible*, Claire's fate is alluded to in the very first scene where she plays dead: her husband, Jim Phelps, shoots her in the closing confrontation between the pair and Hunt. In *Mission: Impossible II*, Nyah injects herself with the deadly chimera virus to allow Hunt to escape a standoff with Ambrose, thwarting his plans to unleash the virus on the city of Sydney. (She is later picked up by Hunt's team and given an antidote).

The later films, from *Mission: Impossible III* onward, center on the fate of Hunt's wife, Julia (Michelle Monaghan), as well as of MI6 agent Isla Faust. Hunt's inability to protect Julia and make a success of married life is suggested to be a consequence of Hunt's work for the IMF. However, it is also indicative of his failure as a man. He is unable to prevent her kidnapping by Davian, which the antagonist uses as leverage to compel Hunt to steal the "rabbit's foot" from a secure unit in Shanghai. (The rabbit's foot is one of several MacGuffins of the *Mission: Impossible* universe—no explanation is offered regarding what it might actually constitute.) Julia must protect Hunt: when the hero discovers that Davian has planted an explosive pellet in his brain, he pleads with her to jolt him with a strong electrical charge. This will stop his heart and deactivate the explosive device. She must then revive him with a set of defibrillators. While Hunt is unconscious, however, Julia must fend off the last of Davian's henchman alone. By the time he has been resuscitated, she has shot and killed all the attackers, singlehandedly protecting him from harm.

Subsequent films in the franchise show Julia has been assigned a new identity, and Hunt can only observe her from a distance to protect her alias. Thus he is prevented from any kind of romantic narrative closure, underlining Hunt's greater commitment to his male peers over any female love interest. This supports Studlar's (2001, 178) statement regarding the "obvious lack of heterosexuality-as-something-that-matters in Cruise's films." It is telling that across the entire *Mission: Impossible* series, only one depicts a romantic ending: *Mission: Impossible II* shows Ethan and Nyah walking hand in hand through a busy Sydney riverside park. The other films close with

Hunt reunited with his IMF teammates. In *Fallout*, his IMF peers gather around the hero's hospital bed where he lies recuperating, perhaps a nod toward Hunt's growing physical vulnerability.

Conclusion: Challenging the Father

The most recent *Mission: Impossible* films show the series' continued commitment to reproducing traits important to Cruise's star persona: his "action exhibitionism" (Purse 2017, 177) through acrobatic stunts and running, the privileging of homosocial bonds over heterosexual coupling, and his failure to ascend to the role of figural patriarch. But have there been any changes in the representation of the star as he grows older? Purse suggests that Cruise's later films, such as *Rogue Nation*, show a greater willingness to acknowledge the aging of the star and place limitations on the kinds of physical feats Cruise performs. She notes that "Cruise frequently now plays characters within whom a tension exists between a hesitating uncertainty about whether the body can still match its younger capacities, and an openness to trying anyway" (2017, 180). This possibility of failure is reflected by recent extra-filmic narratives centering around Cruise's injuries on the set of *Fallout*. The star broke his ankle while filming a stunt that involved jumping between buildings and hitting a wall, which forced the production to be halted. (Footage of the accident is readily available on the web.) Cruise's co-star Henry Cavill disclosed on *Jimmy Kimmel Live* that not only did doctors tell Cruise to rest his leg for six months but that there was also a chance he might never run again. Cruise was back running six weeks later (Clark 2018).

Yet in spite of this increasing sense of the vulnerability of the star's body—partly motivated by audiences' increasing appetite for more impressive stunts—there has been little indication of a shift away from these action set pieces. Cruise is still the ostensible performer of most of these stunts in the *Mission: Impossible* films (though he does employ a stuntman), and Hunt carries most of the stunt work within the film narrative. In the few instances where his teammates do take his place, they are framed in a way to exaggerate their fear, undermine their competency, and remind the audience of Hunt's—and, by extension, Cruise the star's—proper place as a physical performer. That said, his displays in these films are increasingly marked both by physical challenge ("Can he make it?") and comic framing, an indication of the narrative's difficulty in negotiating the star's continued occupation of exhibitionist space as he ages.

Another shift that has occurred in relation to representations of Tom Cruise is the degree of physical suffering his character undergoes within the film narrative. Hunt's increasingly brutalized body onscreen demonstrates a development in the Cruise star persona, which sees his characters move toward challenging the father, which in turn leads to an aggressive retaliation. For example, in *Rogue Nation*, the fifth in the *Mission: Impossible* series, Hunt finds it increasingly hard to escape harm. In an early scene, where he is captured by agents of the Apostles, an anarchist terrorist group that has spun off from the Syndicate, he comes to consciousness and finds that he is bound to a metal pole, his arms above his head. He is topless, the full flank of his torso and arms on display. Yet this is unlike earlier representations of the sexually objectified Cruise body. The instance is more resonant with Steve Neale's ([1983] 1993, 15) account of the disavowal of the exhibitionist male body through screen violence and narratives "marked by sado-masochistic phantasies and scenes." The character now poses a greater challenge to the figural father and is met with the patriarch's castrating rage.

In other recent films featuring Cruise, the threat of patriarchal violence is more sinister and sometimes fatal. A shift in the treatment of his star body appears around the millennium with films such as *Minority Report* (Steven Spielberg, 2002), in which his character, John Anderton, undergoes an invasive eye transplant operation to evade capture by the police. It continues through to works such as *Oblivion* (Joseph Kosinski, 2013) and *Edge of Tomorrow* (Doug Liman, 2014). In *Valkyrie* (Bryan Singer, 2008), Cruise's Colonel Claus Von Stauffenberg is pitted against Hitler, the ultimate in terrifying patriarchs, who ultimately has Von Stauffenberg killed by firing squad. In *Edge of Tomorrow*, Cruise's character US Marine major William Cage finds himself in a temporal loop, in which he must die again and again before he gets his chance at redemption.

Where themes of patriarchal aggression play out in the *Mission Impossible* series, the stakes are lower than in these other films—it would, for example, be unimaginable for Hunt as the lead character in an action franchise to end up dead, especially when the star remains game for more episodes. While Hunt may find himself broken and bruised (literally prostrate on a hospital bed in the closing scene of *Fallout*), there is the suggestion that such injuries are temporary. If he offers up an imperfect performance of manhood, there seem to be limited consequences attached to failure. It remains to be seen if and how the character will evolve from this positioning as the figural son or if the star's aging body will finally catch up with the performer Cruise.

Works Cited

Burger Fiction. 2016. "Every Tom Cruise. Ever." YouTube, October 14, 2016. www.youtube.com/watch?v=U8Q2MgdMskQ.

Bruzzi, Stella. 2013. *Men's Cinema: Masculinity and Mise en Scène in Hollywood*. Edinburgh: Edinburgh University Press.

Clark, Travis. 2018. "Doctors Told Tom Cruise He Might Never Run Again after He Broke His Ankle Filming *Mission: Impossible—Fallout* but He Was Back on Set Sprinting 6 Weeks Later." Business Insider, July 26, 2018. www.businessinsider.com/doctors-told-tom-cruise-he-might-never-run-again-after-mission-impossible-injury-2018-7?r=US&IR=T.

Daily Mail Reporter. 2010. "Action Man Tom Cruise Shows How He Stays in Shape at 48 (albeit an Odd One)." DailyMail.com, October 7, 2010. www.dailymail.co.uk/tvshowbiz/article-1318522/Even-Tom-Cruise-action-man-fight-onset-middle-aged-spread.html.

Dyer, Richard. *Stars*. (1979) 1998. London: British Film Institute.

Gleiberman, Owen. 2018. "Tom Cruise's Stunt Fever." *Variety*, July 31, 2018.

"IMDbrief: Tom Cruise's Best 'Mission: Impossible' Stunts of All Time." IMDb Show, July 24, 2018. www.imdb.com/title/tt8743178/?ref_=vi_md_po.

Kimmel, Michael. 2005. *The Gender of Desire: Essays on Male Sexuality*. New York: State University of New York Press.

Mulhall, Stephen. 2006. "The Impersonation of Personality: Film as Philosophy in 'Mission: Impossible.'" *Journal of Aesthetics and Art Criticism* 64, no.1 (Winter): 97–110. https://www.jstor.org/stable/3700495.

Neale, Steve. (1983) 1993. "Masculinity as Spectacle." In *Screening the Male: Exploring Masculinities in Hollywood Cinema*, edited by Steven Cohan and Ina Rae Hark, 9–22. London: Routledge.

O'Donnell, Ruth. 2015. *Tom Cruise: Performing Masculinity in Post-Vietnam Hollywood*. London: I. B. Tauris.

Purse, Lisa. 2017. "Confronting the Impossibility of Impossible Bodies: Tom Cruise and the Aging Male Action Hero Movie." In *Revisiting Star Studies:*

Cultures, Themes and Methods, edited by Sabrina Qiong Yu and Guy Austin, 162–86. Edinburgh: Edinburgh University Press.

Studlar, Gaylyn. 2001. "Cruise-ing into the Millennium: Performative Masculinity Stardom, and the All-American Boy's Body." 2001. In *Ladies and Gentlemen, Boys and Girls: Gender in Film at the End of the Millennium*, edited by Murray Pomerance, 171–83. Albany: State University of New York Press.

13
STARRING TOM CRUISE AS (DESPERATELY DEFYING) AGING ACTION STAR

Glen Donnar

Building on a long-standing marker of his authenticity as an action star, Tom Cruise's most recent films prominently feature him performing ever-more outlandish stunts and ever-greater physical exertions. Cruise's near-obsessive need to proclaim an undiminished physical capacity and enhanced stunt skill set as he ages is motivated by a number of factors. It cannot be divorced from Scientology's goal to transcend the limitations of the body. It also arguably distinguishes him from an older generation of male action stars, ranging in age from their midfifties into their seventies, including Sylvester Stallone, Arnold Schwarzenegger, and Liam Neeson, whose careers have been revitalized or transformed over the last decade. Broader production and exhibition trends, including industry preferences for sequels/franchises, have supported the (re)emergence of aged action stars. However, distinct shifts in action spectacle have played a conspicuous role, as "the spectacle of once idealized, muscled bodies is concealed and displaced onto oversized guns, fetishized vehicles and younger action bodies," including digital re-creations of their younger selves (Donnar 2016, 2). This chapter uses on-set news, gossip and publicity, and promotional materials from a number of recent films, including three *Mission: Impossible* films—*Ghost Protocol* (Bird 2011), *Rogue Nation* (McQuarrie 2015) and *Fallout* (McQuarrie 2019)—and *The Mummy* (Kurtzman 2017), to interrogate enduring narratives about Cruise's very particular "spectacular" stardom. Responding to Lauren Steimer's (2018, 252) call for scholars to challenge rather than reinforce "the discursive strategies of technologies of action stardom," it argues that these narratives invoke competing discourses about stunt work, generating a steady impression not only of the action spectacle each film will deliver but also of Cruise's professional intensity, commitment, and "crazy," "death-defying" feats. In so doing, both Cruise's renowned stunt work and the on-set injuries he has laudably overcome now evidence anxieties about undeniable aging rather than its undaunted defiance.

Cruise and "Stunting Stardom": Authenticity, Masculinity, and Spectacle

In *Heavenly Bodies*, Richard Dyer (2004, 10) argues that star image is shaped by a "rhetoric of authenticity," a guarantee of sorts "that the star really is what she or he appears to be." The scholarly analysis of Cruise's star image, complexly constructed "out of media texts that can be grouped together as promotion, publicity, films and criticism" (Dyer 1979, 60), has consistently turned on questions of authenticity and spectacle in specific relation to masculinity. However, for Cruise, authenticity has not depended on a presumed coincidence or continuity between his public, performed self and his private, "real" self but instead on the "reality" of his performed body. Discussing his 1980s and 1990s films, Gaylyn Studlar (2001, 176) contends that while Cruise's characters consistently move from an inauthentic "performance of manliness" into "authentic manliness," this remains an exhibitionist masculinity and one, revolving around the appeal of his body and smile, scrutinized "as a construction, a masquerade." Cruise's concerted move into action film shifted associations of this authenticity onto his *stunting* body, initiating the persistent cultural framing of Cruise's stunt work in the two decades since *Mission: Impossible II* (John Woo, 2000). According to Paul McDonald (2013, 184), the "spectacularization of the star" is especially resonant in moments "staged precisely to display the star attraction," from advanced marketing through to the star's entrance in the narrative. The spectacle associated with Cruise and his films consolidates here as a complex function of star image, franchise, and genre—and their collective emphasis on stunt performance. Discussing *Mission: Impossible II*'s opening titles sequence, in which Cruise's Ethan Hunt free-climbs on a rocky mountain face, Manohla Dargis (2000, 20) argues that "precisely because digital effects have become so persuasive," Cruise's (stunting) star body represents "the last stand of the real." By the late noughties, Ruth O'Donnell (2012, 214) observes a shift away from the erotic spectacle of Cruise's mature body, increasingly covered up because it "is no longer able to bear the weight of physical objectification that it once did." Accordingly, moments of spectacle shift onto stunt set pieces that instead affirm an undiminished physical skill and capacity. Echoing Dargis (2000), Gleiberman (2018, 18) writes that Cruise's stunting efforts now not only define his stardom and "lend a cathartic integrity to the action" but also resist "the death of movie stardom itself." As much as Cruise's star image is produced by what his body does—his stunting and running—"the spectacle of risk" is equally a defining feature of Cruise's star image—and crucial to his box office (Hjort 2012, 41). In a period of relative star decline, Cruise's stunt work remains a marker of *undiminished* authenticity and star performance, supported by proliferated online media content that amplifies prevailing narratives about his stunt work in promotional/publicity discourses.

Cruise's fixation on stunt work since *Mission: Impossible II* recalls Jacob Smith's (2004, 35) assertion that the celebration of the stuntman as a heroic figure in 1970s American cinema sought to "remasculinize" an American male culture in the midst of numerous perceived crises, including the decline of the studio system, the rise of civil rights, and the trauma of Vietnam. Initially, this relates to the anticipated anxieties of a would-be "hard-bodied" action star. Cruise performed—and needed to be seen to perform—stunts to *become* an "action star," in a sense mirroring the "narrative of becoming" that Lisa Purse (2011, 34) identifies as common to action film, which articulates a protagonist's trajectory toward achieving full occupation of the heroic action body. It is also, however, wrapped up in longer-standing anxieties around his complex screen masculinity. In contrast to the stunt double, the male film star is ambivalently coded, objectified by the camera, fans, and the press alike; *made* spectacle, he is to be looked at by others, connoting his vulnerability. O'Donnell (2012, 31), among others, observes that the early Cruise's "visual erotic appeal and his roles feature sequences of sexualized spectacle, which position[ed] him in the 'feminine' performance space typically allocated for Hollywood's women." Seeing a stunt double, whose performance marks him as "the structuring Other that facilitated the functioning of the male film star," threatens to "de-masculinize" the male star's constructed image (Smith 2004, 38). In this sense, Cruise's increased emphasis on stunt work and action spectacle becomes a gendered counterpoint to the "feminized" erotic spectacle of his body in his early career.

From the late noughties, the greater emphasis on stunt set pieces is tied to Cruise's desire to (re)establish control over a star image gravely destabilized by a number of infamous appearances on television talk shows. Donna Peberdy (2010, 241) argues Cruise's on- and offscreen performances exhibit what she calls "bipolar masculinity," always in flux between "hard" and "soft" modes. This anticipates his "bizarre" talk-show performances of unstable masculinity in 2005, from jumping on Oprah Winfrey's couch in order to enthusiastically declare his love for then girlfriend Katie Holmes to railing on *Today* against Brooke Shields's use of antidepressants to help with her postpartum depression. Peberdy concludes that these performances eventually overwhelm Cruise's star image, characterizing its inherent instability now in terms of inconsistency and excess, and his public humiliation threatens his specific cultivation of screen masculinity (250). Each episode was deemed evidence of the hold that Scientology had over his behavior and attitudes, and each was endlessly parodied online and in popular culture. The box office backlash was equally extensive with *Mission: Impossible III* (J. J. Abrams, 2006) performing well below expectations, earning US$150 million less than the previous installment and threatening Cruise's continued presence in the series. Yet it would be these problematic notions of excess and intensity that Cruise would build on to realize his star image as a *masculine* star defined by a crazed commitment to training for and performing ever grander and increasingly demanding spectacular action stunts.

The production of film spectacle, typically contrasted with narrative, is arguably as intimately associated with gender as it is with global blockbusters and the action mode. Referring to Cruise's *Ghost Protocol* stunt on the outside of the world's tallest building, Dubai's Burj Khalifa, Stella Bruzzi (2013, 5) describes how what she terms "men's cinema" uses spectacle, visual style, and mise-en-scène "to convey masculinity, not merely to represent it." Likewise, despite the growing prominence of female stunt workers, stunt work is associated not only with spectacle but also with notions of "authentic" masculinity in Hollywood (Smith 2004, 39). For stars like Steve McQueen, "doing one's own stunts became an important part of authenticating a star persona," and this has since become a common trope for the promotion of action films and their stars (39). Yet Smith argues a hierarchical relationship between stunts and narrative is evident both in the production—created by entirely distinct "second units"—and formal structure of films. The emergence of specialized stunt performers, whose role it was to "double" the star, crucially follows creation of the Hollywood star system, under which stars quickly became protected commodities (37). Actors who performed some of their own stunts, such as Buster Keaton, Douglas Fairbanks, and Errol Flynn, became notable exceptions. It is equally "notable that this doubling was kept a secret" so as to preserve the unity of the star's image—and the studio's investment. This unity is reinforced in publicity and promotional materials that implied the star's body was in real danger (37). Paradoxically, Sylvia Martin (2012, 100) observes that while "the image of the stunt is among the most valorized within spectacular films," the labor of stunt performers "is among the most veiled." Stunt doubles "must carefully negotiate with actors in order to create a unified sequence of dangerous bodily spectacle," rendering coherent "what is essentially a fragmented labor process" (98). Ultimately, this requires that the stunt performer be "engulfed by the star's image," his face sutured to the stuntman's body and the stunt performer's labor erased (Smith 2004, 38).

The conspicuous function of stunt work in constructing Cruise's unified star image is clear in his franchise films, advance promotional materials, and publicity, each dominated by references to the extreme physical risk he places himself—and his costars—at. Steimer (2018, 245) observes that all action stars, regardless of their actual involvement in or capacity for stunt work, are discursively constructed in academia as much as the media as "stunting stars." Indeed, Cruise's films are linked in numerous articles less by narrative and character and more by the outlandish stunts performed in each by Cruise. For example, a reference in a *Variety* article to the sixty-four takes Cruise did at zero gravity for the plane crash sequence in the failed franchise reboot of *The Mummy* links not only films across the *Mission: Impossible* series via stunt set pieces but Cruise's star image and filmography as well (Lang 2017). A *Mission: Impossible—Rogue Nation* (Christopher McQuarrie, 2018) stunt in which he clings to the outside of a plane during and after takeoff bookends the film, opening the narrative before being re-presented during the closing credits. A *Hollywood Reporter* piece, despite recognizing how Paramount uses spectacular stunt sequences as a "selling point," lionizes how the stunt "did actually take place," with Robert Elswit, the film's director of photography, insisting, "There's no digital Tom, and there's no fake plane. He's really strapped to an Airbus," a testament to Cruise being "the most obsessive artist" (qtd. in Giardina 2015). An association with authenticity and requisite erasure of stunt workers is similarly evident across the multiple featurettes and cross-promotions for *Mission: Impossible—Fallout* (Christopher McQuarrie, 2018) that aggrandize Cruise's stunt work. A cross-promotional video with Uber features Cooper Adrian, who an *AdWeek* piece describes as "the fictional stunt double Paramount was legally obligated to hire despite him being largely extraneous due to Cruise's impressive work ethic" (Thilk 2018). Cooper becomes an Uber driver to fill out his time. Even Cruise's predilection for running is improbably framed as a stunt in *Fallout*: "Cruise, as always, does all of his own running ... and, boy, is there a lot of it. The amount of running in the film is a stunt unto itself" (Williams 2018). A *New York Daily News* article frames the rigorous testing the stunt coordinator undertook as not alleviating the potential for tragedy: "And make no mistake, Cruise was in real danger during the eight days of filming" (Sacks 2011). By reframing his uncommon intensity as necessary and his "crazy" as a positive, Cruise's films, promotional materials, and publicity productively activated competing and contradictory discourses on stunt performance and spectacle—the professional versus the daredevil.

Cruise as "Stunting Star": Trained Professional and Crazy Daredevil

Despite their typical characterization in the popular imagination as "death-defying" daredevils, stunt professionals predominantly define their work via discourses of professionalism and expertise. These emphasize control, planning and preparation, skill set and training, and commitment. This is not to deny the extreme physical risk their work entails, but stunt performers offset these with "a sense of control over the material conditions under which stunts are performed" (Martin 2012, 107). As one stunt worker further elaborates: "We're trained professionals. We make calculations and we practice and rehearse" (109–10). Far from daredevil, Martin observes that "stuntworkers strive to reduce unpredictability regarding their survival" (99). A *New York Daily News* article about *Mission: Impossible—Ghost Protocol* (Brad Bird, 2011) underscores the planning involved for the scene in which Cruise/Hunt is outside Dubai's Burj Khalifa, the world's tallest building (Sacks 2011). Stunt coordinator Greg Smrz additionally outlines the many safety measures, including constructing a mockup of the building in

Los Angeles, doing countless repetitions, and brake-testing the cabling used at an engineering facility (Sacks 2011). Likewise, in a *Hollywood Reporter* article on *Rogue Nation*, the film's cinematographer emphasizes the safety measures taken to minimize the risk:

> Tom was in a full body harness and he's cabled and wired to the plane through [its] door. Inside the aircraft was an aluminum truss that was carefully bolted to the plane, which held the wires that went through the door, which held Tom. . . . He was also wearing special contact lenses to protect his eyes. . . . They were very careful about cleaning the runway so there were no rocks. And we took off in certain weather conditions; there were no birds. And he's sort of protected by the way the air moves over the wing. (Elswit qtd. in Giardina 2015)

Multiple articles feature members of the production team lauding Cruise's commitment to intense training and preparation. A *Men's Journal* profile (Thorp 2017) on stunt coordinator Wade Eastwood before the release of *Jack Reacher: Never Go Back* (Edward Zwick 2016) serves instead to conspicuously construct Cruise as a stuntperson. Eastwood remarks: "He works hard to build the skill-sets he needs for each project. . . . His skill levels are through the roof. He is incredibly capable. He can do it all." Despite having "doubled" for other "action" stars, Cruise is "of a whole different breed." Eastwood reiterates Cruise's commitment and discipline: "Through programs we get him ready for every movie, and he shows up for every hour. . . . I do the exact same safety protocol with Tom as I do for my own stunt guys." This extends to self-adulation by Cruise himself. In extolling his consummate preparation, Cruise repeatedly not only erases the labor of his stunt team and performers but also subsumes their production role. In the *Men's Journal* profile, Cruise declares: "I spend as much time as possible preparing. . . . There is a tremendous amount of training that goes into it, and, because I have made several movies with Wade, I like to help oversee all the training for the rest of the cast." And in a later *Men's Journal* piece (Thorp 2018) on his stunts in *Fallout*, Cruise begins: "I'm very meticulous about how I prepare both physically and mentally. There are a lot of briefings throughout the shooting day. I like to create a team environment, one where I can push for excellence." Cruise's words here unwittingly invoke Yvonne Tasker's (2018, 382) identification of how "the hero's heightened capacity for action . . . foregrounds the fantastical qualities of the action hero's strength while reinforcing the hierarchies of bodies." In this respect, it is not Cruise's proclamations about his stunt work that carry most import but how easily he excises below-the-line workers from the production.

Despite proclaiming Cruise's training, commitment, and skill set in his discursive construction as the exceptional "stunting star," multiple articles hint at the inevitable gaps between Cruise and a professional stunt performer. As Steimer (2018, 245) reminds us, "One characteristic greatly distinguishes these stars from stunt performers: expert status in a bodily discipline." When Cruise comes for fight training on each film, according to Eastwood, "we take him back to the basics every time" (Thorp 2018). The *Men's Journal* piece on *Fallout* (Thorp 2018) discusses a HALO sky jump sequence and numerously hints at the serious consequences of the experience gap between Cruise and a fully trained professional: "Cruise had a few hundred jumps under his belt, but he was attempting something that usually called for around 10,000 jumps." As a result, the sequence, planned to take a week, ultimately required a month to complete. Eastwood further exposes the unbridgeable gap between Cruise and a professional stuntperson, especially in terms of safety and risk: "He is almost to the point where he is dangerously good . . . because he wants to do everything. It is just not logical to assume that he can also be a world champion motorbike rider; there just aren't enough hours in the day" (Thorp 2017). Eastwood, even in ostensibly acclaiming Cruise's capacity and commitment, here associates him with alternative discourses around stunt work, namely those of the daredevil.

The daredevil, in contrast to the professional stunt performer, is associated with unpredictability, precarity, recklessness, and "craziness." The *Men's Journal* piece on Cruise's stunts in *Fallout* also complexly presents Cruise as daredevil, with director Christopher McQuarrie declaring: "There aren't any rules. We're just with him for the ride" (Thorp 2018). Gleiberman (2018, 18) even aligns Cruise's efforts with the circus and the showman: "Cruise has become his own P. T. Barnum, selling his movie by inviting the audience to step right up and behold whatever crazy thing he's going to do next." Ethan Sacks (2011), in a *New York Daily News* article on *Ghost Protocol*, tellingly reframes discourses around "craziness" in relation to Cruise's stunt work: "After all, only in a screenwriter's vivid imagination would a sane person willingly scale . . . 123 stories up the sheer face of the world's tallest building. . . . Only it really did happen," with Cruise "putting himself in the harness dangling 1,700 feet off the ground." The erasure of the entire stunt production team is most telling. Sacks continues: "During the eight days of shooting the sequence, only a cable with the thickness of a piano wire" prevented Cruise from falling. This is a common refrain across featurettes for later films in the franchise. By obscuring the many safety precautions taken and focusing on the breathless precarity of a single wire, the article invokes Smith's (2004) observation that stunting stars must always appear as if they are in "real danger." Cruise also plays to this daredevil notion in publicity materials. In the same article, director Brad Bird observes that Cruise simply smilingly asked, "When do we go back again," at the end of the shoot. The long association of Cruise's star image with his smile, which once signaled a brash boyishness, now denotes a cavalier disregard for danger. Cruise equally conveys this sense through a tendency to trumpet each stunt set piece as unprecedented and "wild" or "crazy." In discussing *The Mummy* stunt on *The Graham Norton Show*, Cruise speciously exclaims: "Normally stunts take months of prepping, but we just did it. It was wild!" (qtd. in Zakarin 2017). In burnishing his image as an entertainer, Cruise defers his risk taking to others. The manner in which Cruise's stunt spectacles define his star image aligns with Martin's (2012, 99) recognition of "risk taking as a positive undertaking" for stunt performers. However, Cruise's risk-taking, rather than strictly a labor practice, seeks to frame his stunt work as labor *for his fans*. Cruise's status as an action star is especially relevant in *Edge of Tomorrow* (Doug Liman 2014), in which his character "learns to perform to the Tom Cruise-type hero, revealing through the protracted process the labor involved" (Tasker 2018, 396). In this sense, Cruise's stardom mirrors Yvonne Tasker's definition of white military masculinity, here defined in terms of duty to fans *and* labor to produce ever greater stunt spectacles for their pleasure (394). Hjort's (2012) concept of "flamboyant risk taking" is surprisingly relevant for understanding not only Cruise's films but also his stardom. Although discussing documentary film, Hjort accurately captures the *display* of risk in the context of Cruise's star image, including when the risks taken to produce the films are "manifestly present in the finished film" and associated with its visual style (32). In order to achieve their intended effects, his stardom revolves around fans' "ability to grasp the connections between cinematic images and the often physical risks that accompanied their production" (38). Reframing Hjort, rather than "inauthenticity,"

Cruise's "flamboyant risk taking" explicitly constructs his authenticity as a star with the risks he is willing to take. Cruise not only takes avoidable risks but foregrounds them *for his audiences' pleasure*.

Cruise's daredevil defiance of studio entreaties and control are often signaled as a quest for realism for fans, persistently aligning Cruise's stunting efforts with audience expectation and pleasure. A *Variety* article on a production delay on *Fallout* notes that "Cruise has long prided himself on doing his own stunts, even defying studio bosses and insurance companies" (Lang and Keslassy 2017). An earlier *Variety* article on *The Mummy* reiterates this, observing that "Cruise was offered the option to do the scene on a sound stage, but he insisted on filming the sequence in zero gravity, believing it was important that audiences got the most realistic experience possible" (Lang 2017). Even his stunt coordinators and directors are expected to aggrandize Cruise in this respect. Smrz opines about the Dubai building stunt, "We were in meetings, and they said, 'Tom's not going to climb that building. The studio will never allow that.' . . . I said, 'Tom's going to climb the building, I guarantee it'" (qtd. in Sacks 2011). Discussing a helicopter chase sequence among mountains in *Fallout*, Cruise and McQuarrie again fête the star's defiance, declaring, respectively, that "There was a lot of resistance to me doing this stunt" and "Everyone said it wasn't going to be possible" (qtd. in Thorp 2018). Cruise further asserts: "It's all about immersing an audience in extreme action, and doing it practically. . . . The audience can just feel it when it's real. . . . I gave everything I had."[1] Director of *The Mummy*, Alex Kurtzman, suggests that Cruise's daredevil attitude is not merely in service of the audience's pleasure but also essential: "The unpredictability of it is what makes it magical. It puts the audience in the middle of that moment. To make them feel the sheer terror, without any cuts" (Ross 2017). Far from dismissing these stunting (and discursive) efforts, daredevil risk for Cruise was

---

1 The rhetoric about Cruise as a daredevil stunt performer is so pervasive that it even entered promotional discourses for *American Made* (Doug Liman 2017), a "based on a true story" 1980s action-comedy romp. Director Doug Liman described a scene in which Cruise's character dumps drugs from the back of a small airplane he is piloting: "It's one thing to have Tom Cruise alone in the airplane flying it—that's already outrageous—now he's alone and he's not even in the cockpit so he's gone beyond."

equally essential in productively recasting his star image after the damage wrought by his infamous talk-show appearances a decade prior.

Overcoming Injury and Defying Aging: The Vitality of Endurance

The "crazed intensity" Cruise became negatively associated with in the mid-noughties was transformed into Cruise's reworked star image via a complex admixture of stunting and daredevil discourses. O'Donnell (2016, 427) also observes how the critical reception of *Rogue Nation* in particular renegotiated Cruise's intensity in relation to the performance of his own stunts so as "to integrate traits hitherto deemed unpalatable." These collectively proved highly successful, with *Ghost Protocol* and *Rogue Nation* each earning almost US$700 million at the global box office, until the broken ankle Cruise sustained while filming *Fallout*. By elevating daredevil over stunt professional characteristics, Cruise's injury damagingly triggered connotations of wounding and failure closely associated with daredevils and sparked related concerns about diminishing physical capacity related to aging. In puncturing the nearly two-decade-long repeat positioning of Cruise as a "stunting star," Jordan Zakarin (2017) posits a shift in the apparent purpose of these recycled on-set tales, from authenticating Cruise as a masculine action star to authenticating him as *still* an action star, *despite his age*: "He's reaching the point where people can marvel at how he did his own stunts at his advanced age." The dual function of stunt work to alleviate anxieties about Cruise as a "hard-bodied" action star and as a counterpoint to his complex screen masculinity arguably now relate to the anxieties of an undeniably aging action star. This anxiety is apparent in the protagonists Cruise has portrayed onscreen in recent years. In stark contrast to the realities of even the most professional stunt performer, Cruise is variously invulnerable, regenerated, or resurrected in numerous recent films. In *Edge of Tomorrow*, Cruise's character is repeatedly reset on violent death at the hand of invading aliens, returning physically unblemished but martially improved. And following the plane crash sequence in *The Mummy*, Cruise's character is resurrected, before being ultimately deified—fused with the Egyptian god, Set, and able to resurrect others. In each instance, rather than images of a broken body and extended convalescence, markers similarly authenticating his stunt *and* his character's experience, Cruise's body emerges unscathed, even improved. This immunity recalls that of the male action star reliant on the dangerous/invisible labor of his stunt double. However, it has also become associated with discourses around Cruise and his stunt work, which repeatedly marvel over his apparent defiance of aging.

Ironically, the moment Cruise is truly identified with the professional realities of the stunt performer, the greater his star image as the exceptional "stunting star" is most threatened. In discussing 1970s American films about stunt performers, Smith notes that the stuntman's body "slides between the categories of soft and hard," and is "proven by its willingness to continue on in the face of failure and pain, to repeat dangerous stunts even after being rendered profoundly passive" (Smith 2004, 40). This categorical instability suggests the stuntman "operat[es] simultaneously as an icon of authentic masculinity and an acknowledgement of male lack" (43). Cruise, however, cannot abide this association to (re)gain prominence because it recalls the ambivalence of his star image in the mid-noughties and threatens his carefully (re)constructed "stunting star" image. Amateur footage of the incident leaked to gossip media company TMZ shows Cruise hobbling away, before falling and requiring assistance. The accompanying text foregrounds his age, before reiterating Cruise's incapacity in describing the footage. The final sentence notably underscores this sense, recalling the "profound passivity" Smith identifies in adopting a passive construction: "You see Cruise try to limp away and then collapse. He then limps back to the edge of the building and *is pulled away* by crew members on the safety team" ("Tom Cruise Injured" 2017; emphasis added). The incident, and such language, threatened the (precarious) unity of his star image in returning it to earlier, "bipolar masculine" notions—and even a feminized passivity—in positioning his "hard" body as *also/becoming* "soft."

Cruise's on-set injury—or rather the hobbling that followed it—reminded fans of Cruise's advancing age and his otherwise endlessly forestalled "use by" date as an inexhaustible action star. It suggested he had become too old to undertake his own stunts (Gleiberman 2018, 18). The flurry of on-set news and gossip that followed the incident invariably discussed him *as* aging—as opposed to not looking his age. Observations that he attempted the stunt with the assistance of a harness associated a common safety measure, usually a marker of due caution, with lack—of skill and capacity alike. And numerous references to unnamed insiders and rumors about additional injuries exemplified the difficulty—and abiding anxiety—faced by Cruise in controlling his action star image as he ages. The discursive response was immediate. Although production was shut down for six weeks, Paramount repeatedly emphasized that the injury would not delay the film's release. McQuarrie, referring to the ten years he had worked with Cruise, said that he "is in better shape and better form than I have seen him," and pointedly declared that the actor was "*always supposed* to slam into the side of the building" (qtd. in Mumford 2017, emphasis added).[2] In the face of interrelated doubts over Cruise's capacity and age, McQuarrie sought to reframe the accident *as deliberate* and Cruise's physical capacity *as undiminished*, even enhanced.

An orchestrated promotional response, which preceded even the release of any trailers, confirmed the ever-greater lengths an aging Cruise must take to, first, maintain a unified star image through spectacular stunt work and, second, *repair* it through promotional activities *focused on* his endurance. A fixation on numbers, which had signaled a stunt's unprecedented "craziness," now sought to mark Cruise's commitment and exceptionality, detailing how his inexhaustible rehab regime confounded doctors' opinion. This emphasis, including on his age at the time, fifty-five, was repeated across multiple articles. Speaking at CinemaCon, Cruise declared: "I went right into rehab. About 10 hours a day, 12 hours, seven days a week, because six weeks later I had to be on set, and twelve weeks later I had to be sprinting again" (Leasca 2018). Cruise's powers of recovery are also headlined in an article titled "Doctors Told Tom Cruise He Might Never Run Again . . . but He Was Back on Set Sprinting 6 Weeks Later," which highlights the threat this would have represented to Cruise's star image given his predilection for running onscreen (Clark 2018). Each article frames this intensity and commitment, reiterating that he performs his own stunts instead of using a double, in relation to earlier discourses about Cruise's well-known defiance.

Cruise's further attempts to restore (control of) his "stunting star" image in appearances on British and American variety television are even more telling. The prominence of Cruise's stunt work within his star image is in part borrowed from transnational action stars equally defined by

2 Numerous articles mention the complication the planned schedules of other cast members could represent, but there is no mention of the impact on below-the-line performers, whose labor is again rendered invisible.

onscreen physicality. However, unlike Jackie Chan, for example, Cruise typically ensures a clear separation between the creation of stunt sequences and the final film, only "showing" his stunt work in publicity and promotional materials such as featurettes. On *The Graham Norton Show* (Stuart, 2018), Cruise brought along raw footage of the attempted stunt and subsequent injury from multiple camera angles, which also showed the assistance of harnesses. Notably, this "raw" footage, produced by Cruise/Paramount, runs shorter than the amateur footage and cuts prior to Cruise's collapse. Cruise—and Norton—enthusiastically feed the myth of Cruise's intense, even crazed, commitment in discussing his defiance of injury and swift return to shooting:

> NORTON: Is it still broken?
>
> CRUISE: It's still broken, but I'm doing well.
>
> NORTON: No, you're kidding. It's still broken?
>
> CRUISE: Yeah. I mean, it's not fully healed, but we're shooting.
>
> NORTON: But that's nuts, because we've seen the pictures and you're running and doing all the stuff again.

Likewise, on *The Tonight Show Starring Jimmy Fallon* (Michaels, 2018), Cruise positions himself as a veteran stunt performer, and Fallon lauds him for repairing a broken lineage as the sole heir to earlier "stunting stars":

> FALLON: Which one did you break your leg on?
>
> CRUISE: It was the easy one where I'm running and I jump from one building to the next. [Audience laughter and applause]
>
> FALLON: There's no one—No one does it like you anymore.
>
> CRUISE (CONVEYING FALSE MODESTY): Thank you.

Cruise's clear pleasure in Fallon's compliments suggests that his "desire" for risk is accompanied by "the desire to have the reality of the risk taking be acknowledged" (Hjort 2012, 52). More than this, Cruise's appearances confirm an undiminished desire to have his endurance, a sign of his intense commitment, recognized.[3]

Prior to replaying footage from a side angle that includes a slow-motion close-up on his foot as it is injured, Norton invokes many of the discourses associated with Cruise's stunt work: "Here is why Tom Cruise gets paid the big bucks" and "Now anyone else would go, 'Well, that's over.' No! Up he gets and he's running!" The audience laughs, and the camera cuts to Cruise, also laughing. The laughter builds to applause, and then the camera cuts to costars Henry Cavill and Simon Pegg, who join in clapping.

Along with conspicuously substituting hobbling for running, Norton hails Cruise's endurance. Tasker (2018) argues that endurance defines action masculinity in war/action film. Writing about *Edge of Tomorrow*, Tasker observes that because his martial abilities are "learned through labor," Cruise's character highlights "the construction of action masculinity as the ability to endure" (396). Equally true for framing Cruise's stardom, following his injury, this capacity to endure assumes even greater import in repairing his injured star image. Articles succeeding his appearance on Norton's show repeated these discourses, not only aligning his endurance with the intensity and "craziness" of his commitment but also restoring his agency. A *Men's Health* article attested: "Because he's Tom Cruise, he finished the stunt—*then* called cut and went to the hospital" (Leasca 2018; emphasis in original). A *Vanity Fair* article about the episode noted that "the craziest part . . . is that afterward, Cruise *pulls himself up* from the edge of the roof and keeps running. . . . 'I knew instantly it was broken, [Cruise said,] and I ran past the camera. Got the shot—it's in the movie'" (Stefansky 2018; emphasis added). On Norton's show, Cruise repeatedly declares that both the side-angle and front-on shots are "in the movie." Suturing footage of the injury into the final cut equally counters related discourses about incapacity and aging by showing Cruise continue *after* injury, immediately and without delay. Continuity editing functions to erase the six-week production halt his injury caused, seamlessly transitioning Cruise from the injury and onto the next shot as he continues running across the rooftops of Paris after his younger costar, Henry Cavill—Cruise again inexhaustible and invulnerable.

---

3   Cruise's costars are also required to aggrandize his commitment and powers of recovery, as Henry Cavill did during his July 25, 2018, appearance on *Jimmy Kimmel Live!*

Conclusion

Writing about the likely effects of the digital era on Hollywood stardom, Manohla Dargis (2000, 23) contends that Cruise's (stunting) star body ensures that "no movie star is better equipped to combat [such] redundancy." Cruise's attempts to reframe, even celebrate, the injuries he sustains—and overcomes—as related to an undaunted willingness to do his own stunt work seeks to define them as markers of undiminished authenticity and capacity as an action star. However, Cruise's concerted efforts, rather than setting him apart, recall how other aging action stars—and their iconic action characters—similarly resist cultural and professional redundancy and anxieties about becoming superfluous and deprived of one's job, associated status, and worth (Donnar 2016). Such conspicuous physical/star labor—both the stunts and his *recuperative* promotional efforts—chronicles rather than effaces growing anxiety about unavoidable physical decline and suggests a profound reticence toward any cross-examination of his (action) star image *as* aging. His desperate need to have others recognize his feats, and the rhetoric of each stunt/film outdoing the last, suggests that anxieties about undeniable aging, rather than masculine action star legitimacy, now motivate Cruise's defiant performative exertions.

Works Cited

Bruzzi, Stella. 2013. *Men's Cinema: Masculinity and Mise en Scène in Hollywood* (Edinburgh: Edinburgh University Press).

Clark, Travis. 2018. "Doctors Told Tom Cruise He Might Never Run Again after He Broke His Ankle Filming 'Mission: Impossible—Fallout,' but He Was Back on Set Sprinting 6 Weeks Later." Business Insider, July 26, 2018. www.businessinsider.com/doctors-told-tom-cruise-he-might-never-run-again-after-mission-impossible-injury-2018-7/?r=AU&IR=T.

Dargis, Manohla. 2000. "Ghost in the Machine." *Sight & Sound* 10, no. 7 (July): 20–23.

Donnar, Glen. 2016. "Narratives of Cultural and Professional Redundancy: Aging Action Stardom and the 'Geri-Action' Film." *Communication, Politics & Culture* 49 (1): 1–18.

Dyer, Richard. 1979. *Stars*. London: British Film Institute.

———. 2004. *Heavenly Bodies: Film Stars and Society*. London: Routledge.

Giardina, Carolyn. 2015. "How 'Crazy' Was That Tom Cruise 'Mission: Impossible' Plane Stunt? The Movie's Cinematographer Tells All." *Hollywood Reporter*, July 31, 2015. www.hollywoodreporter.com/behind-screen/mission-impossible-plane-stunt-tom-812158.

Gleiberman, Owen. 2018. "Tom Cruise's Stunt Fever." *Variety*, July 31, 2018.

Hjort, Mette. 2012. "Flamboyant Risk Taking: Why Some Filmmakers Embrace Avoidable and Excessive Risks." In *Film and Risk*, edited by Mette Hjort, 31–54. Detroit: Wayne State University Press.

Lang, Brent. 2017. "Tom Cruise's Zero-Gravity Stunt in 'the Mummy' Took 64 Takes." *Vanity Fair*, March 29, 2017. variety.com/2017/film/box-office/mummy-tom-cruise-zero-gravity-stunt-1202018681/.

Lang, Brett, and Elsa Keslassy. 2017. "'Mission: Impossible 6' Faces Production Delay after Tom Cruise Injured," *Variety*, August 16, 2017. variety.com/2017/film/news/mission-impossible-6-faces-production-delay-after-tom-cruise-injured-exclusive-1202528831/.

Leasca, Stacey. 2018. "Tom Cruise Opens Up about That Gruesome 'Mission: Impossible' Ankle Injury." *Men's Health*, April 27, 2018. www.menshealth.com/entertainment/a20085147/tom-cruise-mission-impossible-ankle-injury/.

Martin, Sylvia J. 2012. "Stunt Workers and Spectacle: Ethnography of Physical Risk in Hollywood and Hong Kong." In *Film and Risk*, edited by Mette Hjort, 97–114. Detroit: Wayne State University Press.

McDonald, Paul. 2013. *Hollywood Stardom*. Malden, MA: Wiley-Blackwell.

Michaels, Lorne. 2018. *The Tonight Show Starring Jimmy Fallon*. Season 5, episode 172. Broadway Video and Universal Television, July 23, 2018.

Mumford, Gwilym. "Tom Cruise Injury Halts Filming on Mission Impossible 6." *Guardian*, August 17, 2017. www.theguardian.com/film/2017/aug/17/tom-cruise-injury-halts-filming-on-mission-impossible-6.

O'Donnell, Ruth. 2012. "Performing Masculinity: The Star Persona of Tom Cruise." PhD diss., Royal Holloway, University of London.

———. 2016. "Mission: Impossible? The Rehabilitation of Tom Cruise." *Celebrity Studies* 7 (3): 425–28.

Peberdy, Donna. 2010. "From Wimps to Wild Men: Bipolar Masculinity and the Paradoxical Performances of Tom Cruise." *Men and Masculinities* 13 (2): 231–54.

Purse, Lisa. 2011. *Contemporary Action Cinema*. Edinburgh: Edinburgh University Press.

Ross, Monique. 2017. "The Mummy Director on Tom Cruise, Zero-Gravity Stunts and Universal's Dark Universe," ABC News, June 5, 2017. www.abc.net.au/news/2017-06-06/the-mummy-tom-cruise-universal-dark-universe/8544972.

Sacks, Ethan. 2011. "All about Dangling Tom Cruise 1,700 Feet over Dubai for 'Mission: Impossible—Ghost Protocol,'" *New York Daily News*, December 11, 2011. www.nydailynews.com/entertainment/tv-movies/dangling-tom-cruise-1-700-feet-dubai-mission-impossible-ghost-protocol-article-1.988566.

Smith, Jacob. 2004. "Seeing Double: Stunt Performance and Masculinity." *Journal of Film and Video* 56 (3): 35–53.

Stefansky, Emma. 2018. "Tom Cruise Shows the Gruesome Footage of How He Broke His Ankle on the Set of Mission: Impossible—Fallout," *Vanity Fair*, January 28, 2018. www.vanityfair.com/hollywood/2018/01/tom-cruise-mission-impossible-stunt-video?verso=true.

Steimer, Lauren. 2018. "All Guts and No Glory: Stuntwork and Stunt Performers in Hollywood History." In *A Companion to the Action Film*, edited by James Kendrick, 241–55. Hoboken, NJ: John Wiley.

Stuart, Graham. 2018. *The Graham Norton Show*. Season 22, episode 17. BBC, January 26, 2018.

Studlar, Gaylyn. 2001. "Cruise-Ing into the Millennium: Performative Masculinity Stardom, and the All-American Boy's Body." In *Ladies and Gentlemen, Boys and Girls: Gender in Film at the End of the Millennium*, edited by Murray Pomerance, 171–83. Albany: State University of New York Press.

Tasker, Yvonne. 2018. "X-Men/Action Men: Performing Masculinities in Superhero and Science-Fiction Cinema." In *A Companion to the Action Film*, edited by James Kendrick, 381–97. Hoboken, NJ: John Wiley.

Thilk, Chris. 2018. "While Tom Cruise Is off Doing His Own Stunts, Here's How His Bored Stuntman Keeps Busy." *AdWeek*, July 5, 2018. www.adweek.com/creativity/while-tom-cruise-is-off-doing-his-own-stunts-heres-how-his-bored-stuntman-keeps-busy/.

Thorp, Charles. 2017. "The Man behind Tom Cruise's Most Badass Stunts." *Men's Journal*, February 14, 2017. www.mensjournal.com/entertainment/meet-wade-eastwood-tom-cruises-secret-stunt-weapon-w466942/.

———. 2018. "How Tom Cruise Pulled Off Every Insane 'Mission Impossible: Fallout' Stunt." *Men's Journal*, July 30, 2018. www.mensjournal.com/entertainment/how-tom-cruise-did-every-insane-mission-impossible-fallout-stunt/.

"Tom Cruise Injured in 'Mission Impossible' Stunt." 2017. TMZ, August 13, 2017. www.tmz.com/2017/08/13/tom-cruise-injured-mission-impossible-6-stunt/.

Williams, Trey. 2018. "Did Tom Cruise Really Do All the Stunts in 'Mission: Impossible—Fallout'?" The Wrap, July 28, 2018. www.thewrap.com/tom-cruise-stunts-mission-impossible-fallout/.

Zakarin, Jordan. 2017. "Tom Cruise Has Been Telling the Same Stunt Story for 20 Years." *Inverse*, June 5, 2017. www.inverse.com/article/32528-tom-cruise-the-mummy-stunts-mission-impossible.

14

THE AUTHENTICALLY BRUISED CRUISE

Tom Cruise, *Mission: Impossible*, and Extreme Performative Labor

Justin Owen Rawlins

"How will they know it's my pants?"

In the midst of a then unprecedented 160-minute interview with *The Empire Film Podcast* to promote his latest directorial effort, 2015's *Mission: Impossible—Rogue Nation* (a milestone that would be obliterated by the 352-minute conversation with the same outfit regarding 2018's *Mission: Impossible—Fallout*), Christopher McQuarrie (2015) was searching for an apt description of what it was like to helm a Tom Cruise movie. "It's a dangerous thing having Tom Cruise," he told interviewer Chris Hewitt. The director's anxiety, expressed more candidly by several of his predecessors on previous *Mission: Impossible* installments, had been internalized through a long working relationship with the actor. Echoing other *Mission: Impossible* directors who professed nightmares and bouts of on-set anxiety about the star's risk-taking tendencies, McQuarrie noted that Cruise was both the principal motivating force behind the film's extraordinary stunts *and* the crew member most exposed to potential injury in the process. As the face of the *Mission: Impossible* franchise and one of its producers since the first installment two decades earlier, Cruise's insistence on performing his own stunts seemed to leave no potential danger to the star—as well as the production and possibly the franchise—off the table. Half-jokingly, host Hewitt proposed, Cruise's track record of embracing increasingly dangerous stunts on *Mission: Impossible* films prompted consideration of his—and the production's—limits. "He looks at the underwater shot and he goes, 'Okay we're doing an underwater sequence,'" Hewitt began. "He looks at the model of the plane and goes, 'I can climb on the side of that.' . . . Basically if you suggest anything to him that sounds dangerous, will he do it? 'Rattlesnakes down my pants? Absolutely I will do that!'"

Treating the latter outlandish scenario with the sincerity of a plausible situation, McQuarrie drew on his and Cruise's working process to inform how such a hypothetical conversation would proceed:

> Tom would go, "Okay. How do we know it's my pants? How are you going to shoot it? Because I don't want to stick a rattlesnake down my pants and just have it be an insert of my leg when it could just be anybody's leg." For Tom it is about when you present a stunt to him, Tom is saying, "How can we shoot it in a way that people really know it's me? Because if I'm wearing a helmet on a motorcycle, just put somebody else on the motorcycle, and then why put anybody on the motorcycle because you're not connected to the character anymore. You've got to see my eyes and know it's me or else it's not worth doing."

Consistent with the rest of this conversation and the hours of other interviews, trailers, featurettes, and countless other promotional materials surrounding the *Mission: Impossible* franchise, McQuarrie's hypothetical dialogue with the series' avatar is firmly rooted in an interpretive landscape that frames Tom Cruise's stunt work as *the* distinguishing feature of his performance style. He runs. He jumps. He grimaces. He looks stunned. He runs some more. Indeed, his frantic dashing about is omnipresent, the subject of montages (one of which runs nearly nineteen minutes long). "Does Tom Cruise run?" asks film critic Amy Nicholson (2014, 168) in her monograph on the actor. "Does a fish swim?" Running may be the most enduring element of Cruise's physicality on display in his nearly four-decade filmography, yet it remains but one feature in the broader interpretive matrix that has coalesced around him over the course of his career. His star image—the amalgam of meanings always accumulating from film roles, interviews, promotional materials, publicity, profiles, and other sources pertaining to "Tom Cruise" along all nodes in the media ecosystem—routinely foregrounds an ethos of hard work, passion, and commitment to film production.

In this chapter, I look specifically to the increasingly vital function of Tom Cruise's performative stunt labor in his overall star image. Utilizing reception studies to survey the paratexts—the studio promotion of *Mission: Impossible* films and Cruise as well as the critical reactions to both—I argue that these discourses and representations orbiting *Mission: Impossible* and Cruise collectively constitute an interpretive framework for understanding performance outside of the films themselves. The persistent emphasis on Cruise as a stunt-centric actor and producer, I show, is especially integral to publicity materials for more recent *Mission: Impossible* installments and entwined with the series' durability and profitability. Using his disastrous string of media appearances in 2005 as a touchstone for the fissures in public image undermining Cruise's authenticity and threatening his professional viability, I contend that these paratexts surrounding both star and franchise have been essential in establishing his performances as stunt-centric and thus have become at least as important a venue as the films themselves in in repairing his compromised star image. While the events of 2005 exemplified the dangers of Cruise losing control over both his outward-facing public ("front stage") and his supposedly private ("backstage") selves, I trace a steady effort to hinge the recovery of the star's authenticity on the stunt-centric performances in *Mission: Impossible* that have come to dominate his career of late. In its attempts to carefully curate the star's "back stage" by foregrounding stunt production over his controversial religion and romantic relationships, paratexts have provided ostensibly transparent glimpses into the raw—and thus putatively "real"—work that Cruise accomplishes by subjecting himself to physical extremes. Given the ambivalent reception that continues to greet him, especially with regard to his private life, curating this behind-the-scenes sense of access to Cruise the person may well represent his last viable strategy for reclaiming and maintaining an authenticity requisite to stardom's overall connection with consumers and fans. It also raises broader questions about how and where the meaning of acting can be located, and the work that paratextually constituted performance can do beyond the film text.

Paratexts and Performance

Though "early moving pictures were in many cases like theatrical props . . . gain[ing] meaning only to the extent that performers were able to integrate them into their acts," the preeminence of acting in the filmmaking process was rarely reflected in the discourse of the ossifying industry or film theory (Altman 2006, 61). The emergence of a more formalized star system routinely attenuated greater recognition of acting, often by obscuring the labor of actors and conceding that performers embodied little more than sweat, working for—rather than with—their directors.[1] Early film theory echoed this trend, establishing disciplinary frameworks alienated from acting from the outset (Berke 2016, 177–78). Scholars lagged in recognizing the labor and value of performers even as figures like Lillian Gish, Alice Guy Blaché, Louise Brooks, and Colleen Moore theorized star and performer screen labor in popular forums.[2] Annie Berke (2016, 177) points to the "predominance of the medium specificity concept" behind this trend in early film theory, which dismissed or ignored acting—a vestige, the logic goes, of theater—in order to make the case for cinema's singularity as an art form.

Hollywood's star system has no doubt continued this pattern of obfuscation. Frequently burying acknowledgment of performer preparation, philosophy, and practice beneath an industry veneer asserting that stars were simply being themselves, studios set a precedent for making sense of acting. This interpretive framework remains remarkably intact today in spite of seismic industrial shifts and is evident both in the exceptionalism afforded so-called Method turns by the likes of Daniel Day-Lewis and Christian Bale and in the dismissal of big-budget film leads like Tom Cruise. "He's been hiding in plain sight all this time," affirms Amy Nicholson (qtd. in Hertz 2014, 55), yet "we just reduce him to these weird images of an action star" rather than afford his labor critical consideration or merit.

Meanwhile, studies of film authorship, which have long prioritized directors, have more recently begun to seriously consider the work of the screen performer. James Naremore's (1988, 3–4) seminal contribution to this

---

1 This was often an especially gendered division of imagined labor, where fan magazines and studio advertising campaigns characterized men as working to learn a role-necessitated skill and women as products of others' work.

2 "While most know [Lillian] Gish as a silent film star," writes Annie Berke (2016, 175), "and some know her as an autobiographer and lecturer on the history of early cinema, very few regard her as a film theorist." Amelie Hastie (2007) details the labor of Louise Brooks, Colleen More, and Alice Guy Blaché in ruminating on the motion picture industry and historiography.

shift, best exemplified by his concept of the "performance frame," outlines an analytical structure for examining how screen actors convey meaning to audiences. The performance frame, Naremore asserts, enables viewers to understand the rhetorical conventions of cinema controlling "the ostensiveness of the players, as well as their relative positions within the performing space, and their mode of address to the audience." It also equips them to discern both the role of expressive techniques and the logic of coherence whereby the players stay more or less "in step with changes in the story, more or less in character, and more or less 'true to themselves.'" Beyond the actors, the frame also attends to the role of mise-en-scène in helping to shape the performance through expressive materials, such as inanimate objects, clothing, and accessories (4). Following Naremore, others have looked to the film text for methods to extricate meaning from specific performances and to argue for greater overall valuation of actors and performer labor within the production process. To this end, Cynthia Baron (2007, 38) has called for an end to thinking of screen acting as "inert matter" and argued that "performative choices" are an essential element of montage alongside framing, editing, production, and sound. Extending this intervention further, we could consider how such choices inform—rather than merely coexist with—other characteristics of film. In the case of Cruise, the quality of his acting is up for debate, but an exploration of his trademark professionalism reveals the extent to which he brings his actor's perspective to all phases of the production process. He has never served as a director, yet in the *Mission: Impossible* films especially, Cruise's "performative choices" have transformed him into an official producer, an uncredited screenwriter and cinematographer, and of course a much ballyhooed stuntman.

Though film scholars have not yet responded in force to Rick Altman's (2006, 61) call for performance-centric screen historiography,[3] efforts to pinpoint and validate film performance and performers have made significant inroads. Performance/acting studies scholars seeking to make acting the gravitational center of screen meaning have devised analytical frameworks for extricating acts from the collaborative process of production and imbuing the performer with an agency bordering on (if not outright laying claim to) the authorial. Centering performance in the film text remains a

---

3 One notable response to Altman's provocation is Jacob Smith's (2012) book-length study of the nexus of gender and fame in stunt work's transition to cinema.

crucial intervention, yet this prevailing approach also arouses concern as to how fixation on the film occurs at the expense of other evidentiary and performative possibilities. In other words, efforts to locate meaning in the film convey directly and indirectly the presumption that the act, and thus its potential meanings and uses, is circumscribed by the film. In effect, this precludes opportunities for actors and roles to take on meaning in the texts, spaces, and networks that lie beyond the film in question. Star/celebrity studies scholars have also made crucial inroads in mapping the actor's symbolic and material agency by extensively mining discursive and representational circuits of paratexts for continuities and disruptions. This capacious approach is highly valuable, yet in matters of performance the film retains its primacy and paratexts are relegated to secondary status. As a result, the invaluable interventions working to recenter screen acting within film and to connect paratexts to a star's meaning have occluded how actors' labor may take its prevailing meaning outside of the film altogether and may overlap or diverge entirely from the techniques and philosophies that went into the performance.

This shift in focus toward decentering the screen text reframes many of the underlying assumptions about what constitutes evidence of a film's significance and how far the signifying capacities of acting stretch. Rather than attempt to excavate the essence of the on-screen performance, for example, we may map its relation according to broader cultural and ideological coordinates. This invites us to excavate how performance coalesces through larger circulations of paratextual discourses and representations. Drawing on Gerard Genette's definition of paratexts as "texts that prepare us for other texts," Jonathan Gray argues that paratexts fill up the spaces between texts, their producers, distributors, audiences, and even authors (2010, 25). Films and television programs remain important as the "texts" around which paratexts such as reviews, performer profiles, interviews, DVD and Blu-ray commentaries, newspaper and magazine articles, and studio promotion orbit.

Importantly, paratexts are not secondary to texts. While they can exist without texts (one can read a review but never watch the movie), the inverse is not true given the film or television show's reliance on ubiquitous paratexts to situate the text and its performers within broader frameworks of interpretation and thus to condition, to varying extents, audience relationships with the text. Paratexts do not simply accentuate texts but are instead instrumental in the larger composition of textuality by framing, filtering, and cohering meaning.⁴ In this way, reframing the foundational questions about film meaning directs critical attention toward the paratextual circuits and spaces around and beyond films, prioritizing the contexts and contingencies of actors' symbolic, ideological, and sociocultural work as discursive and representational amalgams. In the case of Cruise and the most recent *Mission: Impossible* films, the stunt-centric promotional videos circulated by Paramount flooded popular paratextual channels like YouTube for months ahead of each installment's theatrical release. Rather than employ polished final cuts of these moments, these videos focused exclusively on foregrounding Cruise's work in performing the stunts through behind-the-scenes style blending of raw footage and interviews with the actor/star/producer as well as other crew testifying to the veracity of what the audience is seeing. The centrality of the stunts to the films—and the extent to which these paratexts cover the stunts—in many ways obviates the need to watch the motion picture at all. This phenomenon also invites exploration of what these Cruise performances are *doing* outside of the *Mission: Impossible* films they seek to promote.

Acting in the Wrong Film

After firing his longtime publicist Pat Kingsley the previous year, actor-turned-superstar Tom Cruise embarked on a disastrous series of media appearances in 2005 originally designed to promote his collaboration with director Steven Spielberg on *War of the Worlds*. Projecting an intensity of emotion far beyond the measured, colloquial intimacy that host Oprah Winfrey had cultivated on her show, Cruise's infamous *Oprah* routine of couch jumping, crouching, fist pumping, aggressive hugging, and declarations of affection for new girlfriend, Katie Holmes (not to mention his decision to forcibly escort her to the stage), suggested a performance geared to match—and then exceed—the adulating fervor displayed by the audience. It was, Barry King (2008, 128) has observed, "an unlicensed presentation of the self" eschewing the star's characteristic disclosures about craft and vision for a confused para-confession seemingly aimed at conveying authenticity

---

4   Says Gray (2010, 3), "Rather than simply serve as extensions of a text, many of these items are filters through which we must pass on our way to the film or program, our first and formative encounters with the text."

through kinetic professions of love. Intentional or not, his actions not only contrasted with that typically expected of Winfrey's celebrity guests, but they became even more jarring through short, decontextualized clips and memes of his dramatic appearance that subsequently circulated online. Cruise's appearance became one of the first hits on the months-old YouTube service—which was just barely older than his romance with Holmes (Knibbs 2018). Cruise's miscalculation highlighted the "visual iterability of the scene itself" in the internet age (DeAngelis 2010, 42). It also foregrounded questions about the place of his acting in his overall symbolic repertoire, previewing a recurring trend that saw his staged passions—for Holmes, his films, and Scientology—from 2005 on increasingly interpreted as suspect, disingenuous, or just plain odd. In the publicity rounds that ensued after the "couch incident," writes Kate Knibbs (2018), "Cruise's over-the-top display of hyper-public affection, possibly made more intense by his desire to prove that his love was real, backfired. Instead of making people think he was a romantic, Cruise just made people think he was weird." This dramatic, tone-setting self-immolation would carry over into inflammatory comments three days after his *Oprah* appearance, during an *Access Hollywood* interview in which Cruise deployed Scientology doctrine to criticize Brooke Shields, postpartum depression sufferers, and antidepressants. An attempted apology several weeks later quickly escalated during an interview with *Today* cohost Matt Lauer, giving way to a lengthy Cruise diatribe against psychiatry. In just over a month's time, "Cruise incinerated over two decades of goodwill" (Nicholson 2014, 144).

Reflecting on the "couch incident," Michael DeAngelis (2010, 42) adroitly observed that "while Cruise's kneeling, jumping, and bouncing may not have been entirely out of character, in this case the 'character' seemed to be appearing in the wrong scene or even the wrong film." Susan J. Douglas and Andrea McDonnell (2019) see a similarly jarring juxtaposition at the heart of this litany of gaffes. Drawing on Erving Goffman's dramaturgical metaphor for conceptualizing social interaction as fundamentally performative, they suggest that figures like Cruise generate such discordant moments by transgressing expectations of how they should act in a given situation. Moments of excess, in the case of Cruise, breach (or at least indicate the existence of) the "back stage"—the machinery and labor that go into, but are not expressly presented in, the "front stage" of the figure's outward-facing presentation (24–47). Successful celebrity performances are convincing and consistent because they "convey sincerity" via self-presentation, thus maintaining the "front stage" veneer while obscuring the "backstage" work and the inconsistencies that arise in outward-facing efforts to meet social or popular expectations. Tom Cruise's 2005 appearances were therefore poorly received because together they conveyed unintended and sustained glimpses backstage. They presented a jarring disjuncture with the carefully managed front stage of the consummate professional, the hardworking star. This unauthorized access also revealed new dimensions of a person whose avowed religious beliefs (alongside the prevailing reception of the Church of Scientology as suspiciously opaque and duplicitous) and sense of propriety undermined his apparent capacity for genuine expressions, thereby threatening his—and stardom's—central precept for connecting with audiences: authenticity (22–23).

These moments and the suspicions they aroused about the "backstage" Cruise no doubt impacted the trajectory and tenor of his career, though to what extent remains a matter of debate. Some suggest that it diminished the box office revenue for *Mission: Impossible III*, which debuted one year later and, while still profitable, has proven so far to be the least financially successful installment in the franchise. Though less lucrative than its two predecessors, the timing of the third *Mission: Impossible* film could not have been more poignant given the series' entanglement with Cruise's performative labor on several registers. In addition to being his most reliably profitable and prolific film property, *Mission: Impossible* represents his first and most sustained venture into producing, suggesting a far greater role in the filmmaking process than even superstar status may confer. This role figures into the discourses of labor as well, serving as further evidence of Cruise's purportedly unmatched commitment to making *Mission: Impossible* movies specifically *and* abetting the performer's, star's, and franchise's attempts to mitigate the "backstage" acts of 2005 and the ensuing fallout (no pun intended).

While the paratexts accompanying every *Mission: Impossible* installment draw attention to Tom Cruise's labor as an actor, star, stuntman, and producer, I home in on examples from the two most recent chapters, *Mission: Impossible—Rogue Nation* and *Mission: Impossible—Fallout* (Christopher McQuarrie 2018). Using the publicity surrounding these films, I illustrate how these paratexts foreground Tom Cruise's stunt-centric acting labor and attempt to curate this "making of" promotional material as a genuine act of transparency. This maneuver replaces the couch-jumping Scientologist with a serious producer and stunt master, in full control of the film's—and his own—"backstage" performances.

The Stunts Are Real

Among the advertisements circulating ahead of the 2015 release of *Rogue Nation*, one prominent promotional video precirculated on platforms like YouTube begins with a question for the viewer. The text "Why do the stunts look real?" lands with a visual and aural thud. Emphasizing its rhetorical nature, the second line unsparingly declares, "Because they **are** real" ("Mission: Impossible Rogue Nation—Stunt Featurette" 2015). The boldface "are" frames the stunt as excessive in the norms of production and thus exceptional. *Rogue Nation* stunt coordinator Wade Eastwood verifies this in narrating the setup as images of an Airbus A400 plane flash across the screen. "Tom wanted to be on the outside of that plane," he tells the audience. Tom Cruise's voice enters over additional shots featuring preparations, meetings, and the A400: "I couldn't sleep the night before, and then came the day." As he appears onscreen for the first time (credited as "Ethan Hunt / Producer"), Cruise continues: "I was like 'Okay, I guess this is really gonna happen.'" He cracks a smile as he folds his arms and leans back toward the out-of-focus backdrop of production equipment. At that, the behind-the-scenes narrative picks up speed as if motivated by Cruise's ensuing "Let's go," uttered from behind a pair of sunglasses as he sheds his coat on the set.

Flashes of preparation follow to convey the linear progression of the A400 shoot, what audiences would later learn was *Rogue Nation*'s opening sequence. The harness is strapped around Cruise's torso to keep him tethered to the plane. Specially designed contact lenses are installed that will allow him to open his eyes for the sake of the shot while staying protected from particles weaponized by the plane's extreme velocity. Over these shots, *Rogue Nation*'s visual effects supervisor, David Vickery, registers his surprise and awe. As the camera cuts to him for a literal eyebrow-raising reveal, he says, "I thought that was a one-take, but he did it *eight* times" (his emphasis). As Cruise is fastened to the plane's exterior and the viewer glimpses crew members and equipment inside the plane just feet away from the star's location, he reminds the audience that the commitment he's made (eight times over, as we just learned) carries significant risk that cannot be immediately addressed and therefore might prove all the more dangerous: "If something went wrong, I can't get into the airplane until we land." At that, the stunt begins. A camera mounted to the side of the A400 and situated roughly ten feet in front of Cruise provides an intimate framing of the actor for the audience, making clear that he, the plane, and the takeoff are all real. A thumbs up from the film's star signals both a readiness and an enthusiasm for stunts reiterated elsewhere in *Rogue Nation* paratexts by McQuarrie, Cruise, and others.

The cut to this camera position also shifts the ad's aesthetic as it provides viewers with their first access to footage intended for the film itself. Now letterboxed, the image conveys a sense of rawness in two ways. The safety harness and cable ensuring Cruise's attachment to the aircraft are visible, as are the metadata concerning the camera and shot in question. Together, these "behind the scene" signifiers strip the shot of the polish that will eventually stitch it into the film's opening sequence and digitally remove the actor's safety apparatus. In the meantime, however, this unvarnished take, the last and longest of the advertisement (clocking in at nearly 20 percent of the total length), is further stripped of the ad's own postproduction features. Voiceovers disappear, and all that remains is one continuous shot of *Rogue Nation*'s star clinging to the plane as the wind screams by and the earth shrinks in the background.

The discourse surrounding the most recent installment, 2018's *Fallout*, extends this stunt-centric framework further. Much like its predecessor, this motion picture's advertising campaign insists on the transparency of action by employing the star as the avatar for this ethos of performative authenticity. Like its predecessor, *Fallout*'s publicity revolves around several "trailers" that, like the A400 advertisement discussed earlier, eschew the conventional subject matter of plot teasers for in-depth studies of particular Tom Cruise stunts such as the HALO jump, payload drop, and helicopter chase.

Unintended—though no less effective—paratexts arose around a stunt gone wrong: a rooftop chase sequence through London that ended with Cruise breaking his ankle during a leap between buildings. So seamless was this unscripted outcome that it was rather effortlessly incorporated into the film's preferred promotional framework. This was perhaps best exemplified by the appearance of Cruise and his costars on *The Graham Norton Show* in late January 2018, one of several videos featuring the accident that circulated widely via platforms like YouTube. Seizing on the promotional

Tom Cruise clings to the side of the Airbus A400 as it lifts off in this *Mission: Impossible—Rogue Nation* (Christopher McQuarrie, 2015) trailer featurette, which emphatically forewarns audiences that the stunts "are real."

opportunity of the accident, the *Graham Norton* appearance occurred while *Fallout* was still in production and the ankle in question, according to Cruise, was still broken (Stuart 2018). Turning toward the audience, Norton acknowledges that the film accident had already been widely circulated and thus was familiar to viewers. Presuming a shared public fascination with the outcome of the stunt ("I think we all kind of thought, 'How did you break an ankle doing that?'"), Norton's rhetorical question cedes the floor to Cruise to both explain the stunt and further demonstrate his expert knowledge of stunt work. The jump was always intended to be the stunt, he declares, rationalizing why it was therefore supposed to look dangerous. Norton's interjection—that Cruise has brought behind-the-scenes footage of the accident to share with the audience—provides visual aids for his explanation of the incident. Ostensibly transported straight from the film set to the television studio, the three camera angles of the same moment proffer a comprehensive and definitive accounting of the injury that verifies Cruise's narrative. The footage also provides performatively transparent access to the extreme physical effort that led to the accident *and* Cruise's dedication to his craft, which saw him complete the shot in question despite the broken ankle.

In the last of the three camera angles, Tom Cruise grimaces from his ankle break a few seconds earlier and begins pulling himself up to run past the camera and complete the shot.

Cruise narrates the three clips in forensic detail. The first follows him from behind as he jumps between buildings, his back obscuring the injury. The second, from the right side, provides the most view of the accident. "[I]t's not for the squeamish," Norton warns everyone. Having established through a zoom-in on the ankle in question—to the groans and cries of Cruise's *Fallout* costars and the studio audience—Norton turns to the third angle. Situated on the building to which the actor is jumping, the camera catches the look on his face when he hit the wall and, as Cruise recalls, knew instantly his ankle was broken. Having already visibly and narratively situated the devastating injury, the third and final camera angle provides the most visceral and intimate evidence of the actor's pain and his commitment to completing the shot. "Here is why," Norton says, preparing the audience before playing the last clip, "Tom Cruise gets paid the big bucks," reminding viewers that the star's value is intimately tied to the performative risks he takes for his roles.

With production crew and safety cables visible behind him, the actor's jump brings him to the middle ground in a violent collision with the building's exterior wall. The grimace on his face registers pain that Norton, Cruise, and others repeatedly invite the audience to read as back stage access to the real Cruise. As he pulls himself up and hobbles through the foreground and beyond the camera, fellow guest and *Fallout* costar Simon Pegg testifies that "everybody said that when you got up and ran out of the shot, 'Oh that's so him.' To complete the shot with your foot hanging off? That's so him.'"

The remainder of the episode, like the segment, was *so him*. The following segment similarly celebrated Cruise's extensive training to pilot a helicopter during *Fallout*'s climactic chase. Even though the final segment—where Cruise teaches audience members to do stunt work by jumping in front of a green screen—is played for laughs, it relies on the same overarching effort to frame Cruise's performative expertise as entwined with stunt work and indicative of who he really is.

Conclusion: "Information is the death of emotion"

While Tom Cruise's feats in these paratexts are no doubt important to the star-centric hype one might expect ahead of a big budget summer release, the particular focus on his labor as an actor–stuntman hybrid seems to strive for something more. This is not to diminish the significance of a broader star image encompassing an array of contradictory signifiers, including the "backstage" Cruise glimpsed on Oprah's couch and suspected elsewhere. Yet the paratexts concerning his performative labor in the *Mission: Impossible* films reflect pointed efforts on behalf of the actor/star and producers to connect his acting to more measured and authentic expressions of passion that not only counter the unintended "backstage" glimpses of Cruise's 2005 PR fiasco but recuperate a newly grounded sense of coherence for Cruise's previously fractured star image. Demonstrating his physical mastery of the risks normally outsourced to stunt professionals is key to this process, seemingly stripping his performances of any sense of artifice and rendering his work visible and tangible. Jacob Smith (2004, 37) has illustrated how historically fluid "boundaries between actor and stunt performer" in early twentieth-century American film gave way to an industrial star system that hardened distinctions between the two while also obscuring the stunt worker. Unlike the "competing logic" of early stardom that prioritized "the affective sensation of realistic thrills" and on-location shooting (Jennifer M. Beam qtd. in Smith 2004, 37), Hollywood studios and the star system ossified the practice of subsuming the stuntman to the male star he doubled, flattening the contrasts between the masculinized and feminized forms of stunt and star labor, and suturing the star's face to the stuntman's body (Smith 2004, 38). For Cruise, repeatedly and unambiguously demonstrating in these paratexts that stunt, star, and performer labor originate in the same actor offers itself as an alternative to the status quo, a marker of his exceptionality, and a corrective to his attributed incongruities epitomized by the events of 2005.

In his marathon 352-minute interview with *The Empire Film Podcast*, *Rogue Nation*, and *Fallout* director Christopher McQuarrie suggested that the guiding logic of both films was to align action, rather than exposition, with affect. "Information," he told interviewer Chris Hewitt, "is the death of emotion" (McQuarrie 2018). What reads at first like a bold statement becomes somewhat less audacious when considering how that sentiment is entwined with the franchise's and lead actor's long-standing efforts to connect with audiences. Not unlike the "competing logic" mentioned earlier, Cruise and the discourses and representations circulating around him seek to construct stunt-oriented narratives through which pains are taken to showcase the star's face and stuntman's body as belonging to the same performer. Rather than subsume the stuntman, the discursive and representational framing of Cruise's acting in *Mission: Impossible* paratexts foregrounds his stunts as action-based means to reveal himself to—and emotionally connect with—the audience. By emphasizing both the need to see his eyes and to know that he is doing the stunts himself, Cruise's performances across *Mission: Impossible* paratexts presume to strip away the artifice of production and offer a carefully curated "backstage" tour free of the performative disjuncture typified by the "couch incident" years earlier. By branding affective attachments through masculinized moments of intimacy and vulnerability as the actor who both stars and stunts, both the performer and the franchise seek to mobilize Tom Cruise's performative labor toward recuperating a sense of authenticity and coherence that aestheticizes transparency and disavows pretense.

At the same time, it is imperative to remind ourselves that exploring what performance *does* also entails probing the extent and limits of that work. In the case of Tom Cruise, the promotional paratexts surrounding the two most recent chapters in the *Mission: Impossible* franchise work tirelessly to foreground his stunt work as the films' central attraction, as the gravitational and affective centers of the respective narratives as well as each film's promotional campaign. Cruise's performance within the constellation of *Mission: Impossible* paratexts is integral to this work. And yet, as other paratexts indicate, efforts to refashion Cruise's perceived intensity and genuineness through stunt-centric acting do not exist in a vacuum. However profitable and powerful, they continue to contend with those fissures epitomized by 2005 and echoed among some observers well into his *Mission: Impossible*–aligned recuperation. As Dave Schilling (2015) observed three days before the release of *Rogue Nation*, "Tom Cruise looks like he's trying *really* hard all the time. That's great when he's pulling off an audacious stunt—less so when he's aiming to approximate what the 'kids' like."

Works Cited

Altman, Rick. 2006. "From Lecturer's Prop to Industrial Product: The Early History of Travel Films." In *Virtual voyages: cinema and travel*, edited by Jeffrey Ruoff, 61–76. Durham, NC: Duke University Press.

Baron, Cynthia. 2007. "Acting Choices/Filmic Choices: Rethinking Montage and Performance." *Journal of Film and Video* 59, no. 2 (Summer): 32–40.

Berke, Annie. 2016. "'Never Let the Camera Catch Me Acting': Lillian Gish as Actress, Star, and Theorist." *Historical Journal of Film, Radio and Television* 36 (2): 175–89. doi.org/10.1080/01439685.2016.1167464.

DeAngelis, Michael. 2010. "Tom Cruise, the 'Couch Incident,' and the Limits of Public Elation." *Velvet Light Trap* 65 (Spring): 42–43. doi.org/10.1353/vlt.0.0080.

Douglas, Susan J., and Andrea McDonnell. 2019. *Celebrity: A History of Fame*. New York: New York University Press.

Gray, Jonathan. 2010. *Show Sold Separately: Promos, Spoilers, and other Media Paratexts*. New York: New York University Press.

Hastie, Amelie. 2007. *Cupboards of Curiosity: Women, Recollection, and Film History*. Durham: Duke University Press.

Hertz, Barry. 2014. "He's Not Dead Yet." *Maclean's*, June 9, 2014.

King, Barry. 2008. "Stardom, Celebrity, and the Para-confession." *Social Semiotics* 18, no. 2 (June): 115–32. doi.org/10.1080/10350330802002135.

Knibbs, Kate. 2018. "The Couch Jump That Rocked Hollywood." The Ringer, August 1, 2018. www.theringer.com/tv/2018/8/1/17631658/tom-cruise-oprah-couch-jump.

McQuarrie, Christopher. 2015. "Christopher McQuarrie Mission: Impossible—Rogue Nation Special." Interview with Chris Hewitt. *Empire Film Podcast*. Podcast audio, December 7, 2015. planetradio.co.uk/podcasts/the-empire-podcast/listen/5905/.

———. 2018. "Mission: Impossible—Fallout Spoiler Special Ft. Christopher McQuarrie Part 1." Interview with Chris Hewitt. *Empire Film Podcast*. Podcast audio, July 31, 2018. planetradio.co.uk/podcasts/the-empire-podcast/listen/10045/.

"Mission: Impossible Rogue Nation—Stunt Featurette." 2015. *YouTube*, July 13, 2015. https://www.youtube.com/watch?v=afS5ks54tms&feature=youtu.be.

Naremore, James. 1988. *Acting in the Cinema*. Berkeley: University of California Press.

Nicholson, Amy. 2014. *Tom Cruise: Anatomy of an Actor*. New York: Phaidon Press, 2014.

Schilling, Dave. 2015. "Tom Cruise Week First-Round Recap: The Motorcycle Dance and the Decline of 'Cool Cruise.'" *Grantland*, July 28, 2015. grantland.com/hollywood-prospectus/tom-cruise-week-first-round-recap-the-motorcycle-dance-and-the-decline-of-cool-cruise/.

Smith, Jacob. 2004. "Seeing Double: Stunt Performance and Masculinity." *Journal of Film and Video* 56, no. 3 (Fall): 35–53.

———. 2012. *The Thrill Makers: Celebrity, Masculinity, and Stunt Performance*. Berkeley: University of California Press.

Stuart, Graham. 2018. "Tom Cruise / Rebecca Ferguson / Henry Cavill / Simon Pegg / Paloma Faith." *The Graham Norton Show*. BBC, January 26, 2018.

15

AGING FOR LIFE

TOM CRUISE IN THE ERA OF FUNCTIONAL FITNESS

Michael DeAngelis

Even before his 2005 fall from grace with the notorious couch-jumping incident on *The Oprah Winfrey Show* in celebration of his love for Katie Holmes, his outburst to *Today* host Matt Lauer about the scam of modern psychiatry, and his tirade against Brooke Shields for taking antidepressant medication to relieve postpartum depression, Tom Cruise could never be considered a dead ringer for the Incredible Hulk. Having entered the realm of action cinema with a version of masculine strength quite different from pumped-up personas of action stars such as Sylvester Stallone or Arnold Schwarzenegger, the last ten years of the actor's career have not brought about the drastic and noticeable changes of body composition shared by many of his colleagues. Cruise has continued to sport a less imposing muscularity accentuated by low levels of body fat, and on the path from *Top Gun* (Tony Scott, 1988) to *Mission: Impossible—Fallout* (Christopher McQuarrie, 2018) his body has never deviated substantially from the "cut/ripped" category.

It is, however, this conspicuous semblance of the "then" and "now" versions of Cruise's physique that fuels ongoing debates surrounding the aging and seeming agelessness of the now fifty-eight-year-old Tom Cruise, often centering on both informed and conjectural accusations that he struggles to preserve his youthful look by resorting to "unnatural" methods of retaining a hard body—not only collagen injections, steroidal supplements, and other technologies of body enhancement but also an irrational obsession with youthfulness that requires countless hours of daily workouts to maintain—so much, in fact, that Cruise brings his private gym with him wherever he goes. Despite such controversies, however, Cruise has indisputably regained his "pre-meltdown" level of popularity, with nine of his thirteen post-2005 films earning a cumulative worldwide gross of over $200,000,000 each, and *Fallout*, the most recently released installment of the *Mission: Impossible* franchise, taking in over $790,000,000 worldwide on its own ("Tom Cruise" n.d.).

As Ruth O'Donnell (2016) suggests, authenticity and sincerity are Cruise's mainstays, and when they are compromised, he loses connection with his audience. This is hardly unique as a phenomenon of celebrity culture, but while contemporary fallen-from-grace stars like Mel Gibson and Russell Crowe have atoned for their verbal and physical transgressions with heartfelt avowals and repeated public apologies, attempts at the public "redemption" of Tom Cruise, along with the recuperation of his authenticity, have played out primarily over the surfaces and contours of the body—*his* body, which continues to deliver optimum-level performance, rarely endures a noticeable setback or sustained injury and, perhaps most emphatically, refuses to be reconciled to a model of aging as a debilitating force whose workings are inevitable. Undoubtedly exacerbated by the star's involvement with the controversial "religion" of Scientology, Cruise's resistant determination fuels the scrutiny to which his body is so often subjected in both celebrity discourse and his film performances.

This chapter examines what has been commonly described as Tom Cruise's "age-defying" tactics by demonstrating their consonance with the philosophy and practices of the popular, contemporary workout phenomenon known as "functional fitness." With its focus on enabling pain-free mobility, pliability, range of motion, and fast-twitch muscle retention, and its dedication to minimizing the threat of injury so commonly associated with traditional fitness training methods, functional fitness has become a movement that offers its benefits both to professional athletes who have promoted and attested to the success of its methods in extending the span of their careers' "prime" years and to Generation Xers and baby boomers enticed by the prospect that getting older doesn't mean having to endure rigorous and extended weight-training exercises to avoid resigning oneself to inertia—generations that now constitute the most popular audience sectors for Cruise's films (Fuster 2018).

Functional Fitness

As a goal and a life strategy, functional fitness is promoted as accessible to just about anyone who positions "optimal performance" as a personal goal. Although Cruise never directly references the phenomenon, with his ability to continue to run, jump, leap, balance, and maneuver elegantly through three-dimensional space, especially in his "post-meltdown" films, Cruise's efforts as a professional actor align closely with the philosophy and practice of functional fitness; as such, what might appear as an "unnatural" aspect of his age defiance needs to be evaluated in the context of a popular health phenomenon that perceives the unquestioned resignation to aging as itself a needless and unnatural surrender to decay. As a result, Cruise's authenticity can be recuperated through the cultural context of a contemporary predisposition to framing body transformation and preservation in terms of contemporary public health discourse, thereby largely evading the perception of a "self-serving" narcissism often associated with the process of bulking up. At the site of the star's body, then, any construction of Cruise as a brainwashed, self-obsessed, manipulative, and dominating fraud contends with a construction that foregrounds sincerity, authentic self-determination, and an unyielding commitment to self-improvement.

Cruise's alliance with this more forgiving self-construction of masculinity attests to a broader cultural shift in idealized images of healthy masculinity circulating in American culture over the past several years.[1] Unlike the pumped-up celebrity bodies that Susan Jeffords (1993) correlates with the impermeable and invulnerable masculinity valued as an emblem of strong American national identity throughout the Reagan era, the ideal hard male body of the first two decades of the twenty-first century is characterized by lean muscle. A 2014 article in *Men's Journal* concurs that "even the type of muscle has changed," and director Tim Burton explains that in terms of male body image, "In the Eighties, it was the bigger the better. . . . Actors rarely bulk up anymore; they're all trying to be [Brad Pitt's character in the 1999 film *Fight Club*] Tyler Durden" (Hill 2015). Personal trainers of celebrity actors echo this transformation: Jason Wimberly confirms that at the present moment, "Shredded trumps pumped" (qtd. in Ginsberg

---

1 In the discussion of cultural shift here and in the subsequent paragraph, I have borrowed heavily from my more extensive treatment of the subject (DeAngelis 2017).

2015). And in a discussion of his reworking of Daniel Craig's body for the *James Bond* series, his trainer Simon Waterston protests that "it wasn't about creating a certain look; it was about creating a certain performance, being functional, and being able to look like one can do shit. The aesthetics was just a byproduct.... Our objective is functional fitness, and not merely the appearance of fitness; actual capacity strengthened confidence, a façade is merely physical" (qtd. in Olesker 2015). Describing the male body currently in highest demand, personal trainer Tim Walker explains that "he looks good, but he's not massive. He's just got really good abs, good arms, and an alright chest. And that's what people want: to be lean, have a six pack" (qtd. in Olesker 2015). Unlike male stars of an earlier era who were more imposingly muscular at the peak of their careers, a look back over the span of Tom Cruise's career reveals a less pronounced long-term shift in body type and a more consistent conformity with the muscular yet leaner version of the masculine ideal popular in the contemporary era. As suggested in a recent article on the physical demands of his character Ethan Hunt in *Mission: Impossible—Fallout*, "muscle size isn't the main focus of his training and it doesn't need to be to gain Cruise's physique. However, some strength and muscle thickness in the right areas, combined with full-body exercises, will develop a pretty impressive physique while maintaining a good level of athleticism" ("Mission Impossible Fallout" 2018).

The ramifications of this cultural shift extend well beyond the training of male celebrities. Whether or not the aesthetics of this version of the male form are primarily a "by-product" of the fitness regimen, and whether or not functional training is less rigorous than traditional training, the less muscularly extreme construction of this more recent configuration of the male body also appeals to a broader client and audience base because it is less imposing, seemingly more attainable as a goal, and more accessible as an object of desire. As an article in *Esquire* suggests, with this form of training, "instead of spending 10 years trying to build mass, you just get really lean" (Olesker 2015).

Functional fitness originated in the field of physical rehabilitation, where treatment plans are tailored to the patient's condition and where the primary goal is to enable the patient to return to a level of physical fitness that he or she enjoyed prior to injury. As Elisabeth Flouts (2017) explains, in the fitness industry "the evolution began when more and more personal trainers started leaving big box gyms filled with traditional equipment to start their own open concept training studios. Less of the expensive and expansive cardio and strength training equipment left more space for trainers to get creative with functional movement training concepts." The movement developed, as Flouts suggests, as fitness culture witnessed the increasing popularity of "outdoor fitness classes and boot camps," leading to the inception of the term "high intensity interval training" (HIIT), and later to the proliferation of multistation fitness apparatuses that facilitated small-group circuit training. As Flouts observes, modern health clubs are increasingly being characterized as "open concept 'functional training spaces'" in which the traditional strength training equipment found in gyms has been replaced by or supplemented with kettlebells, medicine balls, ropes, sledgehammers, and resistance bands ("Functional Fitness Training" 2019). In the fitness industry, then, fitness has evolved into a customizable, individualized, client-centered activity that fosters a closer interaction between trainer and client.

Although its name might render the concept ambiguous, the goals and strategies of "functional fitness" are quite consistent across contexts and client markets. According to the Mayo Clinic, "Functional fitness exercises train your muscles to work together and prepare them for daily tasks simulating common movements you might do at home, at work, or in sports. While using various muscles in the upper and lower body at the same time, functional fitness exercises also emphasize core stability" ("Functional Fitness Training" 2019). The focus on complex, multidirectional movement and the simultaneous engagement of discrete muscle groups serve to further distinguish the methods of functional fitness from traditional strength-training regimens comprising exercises that focus on single muscles and muscle groups as the "topic" of the daily workout, yielding terms such as "abs day" and "legs day." While the goals of functional fitness are largely practical—pain-free mobility, muscle pliability to facilitate increased range of motion, and improved balance and coordination—the means of attaining these goals vary broadly to include loaded movement-specific activities, three-dimensional movement, conditioning designed to strengthen and retains fast-twitch muscle fiber, plyometrics, myofascial manipulation, and exercises that correct postural and foundational anomalies and that improve gait.

It is in the arena of professional sports training where one witnesses the most profound impact of this shift to functional fitness methods: a focus on observing, analyzing, and correcting incongruities in the efficiency of the musculoskeletal system so that it can optimally execute the movements and activities dictated by the demands of a specific sport. Tomahawk Science founder and trainer Ian Mack was recently recognized as a figurehead of this new approach in sports training, with hockey players such as Patrick Kane of the Chicago Blackhawks and J. T. Compher of the Colorado Avalanche attesting to the effectiveness of methods that have led them to championship medals and record-breaking seasons. On the subject of Kane's training, Carol Schram (2019) explains that Ian Mack's system "emphasizes an integrative strategy that includes training, treatment, recovery and nutrition—and de-emphasizes working in the weight room. 'A lot of what we do is movement-specific,' said Mack, who doesn't believe that bulking up is necessarily the best approach for a small trainer like Kane."

Considering professional sports team owners' financial investment in player talent, it is not surprising that the emphasis on optimal athletic performance extends from the level of the individual game to the season and overall career. "A long time ago, our field used to get ranked by how big and strong you guys are," Mack explains. "Now, a lot of times, it's 'How many games did they miss? How healthy was your player and then on top of that, how well did they perform?' I feel like that was a paradigm shift in our industry" (qtd. in Schram 2019). Injury is what led one of the most celebrated members of the American professional athletic community to embrace the concept of functional fitness. After repeated injury prompted doctors to insist upon surgical treatment as his only option, New England Patriots quarterback Tom Brady consulted with trainer Alex Guerrero, who was then able to successfully treat Brady's condition by analyzing, diagnosing, and correcting "biomechanical imbalances" that were disrupting the athlete's range of motion. "I thought: 'Oh, OK, so now that's the way he wants to move? I need to train him for those movement patterns.' And once I started to do that, athletes stopped getting hurt in that same way" (Reilly and Flanagan 2017). Building on his own successful treatment, Brady now sponsors the successful functional fitness organization TB12, which is providing assistance to athletes at locations across the United States.

Despite their origins in professional athletic training, however, organizations such as TB12, Tomahawk Science, and trainer Naudi Aguilar's company, Functional Patterns, are equally adept at promoting the benefits of their methods to a market with which they might not initially seem to have much in common: aging Americans. TB12's promotional materials correlate the two populations most directly, emphasizing the potential benefits of pain-free mobility for the "seventy-seven million baby boomers [who] are at or nearing retirement age" and promising that the principles of TB12 "can help improve your health and well-being—not to mention performance—and your longevity in the 'game' of your choice: whether that's running a marathon, completing a round of golf or tennis match, or being the best parent or grandparent you can" ("Age Is Just a Number" 2019).

Temporality is the key element of this correlation between "life span" and "health span," resting on the premise that whichever efforts one might take to extend one's longevity, the prospect of lengthening the amount of time in which one can expect to physically function in peak form remains largely within one's own control. With the reminder that physical inactivity anticipates muscle loss even for thirty-year-olds ("Age Is Just a Number" 2019) and that most of this loss can be recuperated through high-intensity resistance training, failing to act surfaces as a decision with far-reaching consequences. For the professional athlete, functional fitness discourse prioritizes health span over life span, focusing on the amount of time that one might expect to perform optimally in a sport, and if the most serious threat to sustained peak performance is injury, the ability to render oneself less prone to mishaps that can put a career on hold indefinitely constitutes a significant advantage. Those approaching retirement age also have control over their health span, yet with the number of years past far outnumbering those that are to come, for this group the unspoken context of one's health span *is* life span, and reducing one's susceptibility to injury translates to an ability to maintain independence, to counteract any such focus on longevity as an inevitable end point of life span through the promise of envisioning more of the remaining years of one's life as healthier years.

Accordingly, advertisements, magazine articles, and websites focusing on the health span of the older American adult have significantly expanded under the heading of functional fitness. "You're never too old to get your dream body, and you're never too past it to sculpt a summer six-pack," proclaims leading fitness magazine *Men's Health* ("Ultimate Training Plan" 2019). The American Senior Fitness Association embraces functional fitness as instrumental to a redefinition of "natural aging": "Much of what was earlier commonly thought to be the natural and inevitable result of the 'aging process' is now understood to be mostly the negative result of a sedentary lifestyle" (Therry n.d.). Alerting its audience that "the human body is either in a state of growth or decay," Larson Sports and Orthopaedics, a functional fitness consortium of trainers, HIIT coaches and surgeons, offers the most practical response to the question of "Why you should STILL exercise over 50": "Grandkids and kettlebells weigh the same!" (Bateman 2018). Indeed, organizations like TB12 extend this promotional strategy even further by intimating an alliance between the new older adult client and the organization's celebrity founder: "A TB12 Body Coach will help create a personalized plan that puts it all together . . . helping you to start bending the aging curve just like Tom Brady" ("Age Is Just a Number" 2019).

Clearly much more than just a new workout philosophy, functional fitness has developed into a mind-set that advocates for reconceptualizing the notion of duration, whether temporality is considered in terms of a professional career that demands a high level of physical fitness or of older adults for whom the concerns over "performance" pertain to the repeated and familiar movements necessary to facilitate independent everyday living. And in the discourse of aging surrounding Tom Cruise, whose continued popularity depends on maintaining a level of performance that permits him to continue to do his job well, the process of sustaining the body in a condition of functional strength, pliability and endurance might register only as a "race against time" were it not the case that, in relation to life span and health span, the temporal progression of aging has now been transformed into a more present-centered than end-point-based phenomenon. Certainly one might argue that whatever fit-beyond-their-years celebrities like Tom Brady and Tom Cruise might be attempting to prove to the public about the enduring nature of their professional talents, age will eventually "catch up" with both of them, along with inevitable confrontations with mortality. In the era of functional fitness, however, such a "law" of temporality is at odds with a perspective of time as a continuous present, as potential that is always ready to be activated, rather than as a process of "waiting out," of passively yet anxiously yielding to the changes that signal an inevitable future state of inertia.

"It's mind-boggling to me that we see these benefits of exercise through childhood, young adulthood, and middle age. Then we turn around and create an arbitrary age where we suddenly stop training for life in fear of disability and death," Larson Sports and Orthopaedics admits. "When the very things we're avoiding out of fear *can help prevent or reverse the symptoms of old age*" (Bateman 2019; emphasis in original). Fans of professional athletes like Tom Brady might embrace such a perspective on exercising and aging because fitness is a logical prerequisite to one's definition as a professional athlete. The composite narrative of the athletic professional usually situates the career itself as the area of primary focus, unless scandal or tragedy afflicts the image of the athlete in a way that might alter or recontextualize the significance of career accomplishments. Yet a different set of standards and parameters applies to the aging male actor, whose constructed life story (which gains more credence as less "life" intervenes to potentially disrupt the narrative flow) readily extends beyond the temporal scope of his career, and whose extra-cinematic, offscreen endeavors complicate or even contradict the version of the star persona that emerges solely from screen performances. It is expected that most athletes will cease to be identified as "professional" athletes decades before they die, but a broader ambiguity between "life span" and "health span" emerges in the case of screen actors, since it is not unusual for a career to extend to the end of an actor's life. Taking the traditional Hollywood star biography or biopic as a template for generating a celebrity's life story for public consumption, it becomes clear that the integrity of biographical narratives depends not only on accuracy of information or adherence to "truth" but also on a cohesive narrative structure that, as George Custen (1992) has explicated, relates key elements of character development, foremost among which is the performer's death, which bears the burden of securing cohesiveness through causal investigation, providing an end point to which the narrative trajectory must be directed.

The primacy of the teleological in star narrative construction privileges death as an "ultimate future" that governs the operation of rendering the star's life coherent. The significance of the star's individual accomplishments or experiences lies in their function relative to future life-story developments already known and foretold. Within such parameters, an actor like Cruise, whose physical appearance appears misaligned with one's chronological age-based expectations, disavows the future by challenging the certainty of death, offering a case where the pursuit of a longer health span is construed as a futile, irrational, and disingenuous attempt to disavow mortality. Even the commonly held description of Cruise's physical appearance as "age defying" attests to a future-centered perspective on body development, one that is deemed "unnatural" because it *is* unnatural in the context of a narrative template requiring that the recognizable traces of the aging process register as markings on the body of an actor who has been the subject of public visibility over the course of several decades.

In recent years, this discourse of the unnatural has certainly prevailed in critical commentary aligned with traditional narrative structures that cannot accommodate temporal deviations. Such manifestations of the unnatural are even imposed on visible body sites that are seemingly insusceptible to ageist descriptions. For Cruise, among the most prominent of these involves the controversy surrounding the matter of the "middle tooth." Rendered evident by a series of photos highlighting the celebrity's telltale smile, a 2018 article titled "Tom Cruise's Smile Is Not as Perfect as It Seems" playfully yet insidiously transforms a slight structural anomaly into an emblem of the actor's disingenuousness. The observation that "his teeth aren't exactly symmetrical with the center of his face" becomes the basis for asserting that Cruise has "a rather odd middle tooth," the curiosity rendered yet more strange by close-up photos revealing that "his left incisor [appears] to be bigger than his right one." In this case, the label of "unnatural" resonates as an unwelcome challenge to expectations of absolute symmetry, exacerbated by the intimation that whatever procedure he underwent to "correct" his dental problem only served to accentuate an inherent incorrectness, a reminder of the futility inherent in any pursuit of physical perfection.

Marking the unreconciled conflicts between present-based and future-based constructions of aging, the connection between symmetry, perfection, and authenticity finds a similarly fertile breeding ground in the recent controversy over the seemingly impossibly firm and round appearance of Cruise's gluteus maximus in a single shot of *Valkyrie* (Bryan Singer, 2008). Initiated by Twitter user "swizz keats" with an accompanying gif highlighting the muscle in question, online discussion of the proposition leads to the conjecture of intervention by computer-generated imagery, despite Cruise's pronounced, unyielding disdain for such technologies of digital enhancement; the possibility that a stunt double was used reinforces the context of inauthenticity by intimating deceit in the actor's protestation that he performs his own stunts. Advocates of Cruise counter these accusations by attributing the size and shape of the muscle to his determination to

Colonel Claus von Stauffenberg (Cruise) struggles to regain his balance after a surprise air attack near the beginning of *Valkyrie*.

maintain his physical fitness ("considering he does a ton of his own stunts, it doesn't seem far-fetched to think it's actually from him staying in good shape"), or as evidence that he chose to use a protective safety pad for the stunt featured in the scene in question (Sroczynski 2017).

The most contentious debates regarding Cruise's "unnatural" aging involve a series of full-shot photos of the shirtless, then forty-eight-year-old actor on the set of *Mission: Impossible—Ghost Protocol* (Brad Bird, 2011). Commenting on the photos, a blogger on *Celebitchy* poses the following question: "Tom Cruise Topless: Oddly Lumpy, or Fabulously Hot?" (Kaiser 2010). The author situates his question as one that has prompted a dilemma of perspective: "Now, even though I'm impressed with Tom's body—he really is in wonderful shape for a man his age—I'm also wondering if anyone else think [sic] his stomach is weirdly lumpy? Like I know some (most) of these lumps are gristly muscles. Some of those lumps really are strange, right?" The possible disingenuousness of the inquiry notwithstanding, the posed question generates a series of eighty responses, all but eight of which concur on the side of "oddly lumpy," largely based on perceptions of muscular asymmetry attributed to the workings of age and inefficient metabolism ("He has old man neck, and he's getting old man torso"), sagging pectoral implants, failed liposuction ("he's got a pretty large dent on the right side of his stomach"), and even the presence of tumors ("that lump right above his belly button looks like a lipoma... why he hasn't had it removed boggles the mind"). Recurringly, contributors to this discussion advise Cruise that he is just too old to appear shirtless and that his body is better left covered up.

Relevant to such efforts to de-authenticate Cruise on the basis of age-inappropriate appearance is Lisa Purse's (2017, 167) assertion that the aging celebrity body serves as a sign that triggers the viewer to recall an image of a lost, yet once familiar younger version of this body: "the ageing action star is likely to register with the spectator as an uncanny body because it constitutes a familiar, remembered corporeality and a strange new corporeality simultaneously." Here I would add that the capacity and willingness to reconcile the older with the younger image is based less on any objective, analytical assessment of the two disparately aged versions of the star body than on a cultural reticence thwarting the ability to imagine a representable older-age body in terms other than those of decay and the proximity of death. Lauren Crichton (2018) attributes the problem to prevailing negative stereotypes about aging, and in an insightful article, Brooke Edge (2018) argues that the realm of advertising has confined our cultural imagination of the aging body to images of "deterioration"—that is, when the older adult population is represented at all. To demonstrate her assertion, Edge juxtaposes an image of a lean, fit fifty-five-year-old Cruise as he appears in *Mission: Impossible—Fallout* and who looks fit and quite youthful in comparison with an image of the actor Wilford Brimley in his role as Ben Luckett in *Cocoon* (Ron Howard, 1985) at age fifty. Edge argues that advertising has continued to condition the public to associate age over fifty with the significantly more wrinkled and much less lean figure of Brimley, even though "they're closer to the active and youthful depictions of not just Cruise but any number of his fellow actors who would now be in the 'older adults' demo."

The Brimley/Cruise juxtaposition also resonates as a reminder of American culture's tendency to connect "maturity" not only with age but also with the associated loss of strength, dexterity, and mobility. Cruise's star persona disrupts the seeming integrity of this association by reconfiguring maturity as an adult version of "play" that liberates the transition from boyhood to manhood from the confines of developmental progression. As I suggested in an earlier study of Cruise, many of the actor's early roles, at least until the release of *Born on the Fourth of July* (Oliver Stone, 1989), are invested in the notion of life as play, marked by a sense of adventure and discovery as well as a lack of concern for the consequences of one's actions (DeAngelis 2010). Commenting on the problem of lost authenticity and audience trust in the aftermath of the notorious 2005 incidents, Donna Peberdy asserts in a 2010 piece that any reworking of Cruise's public identity would need to be one in which "Cruise's unstable, excessive maleness becomes the norm" (250). If, on the basis of his last several films (and especially with the expansion of the *Mission: Impossible* series) such a reconfiguration of his public persona has indeed occurred, however, it now seems less an intended counteractive to the off-the-rails behavior that led Paramount to drop the star and more an attempt to secure a continuum with the childlike sense of play and adventure so prevalent in his early films. Such continuity arises from the integrity of this notion of "extended play," intensified by the fact that differences between the younger and current versions of the actor's body are rendered perfectly fit to engage in it.

A more distinctive element of the recent version of Cruise at play is that playfulness is now culturally associated with the enterprising notion of both thinking *and* acting "outside the box," the very quality that continues to make Ethan Hunt of the *Mission: Impossible* series such a successful special agent, that continues to impress his colleagues in the Impossible Mission Force, and that also makes him a challenge for his superiors to explain or manage. Furthermore, although it registers as a set of spontaneous and creative strategies for achieving a desired goal, the play in question, especially across the installments of *Mission: Impossible*, is exceptionally high risk. Whether it involves descending by wire and harness from the high ceiling of a CIA office to a computer terminal below (*Mission: Impossible*; Brian De Palma, 1996), leaping from the face of one Utah rock wall to the next (*Mission: Impossible II*; John Woo, 2000) leaping from the top of one tall Shanghai building to the next (*Mission: Impossible III*; J. J. Abrams, 2006), scaling the sides of the world's tallest building with only support-suction adhesive gloves, one of which fails (*Ghost Protocol*), holding his breath underwater for six minutes while struggling to unlock a compartment containing a data disk (*Mission: Impossible—Rogue Nation*; Christopher McQuarrie, 2015), hanging off the side of an airplane as it accelerates for takeoff (*Rogue Nation* again), or making corkscrew turns while piloting a helicopter roaming through New Zealand canyons, before proceeding to climb down a rope tied to the helicopter and then jumping onto a bag suspended below (*Fallout*), the extreme nature of these stunts, in conjunction with the precision and elegance with which the actor performs them, serves as a physical and visceral extension of the quick, accurate, and razor-sharp decision-making capability that makes Hunt an inimitable leader and clear-thinking strategist.

Conclusion

Born of a more childlike sense of adventure, experimentation, and discovery, however, these stunts, as evidenced by the extensive physical and tactical preparation required to execute them, constitute a form of play that is very much *about* work. Audiences experience only the end result of the effort involved, for example, in Cruise's completion of an accelerated helicopter license program involving nine to eleven hours of daily training over the course of three months (Redman 2018). If critics and commentators label Cruise's authentic stunt work as "death-defying" (Murray 2018), "death" in this context functions ironically as an always unreachable limit, as the trajectory that Cruise's action narratives seem to take, even though the screening audience is always assured of witnessing yet another case of death miraculously averted and, along with it, a return to the present-centered version of temporality that Cruise's star persona inhabits and that reveals him as once again and still not ready to expire, resign, or even age. And it is through this process of maturing without aging, of maintaining a childlike yet hardly naïve sense of adventure through regimens of functional training and performance, that Cruise's fitness efforts align with those of both professional athletes and the aging American males striving to extend a sense of the continuous present through fitness strategies that enable individuals to do their jobs better, in an effort to have "health span" coincide more with the course of "life span." Tapping into a seemingly limitless capacity for age-defying, physical self-improvement, Cruise's efforts embody the familiar principle of leadership by example in this era of functional fitness.

Works Cited

"Age Is Just a Number: 6 Ways Tom Brady Stays Healthy." 2019. TB12, July 2019. tb12sports.com/blog/how-tom-brady-stays-healthy.

Bateman, Jessica. 2018. "Older Athletes Need to Be in Your Gym." Larson Sports and Orthopaedics, October 10, 2018. larsonsportsortho.com/older-athletes-need-your-gym/.

Crichton, Lauren. 2018. "It's Time for Advertising to Stop Perpetuating Negative Stereotypes About Aging." *Adweek*, August 3, 2018. www.adweek.com/creativity/its-time-for-advertising-to-stop-perpetuating-negative-stereotypes-about-aging/.

Custen, George. 1992. *Bio/Pics: How Hollywood Constructed Public History*. New Brunswick, NJ: Rutgers University Press.

DeAngelis, Michael. 2010. "Mel Gibson and Tom Cruise: Rebellion and Conformity." In *Acting for America: Movie Stars of the 1980s*, edited by Robert Eberwein, 77–98. New Brunswick, NJ: Rutgers University Press.

———. 2017. "Soft and Hard: Accessible Masculinity, Celebrity, and Post-Millennial Cuteness." In *The Aesthetics and Affects of Cuteness*, edited by Joshua Paul Dale, Joyce Goggin, Julia Leyda, Anthony P. McIntyre, and Diane Negra, 194–215. London: Routledge.

Edge, Brooke. 2018. "Aging in Advertising and Popular Culture." Priceweber, September 7, 2018, priceweber.com/2018/09/07/aging-in-advertising/.

Flouts, Elisabeth. 2017. "The Modern History of Functional Movement Training." Power Systems, January 9, 2017. blog.powersystems.com/category-spotlight/the-modern-history-of-functional-movement-training/.

"Functional Fitness Training: Is It Right for You?" 2019. Mayo Clinic. September 4, 2019. www.mayoclinic.org/healthy-lifestyle/fitness/in-depth/functional-fitness/art-20047680.

Fuster, Jeremy. 2018. "'Mission: Impossible' Continues to Be the Action Series for Generation X." The Wrap, July 29, 2018. www.thewrap.com/mission-impossible-action-series-for-gen-x-tom-cruise/.

Ginsberg, Merle. 2015. "Introducing the Stromo! Why Straight Male Starts Are Going Gay(ish)." *Hollywood Reporter*, June 26, 2015. www.hollywoodreporter.com/news/introducing-stromo-why-straight-male-804291.

Hill, Logan. 2015. "Building a Bigger Action Hero." *Men's Journal*. May 2014, www.mensjournal.com/features/building-a-bigger-action-hero-20140418/.

Jeffords, Susan. 1993. *Hard Bodies: Hollywood Masculinity in the Reagan Era*. New Brunswick, NJ: Rutgers University.

Kaiser. 2010. "Tom Cruise Topless: Oddly Lumpy, or Fabulously Hot?" *Celebitchy*, October 7, 2010, www.celebitchy.com/120613/tom-cruise-topless-oddly-lumpy-or-fabulously-hot/.

"Mission Impossible Fallout: Tom Cruise Workout." 2018. EasyGym, August 31, 2018. www.easygym.co.uk/blog/tom-cruise-workout.

Murray, Noel. 2018. "10 Most Insane 'Mission: Impossible' Stunts," *Rolling Stone*, July 25, 2018. www.rollingstone.com/movies/movie-features/10-most-insane-mission-impossible-stunts-701200/.

O'Donnell, Ruth. 2016. "Mission: Impossible? The Rehabilitation of Tom Cruise." *Celebrity Studies* 7 (3): 425–28.

Olesker, Max. "The Rise and Fall of the Spornosexual." 2015. *Esquire*, December 1, 2015. www.esquire.com/uk/culture/news/a7588/the-rise-and-rise-of-the-spornosexual/.

Peberdy, Donna. 2010. "From Wimps to Wild Men: Bipolar Masculinity and the Paradoxical Performances of Tom Cruise." *Men and Masculinities* 13 (2): 231–54.

Purse, Lisa. 2017. "Confronting the Impossibility of Impossible Bodies: Tom Cruise and the Ageing Male Action Hero." In *Revisiting Star Studies: Cultures, Themes, and Methods*, edited by Sabrina Qiong Yu and Guy Austin, 162–83. Edinburgh: Edinburgh University Press.

Redman, Justin. 2018. "Tom Cruise Trained for Three Months to Pull Off This Crazy *Mission: Impossible—Fallout* Stunt." 2018. *The Credits: Profiles Below the Line*. Motion Picture Association, July 26, 2018. www.mpaa.org/2018/07/tom-cruise-trained-for-three-months-to-pull-off-this-crazy-mission-impossible-fallout-stunt/.

Reilly, Kevin, and Graham Flanagan. 2017. "How Tom Brady Met His Controversial Personal Trainer Who Was Just Banned from the Patriots' Sideline." Business Insider, December 24, 2017. www.businessinsider.com/tom-brady-alex-guerrero-controversial-personal-trainer-interview-2017-12.

Schram, Carol. 2019. "Patrick Kane Credits Tomahawk Science for Helping Him Hit Peak Performance at Age 30." *Forbes*, May 2, 2019. www.forbes.com/sites/carolschram/2019/05/02/patrick-kane-credits-tomahawk-science-for-helping-him-hit-peak-performance-at-age-30/#78cc65d418c5.

Sroczynski, Jessica. 2017. "Tom Cruise's Fake Butt is the Internet's Newest Conspiracy Theory." Mashable, August 24, 2017. mashable.com/2017/08/24/tom-cruise-fake-butt-valkyrie/.

Therry, Leonard D. n.d. "Goal for Senior Exercisers: FUNCTIONAL FITNESS!" American Senior Fitness Association. Accessed August 17, 2019. www.seniorfitness.net/Therry_Functional.htm.

"Tom Cruise." n.d. Internet Movie Database. Accessed August 25, 2019. www
.imdb.com/name/nm0000129/?ref_=fn_al_nm_1.

"Tom Cruise's Smile Is Not as Perfect as It Seems because of This One Thing."
2018. *Life & Style*, June 9, 2018. www.lifeandstylemag.com/posts/tom-cruise
-middle-tooth-161278/.

"The Ultimate Training Plan for over 50s." 2019. *Men's Health*, May 14, 2019.
www.menshealth.com/uk/building-muscle/a755538/the-over-50s-training
-plan/.

FILMOGRAPHY

Endless Love (Franco Zeffirelli, 1981)
  Billy

Taps (Harold Becker, 1981)
  David Shawn

The Outsiders (Francis Ford Coppola, 1983)
  Steve Randle

Losin' It (Curtis Hanson, 1983)
  Woody

Risky Business (Paul Brickman, 1983)
  Joel Goodson

All the Right Moves (Michael Chapman, 1983)
  Stefen Djordjevic

Legend (Ridley Scott, 1985)
  Jack

Top Gun (Tony Scott, 1986)
  Lt. Pete "Maverick" Mitchell

The Color of Money (Martin Scorsese, 1986)
  Vincent Lauria

Cocktail (Roger Donaldson, 1988)
  Brian Flanagan

Rain Man (Barry Levinson, 1988)
  Charlie Babbitt

Born on the Fourth of July (Oliver Stone, 1989)
  Ron Kovic

Days of Thunder (Tony Scott, 1990)
  Cole Trickle

Far and Away (Ron Howard, 1992)
  Joseph Donnelly

A Few Good Men (Rob Reiner, 1992)
  Lt. Daniel Kaffee

The Firm (Sydney Pollack, 1993)
  Mitch McDeere

Interview with the Vampire (Neil Jordan, 1994)
  Lestat de Lioncourt

Mission: Impossible (Brian De Palma, 1996)
  Ethan Hunt

Jerry Maguire (Cameron Crowe, 1996)
  Jerry Maguire

Eyes Wide Shut (Stanley Kubrick, 1999)
  Dr. William Harford

Magnolia (Paul Thomas Anderson, 1999)
  Frank T. J. Mackey

Mission: Impossible II (*M:I-2*) (John Woo, 2000)
  Ethan Hunt

Stanley Kubrick: A Life in Pictures (Jan Harlan, 2001)
Narrator

Vanilla Sky (Cameron Crowe, 2001)
David Aames

Space Station 3D (Toni Myers, 2002)
Narrator

Minority Report (Steven Spielberg, 2002)
Chief John Anderton

Austin Powers in Goldmember (Jay Roach, 2002)
Himself as Austin Powers

The Last Samurai (Edward Zwick, 2002)
Nathan Algren

Collateral (Michael Mann, 2004)
Vincent

War of the Worlds (Steven Spielberg, 2005)
Ray Ferrier

Mission: Impossible III (J. J. Abrams, 2006)
Ethan Hunt

Lions for Lambs (Robert Redford, 2007)
Senator Jasper Irving

Tropic Thunder (Ben Stiller, 2008)
Les Grossman

Valkyrie (Bryan Singer, 2008)
Col. Claus von Stauffenberg

Knight and Day (James Mangold, 2010)
Roy Miller

Mission: Impossible—Ghost Protocol (Brad Bird, 2011)
Ethan Hunt

Rock of Ages (Adam Shankman, 2012)
Stacee Jaxx

Jack Reacher (Christopher McQuarrie, 2012)
Jack Reacher

Oblivion (Joseph Kosinski, 2013)
Jack Harper

Edge of Tomorrow (Doug Liman, 2014)
Maj. William Cage

Mission: Impossible—Rogue Nation (Christopher McQuarrie, 2015)
Ethan Hunt

Jack Reacher: Never Go Back (Edward Zwick, 2016)
Jack Reacher

The Mummy (Alex Kurtzman, 2017)
Nick Morton

American Made (Doug Liman, 2017)
Barry Seal

Mission: Impossible—Fallout (Christopher McQuarrie, 2018)
Ethan Hunt

Top Gun: Maverick (Joseph Kosinski, 2020)
Capt. Pete "Maverick" Mitchell

Mission: Impossible 7 (Christopher McQuarrie, 2021)
Ethan Hunt

CONTRIBUTORS

Adam Daniel is a member of the Writing and Society Research Centre at Western Sydney University, Australia. His primary research investigates the evolution of horror film, with a focus on the intersection of embodied spectatorship, neuroscience, Deleuzian theory, and new media technologies. His broader research interests include the works of David Lynch, screenwriting, and virtual reality cinema. He is vice president of the Sydney Screen Studies Network.

Michael DeAngelis is a professor of media and cinema studies at DePaul University, Chicago. He is the author of *Rx Hollywood: Cinema and Therapy in the 1960s* (2017) and *Gay Fandom and Crossover Stardom: James Dean, Mel Gibson, and Keanu Reeves* (2001) and editor of the volume *Reading the Bromance: Homosocial Relationships in Film and Television* (2014).

Glen Donnar is a senior lecturer in media and communication at RMIT University in Melbourne, Australia. He has published diversely on action stardom and popular cultural representations of masculinities, monstrosity, and disaster in film and television; the mediation of terror in news media; and the ethics of news viewership. He is the author of *Troubling Masculinities: Terror, Gender, and Monstrous Others in American Film Post-9/11* (2020) and is currently writing a monograph on aging action stars.

Sasha T. Goldberg is a doctoral candidate in gender studies at Indiana University, Bloomington, where her research centers on butch women, female *masculinities*, and lesbian specificity. She also holds an MA in Judaism from the Graduate Theological Union in Berkeley, California. Her research and teaching interests include religion, nationalism, media, masculinities, and LGBT and queer studies.

Loraine Haywood is a conjoint fellow in the Faculty of Education and Arts at the University of Newcastle, Australia. She has a master's of theology and is interested in the uses of biblical master narratives that mediate the Real of apocalypse. In particular, she is engaged with Slavoj Žižek's and Todd McGowan's understanding of Lacanian theory. She has published in the University of Otago's *Performance of the Real Working Papers* (2018) and *SeaChanges* (2016).

TARA LOMAX is completing a PhD in screen studies at the University of Melbourne, Australia, with research on the transtextual poetics of Hollywood franchising. She has published in the journals *Senses of Cinema* and the *Quarterly Review of Film and Video* and in the edited collections *The Palgrave Handbook of Screen Production* (2019), *The Superhero Symbol: Media, Culture, and Politics* (2019), and *Star Wars and the History of Transmedia Storytelling* (2017). Her research spans the topics of media franchising, transmedia storytelling, and visual effects industries.

CARLOS MENÉNDEZ-OTERO holds PhDs in English studies and in communication and journalism, and he is an associate professor at the University of Oviedo, Spain. His main research relates to the Irish audiovisual industry and the Anglo-American classic film about Ireland, on which he has published over twenty papers and the book *Irlanda y los irlandeses en el cine popular (1910–1970)* (2017). Other interests include dubbing, television series, and regional television.

SORCHA NÍ FHLAINN is a senior lecturer in film studies and American studies at Manchester Metropolitan University, United Kingdom. She is a founding member of the Manchester Centre for Gothic Studies and author of *Postmodern Vampires: Film, Fiction, and Popular Culture* (2019). She has published widely on sociocultural history, subjectivity and postmodernism in film studies, American studies, horror studies, and popular culture.

RUTH O'DONNELL is an independent scholar and the author of *Tom Cruise: Performing Masculinity in Post-Vietnam Hollywood* (2015). Her research focuses on psychodynamic theory and representation of masculinities on film.

PATRICK O'NEILL is a senior lecturer in film studies at Kingston University, United Kingdom, and is currently engaged in research that focuses on the portrayal of youth in cinema.

Justin Owen Rawlins is an assistant professor of media and film studies at the University of Tulsa, Oklahoma. He studies stages and screens, the cultures that surround/connect them, and the social identities (race, gender, class, etc.) negotiated through their content and discourses.

Sean Redmond is a professor of screen and design at Deakin University in Melbourne, Australia. He is the author of *Celebrity* (2018), *Liquid Space: Digital Age Science Fiction Film and Television* (2017), *Celebrity and the Media* (2014), and *Flowering Blood: The Cinema of Takeshi Kitano* (2013).

Defne Tüzün is an assistant professor in the Radio, Television and Cinema Department at Kadir Has University, Istanbul. Her research focuses on film theory and criticism, psychoanalytic theory, and narratology.

Alex Wade is a senior research fellow in the School of Education at Birmingham City University, United Kingdom. His most recent book is *The Pac-Man Principle: A User's Guide to Capitalism* (2018).

Brenda R. Weber is a professor of gender studies at Indiana University, Bloomington. Her books include *Latter-day Screens: Gender, Sexuality, and Mediated Mormonism* (2019); *Reality Gendervision: Sexuality and Gender on Transatlantic Reality TV* (2014); *Women and Literary Celebrity in the Nineteenth Century* (2012); and *Makeover TV: Selfhood, Celebrity, and Citizenship* (2009).

Linda Wight is a senior lecturer of literature and screen studies in the School of Arts at Federation University Australia. Her PhD dissertation examined the depiction of masculinities in recent science fiction. She is currently continuing research into depictions of masculinities in science fiction and other popular genres.

INDEX

acting, 6, 67, 108, 129, 140–41, 169, 180, 187, 191, 194, 212, 264–70, 275–76, 291

action: as cinema, 117, 279; and film, 244–45, 257; as genre, 192, 199, 204; as hero, 4, 11, 72, 175; as star, 2, 12, 222–23, 243, 245, 251, 253–55, 258, 265, 290

actor, 6, 13, 38–39, 62, 65, 74, 76, 87, 89, 105, 118, 128–29, 134, 140–43, 149, 184, 187–88, 190, 192, 212, 214, 222, 227, 230, 255, 262–64, 268, 270, 272, 274, 281, 287–90, 292; as producer, 193–95, 198; as stuntman, 275–76. *See also* genre

adaptation, 134–35, 139, 142, 148–49, 155, 189, 199

adolescence, 7, 19–20, 24–28, 30–32. *See also* teen films

aesthetics, 6, 14, 25, 32, 38, 40, 189, 192, 212, 272

aging: and body, 12, 226, 237, 241, 243–44, 253–58, 279–81, 285–90, 292; as star, 6, 12, 226–37, 239, 241. *See also* authenticity; youthful

All the Right Moves (Michael Chapman, 1983), 7, 19, 20–21, 23, 25, 30–33, 129, 213

American dream, 2, 9, 31, 43, 79–80, 82, 95, 106, 108, 125, 137

American Made (Doug Liman, 2017), 223, 252

authenticity: as aging, 11, 12; as heroism, 3, 94, 99; and star, 3–4, 13, 14, 152, 161, 216, 226, 243, 245–48, 252, 258, 264, 268–70, 272, 276, 280, 281, 288, 291

authority figure, 26–28, 30, 100, 162, 229

beard, 40, 78. *See also* sexuality

blockbuster film, 6, 71, 194, 198, 246

body image, 28, 30, 281

Born on the Fourth of July (Oliver Stone, 1989), 7, 8, 32, 37, 46–50, 117, 134, 137, 140, 290

box office appeal, 2, 3, 21, 25, 30, 32, 77, 115, 128, 135, 136, 141, 148, 198, 226, 245, 246, 253, 270

branding, Cruise, 3, 8, 9, 10, 11, 25, 72, 83, 118, 128, 133–34, 141, 150, 185, 187–93, 196–205. *See also* marketing; trademark

capitalism, 21, 43, 46–47, 50, 83. *See also* neoliberalism

casting, Cruise, 10, 133–34, 139–43, 149, 150, 159, 160, 162, 205, 230

celebrity: and Cruise, 4, 44, 71, 74, 75, 78, 87, 90, 141, 144, 188, 195, 211, 216, 220, 270; as culture, 75, 79, 80, 82, 85, 86, 147, 190–91, 204, 280. *See also* persona

closet, 4, 8, 71, 74, 83, 87–90. *See also* sexuality
close-up, shot, 1, 25, 27, 36, 38, 39, 41, 45, 49, 50, 57–58, 63, 66, 201, 229, 257, 288
Cocktail (Roger Donaldson, 1988), 56, 118, 129, 227
Color of Money, The (Martin Scorsese, 1986), 27, 117, 118, 129, 213
controlling, 62, 84, 255, 266
cyborg, 10, 11, 169, 170–73, 175, 179–80, 181, 182, 184, 185

Dark Universe, 11, 187, 189, 191, 193–94, 197, 201–4. *See also* franchise
Days of Thunder (Tony Scott, 1990), 3, 27, 115, 117, 118, 123, 125, 128, 129, 135, 214
disaster, films, 106, 159, 163. *See also* genre
discourse, meaning, 4, 13, 46, 49, 64, 76, 136, 149, 169, 171, 177, 220, 265, 272, 280–81, 285, 286, 288

Edge of Tomorrow (Doug Liman, 2014), 10, 152, 155–56, 160, 163–65, 184, 189, 222, 240, 251, 253, 257
Endless Love (Franco Zeffirelli, 1981), 129
ethnicity, 5, 9, 115, 127–29. *See also* Irishness; race
everyman, 9, 10, 54, 115, 118, 122, 159, 163
Eyes Wide Shut (Stanley Kubrick, 1999), 3, 4, 8, 12, 32, 53–68, 139, 158, 214, 228

family: and Cruise, 211, 213, 217, 218; as ideology, 82, 102–3, 119, 157, 163, 174; and narrative, 46, 49, 56–57, 59, 64, 223. *See also* fatherhood
fans, fan-base, 3, 7, 29, 71, 89, 141, 166, 245, 251, 252, 254, 264
fantasy: and Cruise, 7, 55, 58, 60, 96, 99, 100, 107–8; as narrative, 26, 28, 29, 31, 54, 56, 57, 59–60, 61, 64–65, 98, 146, 237
Far and Away (Ron Howard, 1992), 3, 9, 115, 117–29
fatherhood, 12, 100, 102, 158, 160, 163, 164, 211, 213, 214, 217–23, 230. *See also* family
Few Good Men, A (Rob Reiner, 1992), 60, 143, 214
Firm, The (Sydney Pollack, 1993), 56, 143, 214
franchise: and *Mission Impossible*, 6, 11, 101, 176, 179, 188, 191–93, 198–201, 205, 222, 232; and *The Mummy*, 197, 202–4, 205; star vehicle, 11, 13, 187–90, 194–96, 227, 230, 244, 247, 251, 262–63, 264, 276. *See also* Dark Universe
functional fitness, 13, 279–92

gaze, gazing, 7, 8, 20, 27, 36–37, 38, 39–42, 44, 46–47, 49–50, 57, 60, 63, 66, 98, 104, 107, 146, 148–50, 174, 184–85, 216, 227, 230, 231
gender, 1, 2, 4, 5, 6, 9, 20, 36–37, 40, 41, 42, 46, 50, 74, 75, 117–18, 119, 138, 153–60, 161–66, 220, 227, 246. *See also* masculinity

Index   305

genre, 6, 9, 19, 20–21, 24, 27, 32, 106, 117, 118, 124, 136, 169, 171, 187, 189, 190–92, 198–99, 201–2, 204, 244. *See also* action; gothic; science fiction
gossip, 12, 243, 254
gothic, 9–10, 133–40, 141, 143, 144, 145–46, 148, 149–50. *See also* genre

high-concept, 9, 14, 135–36, 141, 171, 183, 191, 198, 203
Hollywood: and cinema, 11, 21, 29, 54, 65, 72, 107, 135, 136, 137, 144, 154; as Gothic, 10, 134, 135, 136, 148, 149; and ideology, 220, 221; and stars, 2, 5, 14, 36, 56, 79, 84, 116, 141, 144, 163, 187, 188, 189, 204, 246–47, 258, 275, 287
homoerotic, 1, 4, 7, 14, 27, 37–39, 42, 43, 118, 145, 146, 147, 149
homosexuality, 40, 61, 74, 78, 138, 149, 158. *See also* sexuality
homosocial, 4, 7, 14, 37, 39, 41, 118, 147, 228, 239

iconic, 39, 41, 43, 96, 102, 103, 137, 140, 145, 187, 190, 191, 192, 195, 198, 199, 200, 204, 227, 258
iconography, 14, 38, 39, 149, 212
ideology, 2, 3, 4, 5–6, 9, 21, 50, 80, 86, 87, 99, 127, 149, 166, 176, 192, 212, 227, 267–68
intellectual property, 11, 187, 190, 192, 194–95
Interview with the Vampire (Neil Jordan, 1994), 10, 133–50

Irishness, 9, 115–29. *See also* ethnicity

Jack Reacher (Christopher McQuarrie, 2012), 97, 100, 128, 189, 193, 222, 249
Jack Reacher: Never Go Back (Edward Zwick, 2016), 97, 100, 128, 189, 193, 222, 249
Jerry Maguire (Cameron Crowe, 1996), 7–8, 37, 42–46, 48, 50, 56, 77, 139, 143, 154, 219

Knight and Day (James Mangold, 2010), 222

labor, performative, 13, 82, 84, 227, 247–49, 251, 254, 255, 257, 258, 262, 264–76
lack, symbolic, 7, 12, 57, 63–64, 107, 222, 228, 238, 254
Last Samurai, The (Edward Zwick, 2002), 1–2, 154
Legend (Ridley Scott, 1985), 117
lifestyle, 56, 87, 154, 286
Losin' It (Curtis Hanson, 1983), 7, 19, 20, 21, 22–25, 28, 29, 30, 31, 129

Magnolia (Paul Thomas Anderson, 1999), 3, 23, 25, 29, 32, 139, 140, 214, 215–17
marketing, 3, 12, 21–22, 55, 143, 187–91, 197, 202–5, 221, 224. *See also* branding, Cruise
market value, 2–3, 82–83, 118, 282
marriage: and Cruise, 55–56, 213, 220–21; as narrative, 43–44, 54, 56, 100–102, 108, 139, 147

masculinity: and Cruise, 23–25, 28, 32, 39, 41–42, 44–45, 47–50, 55, 57, 58, 60–61, 63–64, 68, 99, 102–3, 117–19, 125, 128–29, 134–35, 143, 149, 152–54, 155–57, 158, 159–64, 165–66, 216–17, 223; and culture, 38, 98, 99, 106, 154, 158, 164, 219, 220; as performativity, 31, 95, 211. *See also* gender
masks, masking, 4, 58–59, 62–63, 66–68, 158, 161, 177, 199, 231, 237
masquerade, 58, 61–68, 216, 228, 244
Minority Report (Steven Spielberg, 2002), 10, 11, 12, 152, 155, 157–58, 161–62, 164, 169, 170–72, 180–85, 214, 217, 240
Mission: Impossible series, 6, 10–11, 13, 72, 86, 95, 97, 99, 100–101, 177, 189, 191, 193, 194, 197, 198–201, 202, 205, 222, 227, 228–29, 231, 234, 235, 236, 237, 239, 240, 262, 263, 264, 266, 268, 275, 276–77, 280, 291
Mission: Impossible (Brian De Palma, 1996), 72, 139, 143, 170, 171, 176–77, 178, 179, 180, 182, 198, 212, 214, 229, 230, 238, 264, 291
Mission: Impossible II (M:I-2) (John Woo, 2000), 198, 232, 234, 235, 238–39, 244, 245, 291
Mission: Impossible III (J. J. Abrams, 2006), 72, 89, 198, 222, 232, 233, 235, 237, 238, 246, 270, 291
Mission: Impossible—Ghost Protocol (Brad Bird, 2011), 12, 72, 198, 222–23, 232, 235, 243, 248, 289, 291

Mission: Impossible—Rogue Nation (Christopher McQuarrie, 2015), 12, 72, 152, 198, 200, 232, 233, 237, 240, 243, 247, 262, 263, 270, 271, 273, 276, 277, 291
Mission: Impossible—Fallout (Christopher McQuarrie, 2018), 3, 12, 72, 95, 101, 108, 184, 198, 200, 223, 227, 230, 232, 233, 239, 243, 248, 262, 270, 274–75, 276, 279, 280, 282, 290
Mummy, The (Alex Kurtzman, 2017), 11, 12, 189, 191, 193, 197, 202–3, 205, 243, 247, 251, 252, 253
myth, 2, 106, 122, 126, 201, 256

neoliberalism, 20, 38, 71, 73–74, 80–90. *See also* capitalism
New York City, 61, 96, 97, 98–99, 103–4, 107, 157
9/11, 97, 102–3, 104–8, 153–55, 157, 159, 160–61, 162, 164, 166

Oblivion (Joseph Kosinski, 2013), 102, 103–6, 108, 152, 155, 159, 163–64, 166
oedipal, 24, 56–60, 227, 230–31
Outsiders, The (Francis Ford Coppola, 1983), 129

paratexts, 13, 36, 37, 264–68, 270–71, 272, 275–76
patriarchal, 5, 11, 12, 26–27, 29, 43–44, 47, 59, 111, 120, 240–41
performative, 2, 3, 4, 5, 12, 13, 27, 31, 45, 211, 228, 236–37, 258, 262, 264–67, 269, 272–76

persona, 7, 9, 12, 19, 20, 22–24, 25–29, 30–33, 36, 55, 72–73, 74, 116–18, 127–29, 134, 139–41, 143–44, 152, 154, 159, 162, 165, 166, 172, 175, 187–88, 192, 198, 211–12, 216–17, 220–21, 222, 226, 229, 231, 239–40, 246, 279, 287, 290–91, 292. *See also* celebrity

phallic, symbol, 12, 41, 59, 60–61, 67, 148, 149

phallus, 59–61, 63, 67

postmodern, 138, 143–44, 177

psychoanalysis, 56, 94–97, 101, 103–4, 106–8

queer, queering, 2, 3, 8, 10, 14, 15, 36–37, 40–42, 46, 74–75, 76, 87–89. *See also* sexuality

race, 2, 44, 45–46, 48, 124–27, 128, 139. *See also* ethnicity

Rain Man (Barry Levinson, 1988), 3, 25, 117, 129, 134, 137, 140, 154, 214

Ray-Bans, 14, 25, 38–39, 43

Reaganism, 7, 20–21, 27, 29, 32, 50, 117, 119, 127, 281

redemption, 10, 102–3, 140, 152–53, 154, 155–66, 219, 280

Risky Business (Paul Brickman, 1983), 7, 19–21, 25–29, 30–31, 32, 117, 129, 134, 140, 169, 170, 185, 213, 227

romance: and narrative, 4, 21, 32, 47, 57–61, 64; public life, 24, 72, 76, 221, 268–69

running, 36, 155, 199, 229, 239, 245, 248, 255–57, 263. *See also* stunt work

science fiction, 9, 10, 102, 106, 152–66, 170–71, 184. *See also* genre

Scientology, 3, 4, 8, 62, 71–90, 171, 192, 220–21, 246, 269, 270, 280

sexuality, 1–2, 4, 5, 7, 9, 19, 22, 24, 25–28, 37, 39–40, 41–42, 43–44, 45–46, 47–50, 55, 56–57, 58, 60, 64, 74, 75, 76, 143, 146–47, 148–50, 230. *See also* closet; queer, queering

simulation, 95–97, 103, 105, 107–8. *See also* virtual

sonhood, 12, 211, 213–17, 218–19, 226, 227, 230, 232

spectacle: Cruise, 4, 10, 14, 24, 38, 139, 143, 145, 192, 198, 227–28, 244–48; and narrative, 27, 61–62, 65, 66, 96–97, 187, 243, 244

spectatorship, 40, 62, 98, 103, 104, 147, 216, 227, 290

stardom: and Cruise, 11, 12, 20, 86, 140–42, 143–45, 146, 149, 150, 189–93, 194–96, 197, 198–201, 202, 204–5, 226, 227, 243–45, 251, 257, 258; as industry, 11, 12, 127, 187, 188, 190–92, 193, 196–98, 202, 203, 275

storyworlds, 11, 188–93, 197–205

stunt work, 12–13, 199, 228, 234–36, 237, 239, 243–58, 263, 264, 268–77, 288–89, 292. *See also* running

Taps (Harold Becker, 1981), 129

teen films, 7, 19, 20–33

Top Gun (Tony Scott, 1986), 5, 7, 10, 11, 13–14, 23, 27, 37–42, 43, 44, 47, 48, 50, 60, 72, 117, 118, 123, 125, 129, 134, 135, 147, 154, 169–76, 177, 180, 185, 189, 193, 213, 227–28, 279
trademark, 44, 134, 158, 192–93, 194–95, 198, 201, 226. *See also* branding, Cruise
transmedia, 11, 190, 192, 196–97

Valkyrie (Bryan Singer, 2008), 240, 288–89

Vanilla Sky (Cameron Crowe, 2001), 4, 10, 152, 154–55, 157–58, 161, 214, 217, 228,
virtual, 71, 95, 99. *See also* simulation
voyeurism, 53–54, 62, 65, 68

War of the Worlds (Steven Spielberg, 2005), 76, 99, 102–3, 108, 152, 155–57, 159–60, 162–64.
white, whiteness, 9, 36, 45, 54, 55, 120, 129

youthful, 6, 8, 25, 27, 37, 39, 40, 54, 136, 144, 158, 232, 279, 290. *See also* aging

www.ingramcontent.com/pod-product-compliance
Lightning Source LLC
Chambersburg PA
CBHW070300240426
43661CB00057B/2600